St. Paul's Church

Clifton

2.8.70

THE NEW ENGLISH BIBLE

THE APOCRYPHA

THE BIBLE

A NEW ENGLISH TRANSLATION

Planned and Directed by Representatives of

THE BAPTIST UNION OF GREAT BRITAIN AND IRELAND

THE CHURCH OF ENGLAND

THE CHURCH OF SCOTLAND

THE CONGREGATIONAL CHURCH IN ENGLAND AND WALES

THE COUNCIL OF CHURCHES FOR WALES

THE IRISH COUNCIL OF CHURCHES

THE LONDON YEARLY MEETING OF
THE SOCIETY OF FRIENDS

THE METHODIST CHURCH OF GREAT BRITAIN

THE PRESBYTERIAN CHURCH OF ENGLAND

THE BRITISH AND FOREIGN BIBLE SOCIETY

THE NATIONAL BIBLE SOCIETY OF SCOTLAND

The publication of the books of the Apocrypha in this translation prepared under the auspices of the Joint Committee on the New Translation of the Bible does not imply that the bodies represented on the Joint Committee hold a common opinion upon the canonical status of these books

THE NEW ENGLISH BIBLE

THE APOCRYPHA

OXFORD UNIVERSITY PRESS
CAMBRIDGE UNIVERSITY PRESS
1970

The New English Bible:
The Apocrypha first published 1970

Printed in Great Britain
at the University Printing House, Cambridge
(Brooke Crutchley, University Printer)

PREFACE TO THE NEW ENGLISH BIBLE

In May 1946 the General Assembly of the Church of Scotland received an overture from the Presbytery of Stirling and Dunblane, where it had been initiated by the Reverend G. S. Hendry, recommending that a translation of the Bible be made in the language of the present day, inasmuch as the language of the Authorized Version, already archaic when it was made, had now become even more definitely archaic and less generally understood. The General Assembly resolved to make an approach to other Churches, and, as a result, delegates of the Church of England, the Church of Scotland, and the Methodist, Baptist, and Congregational Churches met in conference in October. They recommended that the work should be undertaken; that a completely new translation should be made, rather than a revision, such as had earlier been contemplated by the University Presses of Oxford and Cambridge; and that the translators should be free to employ a contemporary idiom rather than reproduce the traditional 'biblical' English.

In January 1947 a second conference, held like the first in the Central Hall, Westminster, included representatives of the University Presses. At the request of this conference, the Churches named above appointed representatives to form the Joint Committee on the New Translation of the Bible. This Committee met for the first time in July of the same year. By January 1948, when its third meeting was held, invitations to be represented had been sent to the Presbyterian Church of England, the Society of Friends, the Churches in Wales, the Churches in Ireland, the British and Foreign Bible Society, and the National Bible Society of Scotland: these invitations were accepted. At a much later stage the hierarchies of the Roman Catholic Church in England and Scotland accepted an invitation to appoint representatives, and these attended as observers.

The Joint Committee provided for the actual work of translation from the original tongues by appointing three panels, to deal, respectively, with the Old Testament, the Apocrypha, and the New Testament. Their members were scholars drawn from various British universities, whom the Committee believed to be representative of competent biblical scholarship at the present time. Apprehending, however, that sound scholarship does not necessarily carry with it a delicate sense of English style, the Committee appointed a fourth panel, of trusted literary advisers, to whom all the work of the translating panels was to be submitted for scrutiny. It should be said that denominational considerations played no part in the appointment of the panels.

The Joint Committee issued general directions to the panels, in pursuance of the aims which the enterprise had in view. The translating panels adopted the following procedure. An individual was invited to submit a draft translation of a particular book, or group of books. Normally he would be a member of the panel concerned. Very occasionally a draft translation was invited from a scholar outside the panel, who was known to have worked specially on the book in question. The draft was circulated in typescript to members of the panel for their consideration. They then met together and discussed the draft round a table, verse by verse, sentence by sentence. Each member brought his view about the meaning of the original to the judgement of his fellows, and discussion went on until they reached a common mind. There are passages where, in the present state of our knowledge, no one could say with certainty which of two (or even more) possible meanings is intended. In such cases, after careful discussion, alternative meanings have been recorded in footnotes, but only where they seemed of sufficient importance. There is probably no member of a panel who has not found himself obliged to give up, perhaps with lingering regret, a cherished view about the meaning of this or that difficult passage, but in the end the panel accepted corporate responsibility for the interpretation set forth in the translation adopted.

The resultant draft was now remitted to the panel of literary advisers. They scrutinized it, once again, verse by verse, sentence by sentence, and took pains to secure, as best they could, the tone and level of language appropriate to the different kinds of writing to be found in the Bible, whether narrative, familiar discourse, argument, law, rhetoric or poetry. The translation thus amended was returned to the translating panel, who examined it to make sure that the meaning intended had not been in any way misunderstood. Passages of peculiar difficulty might on occasion pass repeatedly between the panels. The final form of the version was reached by agreement between the translators concerned and the literary advisers. It was then ready for submission to the Joint Committee.

Since January 1948 the Joint Committee has met regularly twice a year in the Jerusalem Chamber, Westminster Abbey, with four exceptions during 1954–5 when the Langham Room in the precincts of the Abbey was kindly made available. At these meetings the Committee has received reports on the progress of the work from the Conveners of the four panels, and its members have had in their hands typescripts of the books so far translated and revised. They have made such comments and given such advice or decisions as they judged to be necessary, and from time to time they have met members of the panels in conference.

Of the original members of the panels most have happily been able to stay with the work all through, though some have been lost, through death or otherwise, and their places have been filled by fresh appointments.

The Committee has warmly appreciated the courteous hospitality of the Dean of Westminster and of the Trustees of the Central Hall. We owe a great debt to the support and the experienced counsel of the University Presses of Oxford and Cambridge. We recognize gratefully the service rendered to the enterprise by the Reverend Dr G. S. Hendry and the Reverend Professor J. K. S. Reid, who have successively held the office of Secretary to the Committee. To those who have borne special responsibility, as Chairmen of the Joint Committee, we owe more than could readily be told. Dr J. W. Hunkin, Bishop of Truro, our first Chairman, brought to the work an exuberant vigour and initiative without which the formidable project might hardly have got off the ground at all. On his lamented death in 1950 he was succeeded by Dr A. T. P. Williams, then Bishop of Durham and subsequently Bishop of Winchester, who for eighteen years guided our enterprise with judicious wisdom, tact, and benign firmness, but who to our sorrow died when the end of the task was in sight. To both of these we would put on record the gratitude of the Committee and of all engaged in the enterprise.

If we embarked on mentioning the names of those who have served on the various committees and panels, the list would be a long one; and if we mentioned some and not others, the selection would be an invidious one. There are, nevertheless, three names the omission of which would be utterly wrong. As Vice-Chairman and Director, Dr C. H. Dodd has from start to finish given outstanding leadership and guidance to the project, bringing to the work scholarship, sensitivity, and an ever watchful eye. Professor Sir Godfrey Driver, Joint Director since 1965, has also brought to the work a wealth of knowledge and wisdom; to his enthusiasm, tenacity of purpose, and unflagging devotion the whole enterprise is greatly indebted. Professor W. D. McHardy, Deputy Director since 1968, has made an invaluable contribution particularly, but by no means exclusively, in the sphere of the Apocrypha. It is right that the names of these three scholars should always be associated with The New English Bible. Our debt to them is incalculably great.

DONALD EBOR:
Chairman of the Joint Committee

CONTENTS

Preface to The New English Bible — *page* v
Introduction to the Apocrypha — xi
Marginal Numbers — xiv

The First Book of Esdras — 1
The Second Book of Esdras — 26
Tobit — 73
Judith — 93
The Rest of the Chapters of the Book of Esther — 116
The Wisdom of Solomon — 134
Ecclesiasticus or the Wisdom of Jesus son of Sirach — 158
Baruch — 252
A Letter of Jeremiah — 259
The Song of the Three — 263
Daniel and Susanna — 267
Daniel, Bel, and the Snake — 270
The Prayer of Manasseh — 273
The First Book of the Maccabees — 275
The Second Book of the Maccabees — 326

INTRODUCTION

The term 'Apocrypha', a Greek word meaning 'hidden (things)', was early used in different senses. It was applied to writings which were regarded as so important and precious that they must be hidden from the general public and reserved for the initiates, the inner circle of believers. It came to be applied to writings which were hidden not because they were too good but because they were not good enough, because, that is, they were secondary or questionable or heretical. A third usage may be traced to Jerome. He was familiar with the Scriptures in their Hebrew as well as their Greek form, and for him apocryphal books were those outside the Hebrew canon.

The generally accepted modern usage is based on that of Jerome. The Apocrypha as here translated consists of fifteen books or parts of books. They are:

1. The First Book of Esdras
2. The Second Book of Esdras
3. Tobit
4. Judith
5. The Rest of the Chapters of the Book of Esther
6. The Wisdom of Solomon
7. Ecclesiasticus or the Wisdom of Jesus son of Sirach
8. Baruch
9. A Letter of Jeremiah
10. The Song of the Three
11. Daniel and Susanna
12. Daniel, Bel, and the Snake
13. The Prayer of Manasseh
14. The First Book of the Maccabees
15. The Second Book of the Maccabees

These works are outside the Palestinian canon; that is, they form no part of the Hebrew Scriptures, although the original language of some of them was Hebrew. With the exception, however, of the Second Book of Esdras, they are all in the Greek version of the Old Testament made for the Greek-speaking Jews in Egypt. As such they were accepted as biblical by the early Church and were quoted as Scripture by many early Christian writers, for their Bible was the Greek Bible.

In Greek and Latin manuscripts of the Old Testament these books are dispersed throughout the Old Testament, generally in the places most in accord with their contents. The practice of collecting them into a separate unit, a practice which dates back no farther than A.D. 1520, explains why certain of the items are but fragments; they are passages not found in the Hebrew Bible, and so have been removed from the books in which they occur in the Greek version. To help the reader over this disunity and lack of context the present translators have resorted to various devices. We have added the name Daniel to the titles of the stories of Susanna and of Bel and the Snake as a reminder that these tales are to be read with the Book of Daniel. A note we have inserted after the title, The Song of the Three, indicates that this item is to be found in the third chapter of the Greek form of Daniel. And the six additions to the Book of Esther are so disjointed and unintelligible as they stand in most editions of the Apocrypha that we have provided them with a context by rendering the whole of the Greek version of Esther.

The text used in this translation of the Apocrypha is that edited by H. B. Swete in *The Old Testament in Greek according to the Septuagint*. In places Swete includes two texts, and we have chosen to translate the Codex Sinaiticus text of Tobit and Theodotion's version of the additions to the Book of Daniel, namely, The Song of the Three, Daniel and Susanna, and Daniel, Bel, and the Snake. For Ecclesiasticus we have used, in addition to Codex Vaticanus as printed in Swete's edition, the text edited by J. H. A. Hart in *Ecclesiasticus: the Greek Text of Codex 248*, and constant reference has been made to the various forms of the Hebrew text. For the Second Book of Esdras, which apart from a few verses is not extant in a Greek form, we have based our translation on the Latin text of R. L. Bensly's *The Fourth Book of Ezra*. Throughout we have consulted the variant readings given in critical editions of the Greek, the texts of the versions, and the suggestions of editors and commentators.

Alternative readings cited from Greek manuscripts (referred to as *witnesses*) and the evidence of early translations (*Vss.*, that is Versions) are given, as footnotes, only when they are significant either for text or for meaning. In a few places where the text seems to have suffered in the course of transmission and in its present form is obscure or unintelligible we have made a slight change in the text and marked our rendering of it *probable reading*, and we have indicated any evidence other than the evidence afforded by the context. Where an alternative interpretation seemed to deserve serious consideration it has been recorded as a footnote with *Or* as indicator.

In order to preserve the verse numbering of the Authorized (King James) Version of 1611 we have, when necessary, added at the foot of the page those passages which are found in the manuscripts on which the Authorized Version ultimately rests but which are absent from the earlier manuscripts now available.

We have not sought to achieve consistency in the treatment of proper names any more than did our predecessors. We have continued to use familiar English forms, especially when the reference is to well-known Old Testament characters or places. Sometimes as an aid to the correct pronunciation we have had recourse to such expedients as the affixing of an acute accent to the word Sidé or the introduction of a diphthong, as in our Soud for Sud. In general it may be said that Greek spellings have been Latinized, but the Greek forms of place-names have not been brought into line with the Hebrew.

We have not aimed at consistency in our treatment of weights and measures. We have rendered terms into the nearest English equivalents only when these seemed suitable and natural in the context.

In the text of the First and Second Books of the Maccabees the dates given are reckoned according to the Greek or Seleucid era. As a help to the reader we have added at the foot of the page the nearest dates according to the Christian era.

This translation of the Apocrypha shares with other parts of The New English Bible the aim of providing a rendering which will be both faithful to the text translated and genuinely English in idiom. The translators have endeavoured to convey the meaning of the original in language which will be the closest natural equivalent. They have tried to avoid free paraphrase on the one hand and, on the other, formal fidelity resulting in a translation which would read like a translation. It is their hope that by their labours these documents, valuable in themselves and indispensable for the study of the background of the New Testament, have been made more intelligible and more readily accessible.

W. D. McH.

MARGINAL NUMBERS

The conventional verse divisions in the Apocrypha date only from editions printed in the sixteenth century and have no basis in the manuscripts. Any system of division into numbered verses is foreign to the spirit of this translation, which is intended to convey the meaning in continuous natural English.

For purposes of reference, verse numbers are placed in the margin opposite the line in which the first word belonging to the verse in question appears. Sometimes, however, successive verses are combined in a continuous translation, so that the precise point where a new verse begins cannot be fixed; in these cases the verse numbers, joined by a hyphen, are placed at the point where the passage begins.

THE

FIRST BOOK OF

ESDRAS

Exile and return

JOSIAH KEPT the Passover at Jerusalem in honour of 1
his Lord and sacrificed the Passover victims on the fourteenth
day of the first month. The priests, duly robed in their vest- 2
ments, he stationed in the temple of the Lord according to the order
of daily service. He commanded the Levites, who served the temple in 3
Israel, to purify themselves for the Lord, in order to place the holy
Ark of the Lord in the house which was built by King Solomon, son
of David. Josiah said to them, 'You are no longer to carry it on your 4
shoulders. Make yourselves ready now, family by family and clan by
clan, to do service to the Lord your God and to minister to his people
Israel in the manner prescribed by King David and provided for so 5
magnificently by his son Solomon. Take your places in the temple as
Levites in the prescribed order of your families in the presence of
your brother Israelites; sacrifice the Passover victims, and prepare 6
the sacrifices for your brothers. Observe the Passover according to
the ordinance of the Lord which was given to Moses.'

To those who were present Josiah made a gift of thirty thousand 7
lambs and kids and three thousand calves. These he gave from the
royal estates in fulfilment of his promise to the people and to the
priests and Levites. The temple-wardens, Chelkias, Zacharias, and 8
Esyelus, gave the priests two thousand six hundred sheep and three
hundred calves for the Passover. Jechonias, Samaeas, his brother 9
Nathanael, Sabias, Ozielus, and Joram, army officers of high rank,
gave the Levites five thousand sheep and seven hundred calves for
the Passover.

This was the procedure. The priests and the Levites, bearing the 10
unleavened bread, stood in all their splendour before the people, in
the order of their clans and families, to make offerings to the Lord as 11
is laid down in the book of Moses. This took place in the morning.
They roasted the Passover victims over the fire in the prescribed 12

way and boiled the sacrifices in the vessels and cauldrons, and a
13 pleasant smell went up; then they carried portions round to the
whole assembly. After this they made preparations both for them-
14 selves and for their brothers the priests, the sons of Aaron. The
priests went on offering the fat until nightfall, while the Levites made
the preparations both for themselves and for their brothers the
15–16 priests, the sons of Aaron. The sons of Asaph, the temple singers,
with Asaph, Zacharias, and Eddinous of the royal court, and the
door-keepers at each gateway remained at their station according to
the ordinances of David, which prescribe that no one may lawfully
default in his daily duty; their brothers the Levites made the pre-
17 parations for them. All that pertained to the Lord's sacrifice was
18 completed that day: the keeping of the Passover and the offering of
the sacrifices on the altar of the Lord according to the command of
19 King Josiah. The Israelites who were present on this occasion kept
the Passover and the Feast of Unleavened Bread for seven days.
20 Such a Passover had not been kept in Israel since the time of the
21 prophet Samuel; none of the kings of Israel had kept such a Passover as was kept by Josiah, the priests and the Levites, the men of
Judah, and those Israelites who happened to be resident in Jerusalem.
22 It was in the eighteenth year of Josiah's reign that this Passover was
celebrated.

23 All that Josiah did he did rightly and in whole-hearted devotion to
24 his Lord. The events of his reign are to be found in ancient records
which tell a story of sin and rebellion against the Lord graver than
that of any other nation or kingdom, and of offences against him
which brought down his judgement upon Israel.

25 After all these doings of Josiah's it happened that Pharaoh king of
Egypt was advancing to attack Carchemish on the Euphrates, and
26 Josiah took the field against him. The king of Egypt sent him this
27 message: 'What is your business with me, king of Judah? It is not
against you that the Lord God has sent me to fight; my campaign is
on the Euphrates. The Lord is with me, the Lord, I say, is with me,
28 driving me on. Withdraw, and do not oppose the Lord.' Josiah did
not turn his chariot but went forward to the attack. He disregarded
29 what the Lord had said through the prophet Jeremiah and joined
battle with Pharaoh in the plain of Megiddo. Pharaoh's captains
30 swept down upon King Josiah. The king said to his servants, 'Take
me out of the battle, for I am badly hurt.' At once his servants took

him out of the line and lifted him into his second chariot. He was 31
brought back to Jerusalem, and there he died and was buried in his
ancestral tomb.
All Judah mourned Josiah, and the prophet Jeremiah lamented 32
him. The lamentation for Josiah has been observed by the chief men
and their wives from that day to this; it was proclaimed that it should
be a custom for ever for the whole people of Israel. These things are 33
recorded in the book of the histories of the kings of Judah; every deed
that Josiah did which won him fame and showed his understanding
of the law of the Lord, both what he did earlier and what is told of
him here, is related in the book of the kings of Israel and Judah.
His compatriots took Joachaz the son of Josiah and made him king 34
in succession to his father. He was twenty-three years old, and he 35
reigned over Judah and Jerusalem for three months. Then the king
of Egypt deposed him, fined the nation a hundred talents of silver 36
and one talent of gold, and appointed his brother Joakim king of 37
Judah and Jerusalem. Joakim imprisoned the leading men and had 38
his brother Zarius arrested and brought back from Egypt.
Joakim was twenty-five years old when he became king of Judah 39
and Jerusalem; he did what was wrong in the eyes of the Lord. Nebu- 40
chadnezzar king of Babylon marched against him; he put him in
chains of bronze and took him to Babylon. Nebuchadnezzar also took 41
some of the sacred vessels of the Lord, carried them off, and put them
in his temple in Babylon. The stories about Joakim, his sacrilegious 42
and godless conduct, are recorded in the chronicles of the kings.
Joakim was succeeded on the throne by his eighteen-year-old son 43
Joakim. He reigned in Jerusalem for three months and ten days, and 44
did what was wrong in the eyes of the Lord.
A year later Nebuchadnezzar had him deported to Babylon to- 45
gether with the sacred vessels of the Lord. He made Zedekiah king 46
of Judah and Jerusalem. Zedekiah was twenty-one years old and
reigned eleven years. He did what was wrong in the eyes of the Lord 47
and disregarded what the Lord had said through the prophet Jeremiah. King Nebuchadnezzar had made him take an oath of allegi- 48
ance by the Lord, but he broke it and revolted. He was stubborn and
defiant, and transgressed the commandments of the Lord, the God of
Israel.
The leaders of the people and the chief priests committed many 49
wicked and lawless acts, outdoing even the heathen in sacrilege, and

50 they defiled the holy temple of the Lord in Jerusalem. The God of
their fathers sent his messenger to reclaim them, because he wished
51 to spare them and his dwelling-place. But they derided his messengers, and on the very day when the Lord spoke they were scoffing
52 at his prophets. At last he was roused to fury against his people for
their impieties, and ordained that the kings of the Chaldaeans should
53 attack them. These put their young men to the sword all round the
holy temple, sparing neither old nor young, neither boy nor girl; the
54 Lord handed them all over to their enemies. All the sacred vessels of
the Lord, large and small, the furnishings of the Ark of the Lord,
55 and the royal treasures were carried off to Babylon. The house of the
Lord was set on fire, the walls of Jerusalem destroyed, its towers
56 burnt, and all its splendours ruined. Nebuchadnezzar carried off to
57 Babylon the survivors from the slaughter, and they remained slaves
to him and his sons until the Persians took his empire. This fulfilled
58 the word of the Lord spoken by Jeremiah: 'Until the land has run
the full term of its sabbaths, it shall keep sabbath all the time of its
desolation till the end of the seventy years.'

2 1–2 DURING THE FIRST YEAR of Cyrus king of Persia, the Lord, in
order to fulfil his word spoken through Jeremiah, moved Cyrus king
of Persia to make a proclamation throughout his empire, which he
3 also put in writing: 'This is the decree of Cyrus king of Persia: The
Lord of Israel, the most high Lord, has made me king of the world
4 and has directed me to build him a house at Jerusalem in Judaea.
5 Whoever among you belongs to his people, may his Lord be with
him; let him go up to Jerusalem in Judaea and build the house of the
6 Lord of Israel, the Lord who dwells in Jerusalem. Wherever each
7 man lives let his neighbours help him with gold and silver and other
gifts, with horses and pack-animals, together with other things set
aside as votive offerings for the Lord's temple in Jerusalem.'

8 Then the chiefs of the clans of the tribe of Judah and of Benjamin,
the priests, the Levites, came forward, and all whose spirit the Lord
9 had moved to go up to build the Lord's temple in Jerusalem. Their
neighbours helped with everything, with silver and gold, horses and
pack-animals; and many were also moved to help with votive offer-
10 ings in great quantity. King Cyrus brought out the sacred vessels of
the Lord which Nebuchadnezzar had taken away from Jerusalem
11 and set up in his idolatrous temple. Cyrus king of Persia brought

them out and delivered them to Mithradates his treasurer, by whom 12
they were delivered to Sanabassar, the governor of Judaea. This is the 13
inventory: a thousand gold cups, a thousand silver cups, twenty-nine
silver censers, thirty gold bowls, two thousand four hundred and ten
silver bowls, and a thousand other articles. In all, five thousand four 14
hundred and sixty-nine gold and silver vessels were returned, and taken 15
from Babylon to Jerusalem by Sanabassar together with the exiles.

In the time of Artaxerxes king of Persia, Belemus, Mithradates, 16
Tabellius, Rathymus, Beeltethmus, Semellius the secretary, and their
colleagues in office in Samaria and other places, wrote him a letter
denouncing the inhabitants of Judaea and Jerusalem in the following
terms:

To our Sovereign Lord Artaxerxes your servants Rathymus the 17
recorder, Semellius the secretary, the other members of their
council, and the magistrates in Coele-syria and Phoenicia:

This is to inform Your Majesty that the Jews who left you to 18
come here have arrived in Jerusalem and are rebuilding that
wicked and rebellious city. They are repairing its streets and walls
and laying the foundation of the temple. If this city is rebuilt and 19
the walls completed, they will cease paying tribute and will rebel
against the royal house. Since work on the temple is in hand, we 20
have thought it well not to neglect this important matter but to 21
bring it to Your Majesty's notice, in order that, if it is Your
Majesty's pleasure, search may be made in the records left by your
predecessors. You will find in the archives evidence about these 22
matters and will learn that this is a city that has resisted authority
and given trouble to kings and to other states, and has been a 23
centre of armed rebellion by the Jews from the earliest times. That
is why it was laid in ruins. Now we submit to Your Majesty that, 24
if this city be rebuilt and its walls rise again, you will no longer have
access to Coele-syria and Phoenicia.

Then the king wrote to Rathymus the recorder, Beeltethmus, 25
Semellius the secretary, and their colleagues in office in Samaria,
Syria, and Phoenicia this reply:

I have read your letter. I ordered search to be made and it was 26
discovered that this city has always been opposed to its overlords,

27 and its inhabitants have raised rebellions and made wars. There
were kings in Jerusalem, powerful and ruthless men, who in their
time controlled Coele-syria and Phoenicia and exacted tribute from
28 them. I therefore command that the men you mention be prevented from rebuilding the city, and that measures be taken to
29 enforce this order and to check the spread of an evil likely to be a
nuisance to the royal house.

30 When the letter from King Artaxerxes had been read, Rathymus,
Semellius the secretary, and their colleagues set out at once for
Jerusalem with cavalry and a large body of other troops and stopped
the builders. The building of the temple was broken off until the
second year of the reign of Darius king of Persia.

A debate at the Persian court

3 KING DARIUS held a great feast for all those under him, his
2 household, the chief men of Media and Persia, and the satraps
and commanders and governors of his empire in the hundred and
3 twenty-seven satrapies from India to Ethiopia. When they had
eaten and drunk their fill, they went away, and King Darius with-
4 drew to his bedchamber; he went to sleep but woke up again. Then
the three young men of the king's personal bodyguard said to each
5 other: 'Let each one of us name the thing which he judges the
strongest; and to the one whose opinion seems wisest King Darius
6 will give rich gifts and prizes: he shall be clothed in purple, drink
from gold vessels, and sleep on a golden bed; and he shall have a
chariot with gold-studded bridles, and a fine linen turban, and a
7 chain about his neck. His wisdom shall give him the right to sit next
8 to Darius and to be given the title Kinsman of Darius.' Then each
wrote down his own statement, sealed it, and put it under the king's
9 pillow. 'When the king wakes again,' they said, 'the writing will be
given him. The king and the three chief men of Persia shall judge
whose statement is wisest, and the award will be made on the merits
of the written statement.'
10, 11 One wrote 'Wine is strongest', the second wrote 'The king is
12 strongest', and the third wrote 'Women are strongest, but truth

conquers all'. When the king got up he was presented with what 13
they had written. He read it, and summoned all the chief men of 14
Persia and Media, satraps, commanders, governors, and chief
officers. Then he took his seat in the council chamber, and what they 15
had written was read out before them. He said, 'Call the young men 16
and let them expound their statements.' They were called and came
in. They were asked, 'Tell us about what you have written.' 17

The first, who spoke about the strength of wine, began. 'Sirs,' he 18
said, 'how true it is that wine is strongest! It sends astray the wits of
all who drink it; king and orphan, slave and free, rich and poor, it 19
has the same effect on them all. It turns all thoughts to revelry and 20
mirth; it brings forgetfulness of grief and debt. It makes all feel 21
rich, cares nothing for king or satrap, and makes men always talk in
millions. When they are in their cups, they forget to be friendly to 22
friends and relations, and are quick to draw their swords; when they 23
have recovered from their wine, they cannot remember what they
have done. Sirs, is not wine the strongest, seeing that it forces men 24
to behave in this way?' With this he ended.

Then the second, the one who spoke of the strength of the king, **4**
began his speech: 'Sirs, is not man the strongest, man who masters 2
the earth and the sea and all that is in them? But the strongest of 3
men is the king; he is their lord and master, and they obey all his
commands. If he bids them make war upon one another they do it; 4
if he dispatches them against his enemies, they march and level
mountains and walls and towers. They kill and are killed; they do not 5
disobey the king's order. If they are victorious they bring everything
to the king, their spoils and everything else. Or take those who do not 6
serve as soldiers or go to war, but work the land: they sow and reap,
and bring their produce to the king. They compel each other to
bring him their tribute. Though he is no more than one man, if he 7
orders them to kill, they kill; if he orders them to release, they
release; he orders them to attack and they attack, to lay waste and 8
they lay waste, to build and they build, to cut down and they cut 9
down, to plant and they plant. So all his people and his troops obey 10
him. Besides this, while he himself sits at table, eats and drinks, and
goes to sleep, they stand in attendance round about him and none 11
can leave and see to his own affairs; they never disobey him in anything. Sirs, of course the king must be strongest when he commands 12
such obedience!' So he stopped speaking.

13 The third, who spoke about women and truth—and this was
14 Zerubbabel—said: 'Sirs, it is true the king is great, men are many,
and wine is strong, but who rules over them? Who is the sovereign
15 power? Women, surely! The king and all his people who rule land
16 and sea were born of women, and from them they came. Women
brought up the men who planted the vineyards which yield the wine.
17 They make clothes for men and they bring honour to men; men can-
18 not do without women. If they have amassed gold and silver and all
kinds of beautiful things, and then see a woman with a lovely face and
19 figure, they leave all these things to gape and stare at her with open
mouth, and all choose her in preference to gold or silver or beautiful
20 things. A man will desert his father who brought him up, desert
21 even his country, and become one with his wife. He forgets father,
mother, and country, and stays with his wife to the end of his days.
22 Here is the proof that women are your masters: do you not toil and
23 sweat and then bring all you earn and give it to your wives? A man
will take his sword and sally forth to plunder and rob, to sail on sea
24 and river; he faces lions, he travels in the dark; and when he has
robbed and plundered he brings the spoil home to his beloved.

25, 26 'A man loves his wife more than his father or mother. For women's
sakes many men have been driven out of their minds, many have
27 been sold into slavery, many have died or come to grief or ruined their
28 lives. Do you believe me now? Certainly the king wields great
29 authority; no country dare lift a finger against him. Yet I watched
him with Apame, his favourite concubine, daughter of the famous
30 Bartacus. She was sitting on the king's right; she took the diadem
off his head and put it on her own, and slapped his face with her left
31 hand; and the king only gazed at her open-mouthed. When she
laughed at him he laughed; when she was cross with him he coaxed
32 her to make it up. Sirs, if women do as well as this, how can their
33 strength be denied?' The king and the chief men looked at one
another.

34 He then went on to speak about truth: 'Sirs, we have seen that
women are strong. The earth is vast, the sky is lofty, the sun swift in
his course, for he moves through the circle of the sky and speeds
35 home in a single day. How great is he who does all this! But truth
36 too is great and stronger than all else. The whole earth calls on
truth; the sky praises her. All created things shake and tremble;
37 with her there is no injustice. There is injustice in wine, in kings, in

women, in all men, and in all their works, and so forth. There is no
truth in them; they shall perish in their injustice. But truth abides 38
and is strong for ever; she lives and rules for ever and ever. With her 39
there is no favouritism or partiality; she chooses to do justice rather
than what is unjust and evil. All approve her works; in her judge- 40
ments there is no injustice. Hers are strength and royalty, the
authority and majesty of all ages. Praise be to the God of truth!'

So he ended his speech, and all the people shouted and said, 41
'Great is truth: truth is strongest!' Then the king said to him, 'Ask 42
what you will, even beyond what is in the writing, and I will grant it
you. For you have been proved the wisest; and you shall sit by me
and be called my Kinsman.'

Then he said to the king: 'Remember the vow you made on the 43
day when you came to the throne. You promised to rebuild Jerusalem and to send back all the vessels taken from it which Cyrus set 44
aside. When he vowed to destroy Babylon he also vowed to restore
these vessels; and you too made a vow to rebuild the temple which 45
the Edomites burnt when Judaea was ravaged by the Chaldaeans.
This is the favour that I now beg of you, my lord king, this is the 46
magnanimity I request: that you should perform the vow which you
made to the King of heaven.'

King Darius stood up and kissed him, and wrote letters for him to 47
all the treasurers, governors, commanders, and satraps instructing
them to give safe conduct to him and to all those who were going up
with him to rebuild Jerusalem. To all the governors in Coele-syria 48
and Phoenicia and in Lebanon he wrote letters ordering them to
transport cedar-wood from Lebanon to Jerusalem and join with
Zerubbabel in building the city. He gave all Jews going up from the 49
kingdom to Judaea letters assuring their liberties: that no officer,
satrap, governor, or treasurer should interfere with them, that all 50
land which they should acquire should be immune from taxation,
and that the Edomites should surrender the villages they had seized
from the Jews. Each year twenty talents were to be contributed to 51
the building of the temple until it was finished, and a further ten 52
talents annually for[a] burnt-offerings to be sacrificed daily upon the
altar in accordance with their law. All those who were going from 53–54
Babylonia to build the city were to enjoy freedom, and their descendants after them. He gave written orders that all the priests going

[*a*] *Some witnesses add* seventeen.

there should also receive maintenance and the vestments in which they
55 would officiate; that the Levites too should receive maintenance, until
the day when the building of the temple and Jerusalem was com-
56 pleted; and that all who guarded the city should be given land and
57 pay. He sent back all the vessels from Babylon which Cyrus had set
aside. All that Cyrus had commanded, he reaffirmed, ordering
everything to be restored to Jerusalem.

58 When the young man, Zerubbabel, went out, he turned his face
toward Jerusalem, looked up to heaven, and praised the King of
59 heaven. 'From thee comes victory,' he said, 'from thee comes
60 wisdom; thine is the glory and I am thy servant. All praise to thee
who hast given me wisdom; to thee I give thanks, O Lord of our
fathers.'

61 He took the letters and set off for Babylon, where he told his
62 fellow-Jews. They praised the God of their fathers because he had
63 given them full freedom to go and rebuild Jerusalem and the temple
called by his name, and they feasted for a week with music and
rejoicing.

The temple rebuilt

5 AFTER THIS the heads of families, tribe by tribe, were chosen to
go to Jerusalem, with their wives, their sons and daughters, their
2 male and female slaves, and their pack-animals. Darius sent a
thousand horsemen to accompany them until they had brought them
3 safely back to Jerusalem, with a band of drums and flutes, and all
their brothers dancing. So he sent them off with their escort.

4 These are the names of the men who went to Jerusalem, according
5 to their families, tribes, and allotted duties. The priests, the sons of
Phineas son of Aaron, with Jeshua son of Josedek son of Saraeas,
and Joakim his son; and[a] Zerubbabel son of Salathiel of the house of
6 David of the line of Phares of the tribe of Judah, who spoke wise
words before Darius king of Persia. They went in the second year of
his reign, in Nisan the first month.

7 Now these are the men of Judah who came up from amongst the
captive exiles, those whom Nebuchadnezzar king of Babylon had

[a] his son; and: *probable reading* (*compare Nehemiah 12. 10*).

transported to Babylon. They returned to Jerusalem and the rest of 8
Judaea, each to his own city: they came with Zerubbabel and
Jeshua, Nehemiah, Zaraeas, Resaeas, Enenius, Mardochaeus,
Beelsarus, Aspharasus, Reelias, Romelius, and Baana, their leaders.
The numbers of those from the nation who returned with their 9
leaders were: the line of Phoros two thousand one hundred and
seventy-two; the line of Saphat four hundred and seventy-two; the 10
line of Ares seven hundred and fifty-six; the line of Phaath-moab, 11
deriving from the line of Jeshua and Joab, two thousand eight
hundred and twelve; the line of Elam one thousand two hundred and 12
fifty-four; the line of Zathui nine hundred and forty-five; the line of
Chorbe seven hundred and five; the line of Banei six hundred and
forty-eight; the line of Bebae six hundred and twenty-three; the line 13
of Astaa one thousand three hundred and twenty-two. The line of 14
Adonikam six hundred and sixty-seven; the line of Bagoi two
thousand and sixty-six; the line of Adinus four hundred and fifty-
four; the line of Ater son of Hezekias ninety-two; the line of Keilan 15
and Azetas sixty-seven; the line of Azurus four hundred and thirty-
two; the line of Annias one hundred and one; the line of Arom and 16
the line of Bassa three hundred and twenty-three; the line of
Arsiphurith one hundred and twelve; the line of Baeterus three 17
thousand and five. The line of Bethlomon one hundred and twenty-
three; the men of Netophae fifty-five; the men of Anathoth one 18
hundred and fifty-eight; the men of Bethasmoth forty-two; the 19
men of Cariathiarius twenty-five; the men of Caphira and Beroth
seven hundred and forty-three; the Chadasians and Ammidacans 20
four hundred and twenty-two; the men of Kirama and Gabbes
six hundred and twenty-one; the men of Macalon one hundred and 21
twenty-two; the men of Betolio fifty-two; the line of Phinis one
hundred and fifty-six; the line of Calamolalus and Onus seven 22
hundred and twenty-five; the line of Jerechus three hundred and
forty-five; the line of Sanaas three thousand three hundred 23
and thirty.

The priests: the line of Jeddu son of Jeshua, deriving from the line 24
of Anasib, nine hundred and seventy-two. The line of Emmeruth
one thousand and fifty-two. The line of Phassurus one thousand two 25
hundred and forty-seven. The line of Charme one thousand and
seventeen.

The Levites: the line of Jesue, Cadmielus, Bannus, and Sudius 26

27 seventy-four. The temple singers: the line of Asaph one hundred and
twenty-eight.
28 The door-keepers: the line of Salum, of Atar, of Tolman, of
Dacubi, of Ateta, of Sabi, in all one hundred and thirty-nine.
29 The temple-servitors: the line of Esau, of Asipha, of Taboth,
30 of Keras, of Susa, of Phaleas, of Labana, of Aggaba, of Acud, of
Uta, of Ketab, of Gaba, of Subai, of Anan, of Cathua, of Geddur,
31 of Jairus, of Desan, of Noeba, of Chaseba, of Gazera, of Ozius, of
Phinoc, of Asara, of Basthae, of Asana, of Maani, of Naphisi, of
32 Acum, of Achipha, of Asur, of Pharakim, of Baaloth, of Meedda,
of Coutha, of Charea, of Barchue, of Serar, of Thomi, of Nasith, of
33 Atepha. The descendants of Solomon's servants: the line of Asap-
34 phioth, of Pharida, of Jeeli, of Lozon, of Isdael, of Saphythi, of
Hagia, of Phacareth, of Sabie, of Sarothie, of Masias, of Gas, of
35 Addus, of Subas, of Apherra, of Barodis, of Saphat, of Adlon. All
the temple-servitors and the descendants of Solomon's servants
numbered three hundred and seventy-two.
36 The following came from Thermeleth and Thelsas with their
37 leaders Charaathalar and Alar, and could not prove by their families
and genealogies that they were Israelites: the line of Dalan, the line
of Ban, and the line of Necodan six hundred and fifty-two.
38 From among the priests the claimants to the priesthood whose
record could not be traced: the line of Obdia, of Accos, of Joddus,
who married Augia one of the daughters of Zorzelleas, and took his
39 name; when search was made for their family record in the register it
could not be traced, and so they were excluded from priestly service.
40 Nehemiah the governor[a] told them that they should not participate
in the sacred offerings until a high priest arose wearing the breast-
piece of Revelation and Truth.
41 They were in all: Israelites from twelve years old, not counting
slaves male and female, forty-two thousand three hundred and sixty;
42 their slaves seven thousand three hundred and thirty-seven; musicians
43 and singers two hundred and forty-five; camels four hundred and
thirty-five, horses seven thousand and thirty-six, mules two hundred
and forty-five, donkeys five thousand five hundred and twenty-five.
44 Some of the heads of families, when they arrived at the temple of
God in Jerusalem, made a vow to erect the house again on its site as
45 best they could, and to give to the sacred treasury for the fabric fund

[*a*] the governor: *probable meaning; Gk.* and Attharias.

one thousand minas of gold and five thousand minas of silver and one
hundred vestments.

The priests, the Levites, and some of the people settled in Jeru- 46
salem and the neighbourhood, with the temple musicians and the
door-keepers; and all Israel settled in their villages.

WHEN THE SEVENTH MONTH came and the Israelites were in their 47
homes they gathered as one man in the broad square of the first
gateway toward the east. Jeshua son of Josedek and his brother 48
priests and Zerubbabel son of Salathiel and his colleagues came forward and made ready the altar of the God of Israel, to offer on it 49
whole burnt-offerings according to the directions in the book of
Moses the man of God. They were joined[a] by men from the other 50
peoples of the land and they set up the altar on its site (for the peoples
in the land as a whole were hostile to them and were too strong for
them); and they offered sacrifices to the Lord at the proper time,
and whole burnt-offerings morning and evening. They observed 51
the Feast of Tabernacles as enjoined in the law, and the proper
sacrifices day by day; and thereafter the continual offerings, and 52
sacrifices on sabbaths, at new moons, and on all solemn feasts. All 53
who had made a vow to God offered sacrifices to God from the new
moon of the seventh month, although the temple of God was not yet
built. Money was paid to the stonemasons and carpenters; the 54–55
Sidonians and Tyrians were supplied with food and drink, and with
carts to bring cedar-trees from Lebanon, floating them down as rafts
to the anchorage at Joppa, as decreed by Cyrus king of Persia.

In the second month of the second year, Zerubbabel son of Sala- 56
thiel came to the temple of God in Jerusalem and started the work.
There were with him Jeshua son of Josedek, their kinsmen, the
levitical priests, and all who had come to Jerusalem from the exile; 57
and they laid the foundation of the temple of God. This was at the
new moon, in the second month of the second year after they had returned to Judaea and Jerusalem. The Levites from the age of twenty 58
and upwards were set over the works of the Lord. Jeshua, his sons,
his brothers, his brother Cadoel, the sons of Jeshua Emadabun, and
the sons of Joda son of Iliadun with their sons and brothers, all
the Levites, supervisors of the work, were active as one man on the
works in the house of God. While the builders built the temple of

[*a*] *Or* attacked; *the clauses are perhaps in a confused order.*

59 the Lord, the priests in their vestments with musical instruments and
trumpets, and the Levites the sons of Asaph with their cymbals, stood
60 singing to the Lord and praising him as David king of Israel had ap-
61 pointed. They sang psalms praising the Lord, 'for his goodness and
62 glory is for ever toward all Israel'. All the people blew their trumpets
and gave a loud shout, singing to the Lord as the building rose.
63 The priests, the Levites, and heads of families, the older men who
had seen the former house, came to the building of this one with
64 cries of lamentation; and so, while many were sounding the trumpets
65 loudly for joy—so loudly as to be heard far away—the people could
not hear the trumpets for the noise of lamentation.
66 The enemies of Judah and Benjamin heard the noise of the
67 trumpets and came to see what it meant. They found the returned
68 exiles building the temple for the Lord God of Israel; they came to
Zerubbabel and Jeshua and the leaders of the families, and said:
69 'We will build with you; for like you we obey your Lord and have
sacrificed to him from the time of Asbasareth king of Assyria who
70 transported us here.' But Zerubbabel and Jeshua and the leaders of
the families of Israel replied: 'You can have no share in building the
71 house for the Lord our God; we alone will build for the Lord of
72 Israel, as Cyrus king of Persia decreed.' But the peoples of the land
harassed[a] the men of Judaea, blockaded them, and interrupted the
73 building. Their plots, agitations, and riots held up the completion of
the building all the lifetime of King Cyrus. They were prevented
from building for two years until Darius became king.
6 In the second year of the reign of Darius, the prophets Haggai and
Zechariah son of Addo prophesied to the Jews in Judaea and Jeru-
2 salem in the name of the Lord the God of Israel. Then Zerubbabel
son of Salathiel and Jeshua son of Josedek began to rebuild the house of
the Lord in Jerusalem. The prophets of the Lord were at their side
3 to help them. At that time Sisinnes, the governor-general of Syria and
Phoenicia, with Sathrabuzanes and their colleagues, came to them
4 and said: 'Who has authorized you to put up this building, complete
with roof and everything else? Who are the builders carrying out this
5 work?' But, thanks to the Lord who protected the returned exiles,
6 the elders of the Jews were not prevented from building during the
time that Darius was being informed and directions issued.
7 Here is a copy of the letter written to Darius, and sent by Sisinnes,

[*a*] *Probable reading; Gk. obscure.*

the governor-general of Syria and Phoenicia, with Sathrabuzanes
and their colleagues the authorities in Syria and Phoenicia:

To King Darius our humble duty. Be it known to our lord the 8
king: we visited the district of Judaea and entered the city of Jerusalem, and there we found the elders of the Jews returned from
exile building a great new house for the Lord with costly hewn 9
stone and with beams set in the walls. This work was being done 10
with all speed and the undertaking was making good progress; it
was being executed in great splendour and with the utmost care.
We then inquired of these elders by whose authority they were 11
building this house and laying such foundations. We questioned 12
them so that we could inform you in writing who their leaders
were, and asked for a list of their names. They answered as fol- 13
lows: 'We are servants of the Lord who made heaven and earth.
This house was built and completed many years ago by a great 14
and powerful king of Israel. When our fathers sinned against the 15
heavenly Lord of Israel and provoked him, he delivered them over
to Nebuchadnezzar, king of Babylon, king of the Chaldaeans;
and they pulled down the house, set it on fire, and took the people 16
into exile in Babylon. In the first year of the reign of King Cyrus 17
over Babylonia, the king decreed that this house should be rebuilt.
The sacred vessels of gold and silver which Nebuchadnezzar had 18
taken from the house in Jerusalem, and set up in his own temple,
he brought back out of the temple in Babylon and delivered to
Zerubbabel and Sanabassar the governor, with orders to take all 19
these vessels and to put them in the temple at Jerusalem, and to
rebuild this temple of the Lord on the same site as before. Then 20
Sanabassar came and laid the foundations of the house of the Lord
in Jerusalem. From then till now the building has continued and
is still unfinished.' Therefore, if it is Your Majesty's pleasure, let 21
search be made in the royal archives in Babylon, and if it is found 22
that the building of the house of the Lord in Jerusalem took place
with the approval of King Cyrus, and if our lord the king so
decide, let directions be issued to us on this subject.

Then King Darius ordered the archives in Babylon to be searched, 23
and a scroll was found in the castle at Ecbatana in the province of
Media which contained the following record:

24 In the first year of his reign King Cyrus ordered that the house of
the Lord in Jerusalem, where they sacrifice with fire continually,
25 should be rebuilt. Its height should be sixty cubits and its breadth
sixty cubits, with three courses of hewn stone to one of new local
26 timber; the expenses to be met from the royal treasury. The sacred
gold and silver vessels of the house of the Lord which Nebuchadnezzar removed from the house in Jerusalem, and took to Babylon,
should be restored to the house in Jerusalem and replaced where
they formerly were.

27 Darius therefore instructed Sisinnes, the governor-general of
Syria and Phoenicia, with Sathrabuzanes, their colleagues, and the
governors in office in Syria and Phoenicia, to be careful not to interfere with the place, but to allow the servant of the Lord, Zerubbabel,
governor of Judaea, and the elders of the Jews to build the house of
28 the Lord on its old site. 'I have also given instructions', he continued, 'that it should be completely rebuilt, and that they should not
fail to co-operate with the returned exiles in Judaea until the house
29 of the Lord is finished. From the tribute of Coele-syria and Phoenicia let a contribution be duly given to these men for sacrifices to
the Lord, payable to Zerubbabel the governor, for bulls, rams, and
30 lambs; and similarly wheat, salt, wine, and oil are to be provided
regularly each year without question, as the priests in Jerusalem may
31 require day by day. Let all this be expended in order that sacrifices
and libations may be offered to the Most High God for the king and
his children, and that intercession may be made on their behalf.'
32 He also gave these orders: 'If anyone disobeys or neglects any of
these orders written above or here set down, let a beam be taken from
his own house and let him be hanged on it and his estate forfeited to
33 the king. May the Lord himself, therefore, to whom this temple is
dedicated, destroy any king or people who shall lift a finger to delay
34 or damage the Lord's house in Jerusalem. I, Darius the king, decree
that these orders be obeyed to the letter.'
7 Then, in accordance with the orders of King Darius, Sisinnes,
governor-general of Coele-syria and Phoenicia, with Sathrabuzanes
2 and their colleagues, carefully supervised the sacred works, co-
3 operating with the elders of the Jews and the temple officers. With
the encouragement of the prophets Haggai and Zechariah, good
4 progress was made with the sacred works, and they were finished by

the ordinance of the Lord God of Israel and with the approval of
Cyrus, Darius, and Artaxerxes, kings of Persia. It was on the 5
twenty-third of Adar in the sixth year of King Darius that the house
was completed. The Israelites, the priests, the Levites, and the rest 6
of the former exiles who had joined them carried out the directions
in the book of Moses. For the dedication of the temple of the Lord 7
they offered a hundred bulls, two hundred rams, four hundred
lambs, and twelve goats for the sin of all Israel corresponding to the 8
twelve patriarchs of Israel. The priests and the Levites in their vest- 9
ments stood family by family to preside over the services of the Lord
God of Israel according to the book of Moses. The door-keepers
took their stand at every gateway.

The Israelites who had returned from exile kept the Passover on 10
the fourteenth day of the first month. The priests and the Levites
were purified together; not all the returned exiles were purified with 11
the priests, but[a] the Levites were. They slaughtered the Passover 12
victims for all the returned exiles and for their brother priests and for
themselves. All those Israelites participated who had returned from 13
exile and had segregated themselves from the abominations of the
peoples of the land to seek the Lord. They kept the Feast of Un- 14
leavened Bread for seven days, rejoicing before the Lord; for he had 15
changed the policy of the Assyrian king towards them and strengthened them for the service of the Lord the God of Israel.

Ezra in Jerusalem

AFTER THESE EVENTS, in the reign of Artaxerxes king of Persia, 8
came Ezra, son of Saraeas, son of Ezerias, son of Chelkias, son of
Salemus, son of Zadok, son of Ahitub, son of Amarias, son of Ezias, 2
son of Mareroth, son of Zaraeas, son of Savia, son of Bocca, son of
Abishua, son of Phineas, son of Eleazar, son of Aaron the chief
priest. This Ezra came from Babylon as a talented scholar in the law 3
of Moses which had been given by the God of Israel. The king held 4
him in high regard and looked with favour upon all the requests he
made. He was accompanied to Jerusalem by some Israelites, priests, 5
Levites, temple singers, door-keepers, and temple-servitors, in the 6

[*a*] not all...but: *probable meaning; Gk. obscure; some witnesses omit* not.

fifth month of the seventh year of Artaxerxes' reign.[a] They left
Babylon at the new moon in the first month and reached Jerusalem
at the new moon in the fifth month; for the Lord gave them a safe
7 journey. Ezra's knowledge of the law of the Lord and the commandments
was exact in every detail, so that he could teach all Israel
the ordinances and judgements.

8 The following is a copy of the mandate from King Artaxerxes to
Ezra the priest, doctor of the law of the Lord:

9 King Artaxerxes to Ezra the priest, doctor of the law of the Lord,
greeting.

10 I have graciously decided, and now command, that those of the
Jewish nation and of the priests and Levites, in our kingdom, who
11 so choose, shall go with you to Jerusalem. I and my council of
seven Friends have decided that all who so desire may accompany
12 you. Let them look to the affairs of Judaea and Jerusalem in
13 pursuance of the law of the Lord, and bring to Jerusalem for the
Lord of Israel the gifts which I and my Friends have vowed, all
the gold and silver in Babylonia that may be found to belong to
14 the Lord in Jerusalem, together with what has been given by the
nation for the temple of the Lord their God in Jerusalem. Let
the gold and silver be expended upon[b] bulls, rams, lambs, and so
15 forth, so that sacrifices may be offered upon the altar of the Lord
16 their God in Jerusalem. Make use of the gold and silver in whatever
ways you and your colleagues desire, according to the will of
17 your God, and deliver the sacred vessels of the Lord which have
been given you for the use of the temple of your God in Jerusalem.
18 Any other expenses that you may incur for the needs of the
temple of your God you shall defray from the royal treasury.
19 I, Artaxerxes the king, direct the treasurers of Syria and Phoenicia
to give without fail to Ezra the priest, doctor of the law of the Most
20 High God, whatever he may request up to a hundred talents of
silver, and similarly up to a hundred sacks of wheat and a hundred
21 casks of wine, and salt without limit. Let him diligently fulfil in
honour of the Most High God all the requirements of God's law,
so that divine displeasure may not befall the kingdom of the king
22 and of his descendants. You are also informed that no tax or other

[a] *Probable reading; one witness adds* this was the king's second year.
[b] *Or* collected for.

impost is to be laid on the priests, the Levites, the temple singers,
the door-keepers, the temple-servitors, and the lay officers of this
temple; no one is permitted to impose any burden on them. You, 23
Ezra, under God's guidance, are to appoint judges and magistrates
to judge all who know the law of your God in all Syria and
Phoenicia; you yourself shall see to the instruction of those who do
not know it. All who transgress the law of your God and of the 24
king shall be duly punished with death, degradation, fine, or exile.

Then Ezra said: All praise to the Lord alone, who put this into 25
the king's mind, to glorify his house in Jerusalem. He singled me out 26
for honour before the king, his counsellors, and all his Friends and
dignitaries. I took courage from the help of the Lord my God and 27
gathered men of Israel to go up with me.

These are the leaders according to clans and divisions who went 28
with me from Babylon to Jerusalem in the reign of King Artaxerxes:
from the line of Phineas, Gershom; from the line of Ithamar, 29
Gamael; from the line of David, Attus son of Sechenias; from the line 30
of Phoros, Zacharias and a hundred and fifty men with him according to the register; from the line of Phaath-moab, Eliaonias son of 31
Zaraeas and with him two hundred men; from the line of Zathoe, 32
Sechenias son of Jezelus and with him three hundred men; from the
line of Adin, Obeth son of Jonathan and with him two hundred and
fifty men; from the line of Elam, Jessias son of Gotholias and with 33
him seventy men; from the line of Sophotias, Zaraeas son of Michael 34
and with him seventy men; from the line of Joab, Abadias son of 35
Jezelus and with him two hundred and twelve men; from the line of 36
Bani, Assalimoth son of Josaphias and with him a hundred and sixty
men; from the line of Babi, Zacharias son of Bebae and with him 37
twenty-eight men; from the line of Astath, Joannes son of Hacatan 38
and with him a hundred and ten men; last came those from the line 39
of Adonikam, by name Eliphalatus, Jeuel, and Samaeas, and with
them seventy men; from the line of Bago, Uthi son of Istalcurus and 40
with him seventy men.

I assembled them at the river called Theras, where we encamped 41
for three days, and I inspected them. As I found no one there who 42
was of priestly or levitical descent, I sent to Eleazar, Iduelus, 43
Maasmas, Elnathan, Samaeas, Joribus, Nathan, Ennatas, Zacharias, 44
and Mosollamus, who were prominent and discerning men. I told 45

46 them to go to Doldaeus the chief man at the treasury. I instructed
them to speak with Doldaeus, his colleagues, and the treasurers
there, and ask them to send us priests to officiate in the house of our
47 Lord. Under the providence of God they brought us discerning
men from the line of Mooli son of Levi son of Israel, Asebebias and
48 his sons and brothers, eighteen men in all, also Asebias and Annunus
and Hosaeas his brother. Those of the line of Chanunaeus and their
49 sons amounted to twenty men; and those of the temple-servitors
whom David and the leading men appointed for the service of the
Levites amounted to two hundred and twenty. A register of all
these names was compiled.

50 There I made a vow that the young men should fast before our
Lord to beg him to give us a safe journey for ourselves, our children
51 who accompanied us, and our pack-animals. I was ashamed to ask
the king for an escort of infantry and cavalry against our enemies;
52 for we had told the king that the strength of our Lord would ensure
53 success for those who looked to him. So once more we laid all these
things before our Lord in prayer and found him gracious.

54 I set apart twelve men from among the heads of the priestly
families, and with them Sarabias and Asamias and ten of their
55 brother priests. I weighed out for them the silver, the gold, and the
sacred vessels of the house of our Lord; these had been presented by
the king himself, his counsellors, the chief men, and all Israel.
56 When I had weighed it all I handed over to them six hundred and
fifty talents of silver, and vessels of silver weighing a hundred talents,
57 a hundred talents of gold, and twenty pieces of gold plate, and twelve
58 vessels of brass so fine that it gleamed like gold. I said to them: 'You
are consecrated to the Lord, and so are the vessels; the silver and the
59 gold are vowed to the Lord, the Lord of our fathers. Be vigilant and
keep guard until you hand them over at Jerusalem, in the priests'
rooms in the house of our Lord, to the heads of the priestly and
60 levitical families and to the leaders of the clans of Israel.' The
priests and the Levites who received the silver, the gold, and the
vessels in Jerusalem brought them to the temple of the Lord.

61 We left the river Theras on the twelfth day of the first month, and
under the powerful protection which our Lord gave us we reached
Jerusalem. He guarded us against every enemy on our journey, and
62 so we arrived at Jerusalem. Three days passed, and on the fourth the
silver and gold were weighed and handed over in the house of our

Lord to the priest Marmathi son of Uri, with whom was Eleazar son 63
of Phineas. With them also were the Levites Josabdus son of Jeshua
and Moeth son of Sabannus. Everything was numbered and
weighed and every weight recorded there and then. The returned 64, 65
exiles offered sacrifices to the Lord the God of Israel, twelve bulls for
all Israel, with ninety-six rams and seventy-two lambs, and also 66
twelve goats for a peace-offering, the whole as a sacrifice to the Lord.
They delivered the king's orders to the royal treasurers and the 67
governors of Coele-syria and Phoenicia, and so added lustre to the
nation and the temple of the Lord.

WHEN THESE MATTERS had been settled the leaders came to me 68
and said: 'The nation of Israel, the rulers, the priests, and the 69
Levites, have not kept themselves apart from the alien population of
the land with all their pollutions, that is to say the Canaanites,
Hittites, Perizzites, Jebusites, Moabites, Egyptians, and Edomites.
For they and their sons have intermarried with the daughters of 70
these peoples, and the holy race has been mingled with the alien
population of the land; and the leaders and principal men have
shared in this violation of the law from the very beginning.'

As soon as I heard of this I tore my clothes and sacred vestment, 71
plucked out the hair of my head and my beard, and sat down perplexed and miserable. Those who at that time were moved by the 72
word of the Lord of Israel gathered round me, while I grieved over
this disregard of the law, and sat in my misery until the evening
sacrifice. Then I rose from my fast with my clothes and sacred vest- 73
ment torn, and knelt down and, stretching out my hands to the Lord,
said: 74

'O Lord, I am covered with shame and confusion in thy presence.
Our sins tower above our heads; from the time of our fathers our 75–76
offences have reached the sky, and today we are as deep in sin as
ever. Because of our sins and the sins of our fathers, we and our 77
brothers, our kings and our priests, were given over to the kings of
the earth to be killed, taken prisoner, plundered, and humiliated
down to this very day. And now, Lord, how great is the mercy thou 78
hast shown us! We still have a root and a name in the place of thy
sanctuary, and thou hast rekindled our light in the house of our 79
Lord, and given us food in the time of our servitude. Even when we 80
were slaves we were not deserted by our Lord; for he secured for us

81 the favour of the kings of Persia, who have provided our food and
added lustre to the temple of our Lord and restored the ruins of
82 Zion, giving us a firm foothold in Judaea and Jerusalem. And now,
Lord, what are we to say, we who have received all this? For we have
broken thy commandments given us through thy servants the pro-
83 phets. Thou didst say: "The land which you are to occupy is a land
defiled with the pollution of its heathen peoples; they have filled it
84 with their impurities. Do not marry your daughters to their sons nor
85 take their daughters for your sons; never try to make peace with
them if you want to be strong and enjoy the good things of the land
86 and take possession of it for your children for ever." All our misfortunes have come upon us through our evil deeds and our great
sins. Although thou, Lord, hast lightened the burden of our sins
87 and given us so firm a root, yet we have fallen away again and broken
thy law by sharing in the impurities of the heathen peoples of this
88 land. But thou wast not so angry with us, Lord, as to destroy us, root,
89 seed, and name; thou keepest faith, O Lord of Israel; the root is left,
90 we are here today. Behold us, now before thee in our sins; because
of all we have done we can no longer hold up our heads before thee.'
91 While Ezra prayed and made confession, weeping prostrate on the
ground before the temple, a very large crowd gathered, men, women,
and youths of Jerusalem, and there was widespread lamentation among
92 the people. Jechonias son of Jeel, one of the Israelites, called out to
Ezra: 'We have sinned against the Lord in taking alien wives from
the heathen population of this land; and yet there is still hope for
93 Israel. Let us take an oath to the Lord to expel all our wives of alien
94 race with their children, in accordance with your judgement and the
95 judgement of all who are obedient to the law of the Lord. Come
now, set about it, it is in your hands; take strong action and we are
96 with you.' Ezra got up and laid an oath upon the principal priests
and Levites of all Israel that they would act in this way, and they
swore to it.

9 Ezra left the court of the temple and entered the room of the priest
2 Joanan son of Eliasibus. There he stayed, eating no food and drinking no water, while he mourned over the serious violations of the law
3 by the community. A proclamation was made throughout Judaea
and in Jerusalem to all the returned exiles that they should assemble
4 at Jerusalem; those who failed to arrive within two or three days,
according to the decision of the elders in office, were to have their

cattle confiscated for temple use and would themselves be excluded
from the community of the returned exiles.
Three days later all Judah and Benjamin had assembled in Jeru- 5
salem; the date was the twentieth of the ninth month. They all sat 6
together in the open space before the temple, shivering because
winter had set in. Ezra stood up and said to them: 'You have broken 7
the law and married alien wives, bringing a fresh burden of guilt on
Israel. Now make confession to the Lord God of our fathers; do his 8, 9
will and separate yourselves from the heathen population of this land
and from your alien wives.'
The whole company answered with a shout: 'We will do as you 10
have said!' 'But', they said, 'our numbers are great, and we cannot 11
stay here in the open in this wintry weather. Nor is this the work of a
day or two only; the offence is widespread among us. Let the leaders 12
of the community stay here, and let all members of our settlements
who have alien wives attend at an appointed time along with the 13
elders and judges of each place, until we turn away the Lord's anger
at what has been done.'
Jonathan son of Azael and Hezekias son of Thocanus took charge 14
on these terms, and Mosollamus, Levi, and Sabbataeus were their
assessors. The returned exiles duly carried all this out. 15
Ezra the priest selected men by name, all chiefs of their clans, and 16
on the new moon of the tenth month they sat to investigate the
matter. This affair of the men who had alien wives was settled by the 17
new moon of the first month.
Among the priests some of those who had come together were 18
found to have alien wives; these were Mathelas, Eleazar, Joribus, and 19
Joadanus of the line of Jeshua son of Josedek and his brothers, who 20
undertook to send away their wives and to offer rams in expiation of
their error. Of the line of Emmer: Ananias, Zabdaeus, Manes, 21
Samaeus, Jereel, and Azarias; of the line of Phaesus: Elionas, 22
Massias, Ishmael, Nathanael, Okidelus, and Saloas. Of the Levites: 23
Jozabadus, Semis, Colius (this is Calitas), Phathaeus, Judah, and
Jonas. Of the temple singers: Eliasibus, Bacchurus. Of the door- 24, 25
keepers: Sallumus and Tolbanes.
Of the people of Israel there were, of the line of Phoros: Jermas, 26
Jeddias, Melchias, Maelus, Eleazar, Asibias, and Bannaeas. Of the 27
line of Ela: Matthanias, Zacharias, Jezrielus, Oabdius, Jeremoth,
and Aedias. Of the line of Zamoth: Eliadas, Eliasimus, Othonias, 28

29 Jarimoth, Sabathus, and Zardaeas. Of the line of Bebae: Joannes,
30 Ananias, Ozabadus, and Emathis. Of the line of Mani: Olamus,
31 Mamuchus, Jedaeus, Jasubus, Asaelus, and Jeremoth. Of the line of
Addi: Naathus, Moossias, Laccunus, Naidus, Matthanias, Sesthel,
32 Balnuus, and Manasseas. Of the line of Annas: Elionas, Asaeas,
33 Melchias, Sabbaeas, and Simon Chosomaeus. Of the line of Asom:
Altannaeus, Mattathias, Bannaeus, Eliphalat, Manasses, and Semi.
34 Of the line of Baani: Jeremias, Momdis, Ismaerus, Juel, Mandae,
Paedias, Anos, Carabasion, Enasibus, Mamnitanaemus, Eliasis,
Bannus, Eliali, Somis, Selemias, and Nathanias. Of the line of
35 Ezora: Sessis, Ezril, Azael, Samatus, Zambris, and Josephus. Of the
36 line of Nooma: Mazitias, Zabadaeas, Edaes, Juel, and Banaeas. All
these had married alien wives; they sent them away with their
children.

37 THE PRIESTS, the Levites, and such Israelites as were in Jerusalem
and its vicinity, settled down there on the new moon of the seventh
38 month; the other Israelites remained in their settlements. The entire
body assembled as one in the open space before the east gateway of
39 the temple and asked Ezra the high priest and doctor of the law to
40 bring the law of Moses given by the Lord God of Israel. On the new
moon of the seventh month he brought the law to all the multitude
41 of men and women alike, and to the priests, for them to hear. He read
it in the open space before the temple gateway from daybreak until
noon, in the presence of both men and women, and the whole body
42 listened intently. Ezra the priest and doctor of the law stood upon
43 the wooden platform which had been prepared. There stood with him,
on his right, Mattathias, Sammus, Ananias, Azarias, Urias, Hezekias,
44 and Baalsamus, and on his left, Phaldaeus, Misael, Melchias,
45 Lothasubus, Nabarias, and Zacharias. Ezra took up the book of the
law; everyone could see him, for he was seated in a conspicuous place
46 in front of them all, and when he opened it they all stood up. Ezra
47 praised the Lord God the Most High God of hosts, the Almighty. All
the multitude cried 'Amen, Amen', and lifting up their hands fell to
48 the ground and worshipped the Lord. Jeshua, Annus, Sarabias,
Jadinus, Jacubus, Sabbataeas, Autaeas, Maeannas, Calitas, Azarias,
Jozabdus, Ananias, and Phiathas, the Levites, taught the law of the
Lord; they read the law of the Lord to the whole company, at the
same time instilling into their minds what was read.

Then the governor[a] said to Ezra the high priest and doctor of the 49
law and to each of the Levites who taught the multitude: 'This day is 50
holy to the Lord.' All were weeping as they heard the law. 'Go 51
then, refresh yourselves with rich food and sweet wine, and send
shares to those who have none; for the day is holy to the Lord. Let 52
there be no sadness; for the Lord will give you glory.' The Levites 53
issued the command to all the people: 'This day is holy, do not be 54
sad.' So they all departed to eat and drink and make merry, and to
send shares to those who had none, and to hold a great celebration;
because the teaching given them had been instilled into their minds. 55
They gathered together.[b]

[*a*] *Gk.* Attharates. [*b*] *Probably the text originally carried on from this point; compare Nehemiah 8. 13.*

THE SECOND BOOK OF ESDRAS

Israel's rejection and glory to come

1 THE SECOND BOOK of the prophet Ezra, son of Seraiah,
son of Azariah, son of Hilkiah, son of Shallum, son of Zadok,
2 son of Ahitub, son of Ahijah, son of Phinehas, son of Eli, son
of Amariah, son of Aziah, son of Marimoth, son of Arna, son of
Uzzi, son of Borith, son of Abishua, son of Phinehas, son of Eleazar,
3 son of Aaron, of the tribe of Levi.

I, EZRA, WAS a captive in Media in the reign of Artaxerxes, king of
4, 5 Persia, when the word of the Lord came to me: 'Go to my people and
proclaim their crimes; tell their children how they have sinned
6 against me, and let them tell their children's children. They have
sinned even more than their fathers; they have forgotten me and
7 sacrificed to alien gods. Was it not I who rescued them from Egypt,
the country where they were slaves? And yet they have provoked
me to anger and ignored my warnings.
8 'Now, Ezra, pluck out your hair and let calamities loose upon
these people who have disobeyed my law. They are beyond correc-
9 tion. How much longer shall I endure them, I who have lavished on
10 them such benefits? Many are the kings I have overthrown for their
11 sake; I struck down Pharaoh with his court and all his army. I destroyed every nation that stood in their way, and in the east I routed
the peoples of two provinces, Tyre and Sidon, and killed all the
enemies of Israel.
12, 13 'Say to them, "These are the words of the Lord: Was it not I who
brought you through the sea, and made safe roads for you where no
road had been? I gave you Moses as your leader, and Aaron as your
14 priest; I gave you light from a pillar of fire, and performed great
miracles among you. And yet you have forgotten me, says the Lord.
15 '"These are the words of the Lord Almighty: I gave you the quails
as a sign; I gave you a camp for your protection. But all you did

there was to grumble and complain—instead of celebrating the 16
victory I had given you when I destroyed your enemies. From that
day to this you have never stopped complaining. Have you forgotten 17
what benefits I conferred on you? When you were hungry and thirsty
in your journey through the desert, you cried out to me, 'Why have 18
you brought us into this desert to kill us? Better to have remained in
Egypt as slaves than to die here in the desert!' I was grieved by your 19
complaints, and gave you manna for food; you ate the bread of
angels. When you were thirsty, I split open the rock, and out flowed 20
water in plenty. Against the summer heat I gave you the shelter of
leafy trees. I gave you fertile lands to divide among your tribes, 21
expelling the Canaanites, Perizzites, and Philistines who opposed
you. What more could I do for you? says the Lord.

'"These are the words of the Lord Almighty: When you were in 22
the desert, suffering thirst by the stream of bitter water and cursing
me, I did not bring down fire upon you for your blasphemy; I cast a 23
tree into the stream and made the water sweet. What am I to do with 24
you, Jacob? Judah, you have refused to obey me. I will turn to
other nations; I will give them my name, and they will keep my
statutes. Because you have deserted me, I will desert you; when you 25
cry for mercy, I will show you none; when you pray to me, I will not 26
listen. You have stained your hands with blood; you run hot-foot to
commit murder. It is not I whom you have deserted, but yourselves, 27
says the Lord.

'"These are the words of the Lord Almighty: Have I not pleaded 28
with you as a father with his sons, as a mother with her daughters or a
nurse with her children? Have I not said, 'Be my people, and I will 29
be your God; be my sons, and I will be your father'? I gathered you 30
as a hen gathers her chickens under her wings. But now what am
I to do with you? I will toss you away. When you offer me sacrifice, 31
I will turn from you; I have rejected your feasts, your new moons,
and your circumcisions. I sent you my servants the prophets, but you 32
took them and killed them, and mutilated their dead bodies. For
their murder I will call you to account, says the Lord.

'"These are the words of the Lord Almighty: Your house is 33
abandoned. I will toss you away like straw before the wind. Your 34
children shall have no posterity, because like you they have ignored
my commandments and done what I have condemned. I will hand 35
over your home to a people soon to come; a people who will trust me,

though they have not known me; who will do my bidding, though
36 I gave them no signs; who never saw the prophets, and yet will keep
37 in mind what the prophets taught of old. I vow that this people yet to
come shall have my favour. Their little ones shall jump for joy. They
have not seen me with their eyes, but they shall perceive by the spirit
and believe all that I have said."

38 'Now, father Ezra, look with triumph at the nation coming from
39 the east. The leaders I shall give them are Abraham, Isaac, and Jacob,
40 Hosea and Amos, Micah and Joel, Obadiah and Jonah, Nahum,
Habakkuk, and Zephaniah, Haggai and Zechariah, and Malachi,
who is also called the Lord's Messenger.

2 'These are the words of the Lord: I freed this people from slavery,
and gave them commandments through my servants the prophets;
but they shut their ears to the prophets, and let my precepts become
2 a dead letter. The mother who bore them says to them: "Go, my
3 sons; I am widowed and deserted. Joyfully I brought you up; I have
lost you with grief and sorrow, because you have sinned against the
4 Lord God and done what I know to be wrong. What can I do for
you now, widowed and deserted as I am? Go, my sons, ask the Lord
5 for mercy." Now I call upon you, father Ezra, to add your testimony
6 to hers, that her children have refused to keep my covenant; and let
your words bring confusion on them. May their mother be despoiled,
7 and may they themselves have no posterity. Condemn them to be
scattered among the nations, and their name to vanish from the
earth, because they have spurned my covenant.

8 'Woe to you, Assyria, for harbouring sinners! Remember, you
9 wicked nation, what I did to Sodom and Gomorrah: their land lies
buried under lumps of pitch and heaps of ashes. That is how I will
deal with those who have disobeyed me, says the Lord Almighty.

10 'These are the words of the Lord to Ezra: Tell my people that
I will give to them the kingdom of Jerusalem which once I offered to
11 Israel. I will withdraw the splendour of my presence from Israel,
and the home that was to be theirs for ever I will give to my own
12 people. The tree of life shall spread its fragrance over them; they shall
13 not toil or grow weary. Ask, and you shall receive; so pray that your
short time of waiting may be made shorter still. The kingdom is
14 ready for you now; be on the watch! Call heaven, call earth, to
witness: I have cancelled the evil and brought the good into being;
for I am the Living One, says the Lord.

'Mother, cherish your sons. Rear them joyfully as a dove rears her 15
nestlings; teach them to walk without stumbling. You are my chosen
one, says the Lord. I will raise up the dead from their resting-places, 16
and bring them out of their tombs, for I have acknowledged that
they bear my name. Have no fear, mother of many sons; I have 17
chosen you, says the Lord.

'I will send my servants Isaiah and Jeremiah to help you. As they 18
prophesied, I have set you apart to be my people. I have made ready
for you twelve trees laden with different kinds of fruit, twelve 19
fountains flowing with milk and honey, and seven great mountains
covered with roses and lilies. There will I fill your sons with joy.
Champion the widow, defend the cause of the fatherless, give to the 20
poor, protect the orphan, clothe the naked. Care for the weak and 21
the helpless, and do not mock at the cripple; watch over the disabled,
and bring the blind to the vision of my brightness. Keep safe within 22
your walls both old and young.

'When you find the dead unburied, mark them with the sign and 23
commit them to the tomb; and then, when I cause the dead to rise,
I will give you the chief place. Be calm, my people; for your time of 24
rest shall come. Care for your children like a good nurse, and train 25
them to walk without falling. Of my servants whom I have given 26
you not one shall be lost; I will demand them back from among your
number. Do not be anxious when the time of trouble and hardship 27
comes; others shall lament and be sad, but you shall have happiness
and plenty. All nations shall envy you, but shall be powerless against 28
you, says the Lord.

'My power shall protect you, and save your sons from hell. Be 29, 30
joyful, mother, you and your sons, for I will come to your rescue.
Remember your children who sleep in the grave; I will bring them 31
up from the depths of the earth, and show mercy to them; for I am
merciful, says the Lord Almighty. Cherish your children until 32
I come, and proclaim my mercy to them; for my favour flows
abundantly from springs that will never run dry.'

I, EZRA, RECEIVED on Mount Horeb a commission from the Lord 33
to go to Israel; but when I came, they scorned me and rejected the
Lord's commandment. Therefore I say to you Gentiles, you who 34
hear and understand: 'Look forward to the coming of your shepherd,
and he will give you everlasting rest; for he who is to come at the end

35 of the world is close at hand. Be ready to receive the rewards of the
kingdom; for light perpetual will shine upon you for ever and ever.
36 Flee from the shadow of this world, and receive the joy and splen-
37 dour that await you. I bear witness openly to my Saviour. It is he
whom the Lord has appointed; receive him and be joyful, giving
thanks to the One who has summoned you to the heavenly realms.
38 Rise, stand up, and see the whole company of those who bear the
39 Lord's mark and sit at his table. They have moved out of the shadow
of this world and have received shining robes from the Lord.
40 Receive, O Zion, your full number, and close the roll of those
41 arrayed in white who have faithfully kept the law of the Lord. The
number of your sons whom you so long desired is now complete.
Pray that the Lord's kingdom may come, so that your people, whom
he summoned when the world began, may be set apart as his own.'
42 I, Ezra, saw on Mount Zion a crowd too large to count, all singing
43 hymns of praise to the Lord. In the middle stood a very tall young
man, taller than all the rest, who was setting a crown on the head of
each one of them; he stood out above them all. I was enthralled at
44, 45 the sight, and asked the angel, 'Sir, who are these?' He replied,
'They are those who have laid aside their mortal dress and put on the
immortal, those who acknowledged the name of God. Now they are
46 being given crowns and palms.' And I asked again, 'Who is the
young man setting crowns on their heads and giving them palms?',
47 and the angel replied, 'He is the Son of God, whom they acknowledged in this mortal life.' I began to praise those who had stood so
48 valiantly for the Lord's name. Then the angel said to me: 'Go and
tell my people all the great and wonderful acts of the Lord God that
you have seen.'

The mystery of human destiny

3 IN THE THIRTIETH YEAR after the fall of Jerusalem, I, Salathiel
(who am also Ezra), was in Babylon. As I lay on my bed I was
2 troubled; my mind was filled with perplexity, as I considered the
desolation of Zion and the prosperity of those who lived in Babylon.
3 My spirit was deeply disturbed; and I uttered my fears to the Most
4 High. 'My Lord, my Master,' I said, 'was it not you, and you alone,

who in the beginning spoke the word that formed the world? You
commanded the dust, and Adam appeared. His body was lifeless; 5
but yours were the hands that had moulded it, and into it you
breathed the breath of life. So you made him a living person. You 6
led him into paradise, which you yourself had planted before the
earth came into being. You gave him your one commandment to 7
obey; he disobeyed it, and thereupon you made him subject to
death, him and his descendants.

'From him were born nations and tribes, peoples and families, too
numerous to count. Each nation went its own way, sinning against 8
you and scorning you; and you did not stop them. But then again, in 9
due time, you brought the flood upon the inhabitants of the earth and
destroyed them. The same doom came upon all: death upon Adam, 10
and the flood upon that generation. One man you spared—Noah, 11
with his household, and all his righteous descendants.

'The population of the earth increased; families and peoples 12
multiplied, nation upon nation. But then once again they began to
sin, more wickedly than those before them. When they sinned, you 13
chose for yourself one of them, whose name was Abraham; him you 14
loved, and to him alone, secretly, at dead of night, you showed how
the world would end. You made an everlasting covenant with him 15
and promised never to abandon his descendants. You gave him 16
Isaac, and to Isaac you gave Jacob and Esau; of these you chose
Jacob for yourself and rejected Esau; and Jacob grew to be a great
nation.

'You rescued his descendants from Egypt and brought them to 17
Mount Sinai. There you bent the sky, shook[a] the earth, moved the 18
round world, made the depths shudder, and turned creation upside
down. Your glory passed through the four gates of fire and earth- 19
quake, wind and frost; and you gave the commandments of the law
to the Israelites, the race of Jacob. But you did not take away their 20
wicked heart and enable your law to bear fruit in them. For the first 21
man, Adam, was burdened with a wicked heart; he sinned and was
overcome, and not only he but all his descendants. So the weakness 22
became inveterate. Although your law was in your people's hearts, a
rooted wickedness was there too; so that the good came to nothing,
and what was bad persisted.

'Years went by, and when the time came you raised up a servant 23

[*a*] *So some Vss.; Lat.* fixed.

24 for yourself, whose name was David. You told him to build the city
that bears your name and there offer to you in sacrifice what was
25 already your own. This was done for many years; until the inhabi-
26 tants of the city went astray, behaving just like Adam and all his line;
27 for they had the same wicked heart. And so you gave your own city
over to your enemies.

28 'I said to myself: "Perhaps those in Babylon lead better lives, and
29 that is why they have conquered Zion." But when I arrived here,
I saw more wickedness than I could reckon, and these thirty years
30 I have seen many evil-doers with my own eyes. My heart sank, because I saw how you tolerate sinners and spare the godless; how you
have destroyed your own people, but protected your enemies. You
31 have given no hint whatever to anyone how to understand your ways.[a]
32 Is Babylon more virtuous than Zion? Has any nation except Israel
ever known you? What tribes have put their trust in your covenants
33 as the tribes of Jacob have? But they have seen no reward, no fruit
for their pains. I have travelled up and down among the nations, and
have seen how they prosper, heedless though they are of your com-
34 mandments. So weigh our sins in the balance against the sins of the
35 rest of the world; and it will be clear which way the scale tips. Has
there ever been a time when the inhabitants of the earth did not sin
against you? Has any nation ever kept your commandments like
36 Israel? You may find one man here, one there; but nowhere a whole
nation.'

4 The angel who was sent to me, whose name was Uriel, replied:
2 'You are at a loss to explain this world; do you then expect to under-
3 stand the ways of the Most High?' 'Yes, my lord', I replied.

'I have been sent to propound to you three of the ways of this
4 world,' he continued, 'to give you three illustrations. If you can
explain to me any one of them, then I will answer your question
about the way of the Most High, and teach you why the heart is
wicked.'

5 I said, 'Speak, my lord.' 'Come then,' he said, 'weigh me a
pound of fire, measure me a bushel[b] of wind, or call back a day that
has passed.'

6 'How can you ask me to do that?' I replied; 'no man on earth can
7 do it.' He said: 'Suppose I had asked you, "How many dwellings are
there in the heart of the sea? or how many streams to feed the deep?

[a] how...ways: *so some Vss.; Lat. obscure.* [b] *So some Vss.; Lat.* the blast.

or how many watercourses above the vault of heaven? Where are the
paths out of the grave, and the roads into[a] paradise?", you might then 8
have replied, "I have never been down into the deep, I have not yet
gone down into the grave, I have never gone up into heaven." But, as 9
it is, I have only asked you about fire, about wind, and about yester-
day, things you are bound to have met; and yet you have failed to tell
me the answers.

'If then', he went on, 'you cannot understand things you have 10
grown up with, how can your small capacity comprehend the ways of 11
the Most High? A man corrupted by the corrupt world can never
know the way of the incorruptible.'[b]

When I heard that, I fell[c] prostrate and exclaimed: 'Better never 12
to have come into existence than be born into a world of wickedness
and suffering which we cannot explain!' He replied, 'I went out into 13
a wood, and the trees of the forest were making a plan. They said, 14
"Come, let us make war on the sea, force it to retreat, and win
ground for more woods." The waves of the sea made a similar plan: 15
they said, "Come, let us attack the trees of the forest, conquer them,
and annex their territory." The plan made by the trees came to 16
nothing, for fire came and burnt them down. The plan made by the 17
waves failed just as badly, for the sand stood its ground and blocked
their way. If you had to judge between the two, which would you 18
pronounce right, and which wrong?'

I answered, 'Both were wrong; their plans were impossible, for 19
the land is assigned to the trees, and to the sea is allotted a place for
its waves.'

'Yes,' he replied, 'you have judged rightly. Why then have you 20
failed to do so with your own question? Just as the land belongs to 21
the trees and the sea to the waves, so men on earth can understand
earthly things and nothing else; only those who live[d] above the skies
can understand the things above the skies.'

'But tell me, my lord,' I said, 'why then have I been given the 22
faculty of understanding? My question is not about the distant 23
heavens, but about the things which happen every day before our
eyes. Why has Israel been made a byword among the Gentiles; why
has the people you loved been put at the mercy of godless nations?
Why has the law of our fathers been brought to nothing, and the

[*a*] the grave...into: *so some Vss.; Lat. omits.* [*b*] A man...incorruptible: *reading based on other Vss.; Lat. obscure.* [*c*] When...fell: *so some Vss.; Lat. defective.* [*d*] *Or* he who lives.

24 written covenants made a dead letter? We pass like a flight of locusts,
our life is but a vapour, and we are not worth the Lord's pity,
25 though we bear his name; what then will he do for us? These are my
questions.'

26 He answered: 'If you survive, you will see; if you live long
enough, you will marvel.[a] For this present age is quickly passing
27 away; it is full of sorrow and frailties, too full to enjoy what is
28 promised in due time for the godly. The evil about which you ask me
29 has been sown, but its reaping has not yet come. Until the crop of
evil has been reaped as well as sown, until the ground where it was
sown has vanished, there will be no room for the field which has
30 been sown with the good. A grain of the evil seed was sown in the
heart of Adam from the first; how much godlessness has it produced
already! How much more will it produce before the harvest!
31 Reckon this up: if one grain of evil seed has produced so great a crop
32 of godlessness, how vast a harvest will there be when good seeds
beyond number have been sown!'

33 I asked, 'But when? How long have we to wait? Why are our lives
34 so short and so miserable?' He replied, 'Do not be in a greater hurry
than the Most High himself. You are in a hurry for yourself alone;
35 the Most High for many. Are not these the very questions which
were asked by the righteous in the storehouse of souls: "How long
must we stay here? When will the harvest begin, the time when we
36 get our reward?" And the archangel Jeremiel gave them this
answer: "As soon as the number of those like yourselves is complete.
37 For the Lord has weighed the world in a balance, he has measured
and numbered the ages; he will move nothing, alter nothing, until
the appointed number is achieved."'

38 'But, my lord, my master,' I replied, 'we are all of us sinners
39 through and through. Can it be that because of us, because of the
sins of mankind, the harvest and the reward of the just are delayed?'
40 'Go,' he said, 'ask a pregnant woman whether she can keep the child
41 in her womb any longer after the nine months are complete.' 'No,
my lord,' I said, 'she cannot.' He went on: 'The storehouses of souls
42 in the world below are like the womb. As a woman in travail is
impatient to see the end of her labour, so they are impatient to give
43 back all the souls committed to them since time began. Then all your
questions will be answered.'

[a] *So one Vs.; Lat.* live, you will often marvel.

I said, 'If it is possible for you to tell and for me to understand, 44
will you be gracious enough to disclose one thing more: which is the 45
longer—the future still to come, or the past that has gone by?
What is past I know, but not what is still to be.' 'Come and stand on 46, 47
my right,' he said; 'you shall see a vision, and I will explain what it
means.'

So I stood and watched, and there passed before my eyes a blazing 48
fire; when the flames had disappeared from sight, there was still
some smoke left. After that a dark rain-cloud passed before me; 49
there was a heavy storm, and when it had gone over, there were
still some raindrops left. 'Reflect on this', said the angel. 'The 50
shower of rain filled a far greater space than the drops of water,
and the fire more than the smoke. In the same way, the past far
exceeds the future in length; what remains is but raindrops and
smoke.'

'Pray tell me,' I said, 'do you think that I shall live to see those 51
days? Or in whose lifetime will they come?' 'If you ask me what 52
signs will herald them,' he said, 'I can tell you in part. But the
length of your own life I am not commissioned to tell you; of that
I know nothing.

'But now to speak of the signs: there will come a time when the 5
inhabitants of the earth will be seized with panic.[a] The way of truth
will be hidden from sight, and the land will be barren of faith. There 2
will be a great increase in wickedness, worse than anything you now
see or have ever heard of. The country you now see governing the 3
world will become a trackless desert, laid waste for all to see. After 4
the third period (if the Most High grants you a long enough life) you
will see confusion everywhere. The sun will suddenly begin to shine
in the middle of the night, and the moon in the day-time. Trees will 5
drip blood, stones will speak, nations will be in confusion, and the
courses of the stars will be changed. A king unwelcome to the 6
inhabitants of earth will succeed to the throne; even the birds will all
fly away. The Dead Sea will cast up fish, and at night a voice will 7
sound, unknown to the many but heard by all.[b] Chasms[c] will open in 8
many places and spurt out flames incessantly. Wild beasts will range
far afield, women will give birth to monsters, fresh springs will run 9
with salt water, and everywhere friends will become enemies. Then

[*a*] *So some Vss.; Lat. corrupt.* [*b*] *Some Vss. read* and at night one whom the many do not know will utter his voice, and all will hear it. [*c*] *So one Vs.; Lat.* Chaos.

understanding will be hidden, and reason withdraw to her secret
10 chamber. Many will seek her, but not find her; the earth will over-
11 flow with vice and wickedness. One country will ask another, "Has
justice passed your way, or any just man?", and it will answer, "No."
12 In those days men will hope, but hope in vain; they will strive, but
never succeed.
13 'These are the signs I am allowed to tell you. But turn again to
prayer, continue to weep and fast for seven days; and then you shall
hear further signs, even greater than these.'
14 I awoke with a start, shuddering; my spirit faltered, and I was
15 near to fainting. But the angel who had come and talked to me gave
me support and strength, and set me on my feet.
16 The next night Phaltiel, the leader of the people, came to me.
17 'Where have you been?' he asked, 'and why that sad look? Have you
18 forgotten that Israel in exile has been entrusted to your care? Rouse
yourself, take nourishment. Do not abandon us like a shepherd
19 abandoning his flock to savage wolves.' I replied: 'Leave me; for
seven days do not come near me, then you may come again.' When
he heard this, he left me.

20 FOR SEVEN DAYS I fasted, with tears and lamentations, as the
21 angel Uriel had told me to do. By the end of the seven days my
22 mind was again deeply disturbed, but I recovered the power of
thought and spoke once more to the Most High.
23 'My Lord, my Master,' I said, 'out of all the forests of the earth,
24 and all their trees, you have chosen one vine; from all the lands in
the whole world you have chosen one plot; and out of all the flowers
25 in the whole world you have chosen one lily. From all the depths of
the sea you have filled one stream for yourself, and of all the cities
26 ever built you have set Zion apart as your own. From all the birds
that were created you have named one dove, and from all the animals
27 that were fashioned you have taken one sheep. Out of all the countless nations, you have adopted one for your own, and to this chosen
28 people you have given the law which all men have approved. Why
then, Lord, have you put this one people at the mercy of so many?
Why have you humiliated[a] this one stock more than all others, and
29 scattered your own people among the hordes of heathen? Those who
reject your promises have trampled on the people who trust your

[a] *So some Vss.; Lat.* prepared.

covenants. If you so hate your people, they should be punished by 30
your own hand.'

When I had finished speaking, the angel who had visited me that 31
previous night was sent to me again. 'Listen to me,' he said, 'and 32
I will give you instruction. Attend carefully, and I will tell you
more.' 'Speak on, my lord', I replied. 33

He said to me, 'You are in great sorrow of heart for Israel's sake.
Do you love Israel more than Israel's Maker does?' 'No, my lord,' 34
I said, 'but sorrow has forced me to speak; my heart is tortured
every hour as I try to understand the ways of the Most High and to
fathom some part of his judgements.'

He said to me, 'You cannot.' 'Why not, my lord?' I asked. 'Why 35
then was I born? Why could not my mother's womb have been my
grave? Then I should never have seen Jacob's trials and the weari-
ness of the race of Israel.'

He said to me, 'Count me those who are not yet born, collect the 36
scattered drops of rain, and make the withered flowers bloom again;
unlock me the storehouses and let loose the winds shut up there; 37
or make visible the shape of a voice. Then I will answer your
question about Israel's trials.'

'My lord, my master,' I said, 'how can there be anyone with such 38
knowledge except the One whose home is not among men? I am 39
only a fool; how then can I answer your questions?'

He said to me, 'Just as you cannot do any of the things I have put 40
to you, so you will not be able to find out my judgements or the
ultimate purpose of the love I have promised to my people.'

I said, 'But surely, lord, your promise[a] is to those who are alive at 41
the end. What is to be the fate of those who lived before us, or of
ourselves, or of those who come after us?'

He said to me, 'I will compare the judgement to a circle: the 42
latest will not be too late, nor the earliest too early.'

To this I replied, 'Could you not have made all men, past, present, 43
and future, at one and the same time? Then you could have held
your assize with less delay.' But he answered, 'The creation may not 44
go faster than the Creator, nor could the world support at the same
time all those created to live on it.'

'But, my lord,' I said, 'you have told me that you will at one and 45
the same time restore to life every creature you have made; how can

[a] *So one Vs.; Lat. obscure.*

that be? If it is going to be possible for all of them to be alive at the
same time and for the world to support them all, then it could
46 support all of them together now.' 'Put your question in terms of a
woman's womb', he replied. 'Say to a woman, "If you give birth to
ten children, why do you do so at intervals? Why not give birth
47 to ten at one and the same time?"' 'No, my lord, she cannot do that,'
48 I said; 'the births must take place at intervals.' 'True,' he answered;
'and I have made the earth's womb to bring forth at intervals those
49 conceived in it. An infant cannot give birth, nor can a woman who is
too old; and I have made the same rule for the world I have created.'
50 I continued my questions. 'Since you have opened the way,'
I said, 'may I now ask: is our mother that you speak of still young,
51, 52 or is she already growing old?' He replied, 'Ask any mother why the
children she has lately borne are not like those born earlier, but
53 smaller. And she will tell you, "Those who were born in the vigour
of my youth are very different from those born in my old age, when
54 my womb is beginning to fail." Think of it then like this: if you are
55 smaller than those born before you, and those who follow you are
smaller still, the reason is that creation is growing old and losing the
strength of youth.'
56 I said to him, 'If I have won your favour, my lord, show me
6 through whom you will visit your creation.' He said to me, 'Think
of the beginning of this earth: the gates of the world had not yet been
2 set up; no winds gathered and blew, no thunder pealed, no lightning
3 flashed; the foundations of paradise were not yet laid, nor were its
fair flowers there to see; the powers that move the stars were not
4 established, nor the countless hosts of angels assembled, nor the vast
tracts of air set up on high; the divisions of the firmaments had not
received their names. Zion had not yet been chosen as God's own
5 footstool; the present age had not been planned; the schemes of its
sinners had not yet been outlawed, nor had God's seal yet been set on
6 those who have stored up a treasure of fidelity. Then did I think my
thought; and the whole world was created through me and through
me alone. In the same way, through me and through me alone the
end shall come.'
7 'Tell me', I went on, 'about the interval that divides the ages.
8 When will the first age end and the next age begin?' He said, 'The
interval will be no bigger than that between Abraham and Abraham;
for Jacob and Esau were his descendants, and Jacob's hand was

grasping Esau's heel at the moment of their birth. Esau represents 9
the end of the first age, and Jacob the beginning of the next age. The 10
beginning of a man is his hand, and the end of a man is his heel.[a]
Between the heel and the hand, Ezra, do not look for any interval.'
'My lord, my master,' I said, 'if I have won your favour, make 11, 12
known to me the last of your signs, of which you showed me a part
that former night.'
'Rise to your feet,' he replied, 'and you will hear a loud resound- 13
ing voice. When it speaks, do not be frightened if the place where 14–15
you stand trembles and shakes; it speaks of the end, and the earth's
foundations will understand that it is speaking of them. They will 16
tremble and shake; for they know that at the end they must be transformed.' On hearing this I rose to my feet and listened; and a voice 17
began to speak. Its sound was like the sound of rushing waters.
The voice said: 18
'The time draws near when I shall come to judge those who live
on the earth, the time when I shall inquire into the wickedness of 19
wrong-doers, the time when Zion's humiliation will be over, the 20
time when a seal will be set on the age about to pass away. Then
I will perform these signs: the books shall be opened in the sight of
heaven, and all shall see them at the same moment. Children only 21
one year old shall be able to talk, and pregnant women shall give
birth to premature babes of three and four months, who shall live
and leap about. Fields that were sown shall suddenly prove unsown, 22
and barns that were full shall suddenly be found empty. There shall 23
be a loud trumpet-blast and it shall strike terror into all who hear it.
At that time friends shall make war on friends as though they were 24
enemies, and the earth and all its inhabitants shall be terrified.
Running streams shall stand still; for three hours they shall cease to
flow.
'Whoever is left after all that I have foretold, he shall be preserved, 25
and shall see the deliverance that I bring and the end of this world of
mine. They shall all see the men who were taken up into heaven 26
without ever knowing death. Then shall men on earth feel a change
of heart and come to a better mind. Wickedness shall be blotted out 27
and deceit destroyed, but fidelity shall flourish, corruption be over- 28
come, and truth, so long unfruitful, be brought to light.'
While the voice was speaking to me, the ground under me began to 29

[a] The beginning of a man...heel: *reading based on other Vss.; Lat. defective.*

30 quake.[a] Then the angel said to me, 'These, then, are the revelations
31 I have brought you this night.[b] If once again you pray and fast for
32 seven days, then I will return to tell you even greater things.[c] For be
sure your voice has been heard by the Most High. The Mighty God
has seen your integrity and the chastity you have observed all your
33 life. That is why he has sent me to you with all these revelations, and
34 with this message: "Be confident, and have no fear. Do not rush too
quickly into unprofitable thoughts now in the present age; then you
will not act hastily when the last age comes."'

35 THEREUPON I wept and fasted again for seven days in the same
way as before, thus completing the three weeks enjoined on me.
36 On the eighth night I was again disturbed at heart, and spoke to the
37, 38 Most High. With spirit aflame and in great agony of mind I said:
'O Lord, at the beginning of creation you spoke the word. On the
first day you said, "Let heaven and earth be made!", and your word
39 carried out its work. At that time the hovering spirit was there, and
darkness circled round; there was silence, no sound as yet of human
40 voice.[d] Then you commanded a ray of light to be brought out of
your store-chambers, to make your works visible from that time on-
41 wards. On the second day you created the angel[e] of the firmament,
and commanded him to make a dividing barrier between the waters,
42 one part withdrawing upwards and the other remaining below. On
the third day you ordered the waters to collect in a seventh part of
the earth; the other six parts you made into dry land, and from it
43 kept some to be sown and tilled for your service. Your word went
44 forth, and at once the work was done. A vast profusion of fruits
appeared instantly, of every kind and taste that can be desired, with
flowers of the most subtle colours and mysterious scents. These were
45 made on the third day. On the fourth day by your command you
created the splendour of the sun, the light of the moon, and the
46 stars in their appointed places; and you ordered them to be
at the service of man, whose creation was about to take place.
47 On the fifth day you commanded the seventh part, where the
water was collected, to bring forth living things, birds and fishes.
48 And so, at your command, dumb lifeless water brought forth living

[*a*] the ground...quake: *reading based on other Vss.; Lat. obscure.* [*b*] *So one Vs.; Lat.* this coming night. [*c*] *So other Vss.; Lat. adds* in the day-time. [*d*] *So some Vss.; Lat. adds* from you. [*e*] *Literally* spirit.

creatures, and gave the nations cause to tell of your wonders. Then 49
you set apart two creatures: one you called Behemoth and the other
Leviathan. You put them in separate places, for the seventh part 50
where the water was collected was not big enough to hold them both.
A part of the land which was made dry on the third day you gave to 51
Behemoth as his territory, a country of a thousand hills. To Levia- 52
than you gave the seventh part, the water. You have kept them to be
food for whom you will and when you will. On the sixth day you 53
ordered the earth to produce for you cattle, wild beasts, and
creeping things. To crown your work you created Adam, and gave 54
him sovereignty over everything you had made. It is from Adam that
we, your chosen people, are all descended.

'I have recited the whole story of the creation, O Lord, because 55
you have said that you made this first world for our sake, and that all 56
the rest of the nations descended from Adam are nothing, that they
are no better than spittle, and, for all their numbers, no more than a
drop from a bucket. And yet, O Lord, those nations which count for 57
nothing are today ruling over us and devouring us; and we, your 58
people, have been put into their power—your people, whom you
have called your first-born, your only son, your champion, and your
best beloved. Was the world really made for us? Why, then, may we 59
not take possession of our world? How much longer shall it be so?'

When I had finished speaking, the same angel was sent to me as on 7
the previous nights. He said to me, 'Rise to your feet, Ezra, and 2
listen to the message I have come to give you.' 'Speak, my lord', 3
I said.

He said to me: 'Imagine a sea set in a vast open space, spreading
far[a] and wide, but the entrance to it narrow like the gorge of a river. 4
If anyone is determined to reach this sea, whether to set eyes on it or 5
to gain command of it, he cannot arrive at its open waters except
through the narrow gorge. Or again, imagine a city built in a plain, a 6
city full of everything you can desire, but the entrance to it narrow 7
and steep, with fire to the right and deep water to the left. There is 8
only the one path, between the fire and the water; and that is only
wide enough for one man at a time. If some man has been given this 9
city as a legacy, how can he take possession of his inheritance except
by passing through these dangerous approaches?' 'That is the only 10
way, my lord', I agreed.

[a] spreading far: *reading based on other Vss.; Lat.* deep.

11 He said to me: 'Such is the lot of Israel. It was for Israel that
I made the world, and when Adam transgressed my decrees the
12 creation came under judgement. The entrances to this world were
made narrow, painful, and arduous, few and evil, full of perils and
13 grinding hardship. But the entrances to the greater world are broad
14 and safe, and lead to immortality. All men must therefore enter this
narrow and futile existence; otherwise they can never attain the
15 blessings in store. Why then, Ezra, are you so deeply disturbed at the
16 thought that you are mortal and must die? Why have you not turned
your mind to the future instead of the present?'

17 'My lord, my master,' I replied, 'in your law you have laid it
down that the just shall come to enjoy these blessings but the un-
18 godly shall be lost. The just, therefore, can endure this narrow life
and look for the spacious life hereafter; but those who have lived a
wicked life will have gone through the narrows without ever reaching
the open spaces.'

19 He said to me: 'You are not a better judge than God, nor wiser
20 than the Most High. Better that many now living should be lost,
21 than that the law God has set before them should be despised! God
has given clear instructions for all men when they come into this
world, telling them how to attain life and how to escape punishment.
22 But the ungodly have refused to obey him; they have set up their
23 own empty ideas, and planned deceit and wickedness; they have
even denied the existence of the Most High and have not acknow-
24 ledged his ways. They have rejected his law and refused his promises,
have neither put faith in his decrees nor done what he commands.
25 Therefore, Ezra, emptiness for the empty, fullness for the full!

26 'Listen! The time shall come when the signs I have foretold will
be seen; the city which is now invisible[a] shall appear and the
27 country now concealed be made visible. Everyone who has been
delivered from the evils I have foretold shall see for himself my
28 marvellous acts. My son the Messiah[b] shall appear with his companions and bring four hundred years of happiness to all who
29 survive. At the end of that time, my son the Messiah shall die, and
30 so shall all mankind who draw breath. Then the world shall return to
its original silence for seven days as at the beginning of creation, and
31 no one shall be left alive. After seven days the age which is not yet

[a] *So some Vss.; Lat.* the city, the bride, which is now seen... [b] *So some Vss.; Lat.* My son Jesus.

awake shall be roused and the age which is corruptible shall die.
The earth shall give up those who sleep in it, and the dust those who 32
rest there in silence; and the storehouses shall give back the souls
entrusted to them. Then the Most High shall be seen on the judge- 33
ment-seat, and there shall be an end of all pity and patience. Judge- 34
ment alone shall remain; truth shall stand firm and faithfulness be
strong; requital[a] shall at once begin and open payment be made; 35
good deeds shall awake and wicked deeds shall not be allowed to
sleep.[b] Then the place of torment shall appear, and over against it the [36]
place of rest; the furnace of hell shall be displayed, and on the opposite side the paradise of delight.

'Then the Most High shall say to the nations that have been raised [37]
from the dead: "Look and understand who it is you have denied and
refused to serve, and whose commandment you have despised. Look [38]
on this side, then on that: here are rest and delight, there fire and
torments." That is what he will say to them on the day of judgement.

'That day will be a day without sun, moon, or stars; without [39, 40]
cloud, thunder, or lightning; wind, water, or air; darkness, evening,
or morning; without summer, spring, or winter; without heat, frost, [41]
or cold; without hail, rain, or dew; without noonday, night, or [42]
dawn; without brightness, glow, or light. There shall be only the
radiant glory of the Most High, by which all men will see everything
that lies before them. It shall last as it were for a week of years. [43]
Such is the order that I have appointed for the Judgement. I have [44]
given this revelation to you alone.'

I replied: 'My lord, I repeat what I said before: "How blest are [45]
the living who obey the decrees you have laid down!" But as for [46]
those for whom I have been praying, is there any man alive who has
never sinned, any man who has never transgressed your covenant?
I see now that there are few to whom the world to come will bring [47]
happiness, and many to whom it will bring torment. For the wicked [48]
heart has grown up in us, which has estranged us from God's ways,[c]
brought us into corruption and the way of death, opened out to us
the paths of ruin, and carried us far away from life. It has done this,
not merely to a few, but to almost all who have been created.'

The angel replied: 'Listen to me and I will give you further [49]

[*a*] *Probable meaning; literally* work. [*b*] *The passage from verse* [*36*] *to verse* [*105*], *missing from the text of the Authorized Version, but found in ancient witnesses, has been restored.* [*c*] *Literally* from these things.

[50] instruction and correction. It is for this reason that the Most High
[51] has created not one world but two. There are, you say, not many who
are just, but only a few, whereas the wicked are very numerous; well
[52] then, hear the answer. Suppose you had a very few precious stones;
would you add to their number by putting common lead and clay
[53, 54] among them[a]?' 'No,' I said, 'no one would do that.' 'Look at it also
in this way,' he continued; 'speak to the earth and humbly ask her;
[55] she will give you the answer. Say to her: "You produce gold, silver,
[56] and copper, iron, lead, and clay. There is more silver than gold,
more copper than silver, more iron than copper, more lead than iron,
[57] more clay than lead." Then judge for yourself which things are
valuable and desirable—those that are common, or those that are
[58] rare.' 'My lord, my master,' I said, 'the common things are cheaper,
[59] and the rarer are more valuable.' He replied, 'Consider then what
follows from that: the owner of something hard to get has more cause
[60] to be pleased than the owner of what is common. In the same way,
at my promised judgement,[b] I shall have joy in the few who are saved,
because it is they who have made my glory prevail, and through
[61] them that my name has been made known. But I shall not grieve for
the many who are lost; for they are no more than a vapour, they are
like flame or smoke; they catch fire, blaze up, and then die out.'

[62] Then I said: 'Mother Earth, what have you brought forth! Is the
[63] mind of man, like the rest of creation, a product of the dust? Far
better then if the very dust had never been created, and so had never
[64] produced man's mind! But, as it is, we grow up with the power of
thought and are tortured by it; we are doomed to die and we know it.
[65] What sorrow for mankind; what happiness for the wild beasts! What
sorrow for every mother's son; what gladness for the cattle and
[66] flocks! How much better their lot than ours! They have no judgement to expect, no knowledge of torment or salvation after death.
[67] What good to us is the promise of a future life if it is going to be one
[68] of torment? For every man alive is burdened and defiled with
[69] wickedness, a sinner through and through. Would it not have been
better for us if there had been no judgement awaiting us after death?'

[70] The angel replied: 'When the Most High was creating the world
and Adam and his descendants, he first of all planned the judgement
[71] and what goes with it. Your own words, when you said that man

[*a*] by putting...them: *probable reading, based on other Vss.; Lat. obscure.*
[*b*] *Reading based on other Vss.; Lat.* creation.

grows up with the power of thought, will give you the answer. It [72]
was with conscious knowledge that the people of this world sinned,
and that is why torment awaits them; they received the commandments but did not keep them, they accepted the law but violated it.
What defence will they be able to make at the judgement, what [73]
answer at the last day? How patient the Most High has been with the [74]
men of this world, and for how long!—not for their own sake, but for
the sake of the destined age to be.'
Then I said: 'If I have won your favour, my lord, make this plain [75]
to me: at death, when every one of us gives back his soul, shall we be
kept at rest until the time when you begin to create your new world,
or does our torment begin at once?' 'I will tell you that also', he [76]
replied. 'But do not include yourself among those who have despised
my law; do not count yourself with those who are to be tormented.
For you have a treasure of good works stored up with the Most High, [77]
though you will not be shown it until the last days. But now to speak [78]
of death: when the Most High has given final sentence for a man to
die, the spirit leaves the body to return to the One who gave it, and
first of all to adore the glory of the Most High. But as for those who [79]
have rejected the ways of the Most High and despised his law, and
who hate all that fear God, their spirits enter no settled abode, but [80]
roam thenceforward in torment, grief, and sorrow. And this for
seven reasons. First, they have despised the law of the Most High. [81]
Secondly, they have lost their last chance of making a good repen- [82]
tance and so gaining life. Thirdly, they can see the reward in store [83]
for those who have trusted the covenants of the Most High.
Fourthly, they begin to think of the torment that awaits them at the [84]
end. Fifthly, they see that angels are guarding the abode of the [85]
other souls in deep silence. Sixthly, they see that they are soon[a] to [86]
enter into torment. The seventh cause for grief, the strongest cause of [87]
all, is this: at the sight of the Most High in his glory, they break down
in shame, waste away in remorse, and shrivel with fear remembering
how they sinned against him in their lifetime, and how they are soon
to be brought before him for judgement on the last day.
'As for those who have kept to the way laid down by the Most [88]
High, this is what is appointed for them when their time comes to
leave their mortal bodies. During their stay on earth they served the [89]
Most High in spite of constant hardship and danger, and kept to the

[*a*] *So some Vss.; Lat. obscure.*

[90] last letter the law given them by the lawgiver. Their reward is this:
[91] first they shall exult to see the glory of God who will receive them as
his own, and then they shall enter into rest in seven appointed stages
[92] of joy. Their first joy is their victory in the long fight against their
inborn impulses to evil, which have failed to lead them astray from
[93] life into death. Their second joy is to see the souls of the wicked
[94] wandering ceaselessly, and the punishment in store for them. Their
third joy is the good report given of them by their Maker, that
throughout their life they kept the law with which they were en-
[95] trusted. Their fourth joy is to understand the rest which they are
now to share in the storehouses, guarded by angels in deep silence,
[96] and the glory waiting for them in the next age. Their fifth joy is the
contrast between the corruptible world they have escaped and the
future life that is to be their possession, between the cramped
laborious[a] life from which they have been set free and the spacious
[97] life which will soon be theirs to enjoy for ever and ever. Their sixth
joy will be the revelation that they are to shine like stars, never to
[98] fade or die, with faces radiant as the sun. Their seventh joy, the
greatest joy of all, will be the confident and exultant assurance which
will be theirs, free from all fear and shame, as they press forward to
see face to face the One whom they served in their lifetime, and from
whom they are now to receive their reward in glory.

[99] 'The joys I have been declaring are the appointed destiny for the souls of the just; the torments I described before are the sufferings appointed for the rebellious.'

[100] Then I asked: 'When souls are separated from their bodies, will
they be given the opportunity to see what you have described to me?'
[101] 'They will be allowed seven days,' he replied; 'for seven days they
will be permitted to see the things I have told you, and after that
they will join the other souls in their abodes.'

[102] Then I asked: 'If I have won your favour, my lord, tell me more.
On the day of judgement will the just be able to win pardon for the
[103] wicked, or pray for them to the Most High? Can fathers do so for
their sons, or sons for their parents? Can brothers pray for brothers,
relatives and friends[b] for their nearest and dearest?'

[104] 'You have won my favour,' he replied, 'and I will tell you. The day of judgement is decisive,[c] and sets its seal on the truth for all

[*a*] *So some Vss.; Lat. obscure.* [*b*] friends: *so some Vss.; Lat.* the faithful. [*c*] *So one Vs.; Lat.* stern.

to see. In the present age a father cannot send his son in his place,
nor a son his father, a master his slave, nor a man his best friend, to
be ill[a] for him, or sleep, or eat, or be cured for him. In the same way [105]
no one shall ever ask pardon for another; when that day comes,
every individual will be held responsible for his own wickedness
or goodness.'

To this I replied: 'But how is it, then, that we read of intercessions 36 [106]
in scripture? First, there is Abraham, who prayed for the people of
Sodom; then Moses, who prayed for our ancestors when they sinned
in the desert. Next, there is Joshua, who prayed for the Israelites in 37 [107]
the time of Achan, then Samuel in the time of Saul,[b] David during 38 [108]
the plague,[c] and Solomon at the dedication of the temple. Elijah 39 [109]
prayed for rain for the people, and for a dead man that he might be
brought back to life. Hezekiah prayed for the nation in the time 40 [110]
of Sennacherib; and there are many more besides. If, then, in the 41 [111]
time when corruption grew and wickedness increased, the just asked
pardon for the wicked, why cannot it be the same on the day of
judgement?'

The angel gave me this answer: 'The present world is not the end, 42 [112]
and the glory of God does not stay in it continually.[d] That is why the
strong have prayed for the weak. But the day of judgement will be 43 [113]
the end of the present world and the beginning of the eternal world
to come, a world in which corruption will be over, all excess 44 [114]
abolished, and unbelief uprooted, in which justice will be full-
grown, and truth will have risen like the sun. On the day of judge- 45 [115]
ment, therefore, there can be no mercy for the man who has lost his
case, no reversal for the man who has won it.'

I replied, 'But this is my point, my first point and my last: how 46 [116]
much better it would have been if the earth had never produced
Adam at all, or, since it has done so, if he had been restrained from
sinning! For what good does it do us all to live in misery now and 47 [117]
have nothing but punishment to expect after death? O Adam, what 48 [118]
have you done? Your sin was not your fall alone; it was ours also, the
fall of all your descendants. What good is the promise of immortality 49 [119]
to us, when we have committed mortal sins; or the hope of eternity, 50 [120]
in the wretched and futile state to which we have come; or the 51 [121]

[*a*] *So some Vss.; Lat.* to understand. [*b*] in the time of Saul: *so some Vss.; Lat. omits.*
[*c*] during the plague: *so some Vss.; Lat.* for the destruction. [*d*] does...continually:
so some Vss.; Lat. regularly stays in it.

prospect of dwelling in health and safety, when we have lived such
[122] 52 evil lives? The glory of the Most High will guard those who have
led a life of purity; but what help is that to us whose conduct has
[123] 53 been so wicked? What good is the revelation of paradise and its
imperishable fruit, the source of perfect satisfaction and healing?
[124] 54 For we shall never enter it, since we have made depravity our home.
[125] 55 Those who have practised self-discipline shall shine with faces
brighter than the stars; but what good is that to us whose faces are
[126] 56 darker than the night? For during a lifetime of wickedness we have
never given a thought to the sufferings awaiting us after death.'
[127] 57 The angel replied, 'This is the thought for every man to keep in
[128] 58 mind during his earthly contest: if he loses, he must accept the
sufferings you have mentioned, but if he wins, the rewards I have
[129] 59 been describing will be his. For that was the way which Moses in his
time urged the people to take, when he said, "Choose life and live!"
[130] 60 But they did not believe him, nor the prophets after him, nor me
[131] 61 when I spoke to them. Over their damnation there will be no sorrow; there will only be joy for the salvation of those who have
believed.'[a]
[132] 62 'My lord,' I replied, 'I know that the Most High is called
"compassionate", because he has compassion on those yet unborn;
[133] 63 and called "merciful", because he shows mercy to those who repent
[134] 64 and live by his law; and "patient", because he shows patience to those
[135] 65 who have sinned, his own creatures as they are; and "benefactor",
[136] 66 because he prefers giving to taking; and "rich in forgiveness", because
again and again he forgives sinners, past, present, and to come.
[137] 67 For without his continued forgiveness there could be no hope of life
[138] 68 for the world and its inhabitants. And he is called "generous",
because without his generosity in releasing sinners from their sins,
not one ten-thousandth part of mankind could hope to be given life;
[139] 69 and he is also called "judge", for unless he grants pardon to those who
have been created by his word, and blots out their countless offences,
[140] 70 I suppose that of the entire human race only very few would be
spared.'
8 The angel said to me in reply: 'The Most High has made this
2 world for many, but the next world for only a few. Let me give you
an illustration, Ezra. Ask the earth, and it will tell you that it can
produce plenty of clay for making earthenware, but very little

[a] *So some Vss.; Lat.* for those who are convinced of salvation.

gold-dust. The same holds good for the present world: many have 3
been created, but only a few will be saved.'

I SAID: 'My soul, drink deep of understanding and eat your fill of 4
wisdom! Without your consent[a] you came here, and unwillingly 5
you go away; only a brief span of life is given you. O Lord above, if 6
I may be allowed to approach you in prayer, plant a seed in our
hearts and minds, and make it grow until it bears fruit, so that fallen
man may obtain life. For you alone are God, and we are all shaped 7
by you in one mould, as your word declares. The body moulded in 8
the womb receives from you both life and limbs; that which you
create is kept safe amid fire and water; for nine months the body
moulded by you bears what you have created in it. Both the womb 9
which holds safely and that which is safely held will be safe only
because you keep them so. And after the womb has delivered up
what has been created in it, then from the human body itself, that is 10
from the breasts, milk, the fruit of the breasts, is supplied by your
command. For a certain time what has been made is nourished in 11
that way; and afterwards it is still cared for by your mercy. You 12
bring it up to know your justice, train it in your law, and correct it by
your wisdom. It is your creature and you made it; you can put it to 13
death or give it life, as you please. But if you should lightly destroy 14
one who was fashioned by your command with so much labour, what
was the purpose of creating him?

'And now let me say this: about mankind at large, you know best; 15
but it is for your own people that I grieve, for your inheritance that 16
I mourn; my sorrow is for Israel and my distress for the race of
Jacob. For them and for myself, therefore, I will address my prayer 17
to you, since I perceive how low we have fallen, we dwellers on earth;
and I know well how quickly your judgement will follow. Hear my 18, 19
words then, and consider the prayer which I make to you.'

Here begins the prayer which Ezra made, before he was taken up
to heaven.

'O Lord, who dost inhabit eternity, to whom the sky and the 20
highest heavens belong; whose throne is beyond imagining, and 21
whose glory is past conceiving; who art attended by the host of
angels trembling as they turn themselves into wind and fire at thy 22
bidding; whose word is true and constant; whose commands are

[a] Without your consent: *so one Vs.; Lat.* To obey.

23 mighty and terrible; whose glance dries up the deeps, whose anger
24 melts the mountains, and whose truth stands for ever:[a] hear thy
servant's prayer, O Lord, listen to my petition, for thou hast fashioned
25 me, and consider my words. While I live I will speak; while understanding lasts, I will answer.

26 'Do not look upon thy people's offences, look on those who have
27 served thee faithfully; pay no heed to the godless and their pursuits,
but to those who have observed thy covenant and suffered for it.
28 Do not think of those who all their life have been untrue to thee, but
remember those who have acknowledged and feared thee from the
29 heart. Do not destroy those who have lived like animals, but take
30 account of those who have borne shining witness to thy law. Do not
be angry with those judged to be worse than beasts; but show love to
31 those who have put unfailing trust in thy glory. For we and our
fathers have lived in mortal sin,[b] yet it is on our account that thou art
32 called merciful; for if it is thy desire to have mercy on us sinners,
who have no just deeds to our credit, then indeed thou shalt be called
33 merciful. For the reward which will be given to the just, who have
many good works stored up with thee, will be no more than their
own deeds have earned.

34 'What is man, that thou shouldst be angry with him? or the race of
35 mortals, that thou shouldst treat them so harshly? The truth is, no
man was ever born who did not sin; no man alive is innocent of
36 offence. It is through thy mercy towards those with no store of good
deeds to their name that thy justice and kindness, O Lord, will be
made known.'

37 The angel said to me in reply: 'Much of what you have said is just,
38 and it will be as you say. Be sure that I shall not give any thought to
39 sinners, to their creation, death, judgement, or damnation; but I shall
take delight in the just, in their creation, their departure from this
40 world, their salvation, and their final reward. So I have said, and so
41 it is. The farmer sows many seeds in the ground and plants many
plants, but not all the seeds sown come up safely in season, nor do all
the plants strike root. So too in the world of men: not all who are
sown will be preserved.'

42, 43 To that I replied: 'If I have won your favour, let me speak. The
farmer's seed may never come up because it is given no rain at the
44 right time, or it may rot because of too much rain. But man, who

[a] *So some Vss.; Lat.* bears witness. [b] in mortal sin: *so some Vss.; Lat. obscure.*

was formed by your hands and made in your image, and for whose
sake you made everything—will you compare him with seed sown by
a farmer? Surely not, O Lord above! Spare your own people and 45
pity them, for you will be pitying your own creation.'
He answered: 'The present is for those now alive, the future for 46
those yet to come. You cannot love my creation with a love greater 47
than mine—far from it! But never again rank yourself among the
unjust, as you have so often done. Yet the Most High approves of the 48, 49
modesty you have rightly shown; you have not sought great glory by
including yourself among the godly. In the last days, then, the 50
inhabitants of the world will be punished for their arrogant lives by
bitter sufferings. But you, Ezra, should direct your thoughts to 51
yourself and the glory awaiting those like you. For all of you, 52
paradise lies open, the tree of life is planted, the age to come is made
ready, and rich abundance is in store; the city is already built, rest
from toil is assured, goodness and wisdom are brought to perfection.
The root of evil has been sealed off from you; for you there is no more 53
illness, death[a] is abolished, hell has fled, and decay is quite forgotten.
All sorrows are at an end, and the treasure of immortality has been 54
finally revealed. Ask no more questions, therefore, about the many 55
who are lost. For they were given freedom and used it to despise the 56
Most High, to treat his law with contempt and abandon his ways.
Yes, and they trampled on his just servants; they said to themselves, 57, 58
"There is no God", though well aware that they must die. Yours, 59
then, will be the joys I have predicted; theirs the thirst and torments
which are prepared. It is not that the Most High has wanted any man
to be lost, but that those he created have themselves brought dishonour 60
on their Creator's name, and shown ingratitude to the One who had
put life within their reach. My day of judgement is now close at hand, 61
but I have not made this known to all; only to you and a few like you.' 62
'My lord,' I replied, 'you have now revealed to me the many signs 63
which you are going to perform in the last days; but you have not
told me when that will be.'
The angel answered: 'Keep a careful count yourself; when you see 9
that some of the signs predicted have already happened, then you 2
will understand that the time has come when the Most High will
judge the world he has created. When the world becomes the scene 3
of earthquakes, insurrections, plots among the nations, unstable

[*a*] death: *so some Vss.; Lat. omits.*

4 government, and panic among rulers, then you will recognize these
as the events which the Most High has foretold since first the world
5 began. Just as everything that is done on earth has its beginning and
6 end clearly marked,[a] so it is with the times which the Most High has
determined: their beginning is marked by portents and miracles,
their end by manifestations of power.

7 'Whoever comes safely through and escapes destruction, thanks to
8 his good deeds or the faith he has shown, will survive all the dangers
I have foretold and witness the salvation that I shall bring to my
land, the country I have marked out from all eternity as my own.
9 Then those who have misused my law will be taken by surprise;
10 their contempt for it will bring them continual torment. All who in
their lifetime failed to acknowledge me in spite of all the good things
11 I had given them, all who disdained my law while freedom still was
theirs, who scornfully dismissed the thought of penitence while the
12 way was still open—all these will have to learn the truth through
13 torments after death. Do not be curious any more, Ezra, to know
how the godless will be tormented, but only how and when the just
will be saved; the world is theirs and it exists for their sake.'

14, 15 I answered, 'I repeat what I have said again and again: the lost
16 outnumber the saved as a wave exceeds a drop of water.'

17 The angel replied: 'The seed to be sown depends on the soil, the
colour on the flower, the product on the workman, and the harvest
18 on the farmer. There was once a time before the world had been
created for men to dwell in; at that time I was planning it for the sake
19 of those who now exist. No one then disputed my plan, for no one
existed. I supplied this world with unfailing food and a mysterious
20 law; but those whom I created turned to a life of corruption. I looked
at my world, and there it lay spoilt, at my earth in danger from men's
21 wicked thoughts; and at the sight I could scarcely bring myself to
spare them. One grape I saved out of a cluster, one tree out of a
22 forest.[b] So then let it be: destruction for the many who were born in
vain, and salvation for my grape and my tree, which have cost me
such labour to bring to perfection.

23, 24 'You, Ezra, must wait one more week. Do not fast this time, but
go to a flowery field where no house stands, and eat only what grows
25 there—no meat or wine—and pray unceasingly to the Most High.
Then I will come and talk to you again.'

[a] has...marked: *so one Vs.; Lat. defective.* [b] *So some Vss.; Lat.* tribe.

Visions of the last days

SO I WENT OUT, as the angel told me, to a field called Ardat. 26
There I sat among the flowers; my food was what grew in the
field, and I ate to my heart's content. The week ended, and I was 27
lying on the grass, troubled again in mind with all the same per-
plexities. I broke my silence and addressed the Most High. 'O 28, 29
Lord,' I said, 'you showed yourself to our fathers in the desert at the
time of the exodus from Egypt, when they were travelling through the
barren and untrodden waste. You said, "Hear me, Israel; listen to 30
my words, race of Jacob. This is my law, which I sow among you 31
to bear fruit and bring you glory for ever." But our fathers who 32
received your law did not keep it; they did not observe your commandments. Not that the fruit of the law perished; that was impossible, for it was yours. Those who received it perished, because they 33
failed to keep safe the good seed that had been sown in them. Now 34
the usual way of things is that when seed is put into the earth, or a
ship on the sea, or food or drink into a jar, then if the seed, or the
ship, or the contents of the jar should be destroyed, what held or 35
contained them does not perish with them. But with us sinners it is
different. Destruction will come upon us, the recipients of the law, 36
and upon our hearts, the vessel that held the law. The law itself is not 37
destroyed, but survives in all its glory.'

While these thoughts were in my mind, I looked round, and on my 38
right I saw a woman in great distress, mourning and loudly lamenting; her dress was torn, and she had ashes on her head. Abandoning 39
my meditations, I turned to her, and said: 'Why are you weeping? 40
What is troubling you?' 'Sir,' she replied, 'please leave me to my 41
tears and my grief; great is my bitterness of heart, great my distress.'
'Tell me,' I asked, 'what has happened to you?' 'Sir,' she replied, 42, 43
'I was barren and childless through thirty years of marriage. Every 44
hour of every day during those thirty years, day and night alike,
I prayed to the Most High. Then after thirty years, my God answered 45
my prayer and had mercy on my distress; he took note of my
sorrow and granted me a son. What happiness he brought to my
husband and myself and to all our neighbours! What praise we
gave to the Mighty God! I took great pains over his upbringing. 46

47 When he came of age, I chose a wife for him, and fixed the date of
the wedding.
10 'But when my son entered his wedding-chamber, he fell down
2 dead. So we all put out our lamps, and all my neighbours came
to comfort me; I controlled my grief till the evening of the follow-
3 ing day. When they had all ceased urging me to take comfort and
control my grief, I rose and stole away in the night, and came
4 here, as you can see, to this field. I have made up my mind never
to go back to the town, but to stay here eating nothing and drinking
nothing, and to continue my mourning and fasting unbroken till
I die.'

5 At that I interrupted the train of my thoughts, and I spoke sternly
6 to the woman: 'You are the most foolish woman in the world,'
7 I said; 'are you blind to the grief and sufferings of our nation? It is
for the sorrow and humiliation of Zion, the mother of us all, that you
8 should mourn so deeply; you should share in our common mourn-
9 ing and sorrow. But you are deep in sorrow for your one son. Ask
the earth and she will tell you; she must mourn for the thousands
10 and thousands who come to birth upon her. From her we all originally sprang, and there are more to come. Almost all her children go
11 to perdition, and their vast numbers are wiped out. Who then has the
better right to be in mourning—the earth, who has lost such vast
12 numbers, or you, whose sorrow is for one alone? You may say to me,
"But my grief is very different from the earth's grief; I have lost the
fruit of my own womb, which I brought to birth with pain and
13 travail, but it is only in the course of nature that the vast numbers
now alive on earth should depart in the same way as they have come."
14 My answer to that is: at the cost of pain you have been a mother, but
in the same way the earth has always been the mother of mankind,
bearing fruit to earth's creator.

15 'Keep your sorrow to yourself, therefore, and bear your mis-
16 fortunes bravely. If you will accept God's decree as just, then in due
time you will receive your son back again, and win an honoured name
17 among women. So go back to the town and to your husband.'

18 'No, I will not,' she replied; 'I will not go back to the town; I will
stay here to die.'

19, 20 But I continued to argue with her. 'Do not do what you say,'
I urged; 'be persuaded because of Zion's misfortunes, and take
21 comfort to yourself from the sorrow of Jerusalem. You see how our

sanctuary has been laid waste, our altar demolished, and our temple
destroyed. Our harps are unstrung, our hymns silenced, our shouts 22
of joy cut short; the light of the sacred lamp is out, and the ark of our
covenant has been taken as spoil; the holy vessels are defiled, and the
name which God has conferred on us is disgraced; our leading men[a]
have been treated shamefully, our priests burnt alive, and the
Levites taken off into captivity; our virgins have been raped and our
wives ravished, our godfearing men carried off, and our children
abandoned; our youths have been enslaved, and our strong warriors
reduced to weakness. Worst of all, Zion, once sealed with God's own 23
seal, has forfeited its glory and is in the hands of our enemies. Then 24
throw off your own heavy grief, and lay all your sorrows aside; may
the Mighty God restore you to his favour, may the Most High give
you rest and peace after your troubles!'

Suddenly, while I was still speaking to the woman, I saw her face 25
begin to shine; her countenance flashed like lightning, and I shrank
from her in terror. While I wondered what this meant, she suddenly 26
uttered a loud and terrible cry, which shook the earth. I looked up 27
and saw no longer a woman but a complete city, built[b] on massive
foundations. I cried aloud in terror, 'Where is the angel Uriel, who 28
visited me before? It is his doing that I have fallen into this be-
wilderment, that all my hopes are shattered,[c] and all my prayers in
vain.'

I was still speaking when the angel appeared who had visited me 29
before. When he saw me lying in a dead faint, unconscious on the 30
ground, he grasped me by my right hand, put strength into me, and
raised me to my feet. 'What is the matter?' he asked. 'Why are you 31
overcome? What was it that disturbed your mind and made you
faint?' 'It was because you deserted me', I replied. 'I did what 32
you told me: I came out to the field; and what I have seen here and
can still see is beyond my power to relate.'

'Stand up like a man,' he said, 'and I will explain it to you.' 33

'Speak, my lord,' I replied; 'only do not abandon me and leave me 34
to die unsatisfied. For I have seen and I hear things beyond my 35
understanding—unless this is all an illusion and a dream. I beg you 36, 37
to tell me, my lord, the meaning of my vision.'

'Listen to me,' replied the angel, 'while I explain to you the 38

[*a*] *So some Vss.; Lat.* our children. [*b*] *Probable meaning, based on other Vss.; Lat.* but a city was being built... [*c*] *Or* that my destiny turns out to be corruption.

meaning of the things that terrify you; for the Most High has revealed
39 many secrets to you. He has seen your blameless life, your unceasing
40 grief for your people, and your deep mourning over Zion. Here then
41 is the meaning of the vision. A little while ago you saw a woman in
42 mourning, and tried to give her comfort; now you no longer see that
43 woman, but a whole city. She told you she had lost her son, and this
44 is the explanation. The woman you saw is Zion, which you now see as
45 a city with all its buildings. She told you she was childless for thirty
years; that was because there were three thousand years in which
46 sacrifices were not yet offered in Zion. But then, after the three
thousand years, Solomon built the city and offered the sacrifices;
47 that was the time when the barren woman bore her son. She took
great pains, she said, over his upbringing; that was the period when
48 Jerusalem was inhabited. Then she told you of the great loss she
suffered, how her son died on the day he entered his wedding-
49 chamber; that was the destruction which overtook Jerusalem. Such
then was the vision that you saw—the woman mourning for her son
—and you tried to comfort her in her sufferings; this was the revela-
50 tion you had to receive. Seeing your sincere grief and heartfelt
sympathy for the woman, the Most High is now showing you her
51 radiant glory and her beauty. That was why I told you to stay in a
52 field where no house stood, for I knew that the Most High intended
53 to send you this revelation. I told you to come to this field, where no
54 foundation had been laid for any building; for in the place where the
city of the Most High was to be revealed, no building made by man
could stand.

55 'Have no fear then, Ezra, and set your trembling heart at rest; go
into the city, and see the magnificence of the buildings, so far as your
56 eyes have power to see it all. Then, after that, you shall hear as much
57 as your ears have power to hear. You are more blessed than most other
58 men, and few have such a name with the Most High as you have. Stay
59 here till tomorrow night, when the Most High will show you in
dreams and visions what he intends to do to the inhabitants of earth
in the last days.' I did as I was told and slept there that night and
the next.

11 ON THE SECOND NIGHT I had a vision in a dream; I saw, rising
2 from the sea, an eagle with twelve wings and three heads. I saw it
spread its wings over the whole earth; and all the winds blew on it,

and the clouds[a] gathered. Out of its wings I saw rival wings sprout, 3
which proved to be only small and stunted. Its heads lay still; even 4
the middle head, which was bigger than the others, lay still between
them. As I watched, the eagle rose on its wings to set itself up as 5
ruler over the earth and its inhabitants. I saw it bring into subjection 6
everything under heaven; it met with no opposition at all from any
creature on earth. I saw the eagle stand erect on its talons, and it 7
spoke aloud to its wings: 'Do not all wake at once,' it said; 'sleep in 8
your places, and each wake up in turn; the heads are to be kept till 9
the last.' I saw that the sound was not coming from its heads, but 10
from the middle of its body. I counted its rival wings, and saw that 11
there were eight of them.

As I watched, one of the wings on its right side rose and became 12
ruler over the whole earth. After a time, its reign came to an end, 13
and it disappeared from sight completely. Then the next one arose
and established its rule, which it held for a long time. When its reign 14
was coming to an end and it was about to disappear like the first one,
a voice could be heard saying to it: 'You have ruled the world for so 15, 16
long; now listen to my message before your time comes to disappear.
None of your successors will achieve a reign as long as yours, nor 17
even half as long.' Then the third wing arose, ruled the world for a 18
time like its predecessors, and like them disappeared. In the same 19
way all the wings came to power in succession, and in turn disappeared from sight.

As time went on, I saw the wings on the left[b] side also raise them- 20
selves up to seize power. Some of them did so, and passed immediately from sight, while others arose but never came to power. At this 21, 22
point I noticed that two of the little wings were, like the twelve, no
longer to be seen. Nothing was now left of the eagle's body except 23
the three motionless heads and six little wings. As I watched, two of 24
the six little wings separated from the rest and took up a place under
the head on the right. The other four remained where they were;
and I saw them planning to rise up and seize power. One rose, but 25, 26
disappeared immediately; so too did the second, vanishing even 27
more quickly than the first. I saw the last two planning to seize the 28
kingship for themselves. But while they were still plotting, suddenly 29
one of the heads woke from sleep, the one in the middle, the biggest
of the three. I saw how it joined with the other two heads, and along 30, 31

[*a*] the clouds: *so some Vss.; Lat. omits.* [*b*] *So one Vs.; Lat.* right.

with them turned and devoured the two little wings which were
32 planning to seize power. This head got the whole earth into its grasp,
establishing an oppressive rule over all its inhabitants and a world-
33 wide kingdom mightier than any of the wings had ruled. But after
that I saw the middle head vanish just as suddenly as the wings
34 had done. There were two heads left, and they also seized power over
35 the earth and its inhabitants, but as I watched, the head on the right
devoured the head on the left.

36 Then I heard a voice which said to me: 'Look carefully at what
37 you see before you.' I looked, and saw what seemed to be a lion
roused from the forest; it roared as it came, and I heard it address
38 the eagle in a human voice. 'Listen to what I tell you', it said. 'The
39 Most High says to you: Are you not the only survivor of the four
beasts to which I gave the rule over my world, intending through
40–41 them to bring my ages to their end? You are the fourth beast, and
you have conquered all who went before, ruling over the whole
world and holding it in the grip of fear and harsh oppression. You
have lived[a] long in the world, governing it with deceit and with no
42 regard for truth. You have oppressed the gentle and injured the
peaceful, hating the truthful and loving liars; you have destroyed the
homes of the prosperous, and razed to the ground the walls of those
43 who had done you no harm. Your insolence is known to the Most
44 High, and your pride to the Mighty One. The Most High has
surveyed the periods he has fixed: they are now at an end, and his
45 ages have reached their completion. So you, eagle, must now disappear and be seen no more, you and your terrible great wings, your
evil small wings, your cruel heads, your grim talons, and your whole
46 worthless body. Then all the earth will feel relief at its deliverance
from your violence, and look forward hopefully to the judgement
and mercy of its Creator.'

12 1, 2 While the lion was still addressing the eagle, I looked and saw the
one remaining head disappear. Then the two[b] wings which had gone
over to him arose and set themselves up as rulers. Their reign was
3 short and troubled, and when I looked at them they were already
vanishing. Then the eagle's entire body burst into flames, and the
earth was struck with terror.

So great was my alarm and fear that I awoke, and said to myself:

[a] You are the fourth...lived: *so some Vss.; Lat.* The fourth beast came and conquered ...It has lived... [b] *So other Vss.; Lat. corrupt.*

'See the result of your attempt to discover the ways of the Most 4
High! My mind is weary; I am utterly exhausted. The terrors of this 5
night have completely drained my strength. So I will now pray to 6
the Most High for strength to hold out to the end.' Then I said: 'My 7
Master and Lord, if I have won your favour and stand higher in your
approval than most men, if it is true that my prayers have reached
your presence, then give me strength; reveal to me, my Lord, the 8
exact interpretation of this terrifying vision, and so bring full consolation to my soul. For you have already judged me worthy to be 9
shown the end of the present age.'

He said to me: 'Here is the interpretation of your vision. The eagle 10, 11
you saw rising from the sea represents the fourth kingdom in the
vision seen by your brother Daniel. But he was not given the inter- 12
pretation which I am now giving you or have already given you. The 13
days are coming when the earth will be under an empire more terrible than any before. It will be ruled by twelve kings, one after 14
another. The second to come to the throne will have the longest 15
reign of all the twelve. That is the meaning of the twelve wings you 16
saw.

'As for the voice which you heard speaking from the middle of the 17
eagle's body, and not from its heads, this is what it means: After this 18
second king's reign, great conflicts will arise, which will bring the
empire into danger of falling; and yet it will not fall then, but will be
restored to its original strength.

'As for the eight lesser wings which you saw growing from the 19
eagle's wings, this is what they mean: The empire will come under 20
eight kings whose reigns will be trivial and short-lived; two of them 21
will come and go just before the middle of the period, four will be
kept back until shortly before its end, and two will be left until the
end itself.

'As for the three heads which you saw sleeping, this is what they 22
mean: In the last years of the empire, the Most High will bring to 23
the throne three kings, who will restore much of its strength, and
rule[a] over the earth and its inhabitants more oppressively than any- 24
one before. They are called the eagle's heads, because they will 25
complete and bring to a head its long series of wicked deeds. As for 26
the greatest head, which you saw disappear, it signifies one of the
kings, who will die in his bed, but in great agony. The two that 27

[*a*] who...rule: *so some Vss.; Lat.* and he will restore...and they will rule...

28 survived will be destroyed by the sword; one of them will fall by the
sword of the other, who will himself fall by the sword in the last
days.
29 'As for the two little wings that went over to the head on the right
30 side, this is what they mean: They are the ones whom the Most
High has reserved until the last days, and their reign, as you saw, was
short and troubled.
31 'As for the lion which you saw coming from the forest, roused
from sleep and roaring, which you heard addressing the eagle,
32 taxing it with its wicked deeds and words, this is the Messiah whom
the Most High has kept back until the end. He will address[a] those
rulers, taxing them openly with their sins, their crimes, and their
33 defiance. He will bring them alive to judgement; he will convict
34 them and then destroy them. But he will be merciful to those of my
people that remain, all who have been kept safe in my land; he will
set them free and give them gladness, until the final day of judgement comes, about which I told you at the beginning.
35, 36 'That, then, is the vision which you saw, and its meaning. It is the
secret of the Most High, which no one except yourself has proved
37 worthy to be told. What you have seen you must therefore write in a
38 book and deposit it in a hiding-place. You must also disclose these
secrets to those of your people whom you know to be wise enough to
39 understand them and to keep them safe. But stay here yourself for
seven more days, to receive whatever revelation the Most High
thinks fit to send you.' Then the angel left me.
40 When all the people heard that seven days had passed without my
41 returning to the town, they assembled and came to me. 'What wrong
or injury have we done you,' they asked me, 'that you have deserted
42 us and settled here? Out of all the prophets you are the only one left
to us. You are like the last cluster in a vineyard, like a lamp in the
43 darkness, or a safe harbour for a ship in a storm. Have we not suf-
44 fered enough? If you desert us, we had far better have been
45 destroyed in the fire that burnt up Zion. We are no better than
those who perished there.' Then they raised a loud lamentation.
46 I replied: 'Take courage, Israel; house of Jacob, lay aside your
47 grief. The Most High bears you in mind, and the Mighty One has
48 not for ever[b] forgotten you. I have not left you, nor abandoned you;
I came here to pray for Zion in her distress, and to beg for mercy for

[a] He will address: *probable reading; Lat. defective.* [b] *So one Vs.; Lat.* in strife.

your sanctuary that has fallen so low. Go to your homes now, every 49
one of you; and in a few days' time I will come back to you.'
So the people returned to the town as I told them, while I re- 50, 51
mained in the field. I stayed there for seven days in obedience to the
angel, eating nothing but what grew in the field, and living on that
for the whole of the time.

THE SEVEN DAYS passed; and the next night I had a dream. In 13 1, 2
my dream, a wind came up out of the sea and set the waves in
turmoil. And this wind brought a human figure rising from the 3
depths,[a] and as I watched, this man came flying[b] with the clouds of
heaven. Wherever he turned his eyes, everything that they fell on
was seized with terror; and wherever the sound of his voice reached, 4
all who heard it melted like wax at the touch of fire.
Next I saw an innumerable host of men gathering from the four 5
winds of heaven to wage war on the man who had risen from the sea.
I saw that the man hewed out a vast mountain for himself, and flew 6
up on to it. I tried to see from what quarter or place the mountain 7
had been taken, but I could not. Then I saw that all who had 8
gathered to wage war against the man were filled with fear, and yet
they dared to fight against him. When he saw the hordes advancing 9
to attack, he did not so much as lift a finger against them. He had no
spear in his hand, no weapon at all; only, as I watched, he poured 10
what seemed like a stream of fire out of his mouth, a breath of flame
from his lips, and a storm of sparks from his tongue. All of them 11
combined into one mass—the stream of fire, the breath of flame, and
the great storm. It fell on the host advancing to join battle, and
burnt up every man of them; suddenly all that enormous multitude
had disappeared, leaving nothing but dust and ashes and a reek of
smoke. I was dumbfounded at the sight.
After that, I saw the man coming down from the mountain and 12
calling to himself a different company, a peaceful one. He was joined 13
by great numbers of men, some with joy on their faces, others with
sorrow. Some came from captivity; some brought others to him as
an offering. I woke up in terror, and prayed to the Most High.
I said, 'You have revealed these marvels to me, your servant, all the 14
way through; you have judged me worthy to have my prayers
answered. Now show me the meaning of this dream also. How 15, 16

[a] And...depths: *so other Vss.; Lat. defective.* [b] *So other Vss.; Lat.* grew strong.

terrible, to my thinking, it will be for all who survive to those days!
17 But how much worse for those who do not survive! Those who do
18 not survive will have the sorrow of knowing what is in store in the
19 last days and yet missing it. Those who do survive are to be pitied
for the terrible dangers and trials which, as these visions show, they
20 will have to face. But perhaps after all it is better to endure the
dangers and reach the goal than to vanish out of the world like a cloud
and never see the events of the last days.'

21 'Yes,' he replied, 'I will explain the meaning of this vision, and
22 tell you all that you ask. As for your question about those who sur-
23 vive, this is the answer: the very person from whom the danger will
then come will protect in danger those who have works and fidelity
24 laid up to their credit with the Most High. You may be assured
that those who survive are more highly blessed than those who die.

25 'This is what the vision means: The man you saw rising from the
26 depths of the sea is he whom the Most High has held in readiness
through many ages; he will himself deliver the world he has made,
27 and determine the lot of those who survive. As for the breath, fire,
28 and storm which you saw pouring from the mouth of the man, so that
without a spear or any weapon in his hand he destroyed the hordes
29 advancing to wage war against him, this is the meaning: The day is
near when the Most High will begin to bring deliverance to those on
30, 31 earth. Then men will all be filled with great alarm; they will plot to
make war on one another, city on city, region on region, nation on
32 nation, kingdom on kingdom. When this happens, and all the signs
that I have shown you come to pass, then my son will be revealed,
33 whom you saw as a man rising from the sea. On hearing his voice, all
the nations will leave their own territories and their separate wars,
34 and unite in a countless host, as you saw in your vision, with a
35 common intent to go and wage war against him. He will take his
36 stand on the summit of Mount Zion, and Zion will come into sight
before all men, complete and fully built. This corresponds to the
37 mountain which you saw hewn out, not by the hand of man. Then
my son will convict of their godless deeds the nations that confront
38 him. This will correspond to the storm you saw. He will taunt them
with their evil plottings and the tortures they are soon to endure. This
corresponds to the flame. And he will destroy them without effort
by means of[a] the law—and that is like the fire.

[a] by means of: *so one Vs.; Lat.* and.

'Then you saw him collecting a different company, a peaceful one. 39
They are the ten tribes which were taken off into exile in the time of 40
King Hoshea, whom Shalmaneser king of Assyria took prisoner. He
deported them beyond the River, and they were taken away into a
strange country. But then they resolved to leave the country popu- 41
lated by the Gentiles and go to a distant land never yet inhabited by
man, and there at last to be obedient to their laws, which in their 42
own country they had failed to keep. As they passed through the 43
narrow passages of the Euphrates, the Most High performed miracles 44
for them, stopping up the channels of the river until they had crossed
over. Their journey through that region, which is called Arzareth, 45
was long, and took a year and a half. They have lived there ever since, 46
until this final age. Now they are on their way back, and once more 47
the Most High will stop the channels of the river to let them cross.

'That is the meaning of the peaceful assembly that you saw. With 48
them too are the survivors of your own people, all who are found
inside my sacred boundary. So then, when the time comes for him 49
to destroy the nations assembled against him, he will protect his
people who are left, and show them many prodigies.' 50

'My lord, my master,' I asked, 'explain to me why the man that 51
I saw rose up out of the depths of the sea.' He replied: 'It is beyond 52
the power of any man to explore the deep sea and discover what is in
it; in the same way no one on earth can see my son and his company
until the appointed day. Such then is the meaning of your vision. 53
The revelation has been given to you, and to you alone, because you 54
have given up your own affairs, and devoted yourself entirely to
mine, and to the study of my law. You have taken wisdom as your 55
guide in everything, and called understanding your mother. That is 56
why I have given this revelation to you; there is a reward in store for
you with the Most High. In three days' time I will speak with you
again, and tell you some momentous and wonderful things.'

So I went away to the field, giving worship and praise to the Most 57
High for the wonders he performed from time to time and for his 58
providential control of the passing ages and what happens in them.
There I remained for three days.

The writing of the sacred books

14 ON THE THIRD DAY I was sitting under an oak-tree, when a
2 voice came to me from a bush, saying, 'Ezra, Ezra!' 'Here
3 I am, Lord', I answered, and rose to my feet. The voice went on:
'I revealed myself in the bush, and spoke to Moses, when my people
4 Israel was in slavery in Egypt, and sent him to lead my people out of
Egypt. I brought him up on to Mount Sinai, and kept him with me
5 for many days. I told him of many wonders, showing him the
6 secrets of the ages and the end of time, and instructed him what to
7 make known and what to conceal. So too I now give this order to you:
8 commit to memory the signs I have shown you, the visions you have
9 seen, and the explanations you have been given. You yourself are
about to be taken away from the world of men, and thereafter you
will remain with my son and with those like you, until the end of
10, 11 time. The world has lost its youth, and time is growing old. For the
whole of time is in twelve divisions; nine[a] divisions and half the
12, 13 tenth have already passed, and only two and a half still remain. Set
your house in order, therefore; give warnings to your nation, and
comfort to those in need of it; and take your leave of mortal life.
14 Put away your earthly cares, and lay down your human burdens;
15 strip off your weak nature, set aside the anxieties that vex you, and be
16 ready to depart quickly from this life. However great the evils you
17 have witnessed, there are worse to come. As this ageing world grows
18 weaker and weaker, so will evils increase for its inhabitants. Truth
will move farther away, and falsehood come nearer. The eagle that
you saw in your vision is already on the wing.'
19, 20 'May I speak[b] in your presence, Lord?' I replied. 'I am to
depart, by your command, after giving warning to those of my people
who are now alive. But who will give warning to those born hereafter? The world is shrouded in darkness, and its inhabitants are
21 without light. For your law was destroyed in the fire, and so no one
22 can know about the deeds you have done or intend to do. If I have
won your favour, fill me with your holy spirit, so that I may write
down the whole story of the world from the very beginning, everything that is contained in your law; then men will have the chance

[a] *Probable reading; Lat.* ten. [b] May I speak: *so other Vss.; Lat. omits.*

to find the right path, and, if they choose, gain life in the last
days.'
'Go,' he replied, 'call the people together, and tell them not to 23
look for you for forty days. Have a large number of writing-tablets 24
ready, and take with you Seraiah and Dibri, Shelemiah, Ethan, and
Asiel, five men all trained to write quickly. Then return here, and 25
I will light a lamp of understanding in your mind, which will not go
out until you have finished all that you are to write. When your work 26
is complete, some of it you must make public; the rest you must give
to wise men to keep secret. Tomorrow at this time you shall begin to
write.'

I went as I was ordered and summoned all the people, and said: 27
'Israel, listen to what I say. Our ancestors lived originally in Egypt 28, 29
as foreigners. They were rescued from that land, and were given the 30
law which offers life. But they disobeyed it, and you have followed
their example. Then you were given a land of your own, the land of 31
Zion; but you, like your ancestors, sinned and abandoned the way
laid down for you by the Most High. Because he is a just judge he 32
took away from you in due time what he had given. And so you are 33
now here in exile, and your fellow-countrymen are still farther away.
If then you will direct your understanding and instruct your minds, 34
you shall be kept safe in life and meet with mercy after you die. For 35
after death will come the judgement; we shall be restored to life, and
then the names of the just will be known and the deeds of the godless
exposed. From this moment no one must come to talk to me, nor 36
look for me for the next forty days.'

I took with me the five men as I had been told, and we went away 37
to the field, and there we stayed. On the next day I heard a voice 38
calling me, which said: 'Ezra, open your mouth and drink what
I give you.' So I opened my mouth, and was handed a cup full of 39
what seemed like water, except that its colour was the colour of fire.
I took it and drank, and as soon as I had done so my mind began to 40
pour forth a flood of understanding, and wisdom grew greater and
greater within me, for I retained my memory unimpaired. I opened 41
my mouth to speak, and I continued to speak unceasingly. The Most 42
High gave understanding to the five men, who took turns at writing
down what was said, using characters[a] which they had not known
before. They remained at work through the forty days, writing all

[*a*] *Probable reading, based on other Vss.; Lat. corrupt.*

43 day, and taking food only at night. But as for me, I spoke all through
44 the day; even at night I was not silent. In the forty days, ninety-
45 four[a] books were written. At the end of the forty days the Most
High spoke to me. 'Make public the books you wrote first,' he said,
46 'to be read by good and bad alike. But the last seventy books are to be
47 kept back, and given to none but the wise among your people. They
contain a stream of understanding, a fountain of wisdom, a flood of
48 knowledge.' And I did so.

Prophecies of doom

15 PROCLAIM TO MY PEOPLE the words of prophecy which I give
2 you to speak, says the Lord; and have them written down, because
3 they are trustworthy and true. Have no fear of plots against you,
4 and do not be troubled by the unbelief of those who oppose you. For
everyone who does not believe will die because of his unbelief.[b]
5 Beware, says the Lord, I am letting loose terrible evils on the
6 world, sword and famine, death and destruction, because wickedness
has spread over the whole earth and there is no room for further
7, 8 deeds of violence. Therefore the Lord says, I will not keep silence
about their godless sins; I will not tolerate their wicked deeds. See
how the blood of innocent victims cries to me for vengeance, and the
9 souls of the just never cease to plead with me! I will most surely
avenge them, says the Lord, and will hear the plea of all the innocent
10 blood that has been shed. My people are being led to the slaughter
11 like sheep. I will no longer allow them to remain in Egypt, but will
use all my power to rescue them; I will strike the Egyptians with
12 plagues, as I did before, and destroy their whole land. How Egypt
will mourn, shaken to its very foundations, when it is scourged and
13 chastised by the Lord! How the tillers of the soil will mourn, when
the seed fails to grow, and when their trees are devastated by blight
14 and hail and terrible storm![c] Alas for the world and its inhabitants!
15 The sword that will destroy them is not far away. Nation will draw
16 sword against nation and go to war. Stable government will be at an
end; one faction will prevail over another, caring nothing in their

[a] *So other Vss.; Lat. corrupt.* [b] *Or* in his unbelief. [c] *Probable meaning; Lat. obscure.*

day of power for king or leading man of rank. A man may want to 17
visit a city, but will not be able to do so; for ambition and rivalry will 18
have reduced cities to chaos, destroyed houses, and filled men with
panic. A man will violently assault his neighbour's house and 19
plunder his goods; no pity will restrain him, when he is in the grip of
famine and grinding misery.

See how I summon before me all the kings of the earth, says God, 20
from sunrise and south wind, from east and south,[a] to turn back and
repay what they have been given. I will do to them as they are doing 21
to my chosen people even to this day; I will pay them back in their
own coin.

These are the words of the Lord God: I will show sinners no pity; 22
the sword will not spare those murderers who stain the ground with
innocent blood. The Lord's anger has overflowed in fire to scorch 23
the earth to its foundations and consume sinners like burning straw.
Alas for sinners who flout my commands! says the Lord; I will show 24, 25
them no mercy. Away from me, you rebels! Do not bring your
pollution near my holiness. The Lord well knows all who sin against 26
him, and has consigned them to death and destruction. Already 27
disaster has fallen upon the world, and you will never escape it; God
will refuse to rescue you, because you have sinned against him.

How terrible the sight of what is coming from the east! Hordes of 28, 29
dragons from Arabia will sally forth with countless chariots, and
from the first day of their advance their hissing will spread across the
land, to fill all who hear them with fear and consternation. The 30
Carmanians, mad with rage, will rush like wild boars out of the
forest, advancing in full force to join battle with them, and will
devastate whole tracts of Assyria with their tusks. But then the 31
dragons will summon up their native fury, and will prove the
stronger. They will rally and join forces, and fall on them with over-
whelming might until they are routed, until their power is silenced, 32
and every one of them turns to flight. Then their way will be blocked 33
by a lurking enemy from Assyria, who will destroy one of them. Fear
and panic will spread in their army, and wavering among their kings.

See the clouds stretching from east and north to south! Their 34
appearance is hideous, full of fury and tempest. They will clash 35
together, they will pour over the land a vast storm;[b] blood, shed by
the sword, will reach as high as a horse's belly, a man's thigh, or a 36

[*a*] south: *probable reading; Lat.* Lebanon. [*b*] storm: *probable meaning; Lat. obscure.*

37 camel's hock. Terror and trembling will cover the earth; all who see
38 the raging fury will shudder and be stricken with panic. Then vast
storm-clouds will approach from north and south, and others from
39 the west. But the winds from the east will be stronger still, and will
hold in check the raging cloud and its leader; and the storm[a] which
was bent on destruction will be fiercely driven back to the south and
40 west by the winds from the east. Huge mighty clouds, full of fury,
will mount up and ravage the whole land and its inhabitants; a
41 terrible storm[a] will sweep over the great and the powerful, with fire
and hail and flying swords; and a deluge of water will flood all the
42 fields and rivers. They will flatten to the ground cities and walls,
43 mountains and hills, trees in the woods and crops in the fields. They
44 will advance all the way to Babylon, and blot it out. When they reach
it, they will surround it, and let loose a storm[a] in all its fury. The dust
and smoke will reach the sky, and all her neighbours will mourn for
45 Babylon. Any of her survivors will be enslaved by her destroyers.
46 And you, Asia, who have shared the beauty and the splendour of
47 Babylon, alas for you, poor wretch! Like her you have dressed up
your daughters as whores, to attract and catch your lovers who have
48 always lusted for you. You have copied all the schemes and practices
49 of that vile harlot. Therefore God says, I will bring upon you terrible
evils: widowhood and poverty, famine, sword, and plague, bringing
50 ruin to your homes, bringing violence and death. Your strength and
splendour will wither like a flower, when that scorching heat bears
51 down upon you. Then you will be a poor weak woman, bruised,
beaten, and wounded, unable to receive your wealthy lovers any
52, 53 more. Should I be so fierce with you, says the Lord, if you had not
killed my chosen ones continually, gloating over the blows you struck
them, and hurling your drunken taunts at their corpses?
54, 55 Paint your face; make yourself beautiful! The harlot's pay shall be
56 yours; you will get what you have earned. What you do to my chosen
people, God will do to you, says the Lord; he will consign you to a
57 terrible fate. Your children will die of hunger; you will fall by the
sword, your cities will be blotted out, and all your people will fall on
58 the field of battle. Those who are up on the mountains will be dying
of hunger, and their hunger and thirst will force them to gnaw their
59 own flesh and drink their own blood. You will be foremost in misery,
60 and still there will be more to come. As the victors go past on their

[*a*] storm: *probable meaning; Lat. obscure.*

way home from the sack of Babylon, they will smash your peaceful
city, destroy a great part of your territory, and bring much of your
splendour to an end. They will destroy you—you will be stubble, 61
and they the fire. They will completely devour you and your cities, 62
your land and your mountains, and will burn all your forests and
your fruit-trees. They will make your children prisoners and plunder 63
your property; and not a trace will be left of your splendid beauty.
Alas for you, Babylon and Asia! Alas for you, Egypt and Syria! **16**
Put on sackcloth and hair-shirt, and raise a howl of lamentation for 2
your sons; your doom is close at hand. The sword is let loose against 3
you, and who will turn it aside? Fire is let loose upon you, and who 4
will put it out? Calamities have been let loose against you, and who 5
is there to stop them? Can any man stop a hungry lion in a forest, or 6
put out a fire among the stubble once it has begun to blaze? Can 7
any man stop an arrow shot by a strong archer? When the Lord God 8
sends calamities, who can stop them? When his anger overflows in 9
fire, who can put it out? When the lightning flashes, who will not 10
tremble? When it thunders, who will not shake with dread? When it 11
is the Lord who utters his threats, is there any man who will not be
crushed to the ground at his approach? The earth is shaken to its 12
very foundations, and the sea is churned up from its depths; the
waves and all the fish with them are in turmoil before the presence of
the Lord and the majesty of his strength. For strong is his arm 13
which bends the bow, and sharp the arrows which he shoots; once
they are on their way, they will not stop before they reach the ends of
the earth. Calamities are let loose, and will not turn back before 14
they strike the earth. The fire is alight and will not be put out until it 15
has burnt up earth's foundations. An arrow shot by a powerful 16
archer does not turn back; no more will the calamities be recalled
which are let loose against the earth.
Alas, alas for me! Who will rescue me on that day? When troubles 17, 18
come, many will groan; when famine strikes, many will die; when
wars break out, empires will tremble; when the calamities come, all
will be filled with terror. What will men do then, in the face of
calamity? Famine and plague, suffering and hardship, are scourges 19
sent to teach men better ways. But even so they will not abandon 20
their crimes, nor keep in mind their scourging. A time will come 21
when food grows cheap, so cheap that they will imagine they have
been sent peace and prosperity. But at that very moment the earth

22 will become a hotbed of disasters—sword, famine, and anarchy. Most
of its inhabitants will die in the famine; and those who survive the
23 famine will be destroyed by the sword. The dead will be tossed out
like dung, and there will be no one to offer any comfort. For the
24 earth will be left empty, and its cities a ruin. None will be left to till
25 the ground and sow it. The trees will bear their fruits, but who will
26 pick them? The grapes will ripen, but who will tread them? There
27 will be vast desolation everywhere. A man will long to see a human
28 face or hear a human voice. For out of a whole city, only ten will
survive; in the country-side, only two will be left, hiding in the
29 forest or in holes in the rocks. Just as in an olive-grove three or four
30 olives might be left on each tree, or as a few grapes in a vineyard
31 might be overlooked by the sharp-eyed pickers, so also in those days
three or four will be overlooked by those who search the houses to
32 kill. The earth will be left a desert, and the fields will be overrun
with briers; thorns will grow over all the roads and paths, because
33 there will be no sheep to tread them. Girls will live in mourning
with none to marry them, women will mourn because they have no
husbands, their daughters will mourn because they have no one to
34 support them. The young men who should have married them will
be killed in the war, and the husbands wiped out by the famine.

35 BUT LISTEN to me, you who are the Lord's servants, and take my
36 words to heart. This is the word of the Lord. Receive it, and do
37 not disbelieve what he says. Calamities are here, close at hand, and
38 will not delay. When a pregnant woman is in the ninth month, and
the moment of her child's birth is drawing near, there will be two or
three hours in which her womb will suffer pangs of agony, and then
39 the child will come from the womb without a moment's delay; in the
same way calamities will come on the earth without delay, and the
world will groan under the pangs that grip it.

40 Listen to my words, my people; get ready for battle, and when the
calamities surround you, be as though you were strangers on earth.
41 The seller must expect to have to run for his life, the buyer to lose
42 what he buys; the merchant must expect to make no profit, the
43 builder never to live in the house he builds. The sower must not
44 expect to reap, nor the pruner to gather his grapes. Those who
marry must expect no children; the unmarried must think of them-
45, 46 selves as widowed. For all labour is labour in vain. Their fruits will

be gathered by foreigners, who will plunder their goods, pull down
their houses, and take their children captive. If they have children,
they will have been bred only for captivity and famine; any who 47
make money do so only to have it plundered. The more care they
lavish on their cities, houses, and property, and on their own persons,
the fiercer will be my indignation against their sins, says the Lord. 48
Like the indignation of a virtuous woman towards a prostitute, so 49, 50
will be the indignation of justice towards wickedness with all her
finery; she will accuse her to her face, when the champion arrives to
expose all sin upon earth. Do not imitate wickedness, therefore, and 51
her actions. For in a very short time she will be swept from the earth, 52
and the reign of justice over us will begin.

The sinner must not deny that he has sinned; he will only bring 53
burning coals on to his own head if he says, 'I have committed no
sin against the majesty of God.' For the Lord knows all that men do; 54
he knows their plans, their schemes, and their inmost thoughts. He 55
said, 'Let the earth be made', and it was made; and 'Let the heavens
be made', and they were made. It was by the Lord's word that the 56
stars were fixed in their places; the number of the stars is known to
him. He looks into the depths with their treasures; he has measured 57
the sea and everything it contains. By his word he confined the sea 58
within the bounds of the waters, and above the water he suspended
the land. He spread out the sky like a vault, and made it secure upon 59
the waters. He provided springs in the desert, and pools on the 60
mountain-tops as the source of rivers flowing down to water the
earth. He created man, and placed a heart in the middle of his body; 61
he gave him spirit, life, and understanding, the very breath of 62
Almighty God who created the whole world and searches out secret
things in secret places. He knows well your plans and all your 63
inward thoughts. Alas for sinners who try to hide their sins! The 64
Lord will scrutinize all their deeds; he will call you all to account.
You will be covered with confusion, when your sins are brought into 65
the open, and your wicked deeds stand up to accuse you on that day.
What can you do? How can you hide your sins from God and his 66
angels? God is your judge: fear him! Abandon your sins, and have 67
done with your wicked deeds for ever! Then God will set you free
from all distress.

Fierce flames are being kindled to burn you. A great horde will 68
descend on you; they will seize some of you and make you eat pagan

69 sacrifices. Those who give in to them will be derided, taunted, and
70 trampled on. In place after place[a] and in all the neighbourhood
71 there will be a violent attack on those who fear the Lord. Their
enemies will be like madmen, plundering and destroying without
72 mercy all who still fear the Lord. They will destroy and plunder their
73 property, and throw them out of their homes. Then it will be seen
that my chosen people have stood the test like gold in the assayer's
fire.

74 Listen, you whom I have chosen, says the Lord; the days of harsh
75 suffering are close at hand, but I will rescue you from them. Away
76 with your fears and doubts! For God is your leader. You who
follow my commandments and instructions, says the Lord God,
must not let your sins weigh you down, nor your wicked deeds get
77 the better of you. Alas for those who are entangled in their sins, and
overrun with their wicked deeds! They are like a field overrun by
78 bushes, with brambles across the path and no way through, completely shut off and doomed to destruction by fire.

[*a*] In place after place: *possible meaning; Lat. obscure.*

TOBIT

The troubles of Tobit

THIS IS THE STORY of Tobit, son of Tobiel, son of 1
Hananiel, son of Aduel, son of Gabael, son of Raphael, son
of Raguel, of the family of Asiel, of the tribe of Naphtali.
He was taken captive in the time of Shalmaneser[a] king of Assyria, 2
from Thisbe which is south of Kedesh Naphtali in Upper Galilee
above Hazor, behind the road to the west, north of Peor.

I, TOBIT, MADE truth and righteousness my lifelong guide; I did 3
many acts of charity for my kinsmen, those of my nation who had
gone into captivity with me at Nineveh in Assyria. When I was quite 4
young in my own country, Israel, the whole tribe of Naphtali my
ancestor broke away from the dynasty of David,[b] and from Jerusalem, the city chosen out of all the tribes of Israel as the one place of
sacrifice. It was there that God's dwelling-place, the temple, had
been consecrated, built to last for all generations. All my kinsmen, 5
the whole house of Naphtali my ancestor, sacrificed on the mountains of Galilee to the calf which Jeroboam, king of Israel, had made
in Dan; at the festivals I was the only one to make the frequent 6
journey to Jerusalem prescribed for all Israel as an eternal commandment. I used to hurry off to Jerusalem with the firstfruits of crops
and herds, the tithes of the cattle, and the first shearings of the sheep;
and I gave them to the priests of Aaron's line for the altar, and the 7
tithe of wine, corn, olive oil, pomegranates and other fruits to the
Levites ministering in Jerusalem. The second tithe for the six years
I converted into money, and I went and distributed it in Jerusalem
year by year among the orphans and widows, and the converts who 8
had attached themselves to Israel. Every third year when I brought
it and gave it to them, we held a feast according to the rule laid down
in the law of Moses and the instructions given by Deborah the
mother of Hananiel our grandfather; for my father had died leaving
me an orphan.

When I came of age I took a wife from our kindred, and had a son 9

[*a*] *Gk.* Enemessaros. [*b*] *Gk. adds* my ancestor.

10 by her whom I called Tobias. After the deportation to Assyria when
I was taken captive and came to Nineveh, everyone of my kindred
11 and nation ate gentile food; but I myself scrupulously avoided doing
12, 13 so. Since I was whole-heartedly mindful of my God, the Most High
endowed me with a presence which won me the favour of Shal-
14 maneser, and I became his buyer of supplies. As long as he lived
I used to travel to Media and buy for him there. I deposited bags of
money to the value of ten talents of silver with my kinsman Gabael
15 son of Gabri in Media. When Shalmaneser died and was succeeded
by his son Sennacherib, the roads to Media passed out of Assyrian
control and I could no longer make the journey.

16 In the time of Shalmaneser, I did many acts of charity for my
17 fellow-countrymen: I shared my food with the hungry and provided
clothes for the naked. If I saw the dead body of any man of my race
18 lying outside the wall of Nineveh, I buried it. I buried all those who
fell victim to Sennacherib after his flight from Judaea, when the
King of heaven executed judgement on him for all his blasphemies,
and in his rage he killed many of the Israelites. I stole their bodies
away and buried them, and Sennacherib looked for them but could
19 not find them. One of the Ninevites informed the king that I was
giving burial to his victims; so I went into hiding. When I learnt
that the king knew about me and that I was wanted for execution,
20 I took fright and ran away. All my property was seized and put into
the royal treasury; I was left with nothing but Anna my wife and my
21 son Tobias. However, less than forty days afterwards, the king was
murdered by two of his sons. They took refuge in the mountains of
Ararat, and his son Esarhaddon succeeded him. He appointed
Ahikar son of my brother Anael to supervise all the finances of his
22 kingdom; he had control of the entire administration. Then Ahikar
interceded on my behalf and I came back to Nineveh. For he had
been chief cupbearer, keeper of the privy seal, comptroller, and
treasurer when Sennacherib was king of Assyria; and Esarhaddon
renewed the appointments. Ahikar was my nephew and so one of my
kinsmen.

2 DURING THE REIGN of Esarhaddon, I returned to my house, and
my wife Anna and my son Tobias were restored to me. At our
festival of Pentecost, that is the Feast of Weeks, a good dinner was
2 prepared for me and I sat down to eat. The table was laid and a

lavish meal was put before me. I said to my son Tobias: 'Go, my
boy, and if you can find any poor man of our captive people in
Nineveh who is whole-heartedly mindful of God, bring him and he
shall share my dinner. I will wait for you until you return.' Tobias 3
went to look for a poor man of our people, but he came back and
said, 'Father!' 'Yes, my son?' I replied. He answered, 'Father, one
of our nation has been murdered and his body is lying in the market-
place. He was strangled only a moment ago.' I jumped up and left 4
my dinner untasted. I took the body from the square and put it
in one of the outbuildings until sunset when I could bury it;
then I went home, duly bathed myself, and ate my food in sorrow. 5
I recalled the saying of the prophet Amos in the passage about 6
Bethel:

> 'Your feasts shall be turned into mourning,
> and all your songs[a] into lamentation',

and I wept. After sunset I went and dug a grave and buried the 7
body. The neighbours jeered at me and said: 'Is he no longer afraid? 8
He ran away last time, when they were hunting for him to put him to
death for this very offence; and here he is burying the dead again!'
That night I bathed myself and went into my courtyard. I lay down 9
to sleep by the courtyard wall, leaving my face uncovered because of
the heat. I did not know that there were sparrows in the wall above 10
me; and their droppings fell, still warm, right into my eyes and
produced white patches. I went to the doctors to be cured, but the
more they treated me with their ointments, the more my eyes were
blinded by the white patches, until I lost my sight. For four years
I was blind. All my kinsmen grieved for me, and Ahikar looked after
me for two years until he moved to Elymais.

During that time my wife Anna used to earn money by women's 11
work. When she took what she had done to her employers they would 12
pay her wages. One day, the seventh of Dystrus, when she had cut off
the piece she had woven and delivered it, the owners not only paid
her in full, but also gave her a kid from their herd of goats to take
home. When my wife came in to me the kid began to bleat. I called 13
out to her: 'Where does that kid come from? I hope it was not
stolen? Give it back to its owners; we have no right to eat anything
stolen.' She assured me: 'It was given me as a present, over and 14

[*a*] *So one Vs.* (*compare Amos 8. 10*); *Gk.* ways.

above my wages.' I did not believe her and insisted that she should
give it back to its owners, and I blushed with shame for what she had
done. She retorted: 'So much for all your good works and acts of
charity! Now we can see what you are!'

3 In deep distress I groaned and wept, and as I groaned I prayed:
2 'Thou art just, O Lord, and all thy acts are just; in all thy ways
3 thou art merciful and true; thou art judge of the world. Remember
me now, Lord, and look upon me. Do not punish me for the sins and
4 errors which I and my fathers have committed. We have sinned
against thee and disobeyed thy commandments, and thou hast given
us up to plunder, captivity, and death, until we have become a byword,
a proverb, and a taunt to all the nations among whom thou hast
5 scattered us. I acknowledge the justice of thy many judgements, the
due penalty for my sins, for we have not obeyed thy commandments
6 and have not lived in loyal obedience before thee. And now deal
with me at thy pleasure, and command that my life be taken away, so
that I may be removed from the face of the earth and turned to
earth. I should be better dead than alive, for I have had to hear
undeserved reproaches and am in deep grief. Lord, command that
I may be released from this misery; let me go to my long home; do
not turn thy face from me, O Lord. It is better for me to die than to
live in such misery and to hear such reproaches.'

7 On that same day it happened that Sarah, the daughter of Raguel
who lived at Ecbatana in Media, also had to listen to reproaches from
8 one of her father's maidservants, because she had been given in
marriage to seven husbands, and before the marriage could be
regularly consummated they had all been killed by the wicked demon
Asmodaeus. The maidservant said to her: 'It is you who kill your
husbands! You have already been given in marriage to seven, and
9 you have not borne the name of any one of them. Why punish us
because they are dead? Go and join your husbands! I hope we never
see son or daughter of yours!'

10 She was sad at heart that day, and went in tears up to the attic in
her father's house meaning to hang herself. But she had second
thoughts and said to herself: 'Perhaps they will reproach my father
and say to him, "You had one dear daughter and she hanged herself
because of her troubles", and so I shall bring my aged father in sorrow
to the grave. No, I will not hang myself; it would be better to beg
11 the Lord to let me die and not live on to hear such reproaches.' Then

at once she spread out her hands towards the window in prayer and
said: 'Praise to thee, merciful God, praise to thy name for ever; let
all thy works praise thee for evermore. Now I lift up my eyes and 12
look to thee. Command me to be removed from this earth so that 13
I may no longer hear such reproaches. Thou knowest, Lord, that 14
I am a virgin, guiltless of intercourse with any man; I have not dis- 15
graced my name nor my father's name in the land of my exile. I am
my father's only child; he has no other to be his heir, nor has he any
near kinsman or relative who might marry me, and for whom I should
stay alive. Already seven husbands of mine have died. What have
I to live for any longer? If it is not thy will, O Lord, to let me die,
listen now to my complaint.'

At that very time the prayers of both of them were heard in the 16
glorious presence of God. His angel Raphael was sent to cure them 17
both of their troubles: Tobit, by removing the white patches from
his eyes so that he might see God's light again, and Sarah daughter
of Raguel by giving her in marriage to Tobias son of Tobit and by
setting her free from the wicked demon Asmodaeus; for it was the
destiny of Tobias and not of any other suitor to possess her. At the
moment when Tobit went back from the courtyard into his house,
Sarah daughter of Raguel came down from the attic.

The adventures of Tobias

THAT SAME DAY Tobit remembered the silver that he had 4
deposited with Gabael at Rages in Media, and he said to himself, 2
'I have asked for death; before I die ought I not to send for my son
Tobias and explain to him about this money?' So he sent for Tobias, 3
and when he came he said to him: 'Give me decent burial. Show
proper respect to your mother, and do not leave her in the lurch as
long as she lives; do what will please her, and never grieve her heart
in any way. Remember, my son, all the dangers she faced for your 4
sake while you were in her womb. When she dies, bury her beside
me in the same grave. And remember the Lord every day of your 5
life. Never deliberately do what is wrong or break his commandments. As long as you live do what is right. Do not fall into evil
ways; for an honest life leads to prosperity. To all who keep the law, 6

19 the Lord gives good guidance, and as he chooses he humbles men to
the grave below.[a] Now, my son, remember these commands; let
them never be effaced from your mind.

20 'Well now, my boy, let me tell you that I have ten talents of silver
21 on deposit with Gabael son of Gabri, at Rages in Media. Do not be
anxious because we have become poor; there is great wealth waiting
for you, if only you fear God and avoid all wickedness and do what is
good in the sight of the Lord your God.'

5 Then Tobias said: 'I will do all that you have told me, father.
2 But how shall I be able to get this money from him, since he does not
know me and I do not know him? What proof of identity shall I give
him to make him believe me and give me this money? Also I do not
3 know the roads to Media or how to get there.' To this Tobit replied:
'He gave me his note of hand, and I gave him mine, which I divided
in two. We took one part each, and I put mine with the money. It is
twenty years since I made this deposit. And now, my boy, find
someone reliable to go with you, and we will pay him up to the time
of your return; then go and recover the money from Gabael.'

4 Tobias went out to find a man who knew the way and would

[*a*] To all...below: *in place of these words some witnesses have* To all who keep the law (7) give alms from what you possess and never give with a grudging eye. Do not turn your face away from any poor man, and God will not turn away his face from you. (8) Let your almsgiving match your means. If you have little, do not be ashamed to give the little you can afford; (9) you will be laying up a sound insurance against the day of adversity. (10) Almsgiving saves the giver from death and keeps him from going down into darkness. (11) All who give alms are making an offering acceptable to the Most High.

(12) 'Beware, my son, of fornication; above all choose your wife from the race of your ancestors. Do not take a foreign wife who is not of your father's tribe, because we are descendants of the prophets. Remember, my son, that Noah, Abraham, Isaac, and Jacob, our ancestors, back to the earliest days, all chose wives from their kindred. They were blessed in their children, and their descendants shall possess the earth. (13) And you like them, my son, must love your kindred. Do not be too proud to take a wife from among the women of your own nation. Pride breeds ruin and anarchy, and the waster declines into poverty; waste is the mother of starvation.

(14) 'Pay your workmen their wages the same day; do not make any man wait for his money. If you serve God you will be repaid. Be circumspect, my son, in all that you do, and show yourself well-bred in all your behaviour. (15) Do not do to anyone what you yourself would hate. Do not drink to excess and so let drunkenness become a habit. (16) Give food to the hungry and clothes to the naked. Whatever you have beyond your own needs, give away to the poor, and do not give grudgingly. (17) Pour out your wine and offer your bread on the tombs of the righteous; but give nothing to sinners. (18) Ask any sensible man for his advice; do not despise any advice that may help you. (19) Praise the Lord God at all times and ask him to guide your course. Then all you do and all you plan will turn out well. The heathen all lack such guidance; it is the Lord himself who gives all good things, or humbles men at will, as he chooses.

accompany him to Media, and found himself face to face with the
angel Raphael. Not knowing he was an angel of God, he questioned 5
him: 'Where do you come from, young man?' 'I am an Israelite,'
he replied, 'one of your fellow-countrymen, and I have come here to
find work.' Tobias asked, 'Do you know the road to Media?' 'Yes,' 6
he said, 'I have often been there; I am familiar with all the routes and
know them well. I have often travelled into Media and used to lodge
with Gabael our fellow-countryman who lives there in Rages.[a] It is
two full days' journey from Ecbatana to Rages; for Rages is in the
hills, and Ecbatana is in the middle of the plain.' Tobias said: 'Wait 7
for me, young man, while I go in and tell my father. I need you to
go with me and will pay you your wages.' 'All right, I will wait,' he 8
said; 'only do not be too long.'

Tobias went in and told his father. 'I have found a fellow-Israelite to accompany me', he said. His father replied, 'Call the man in, my son. I want to find out his family and tribe and make sure that he will be a trustworthy companion for you.'

Tobias went out and called him: 'Young man, my father is asking 9
for you.' He went in, and Tobit greeted him first. To Raphael's
reply, 'May all be well with you!', Tobit retorted: 'How can anything be well with me now? I am a blind man; I cannot see the light
of heaven, but lie in darkness like the dead who cannot see the light.
Though still alive, I am as good as dead. I hear men's voices, but the
men I do not see.' Raphael answered: 'Take heart; in God's design
your cure is at hand. Take heart.' Tobit went on: 'My son Tobias
wishes to travel to Media. Can you go with him as his guide? I will
pay you, my friend.' 'Yes,' he said, 'I can go with him; I know all
the roads. I have often been to Media; I have travelled over all the
plains and mountains there, and am familiar with all its roads.' Tobit 10
said to him, 'Tell me, my friend, what family and tribe you belong
to.' He asked, 'Why need you know my tribe?' Tobit said, 'I do 11
indeed wish to know whose son you are, my friend, and what your
name is.' 'I am Azarias,' he replied, 'son of the older Ananias, one of 12
your kinsmen.'

Tobit said to him: 'Good luck and a safe journey to you! Do not 13
be angry with me, my friend, because I wished to know the facts of
your descent. It turns out that you are a kinsman, and a man of good
family. I knew Ananias and Nathan the two sons of the older

[a] *Probable reading (compare 4.1); Gk.* Ecbatana.

Semelias. They used to go with me to Jerusalem and worship with
me there; they never went astray. Your kinsmen are worthy men;
14 you come of a sound stock. Good luck go with you.' Tobit added:
'I will pay you a drachma a day and allow you the same expenses as
15 my son. Keep him company on his travels, and I will add something
16 to your wages.' Raphael answered: 'I will go with him. Never fear;
we shall travel there and back without mishap, because the road is
safe.' Tobit replied, 'God bless you, my friend.' He called his son
and said to him: 'My boy, get ready what you need for the journey,
and set off with your kinsman. May God in heaven keep both of you
safe on your journey there and restore you to me unharmed. May
his angel safely escort you both.' Before setting out Tobias kissed his
father and mother, and Tobit said to him, 'Goodbye, and a safe
journey!'

17 Then his mother burst into tears. 'Why have you sent my boy
away?' she said to Tobit. 'Is he not our prop and stay? Has he not
18 always been at home with us? Why send money after money? Write
19 it off for the sake of our boy! Let us be content to live the life the
20 Lord has appointed for us.' Tobit said to her: 'Do not worry; our
son will go safely and come back safely, and you will see him with
your own eyes on the day of his safe return. Do not worry or be
21 anxious about them, my dear. A good angel will go with him, and his
22 journey will prosper, and he will come back safe and sound.' At that
she stopped crying.

6 THE BOY and the angel left the house together, and the dog came
out with him and accompanied them. They travelled until night
2 overtook them, and then camped by the river Tigris. Tobias went
down to bathe his feet in the river, and a huge fish leapt out of the
3 water and tried to swallow the boy's foot. He cried out, and the
angel said to him, 'Seize the fish and hold it fast.' So Tobias seized
4 it and hauled it on to the bank. The angel said to him: 'Split the fish
open and take out its gall, heart, and liver; keep them by you, but
throw the guts away; the gall, heart, and liver can be used as
5 medicine.' Tobias split the fish open, and put together its gall, heart,
and liver. He cooked and ate part of the fish; the rest he salted and
kept.

They continued the journey together until they came near Media.
6 Then the boy asked the angel: 'Azarias, my friend, what medicine is

there in the fish's heart, liver, and gall?' He said: 'You can use the 7
heart and liver as a fumigation for any man or woman attacked by a
demon or evil spirit; the attack will cease, and it will give no further
trouble. The gall is for anointing a man's eyes when white patches 8
have spread over them, or for blowing on the white patches in the
eyes; the eyes will then recover.'

When he had entered Media and was now approaching Ecbatana, 9
Raphael said to the boy, 'Tobias, my friend.' 'Yes?' he re- 10
plied. Raphael said: 'We must stay the night with Raguel. He is
your kinsman and he has a daughter named Sarah. Apart from Sarah
he has neither son nor daughter. You are her next of kin and have the 11
right to marry her and inherit her father's property. The girl is 12
sensible, brave, and very beautiful, and her father is an honourable
man.' He went on: 'It is right that you should marry her. Be guided by me, my friend; I will speak to her father about the girl this very night and ask for her hand as your bride, and on our return from Rages we will celebrate her marriage. I know that Raguel cannot withhold her from you or betroth her to another man without incurring the death penalty according to the ordinance in the book of Moses; and he is aware that his daughter belongs by right to you rather than to any other man. Now be guided by me, my friend; we will talk about the girl tonight and will betroth her to you, and when we return from Rages we shall take her back with us to your home.'

Then Tobias answered Raphael: 'Azarias, my friend, I have heard 13
that she has already been given to seven husbands and they died the
very night they went into the bridal chamber to her. I have been 14
told that it is a demon who kills them. And now it is my turn to be
afraid; he does her no harm, but kills any man who tries to come
near her. I am my father's only child; I am afraid that if I die I shall
bring my father and mother to the grave with grief for me. They
have no other son to bury them.' Raphael said to him: 'Have you 15
forgotten the orders your father gave you? He told you to take a wife
from your father's kindred. Now be guided by me, my friend: do
not worry about the demon, but marry her. I am sure that this night
she shall be given you as your wife. When you enter the bridal 16
chamber, take some of the fish's liver and its heart, and put them on
the smoking incense. The smell will spread, and when the demon 17
smells it he will make off and never be seen near her any more.

When you are about to go to bed with her, both of you must first stand up and pray, beseeching the Lord of heaven to grant you mercy and deliverance. Have no fear; she was destined for you before the world was made. You shall rescue her and she shall go with you. No doubt you will have children by her and they will be very dear to you.[a] So do not worry!' When Tobias heard what Raphael said, and learnt that she was his kinswoman and of his father's house, he was filled with love for her and set his heart on her.

7 WHEN THEY REACHED Ecbatana, Tobias said, 'Azarias, my
friend, take me straight to our kinsman Raguel.' So Azarias
brought him to Raguel's house, and they found him sitting by the
courtyard door. They greeted him first, and he replied, 'A hearty
welcome to you, friends. I am glad to see you well after your
2 journey.' He took them into his house and said to Edna his wife, 'Is
3 not this young man like my kinsman Tobit?' Edna asked them,
'Where do you come from, friends?' 'We belong to the tribe of
4 Naphtali,' they answered, 'now in captivity at Nineveh.' 'Do you
know our kinsman Tobit?' she asked, and they replied, 'Yes, we do.'
5 'Is he well?' she said. 'He is alive and well', they answered, and
6 Tobias added, 'He is my father.' Raguel jumped up and, with tears
7 in his eyes, he kissed him and said, 'God bless you, my boy, son of a
good and noble father. But what grievous news that so good and
charitable a man has gone blind!' He embraced Tobias his kinsman
8 and wept; and Edna his wife and their daughter Sarah also wept for
Tobit. Then Raguel slaughtered a ram from the flock and made them
warmly welcome.

After they had taken a bath and washed their hands, and had sat
down to dinner, Tobias said to Raphael, 'Azarias, my friend, ask
9 Raguel to give me Sarah my kinswoman.' Raguel overheard and said
10 to the young man: 'Eat, drink, and be happy tonight. There is no
one but yourself who should have my daughter Sarah; indeed I have
no right to give her to anyone else, since you are my nearest kins-
11 man. But I must tell you the truth, my son: I have given her in
marriage to seven of our kinsmen, and they all died on their wedding
night. My son, eat now and drink, and may the Lord deal kindly
with you both.' Tobias answered, 'I will not eat or drink anything
12 here until you have disposed of this business of mine.' Raguel said

[a] *Literally* be like brothers to you.

to him, 'I will do so: I give her to you as the ordinance in the book of
Moses prescribes. Heaven has ordained that she shall be yours.
Take your kinswoman. From now on, you belong to her and she to
you; she is yours for ever from this day. The Lord of heaven prosper
you both this night, my son, and grant you mercy and peace.'

Raguel sent for his daughter Sarah, and when she came he took 13
her hand and gave her to Tobias, saying: 'Take her to be your
wedded wife in accordance with the law and the ordinance written in
the book of Moses. Keep her and take her home to your father; and
may the God of heaven keep you safe and give you peace and
prosperity.' Then he sent for her mother and told her to bring paper, 14
and he wrote out a marriage contract granting Sarah to Tobias as his
wife, as the law of Moses ordains. After that they began to eat and 15
drink.

Raguel called his wife and said, 'My dear, get the spare room 16
ready and take her in there.' Edna went and prepared the room as he 17
had told her, and took Sarah into it. Edna cried over her, then dried
her tears and said: 'Courage, dear daughter; the Lord of heaven give 18
you joy instead of sorrow. Courage, daughter!' Then she went out.

When they had finished eating and drinking and were ready for **8**
bed, they escorted the young man to the bridal chamber. Tobias 2
recalled what Raphael had told him; he took the fish's liver and heart
out of the bag in which he kept them, and put them on the smoking
incense. The smell from the fish held the demon off, and he took 3
flight into Upper Egypt; and Raphael instantly followed him there
and bound him hand and foot.

When they were left alone and the door was shut, Tobias rose 4
from the bed and said to Sarah, 'Get up, my love; let us pray and
beseech our Lord to show us mercy and keep us safe.' She got up 5
and they began to pray that they might be kept safe. Tobias said:
'We praise thee, O God of our fathers, we praise thy name for ever
and ever. Let the heavens and all thy creation praise thee for ever.
Thou madest Adam, and Eve his wife to be his helper and support; 6
and those two were the parents of the human race. This was thy
word: "It is not good for the man to be alone; let us make him a
helper like him." I now take this my beloved to wife, not out of lust 7
but in true marriage. Grant that she and I may find mercy and
grow old together.' They both said 'Amen', and slept through the 8, 9
night.

Raguel got up and summoned his servants, and they went out and
10 dug a grave. For he said, 'He may have been killed, and then we
11 shall have to face scorn and disgrace.' When they had finished dig-
12 ging the grave, Raguel went into the house and called his wife: 'Send
one of the maidservants', he said, 'to go in and see if he is alive. If he
13 is dead, let us bury him so that no one may know.' They lit a lamp,
opened the door, and sent a maidservant in; and she found them
14 sound asleep together. She came out and told them: 'He is alive and
has come to no harm.'

15 Then they praised the God of heaven: 'We praise thee, O God,
we praise thee with all our heart. Let men praise thee throughout all
16 ages. Praise to thee for the joy thou hast given me; the thing
I feared has not happened, but thou hast shown us thy great mercy.
17 Praise to thee for the mercy thou hast shown to these two, these only
children. Lord, show them mercy, keep them safe, and grant them a
18 long life of happiness and affection.' Then he ordered his servants to
fill in the grave before dawn came.

19 He told his wife to bake a great batch of bread; he went to the herd
and brought two oxen and four rams and told his servants to get them
20 ready; so they set about the preparations. He then called Tobias
and said: 'You shall not stir from here for two weeks. Stay with us;
let us eat and drink together and cheer my daughter's heart after all
21 her suffering. Here and now take half of all I have, and go home to
your father safe and sound; and the other half will come to you both
when my wife and I die. Be reassured, my son, I am your father and
Edna is your mother; we are as close to you as to your wife, now and
always. You have nothing to fear, my son.'

9 1, 2 Tobias called Raphael and said to him: 'Azarias, my friend, take
four servants with you, and two camels, and make your way to
Rages. Go to Gabael's house, give him the bond and collect the
4 money, and bring him with you to the wedding-feast. You know that
my father will be counting the days and, if I am even one day late, it
3 will distress him. You see what Raguel has sworn, and I cannot go
5 against his oath.' Raphael went with the four servants and the two
camels to Rages in Media and lodged there with Gabael. He gave
him his bond and informed him that Tobit's son Tobias had taken
a wife and was inviting him to the wedding-feast. At once Gabael
counted out the bags to him with their seals intact, and they put
6 them together. They all made an early start and came to the wedding.

When they entered Raguel's house and found Tobias at the feast, he jumped up and greeted Gabael. With tears in his eyes Gabael blessed him and said: 'Good sir, worthy son of a worthy father, that upright and charitable man, may the Lord give Heaven's blessing to you and your wife, your father and your mother-in-law. Praise be to God that I have seen my cousin Tobias, so like his father.'

Tobias's homecoming

NOW DAY BY DAY Tobit was keeping count of the time Tobias **10**
would take for his journey there and back. When the days had
passed and his son had not returned, Tobit said: 'Perhaps he has 2
been detained there. Or perhaps Gabael is dead and there is no one
to give him the money.' And he grew anxious. Anna his wife said: 3, 4
'My child has perished. He is no longer in the land of the living.'
She began to weep and lament for her son: 'O my child, the light of 5
my eyes, why did I let you go?' Tobit said to her: 'Hush, do not 6
worry, my dear; he is all right. Something has happened there to
distract them. The man who went with him is one of our kinsmen
and can be trusted. Do not grieve for him, my dear; he will soon be
back.' But she answered: 'Be quiet! Leave me alone! Do not try to 7
deceive me. My boy is dead.' Each day she would rush out and look
down the road her son had taken, and would listen to no one; and
when she came indoors at sunset she could never sleep, but wept and
lamented the whole night long.

The two weeks of wedding celebrations which Raguel had sworn to
hold for his daughter came to an end, and Tobias went up to him and
said: 'Let me be off on my journey; for I am sure that my parents
are thinking they will never see me again. I beg you, father, let me
go home now to my father Tobit. I have already told you how I left
him.' Raguel said to Tobias: 'Stay, my son. Stay with me, and 8
I will send news of you to your father.' But Tobias answered: 'No; 9
please let me go home to my father.' Then without further delay 10
Raguel handed over to Tobias Sarah his bride and half of all that he
possessed, male and female slaves, sheep and cattle, donkeys and
camels, clothes, money, and furniture. He saw them safely off and 11
embraced Tobias, saying: 'Goodbye, my son; a safe journey to you!

May the Lord of heaven give prosperity to you and Sarah your wife;
12 and may I live to see your children.' To his daughter Sarah he said:
'Go to your father-in-law's house; they are now your parents as
much as if you were their own daughter. Go in peace, my child;
I hope to hear good news of you as long as I live.' He bade them
both goodbye and sent them on their way. Edna said to Tobias:
'Child and beloved cousin, may the Lord bring you safely home, you
and my daughter Sarah, and may I live long enough to see your
children. In the sight of the Lord I entrust my daughter to you; do
nothing to hurt her as long as you live. Go in peace, my son. From
now on I am your mother and Sarah is your beloved wife. May we
all be blessed with prosperity to the end of our days!' She kissed
11 them both and saw them safely off. Tobias parted from Raguel in
good health and spirits, thankful to the Lord of heaven and earth,
the king of all, for the success of his journey. Raguel's last words to
him were: 'May the Lord give you the means to honour your parents
all their lives.'

2 When they reached Caserin close to Nineveh, Raphael said: 'You
3 know how your father was when we left him; let us hurry on ahead
of your wife and see that the house is ready before the others arrive.'
4 As the two of them went on together Raphael said: 'Take the fish-
gall in your hand.' The dog went with the angel and Tobias, following at their heels.

5, 6 Anna sat watching the road by which her son would return. She
saw him coming and exclaimed to his father, 'Here he comes, your
7 son and the man who went with him!' Before Tobias reached his
father's house Raphael said: 'I know for certain that his eyes will be
8 opened. Spread the fish-gall on his eyes, and the medicine will make
the white patches shrink and peel off. Your father will get his sight
9 back and see the light of day.' Anna ran forward and flung her arms
round her son. 'Here you are, my boy; now I can die happy!' she
cried out with tears in her eyes.

10 Tobit rose to his feet and came stumbling out through the court-
11 yard door. Tobias went up to him with the fish-gall in his hand and
blew it into his father's eyes, and took him by the arm and said: 'It
12 will be all right, father.' Then when he had put the medicine on and
13 applied it, using both hands he peeled off the patches from the
14 corners of Tobit's eyes. Tobit flung his arms round him and burst
into tears. 'I can see you, my son, the light of my eyes!' he cried.

'Praise be to God, and praise to his great name, and to all his holy
angels. May his great name rest upon us. Praised be all the angels
for ever. He laid his scourge on me, and now, look, I see my son 15
Tobias!'

Tobias went in, rejoicing and praising God with all his strength.
He told his father about the success of his journey, how he had
brought the money with him and had married Sarah daughter of
Raguel. 'She is on her way,' he said, 'quite close to the city gate.'
Tobit went out joyfully to meet his daughter-in-law at the gate, 16
praising God as he went. At the sight of him passing through the
city in full vigour and walking without a guide, the people of
Nineveh were astonished; and Tobit gave thanks to God before them 17
all for his mercy in opening his eyes. When he met Sarah, the wife
of his son Tobias, he blessed her and said to her: 'Come in, my
daughter, and welcome. Praise be to your God who has brought you
to us, my daughter. Blessings on your father, and on my son Tobias,
and blessings on you, my daughter. Come into your home, and may
health, blessings, and joy be yours; come in, my daughter.' It was a
day of joy for all the Jews in Nineveh; and Ahikar and Nadab, Tobit's 18
cousins, came to share his happiness.

When the marriage-feast was over, Tobit called Tobias and said, **12**
'My son, see that you pay the man who went with you, and give him
something extra, over and above his wages.' Tobias said: 'Father, 2
how much shall I pay him? It would not hurt me to give him
half the money he and I brought back. He has kept me safe, 3
cured my wife, helped me bring the money, and healed you. How
much extra shall I pay him?' Tobit replied, 'It is right, my son, for 4
him to be given half of all that he has brought with him.' So Tobias 5
sent for him and said, 'Half of all that you have brought with you is
yours for your wages; take it, and fare you well.'

Then Raphael called them both aside and said to them: 'Praise 6
God and thank him before all men living for the good he has done
you, so that they may sing hymns of praise to his name. Proclaim to
all the world what God has done, and pay him honour; do not be slow
to give him thanks. A king's secret ought to be kept, but the works 7
of God should be acknowledged publicly. Acknowledge them,
therefore, and pay him honour. Do good, and evil shall not touch
you. Better prayer with sincerity, and almsgiving with righteousness, 8
than wealth with wickedness. Better give alms than hoard up gold.

9 Almsgiving preserves a man from death and wipes out all sin.
10 Givers of alms will enjoy long life; but sinners and wrong-doers are
their own worst enemies.
11 'I will tell you the whole truth; I will hide nothing from you.
Indeed I told you just now when I said, "A king's secret ought to be
12 kept, but the works of God should be publicly honoured." When you
and Sarah prayed, it was I who brought your prayers into the glorious
presence of the Lord; and so too whenever you buried the dead.
13 That day when you got up from your dinner without hesitation to go
14 and bury the corpse, I was sent to test you; and again God sent me to
cure both you and Sarah your daughter-in-law at the same time.
15 I am Raphael, one of the seven angels who stand in attendance on the
Lord and enter his glorious presence.'
16, 17 The two men were shaken, and prostrated themselves in awe. But
he said to them: 'Do not be afraid, all is well; praise God for ever.
18 It is no thanks to me that I have been with you; it was the will of
19 God. Worship him all your life long, sing his praise. Take note that
20 I ate no food; what appeared to you was a vision. And now praise
the Lord, give thanks to God here on earth; I am ascending to him
who sent me. Write down all these things that have happened to you.'
21 He then ascended, and when they rose to their feet, he was no longer
22 to be seen. They sang hymns of praise to God, giving him thanks
for these great deeds he had done when his angel appeared to them.

13 TOBIT said:

'Praise to the ever-living God and to his kingdom.
2 He punishes and he shows mercy;
he brings men down to the grave below,
and up from the great destruction.
Nothing can escape his power.
3 Give him thanks, men of Israel, in the presence of the nations,
for he has scattered you among them;
4 there he has shown you his greatness.
Exalt him in the sight of every living creature,
for he is our Lord and God;
he is our Father and our God for ever.
5 He will punish you for your wickedness,
and he will show mercy to you all,

gathering you from among all the nations
wherever you have been scattered.
When you turn to him with all your heart and soul 6
and act in loyal obedience to him,
then he will turn to you
and hide his face from you no longer.
Consider now the deeds he has done for you,
and give him thanks with full voice;
praise the righteous Lord
and exalt the King of ages.[a]

'Your sanctuary[b] shall be rebuilt for you with rejoicing. 10
May he give happiness to all your exiles
and cherish all who mourn and your descendants for ever.
Your light shall shine brightly to all the ends of the earth. 11
Many nations shall come to you from afar,
from all the corners of the earth to your holy name;
they shall bring gifts in their hands for the King of heaven.
In you endless generations shall utter their joy;
the name of the chosen city shall endure for ever and ever.
There shall be a curse upon all who speak harshly to you, 12
upon all who destroy you and pull down your walls,
upon all who demolish your towers and burn your houses;
but blessings shall be for evermore upon those who hold you in reverence.
Come then, be joyful for the righteous, 13
for they shall all be gathered together
and shall praise the eternal Lord.

[*a*] *Some witnesses add*
In the land of my exile I give thanks to him
and declare his might and greatness to a sinful nation.
Turn, you sinners, and do what is right in his eyes;
who knows whether he may not welcome you and show you mercy?
I will exalt my God 7
and rejoice in the King of heaven.
Let all men tell of his majesty 8
and give him thanks in Jerusalem.
O Jerusalem, the holy city, 9
he will punish you for what your sons have done,
but he will again show mercy on the righteous.
Thank the good Lord and praise the King of ages. 10

[*b*] *Or* home.

14 How happy shall they be who love you and rejoice in your prosperity,
happy all who grieve for you in your afflictions;
they shall rejoice over you and for ever be witness of your joy.
15 My soul, praise the Lord, the great king,
16 for Jerusalem shall be built as a city for him to dwell in for ever.
How happy I shall be when the remnant of my descendants shall see your splendour
and give thanks to the King of heaven.
The gates of Jerusalem shall be built of sapphire and emerald,
and all your walls of precious stones.
The towers of Jerusalem shall be built of gold,
their battlements of the finest gold.
17 The streets of Jerusalem shall be paved with garnets and jewels of Ophir.
18 The gates of Jerusalem shall sing hymns of joy
and all her houses shall say Alleluia,
praise to the God of Israel!
Blessed by him, they shall bless his holy name for ever and ever.'

14 SO ENDED Tobit's thanksgiving. He died peacefully at the age of
a hundred and twelve, and was given honourable burial in Nineveh.
2 He was sixty-two years old when his eyes were injured, and
after he recovered his sight he lived in prosperity, doing his
acts of charity and never ceasing to praise God and proclaim his
majesty.
3 When he was dying he sent for his son Tobias, and gave him these
4 instructions: 'My son, you must take your children and make your
escape to Media, for I believe God's word against Nineveh spoken
by Nahum. It will all come true; everything will happen to Asshur
and Nineveh that was spoken by the prophets of Israel whom God
sent. Not a word of it will fall short; everything will be fulfilled
when the time comes. It will be safer in Media than in Assyria and
Babylon; I know, I am convinced, that all God's words will be
fulfilled. It will be so; not one of them will fail. Our countrymen who live in Israel will all be scattered and carried off into
captivity out of that good land, and the whole territory of Israel

laid waste. Samaria and Jerusalem will lie waste, and for a time
the house of God will be in mourning; it will be burnt to the
ground.

'Then God will have mercy on them again and will bring them 5
back to the land of Israel. They will rebuild the house of God, but
not as it was before, not until the time of fulfilment comes. Then
they will all return from their captivity and rebuild Jerusalem
gloriously; then indeed the house will be built in her as the prophets
of Israel foretold. All the nations of the world will be converted to 6
the true worship of God; they will abandon their idols which led
them astray into falsehood, and praise the eternal God according to 7
his law. All the Israelites who survive at that time and are firm in
their loyalty to God will be brought together; they will come to
Jerusalem to take possession of the land of Abraham, and live there
for ever in safety. Those who love God in truth will rejoice; and
sinners and wrong-doers will disappear from the earth. Now, my 8
children, I give you this command: serve God in truth and do what
pleases him. Train your children to do what is right and give alms, 9
to keep God in mind at all times and praise his name in sincerity with
all their strength.

'And now, my son, you must leave Nineveh. Do not stay here; 10
once you have laid your mother in the grave with me, do not spend
another night within the city boundaries. For I see that the place is
full of wickedness and shameless dishonesty. My son, think what
Nadab did to Ahikar who brought him up: he forced him to hide in a
living grave. Ahikar survived to see God requite the dishonour done
to him; he came out into the light of day, but Nadab passed into
eternal darkness for his attempt to kill Ahikar. Because I gave alms,
Ahikar escaped from the fatal trap Nadab set for him, and Nadab fell
into the trap himself and was destroyed. So, my children, see what 11
comes of almsgiving, and see what comes of wickedness—death.
But now my strength is failing.'

Then they laid him on his bed, and he died; and they gave him
honourable burial. When his mother died, Tobias buried her beside 12
his father. He and his wife went away to Media and settled at Ecbatana
with his father-in-law Raguel. He honoured and cared for his wife's 13
parents in their old age. He buried them at Ecbatana in Media, and
he inherited the estate of Raguel as well as that of his father Tobit.
He died greatly respected at the age of one hundred and seventeen. 14

15 He lived long enough to hear of the destruction of Nineveh by
Ahasuerus king of Media and to see his prisoners of war brought
from there into Media. So he praised God for all that he had done to
the people of Nineveh and Asshur; and before he died he rejoiced
over the fate of Nineveh and praised the Lord God who lives for ever
and ever.

Amen.

JUDITH

The Assyrian invasion

IN THE TWELFTH YEAR of the reign of Nebuchadnezzar, 1
who reigned over the Assyrians from his capital, Nineveh,
Arphaxad was ruling the Medes from Ecbatana. He it was who 2
encircled Ecbatana with a wall built of hewn stones which were four
and a half feet thick and nine feet long.[a] He made the wall a hundred
and five feet high and seventy-five feet thick, and at the city gates he 3
set up towers a hundred and fifty feet high with foundations ninety
feet thick; and he made the gates a hundred and five feet high and 4
sixty feet wide to allow his army to march out in full force with his
infantry in formation. It was in those days, then, that King Nebu- 5
chadnezzar waged war against King Arphaxad in the great plain on
the borders of Ragau. Nebuchadnezzar was opposed by all the 6
inhabitants of the hill-country, by all those who lived along the
Euphrates, the Tigris, and the Hydaspes; and, on the plain, by
Arioch king of Elam; and many tribes of the Chelodites joined forces
with them.

Then Nebuchadnezzar king of Assyria sent a summons to all the 7
inhabitants of Persia, and to all who lived in the west: the inhabitants of Cilicia and Damascus, Lebanon and Antilebanon, all who
lived near the coast, the peoples in Carmel and Gilead, Upper 8
Galilee, and the great plain of Esdraelon, all who were in Samaria 9
and its towns, and on the west of Jordan as far as Jerusalem, Betane,
Chelus, Cadesh, and the frontier[b] of Egypt, those who lived in
Tahpanhes, Rameses, and the whole land of Goshen as far as Tanis 10
and Memphis, and all the inhabitants of Egypt as far as the borders
of Ethiopia. But the entire region disregarded the summons of 11
Nebuchadnezzar king of Assyria and did not join him in the war.
They were not afraid of him, for he seemed to them to stand alone[c]
and unsupported; and they treated his envoys with contempt and
sent them back empty-handed.

This roused Nebuchadnezzar to fury against the whole region, 12

[*a*] *In verses 2–4 the measurements are given in cubits in the Greek.* [*b*] *Literally* river.
[*c*] *One witness reads* to be no more than their equal...

and he swore by his throne and his kingdom that he would have his
revenge on all the territories of Cilicia, Damascus, and Syria, and put
their inhabitants to the sword, along with the Moabites, the Ammonites, and the people in all Judaea and in Egypt as far as the
shores of the two seas.
13 In the seventeenth year of his reign he marshalled his forces
against King Arphaxad and defeated him in battle, routing his entire
14 army, cavalry, chariots, and all. He occupied his towns; and when he
reached Ecbatana he captured its towers, looted its bazaars, and
15 turned its splendour to abject ruin. He caught Arphaxad in the
mountains of Ragau, speared him through, and so made an end of
16 him. Then he returned with his spoils to Nineveh, he and his combined forces, an immense host of warriors. There he rested and
feasted with his army for four months.
2 In the eighteenth year, on the twenty-second day of the first
month, a proposal was made in the palace of Nebuchadnezzar king
of Assyria to carry out his threat of vengeance on the whole region.
2 Assembling all his officers and nobles, the king laid before them his
personal decision about the region and declared his intention of
3 putting an end to its disaffection. They resolved that everyone who
had not obeyed his summons should be put to death.
4 When his plans were completed,[a] Nebuchadnezzar king of Assyria
summoned Holophernes, his commander-in-chief, who was second
5 only to himself, and said to him, 'This is the decree of the Great
King, lord of all the earth: Directly you leave my presence, you are to
take under your command an army of seasoned troops, a hundred
and twenty thousand infantry with a force of twelve thousand
6 cavalry, and march out against all the peoples of the west who have
7 dared to disobey my command. Tell them to have ready their
offering of earth and water, for I am coming to vent my wrath on
them. Their whole land will be smothered by my army, and I will
8 give them up to be plundered by my troops. Their dead will fill the
9 valleys, and every stream and river will be choked with corpses; and
10 I will send them into captivity to the ends of the whole earth. Now
go and occupy all their territory for me. If they surrender to you,
11 hold them for me until the time comes to punish them. But show no
mercy to those who resist; let them be slaughtered and plundered
12 throughout the whole region. By my life and my royal power I swear:

[a] *Or* When he had finished stating his purpose...

I have spoken and I will be as good as my word. As for you, do not 13
disobey a single one of my orders, but see that you carry them out
exactly as I your sovereign have commanded you. Do this without
delay.'

After leaving his sovereign's presence, Holophernes assembled all 14
the marshals, generals, and officers of the Assyrian army, and 15
mustered picked men, as the king had commanded, a hundred and
twenty thousand infantry and twelve thousand mounted archers,
drawing them up in battle order. He took an immense number of 16, 17
camels, asses, and mules for their baggage, innumerable sheep, oxen,
and goats for provisions, and ample rations for every man, as well as a 18
great quantity of gold and silver from the royal palace. Then he set 19
out with all his army to go ahead of King Nebuchadnezzar and to
overrun the entire region to the west with chariots, cavalry, and
picked infantry. Along with them went a motley host like a swarm of 20
locusts, countless as the dust of the earth.

From Nineveh they marched for three days towards the plain of 21
Bectileth, and encamped beside Bectileth near the mountain north of
Upper Cilicia. From there, Holophernes advanced into the hill- 22
country with his whole army, infantry, cavalry, and chariots. He 23
devastated Put and Lud, and plundered all the people of Rassis, and
the Ishmaelites on the edge of the desert south of the land of the
Cheleans. Then he followed[a] the Euphrates and traversed Mesopo- 24
tamia, destroying all the fortified towns along the river Abron as far
as the sea. He occupied the territory of Cilicia and cut down all who 25
resisted him. Then he came south to the borders of Japheth fronting
Arabia. He surrounded the Midianites, burnt their encampments, 26
and plundered their sheepfolds. At the time of wheat harvest he 27
went down to the plain of Damascus, burnt their crops, exterminated their flocks and herds, sacked their towns, laid waste their
fields, and put all their young men to the sword. Fear and dread of 28
him fell on all the inhabitants of the coast at Tyre and Sidon, of Sur
and Okina, and of Jemnaan; the people of Azotus and Ascalon were
terrified of him.

They sent envoys to sue for peace, who said: 'We are servants of **3** 1, 2
the Great King Nebuchadnezzar, we lie prostrate before you; do
with us as you please. Our buildings, our territory, our wheat fields, 3
our flocks and herds and every sheepfold in our encampments, all are

[*a*] *Or* crossed.

4 yours to do with as you wish. Our towns and their inhabitants are
subject to you; come and deal with them as you think fit.'
5, 6 When the envoys came to Holophernes with this message, he went
down to the coast with his army and garrisoned all the fortified
7 towns, taking from them picked men as auxiliaries. Both there and
in all the surrounding country he was welcomed with garlands,
8 dancing, and tambourines. He demolished all their sanctuaries[a] and
cut down their sacred groves, for he had been commissioned to
destroy all the gods of the land, so that Nebuchadnezzar alone
should be worshipped by every nation and invoked as a god by men of
every tribe and tongue.
9 Holophernes then advanced towards Esdraelon, near Dothan,
10 which faces the great ridge of Judaea, and encamped between Geba
and Scythopolis, where he remained for a whole month to collect
supplies for his army.

4 WHEN THE ISRAELITES who lived in Judaea heard of all that
had been done to the nations by Holophernes, the commander-
in-chief of Nebuchadnezzar king of Assyria, and how he had
2 plundered and totally destroyed all their temples, they were terrified
at his approach. They were in great alarm for Jerusalem and for the
3 temple of the Lord their God. For they had just returned from
captivity, and it was only recently that the people had been re-united
in Judaea, and the sacred vessels, the temple, and the altar sanctified
4 after their profanation. So they sent out a warning to the whole of
Samaria, Cona, Beth-horon, Belmain and Jericho, Choba and Aesora
5 and the valley of Salem, and occupied the tops of all the high hills.
They fortified the villages on them and laid up stores of food in pre-
6 paration for war; for their fields had just been harvested. Joakim,
who was high priest in Jerusalem at the time, wrote to the people of
Bethulia and Bethomesthaim, which is opposite Esdraelon facing the
7 plain near Dothan. He ordered them to occupy the passes into the
hill-country, because they controlled access to Judaea, and it was
easy to hold up an advancing army, for the approach was only wide
8 enough for two men. The Israelites obeyed the orders of the high
9 priest Joakim and the senate of all Israel in Jerusalem. Fervently
they sent up a cry to God, every man of Israel, and fervently they
10 humbled themselves before him. They put on sackcloth—they

[*a*] *So one Vs.; Gk.* borders.

themselves, their wives, their children, their livestock, and every
resident foreigner, hired labourer, and slave—and all the inhabitants 11
of Jerusalem, men, women, and children, prostrated themselves in
front of the sanctuary, and, with ashes on their heads, spread out
their sackcloth before the Lord. They draped the altar in sackcloth,
and with one voice they earnestly implored the God of Israel not to 12
allow their children to be captured, their wives carried off, their
ancestral cities destroyed, and the temple profaned and dishonoured,
to the delight of the heathen. The Lord heard their prayer and pitied 13
their distress.

For many days the whole population of Judaea and Jerusalem
fasted before the sanctuary of the Lord Almighty. Joakim the high 14
priest and the priests who stood in the presence of the Lord, and all
who served in the temple, wore sackcloth when they offered the
regular burnt-offering and the votive and freewill offerings of the
people; and with ashes on their turbans they cried aloud to the Lord 15
to look favourably on the whole house of Israel.

When it was reported to Holophernes, the Assyrian commander- **5**
in-chief, that the Israelites had prepared for war, and that they had
closed the passes in the hill-country, fortified all the heights, and dug
pitfalls in the plains, he was furious. He summoned all the rulers of 2
Moab, the Ammonite commanders, and all the governors of the
coastal region, and said to them, 'Tell me, you Canaanites, what 3
nation is this that lives in the hill-country? What towns do they
inhabit? How big is their army? What gives them their power and
strength? Who is the king that commands their forces? Why are they 4
the only people of the west who have refused to come and meet me?'

Then Achior, the leader of all the Ammonites, said to him, 'My 5
lord, if you will allow your servant to speak, I will tell you the truth
about this nation that lives in the hill-country near here; and no lie
shall pass my lips. They are descended from the Chaldaeans; and at 6, 7
one time they settled in Mesopotamia, because they refused to
worship the gods their fathers had worshipped in Chaldaea. They 8
abandoned the ways of their ancestors and worshipped the God of
Heaven, the god whom they now acknowledged. When the Chaldaeans drove them out from the presence of their gods, they fled to
Mesopotamia, where they lived for a long time. Then their god told 9
them to leave their new home and go on to Canaan. They settled
there and acquired great wealth in gold, silver, and livestock.

10 'Because of a famine which spread over the whole of Canaan, they
went down to Egypt and lived there as long as they were supplied
with food. While in Egypt, they multiplied so greatly that their
11 numbers could not be reckoned, and the king of Egypt turned
against them. He exploited them by setting them to hard labour
12 making bricks, and he reduced them to abject slavery. They cried
out to their god, and he inflicted incurable plagues on the whole of
13 Egypt. So the Egyptians turned them out; and their god dried up the
14 Red Sea for them and led them on to Sinai and Cadesh-barnea. Then
15 they drove out all the inhabitants of the wilderness and settled in the
land of the Amorites, and they destroyed all the people of Heshbon
by force of arms. After that they crossed the Jordan and occupied
16 all the hill-country, driving out the Canaanites, the Perizzites, the
Jebusites, the Shechemites, and all the Girgashites. There they settled
for a long time.

17 'As long as they did not sin against their god, they prospered; for
18 theirs is a god who hates wickedness. But when they left the path he
had laid down for them, they suffered heavy losses in many wars and
were carried captive to a foreign country; the temple of their god was
razed to the ground, and their towns were occupied by their enemies.
19 But now that they have returned to their god, they have come back
from the places where they had been dispersed, and have taken
possession of Jerusalem, where their sanctuary is, and have settled in
the hill-country, because it was uninhabited.

20 'Now, my lord and master, if these people are guilty of an error
and are sinning against their god, and if we find out that they have
21 committed this offence, then we may go and make war on them. But
if these people have committed no wickedness, leave them alone, my
lord, for fear the god they serve should protect them and we become
22 the laughing-stock of the world.' When Achior stopped speaking
there were protests from all those who stood round the tent. Holophernes' officers and all the people from the coastal region and from
23 Moab demanded that Achior should be cut to pieces. 'We are not
going to be afraid of the Israelites,' they said, 'a people quite
24 incapable of putting an effective army in the field. Let us go ahead,
Lord Holophernes; your great army will swallow them whole.'

6 When the hubbub among the men around the council had sub-
sided, Holophernes, the Assyrian commander-in-chief, said to Achior
and all the Ammonites, in the presence of the assembled foreigners:

'And who are you, Achior, you and your Ammonite mercenaries, to 2
play the prophet among us as you have done today, telling us not to
make war against the people of Israel because their god will protect
them? What god is there but Nebuchadnezzar? He will exert his 3
power and wipe them off the face of the earth; and their god will not
rescue them. We who serve Nebuchadnezzar will strike them all
down as if they were only one man. They will not be able to stand up
to the weight of our cavalry; we shall overwhelm them. Their 4
mountains will be drenched with blood, and their plains filled with
their dead. They cannot stand their ground against us; they will be
completely wiped out. This is the decree of King Nebuchadnezzar,
lord of the whole earth. He has spoken; and what he has said will be
made good. As for you, Achior, you Ammonite mercenary, the 5
words you have spoken today are treason, so from today you shall not
see my face again until I have taken vengeance on this brood of run-
aways from Egypt. But when I come back, the warriors of my body- 6
guard will run you through and add you to their victims. My men 7
are going to take you away now to the hill-country and leave you in
one of the towns in the passes. You will not die until you share their 8
fate. If you are so confident that they will not fall into our hands, 9
you need not look downcast. I have spoken; and nothing that I have
said will fail to come true.'

Then Holophernes ordered his men, who were standing by in his 10
tent, to seize Achior, take him off to Bethulia, and hand him over to
the Israelites. So they seized him and took him outside the camp to 11
the plain, and from there into the hill-country, until they arrived at
the springs below Bethulia. When the men of the town saw them, 12
they picked up their weapons and came out of the town to the top of
the hill; then all the slingers pelted the enemy with stones to prevent
them from coming up. But they slipped through under cover of the 13
hill, tied Achior up and left him lying at the foot of it, and went back
to their master. When the Israelites came down from the town and 14
found him there, they untied him and took him into Bethulia, where
they brought him before the town magistrates then in office, Ozias 15
son of Mica, of the tribe of Simeon, and Chabris son of Gothoniel,
and Charmis son of Melchiel. The magistrates summoned all the 16
elders of the town; and all the young men and women came running
to the assembly. When Achior had been brought before the people,
Ozias asked him what had happened. He answered by telling them 17

all that had taken place in Holophernes' council, what he himself had
said in the presence of the Assyrian commanders, and how Holo-
18 phernes had boasted of what he would do to Israel. Then the people
19 prostrated themselves in worship and cried out to God: 'O Lord,
God of heaven, mark their arrogance; pity our people in their
20 humiliation; show favour this day to those who are thy own.' Then
21 they reassured Achior and commended him warmly. Ozias took
him from the assembly to his own house, and gave a feast for the
elders; and all that night they invoked the help of the God of Israel.

7 THE NEXT DAY Holophernes ordered his whole army and all his
allies to strike camp and march on Bethulia, seize the passes into
2 the hill-country, and make war on the Israelites. So the whole force
set out that day, an army of a hundred and seventy thousand infantry
and twelve thousand cavalry, not counting the baggage train of the
3 infantry, an immense host. They encamped in the valley near
Bethulia, beside the spring; and their camp extended in breadth
towards Dothan as far as Belbaim, and in length from Bethulia to
4 Cyamon which faces Esdraelon. When the Israelites saw their
numbers they said to each other in great alarm, 'These men will strip
the whole country bare; the high mountains, the valleys, and the hills
5 will never be able to bear the burden of them.' Then each man stood
to arms; and they lit the beacons on the towers and remained on
guard all that night.

6 On the following day Holophernes led out all his cavalry in full
7 view of the Israelites in Bethulia, and reconnoitred the approaches to
their town. He inspected the springs and seized them; and when he
had stationed detachments of soldiers there, he returned to his army.
8 Then all the rulers of the Edomites and all the leaders of Moab and
the commanders from the coastal region came to him and said,
9 'Listen to our advice, Lord Holophernes, and save your army from a
10 crushing defeat. These Israelites do not trust in their spears but in
the height of the mountains where they live; for it is no easy task to
11 get up to the tops of these mountains of theirs. Now, Lord Holophernes, avoid fighting a pitched battle with them, and you will not
12 lose a single man. Remain in your camp and keep your men in their
quarters; but let your servants take possession of the spring at the
13 foot of the hill, for that is where all the townspeople of Bethulia get
their water. When they are dying of thirst they will surrender the

town. Meanwhile, we and all our people will go up to the tops of the
neighbouring hills and camp there to see that not a man gets away
from the town. They and their wives and children will waste away 14
with famine; and before the sword reaches them, their streets will be
strewn with their corpses. So you will make them pay heavily for 15
rebelling against you, instead of receiving you peaceably.' Holo- 16
phernes and all his staff approved this plan; and he gave orders that
it should be carried out. The Moabite force moved forward in com- 17
pany with five thousand Assyrians and encamped in the valley,
where they seized the springs which were the Israelites' water-supply.
Then the Edomites and Ammonites went up and encamped in the 18
hill-country opposite Dothan, and sent some of their number south-
east[a] in the direction of Egrebel, which is near Chus on the Mochmur
ravine. The rest of the Assyrian army encamped on the plain. They
filled the entire country-side, their tents and baggage train forming
an immense encampment, for they were a vast host.

Then the Israelites cried out to the Lord their God. Their 19
courage failed, because all their enemies had surrounded them and
there was no way of escape. The whole Assyrian army, infantry, 20
cavalry, and chariots, kept them blockaded for thirty-four days.
The citizens of Bethulia came to the end of their household supplies
of water. The cisterns too were running dry; drinking-water was so 21
strictly rationed that there was never a day when their needs were
satisfied. The children were lifeless, the women and young men faint 22
with thirst. They collapsed in the streets and gateways from sheer
exhaustion.

Then all the people, young men, women, and children, gathered 23
round Ozias and the magistrates of the town, shouting loudly. In the
presence of the elders they said: 'May God judge between us, for 24
you have done us a great wrong in not coming to terms with the
Assyrians. Now we have no one to help us. God has sold us into 25
their power; they will find us dead of thirst, and the ground strewn
with our corpses. Surrender to them; let Holophernes' people and 26
his army sack the town. It is better for us to be taken prisoner; for 27
even as slaves we shall still be alive, and shall not have to watch our
babies dying before our eyes, and our wives and children at their last
gasp. We call heaven and earth to witness, we call our God, the Lord 28
of our fathers, to witness against you—the God who is punishing us

[a] *Or* south and east.

for our sins and for the sins of our fathers. We pray that he may not
29 let our forebodings come true this day.' Then the whole assembly
30 broke into loud lamentation and cried to the Lord God. Ozias said
to them, 'Courage, my friends! Let us hold out for five more days;
by that time the Lord our God may show us his mercy again. Surely
31 he will not finally desert us. But if by the end of that time no help
32 has reached us, then I will do what you ask.' Then he dismissed the
men to their various posts; and they went off to the walls and towers
of the town. The women and children he sent indoors. Throughout
the town there was deep dejection.

Judith kills Holophernes

8 NEWS OF WHAT was happening reached Judith, daughter of
Merari, son of Ox, son of Joseph, son of Oziel, son of Helkias,
son of Elias, son of Chelkias, son of Eliab, son of Nathanael, son of
2 Salamiel, son of Sarasadae, son of Israel. Her husband Manasses,
who belonged to her own tribe and clan, had died at the time of barley
3 harvest. While he was out in the fields supervising the binding of the
sheaves, he got sunstroke, took to his bed, and died in Bethulia his
native town; and they buried him beside his ancestors in the field
4 between Dothan and Balamon. For three years and four months
5 Judith had lived at home as a widow; she had a shelter erected on the
roof of her house; she put on sackcloth and always wore mourning.
6 After she became a widow she fasted every day except sabbath eve,
the sabbath itself, the eve of the new moon, the new moon, and the
7 Israelite feasts and days of public rejoicing. She was a very beautiful
and attractive woman. Her husband Manasses had left her gold and
silver, male and female slaves, livestock and land, and she lived on her
8 estate. No one spoke ill of her, for she was a very devout woman.
9 When Judith heard of the shameful attack which the people had
made upon Ozias the magistrate, because they were demoralized by
the shortage of water, and how he had sworn to surrender the town
10 to the Assyrians after five days, she sent her maid who had charge of
all her property to ask Ozias, Chabris, and Charmis, the elders of the
11 town, to come and see her. When they arrived she said to them:
'Listen to me, magistrates of Bethulia. You had no right to speak as

you did to the people today, and to bind yourselves by oath before
God to surrender the town to our enemies if the Lord sends no relief
within so many days. Who are you to test God at a time like this, and 12
openly set yourselves above him? You are putting the Lord Almighty 13
to the proof. You will never understand! You cannot plumb the 14
depths of the human heart or understand the way a man's mind
works; how then can you fathom man's Maker? How can you know
God's mind, and grasp his thought? No, my friends, do not rouse
the anger of the Lord our God. For even if he does not choose to 15
help us within the five days, he is free to come to our rescue at any
time he pleases, or equally to let us be destroyed by our enemies.
It is not for you to impose conditions on the Lord our God; God will 16
not yield to threats or be bargained with like a mere man. So we 17
must wait for him to deliver us, and in the mean time appeal to him
for help. If he sees fit he will hear us.

'There is not one of our tribes or clans, districts or towns, that 18
worships man-made gods today, or has done so within living memory.
This did happen in days gone by, and that was why our ancestors 19
were abandoned to their enemies to be slaughtered and pillaged, and
great was their downfall. But we acknowledge no god but the Lord, 20
and so we are confident that he will not spurn us or any of our race.
For our capture will mean the loss of all Judaea, and our temple will 21
be looted; and God will hold us responsible for its desecration.
The slaughter and deportation of our fellow-countrymen, and the 22
laying waste of the land we inherited, will bring his judgement upon
us wherever we become slaves among the Gentiles. Our masters will
regard us with disgust and contempt. There will be no happy ending 23
to our servitude, no return to favour; the Lord our God will use it
to dishonour us.

'So then, my friends, let us set an example to our fellow-country- 24
men; for their lives depend on us, and the fate of the sanctuary, the
temple, and the altar rests with us. We have every reason to give 25
thanks to the Lord our God; he is putting us to the test as he did our
ancestors. Remember how he dealt with Abraham and how he tested 26
Isaac, and what happened to Jacob in Syrian Mesopotamia when he
was working as a shepherd for his uncle Laban. He is not subjecting 27
us to the fiery ordeal by which he tested their loyalty, or taking
vengeance on us: it is for discipline that the Lord scourges his
worshippers.'

28 Ozias replied, 'You are quite right; everything you say is true, and
29 no one can deny it. This is not the first time that you have given proof
of your wisdom. Throughout your life we have all recognized your
30 good sense and the soundness of your judgement. But the people
were desperate with thirst and compelled us to make this promise
31 and to pledge ourselves by an oath we may not break. Now, you are
a devout woman; pray for us and ask the Lord to send rain to fill our
cisterns, and then we shall no longer faint for lack of water.'

32 'Hear what I have to say', replied Judith. 'I am going to do a
deed which will be remembered among our people for all generations.
33 Be at the gate tonight yourselves, and I will go out with my maid.
Before the day on which you have promised to surrender the town to
34 our enemies, the Lord will deliver Israel by my hand. But do not try
to find out my plan; I will not tell you until I have accomplished
35 what I mean to do.' Ozias and the magistrates said to her, 'Go with
our blessing, and may God be with you to take vengeance on our
36 enemies.' So they left the roof-shelter and returned to their posts.

9 Then Judith prostrated herself, put ashes on her head, and uncovered the sackcloth she was wearing; and at the time when the
evening incense was being offered in the temple in Jerusalem, she
2 cried to the Lord: 'O Lord, the God of my forefather Simeon! Thou
didst put in his hand a sword to take vengeance on those foreigners
who had stripped off a virgin's veil to defile her, uncovered her thighs
to shame her, and polluted her womb to dishonour her. Thou didst
3 say, "It shall not be done"; yet they did it. So thou didst give up
their rulers to be slain, and their bed, which blushed for their
treachery, to be stained with blood; beneath thy stroke slaves fell
dead upon the bodies of princes, and princes upon their thrones.
4 Thou didst give up their wives as booty, and their daughters as
captives, and all their spoils to be divided among thy beloved sons,
who, aflame with zeal for thy cause and aghast at the pollution of
their blood, called on thee to help them. O God, thou art my God,
5 hear now a widow's prayer. All that happened then, and all that
happened before and after, thou didst accomplish. The things that
are now, and are yet to be, thou hast designed; and what thou didst
6 design has come to pass. The things thou hast foreordained present
themselves and say, "We are here." Thy ways are prepared beforehand: foreknowledge determines thy judgement.

7 'Thou seest the Assyrians assembled in their strength, proud of

their horses and riders, boasting of the power of their infantry, and
putting their faith in shield and javelin, bow and sling. They do not
know that thou art the Lord who stamps out wars; the Lord is thy
name. Shatter their strength by thy power and crush their might in 8
thy anger. For they have planned to desecrate thy sanctuary, to
pollute the dwelling-place of thy glorious name, and to strike down
the horns of thy altar with the sword. Mark their arrogance, pour 9
thy wrath on their heads, and give to me, widow as I am, the strength
to achieve my end. Use the deceit upon my lips to strike them dead, 10
the slave with the ruler, the ruler with the servant; shatter their pride
by a woman's hand. For thy might lies not in numbers nor thy 11
sovereign power in strong men; but thou art the God of the humble,
the help of the poor, the support of the weak, the protector of the
desperate, the deliverer of the hopeless. Hear, O hear, thou God of 12
my forefather, God of Israel's heritage, ruler of heaven and earth,
creator of the waters, king of all thy creation, hear thou my prayer.
Grant that my deceitful words may wound and bruise them; for they 13
have cruel designs against thy covenant, thy sacred house, the summit
of Zion, and thy children's home, their own possession. Give thy 14
whole nation and every tribe the knowledge that thou alone art God,
God of all power and might, and that thou and thou alone art
Israel's shield.'

When Judith had ended her prayer, prostrate before the God of 10 1–2
Israel, she rose, called her maid, and went down into the house,
where she was accustomed to spend her sabbaths and festivals. She 3
removed the sackcloth she was wearing and took off her widow's
weeds; then she washed, and anointed herself with rich perfume.
She did her hair, put on a headband, and dressed in her gayest
clothes, which she used to wear when her husband Manasses was
alive. She put on sandals and anklets, bracelets and rings, her ear- 4
rings and all her ornaments, and made herself very attractive, so as to
catch the eye of any man who might see her. She gave her maid a 5
skin of wine and a flask of oil; then she filled a bag with roasted grain,
cakes of dried figs, and the finest bread, packed everything up, and
gave it all to her maid to carry.

They went out towards the gate of Bethulia and found Ozias 6
standing there, with Chabris and Charmis the elders of the town.
When they saw Judith transformed in appearance and quite dif- 7
ferently dressed, they were filled with admiration of her beauty, and

8 said to her, 'The God of our fathers grant you favour and fulfil your
plans, so that Israel may triumph and Jerusalem may be exalted!'
9 Judith bowed to God in worship. Then she said to them, 'Order the
gate to be opened for me, and I will go out to accomplish all that you
say.' They ordered the young men to open the gate as she had asked.
10 When they had done so, Judith went out, accompanied by her maid;
and the men of the town watched her until she had gone down the
hill-side and crossed the valley, and then they lost sight of her.

11 The women went straight across the valley and were met by an
12 Assyrian outpost; they seized Judith and questioned her: 'What is
your nationality? Where have you come from? Where are you
going?' 'I am a Hebrew,' she replied; 'but I am running away from
my people, because they are going to fall into your hands and be
13 devoured. I am on my way to Holophernes, your commander-in-
chief, with reliable information. I will show him a route by which he
can gain command of the entire hill-country without losing a single
man.'

14 As the men listened to her story they looked at her face and were
15 amazed at her beauty. 'You have saved your life', they said, 'by
coming down at once to see our master. Go to his tent straight away.
16 Some of us will escort you and hand you over to him. When you are
in his presence, do not be afraid; just tell him what you have told us,
17 and he will treat you kindly.' They detailed a hundred of their
number to accompany her and her maid, and they brought the two
women to Holophernes' tent.

18 AS THE NEWS of her arrival spread from tent to tent, men came
running from all parts of the camp. They gathered round her as
she stood outside Holophernes' tent waiting until he had been told
19 about her. Her wonderful beauty made them think that the Israelites
must be a wonderful people. They said to each other, 'Who can
despise a nation which has such women as this? We had better not
leave a man of them alive, for if they get away they will be able to
outwit the whole world.'

20 Then Holophernes' bodyguard and all his attendants came out and
21 took her into the tent. He was resting on his bed under a mosquito-
net of purple interwoven with gold, emeralds, and precious stones.
22 When Judith was announced he came out into the front part of the
23 tent, with silver lamps carried before him. He and his attendants

were all amazed at the beauty of her face as she stood before them.
She prostrated herself and did obeisance to him; but his slaves raised
her up.
'Take heart, madam,' said Holophernes; 'do not be afraid. I have 11
never harmed anyone who chose to serve Nebuchadnezzar, king of all
the earth. I should never have raised my spear against your people 2
in the hill-country if they had not insulted me; they brought it on
themselves. Now tell me why you have run away from them and 3
joined us. By coming here you have saved your life. Take heart! You
are in no danger tonight or in the future; no one will harm you. You 4
will enjoy the good treatment which is given to the subjects of my
master King Nebuchadnezzar.'
Judith replied, 'My lord, grant your slave a hearing and listen to 5
what I have to say to you. The information I am giving you tonight
is the truth. If you follow my advice, God will do some great thing 6
through you, and my lord will not fail to attain his ends. By the life 7
of Nebuchadnezzar, king of all the earth, and by the living might of
him who sent you to bring order to all creatures, I swear: not only do
men serve him, thanks to you, but wild animals also, cattle, and
birds, will owe their lives to your power as long as Nebuchadnezzar
and his dynasty reign.[a] We have heard how wise and clever you are. 8
You are known throughout the world as the man of ability unrivalled
in the whole empire, of powerful intelligence and amazing skill in the
art of war. We know about the speech that Achior made in your 9
council, because the men of Bethulia rescued him, and he told them
what he had said to you. Do not disregard what he said, my lord and 10
master, but give full weight to his words. They are true. No punishment ever falls on our race and the sword does not subdue them,
except when they sin against their God. But now, my lord, you are 11
not to be thwarted and cheated of success, for they are doomed to
die. Sin has them in its power, and when they do wrong they will
arouse their God's anger. Because they have run out of food and 12
their water-supply is low, they have decided to lay hands on their
cattle; they mean to consume everything that God by his laws has
prohibited as food; and they have resolved to use up the firstfruits of 13
the grain and the tithes of wine and oil, although these are dedicated

[a] not only...reign: *or* thanks to you and to your power, not only do men serve him, but wild animals also, cattle, and birds, will live at the disposal of Nebuchadnezzar and his household; *the text and meaning are uncertain.*

and reserved for the priests who stand in attendance before our God
14 in Jerusalem, and no layman may so much as handle them. They
have sent men to Jerusalem to get permission from the senate,
15 because even the people there have done this. As soon as ever word
reaches them and they act on it, on that very day they will be given
up to you to be destroyed.
16 'So, my lord, when I learnt all this, I ran away from them; and
God has sent me to do with you things that will be the wonder of the
17 world, wherever men hear about them. For I, your servant, am a
religious woman: day and night I worship the God of heaven. I will
stay with you now, my lord; and each night I shall go out into the
valley and pray to God, and he will tell me when they have committed
18 their sins. Then, when I return and bring you word, you may lead
out your whole army, and you will meet with no resistance from any
19 of them. I will guide you across Judaea until you reach Jerusalem,
and I will set up your throne in the heart of the city. They will follow
you like sheep that have lost their shepherd, and not a dog will so
much as growl at you. I have been given foreknowledge of this. It
has been revealed to me, and I have been sent to announce it to you.'
20 Judith's words delighted Holophernes and all his attendants, and
21 they were amazed at her wisdom. 'In the whole wide world', they
said, 'there is not a woman to compare with her for beauty of face or
22 shrewdness of speech.' Holophernes said to her, 'Thank God for
sending you out from your people, to bring strength to us and
23 destruction to those who have insulted my lord! You are a beautiful
woman and your words are good. If you do as you have promised,
your God shall be my God, and you shall live in King Nebuchadnezzar's palace and be renowned throughout the world.'
12 Holophernes then commanded them to bring her in where his
silver was set out, and he ordered a meal to be served for her from
2 his own food and wine. But Judith said, 'I will not eat any of it, in
case I should be breaking our law. What I have brought with me will
3 meet my needs.' Holophernes said to her, 'But if you use up all you
have with you, where can we get you a fresh supply of the same kind?
4 There is no one of your race here among us.' Judith replied, 'As
sure as you live, my lord, I shall not finish what I have brought with
me before the Lord accomplishes through me what he has planned.'
5 Holophernes' attendants brought her into the tent; and she slept
6 until midnight. Shortly before the morning watch she got up and

sent this message to Holophernes: 'My lord, will you give orders for
me to be allowed to go out and pray?' Holophernes ordered his 7
bodyguard to let her pass. She remained in the camp for three days,
going out each night into the valley of Bethulia and bathing in the
spring. When she came up from the spring, she prayed the Lord, the 8
God of Israel, to prosper her undertaking to restore her people.
Then she returned to the camp purified, and remained in the tent 9
until she took her meal towards evening.

ON THE FOURTH DAY Holophernes gave a banquet for his 10
personal servants only, and did not invite any of the army
officers. He said to Bagoas, the eunuch in charge of all his affairs: 11
'Go to the Hebrew woman who is in your care, and persuade her to
join us and to eat and drink with us. It would be a disgrace if we let 12
such a woman go without enjoying her company. If we do not win
her favours she will laugh at us.' Bagoas left Holophernes' presence, 13
and went to Judith and said, 'Now, my beauty, do not be bashful;
come along to my master and give yourself the honour of his
company. Drink with us and enjoy yourself, and behave today like
one of the Assyrian women in attendance at Nebuchadnezzar's
palace.' 'Who am I to refuse my master?' said Judith. 'I am eager 14
to do whatever pleases him; and it will be something to boast of
till my dying day.' She proceeded to dress herself up and put on all 15
her feminine finery. Her maid went ahead of her, and spread on the
ground in front of Holophernes the fleeces which she had received
from Bagoas for her daily use, so that she might recline on them
when she ate. When Judith came in and took her place, Holophernes 16
was beside himself with desire for her. He shook with passion and
was filled with an ardent longing to possess her; indeed he had been
looking for an opportunity to seduce her ever since he first set eyes
on her. So he said to her, 'Drink and enjoy yourself with us.' 17
'Indeed I will, my lord,' said Judith; 'today is the greatest day of my 18
whole life.' Then she took what her servant had prepared, and ate 19
and drank in his presence. Holophernes was delighted with her, and 20
drank a great deal of wine, more, indeed, than he had ever drunk on
any single day since he was born.

When it grew late, Holophernes' servants quickly withdrew. **13**
Bagoas closed the tent from outside, shutting out all the attendants
from his master's presence, and they went to bed; the banquet had

2 lasted so long that they were all worn out. Judith was left alone in
the tent, with Holophernes lying sprawled on his bed, dead drunk.
3 Judith had told her maid to stand outside the sleeping-apartment
and wait for her mistress to go out, as she did every day; she had said
that she would be going out to pray, and had explained this to
4 Bagoas also. When they had all gone and not a soul was left, Judith
stood beside Holophernes' bed and prayed silently: 'O Lord, God of
all power, look favourably now on what I am about to do to bring
5 glory to Jerusalem, for now is the time to help thy heritage and to
give success to my plan for crushing the enemies who have risen up
6 against us.' She went to the bed-rail beside Holophernes' head and
7 took down his sword, and stepping close to the bed she grasped his
8 hair. 'Now give me strength, O Lord, God of Israel', she said; then
she struck at his neck twice with all her might, and cut off his head.
9 She rolled the body off the bed and took the mosquito-net from its
posts; a moment later she went out and gave Holophernes' head to
10 the maid, who put it in her food-bag. The two of them went out
together, as they had usually done for prayer. Through the camp
they went, and round that valley, and up the hill to Bethulia till
they reached the gates.

11 From a distance Judith called to the sentries at the gates: 'Open!
Open the gate! God, our God, is with us, still showing his strength
in Israel and his might against our enemies. He has shown it today!'
12 When the citizens heard her voice, they hurried down to the gate and
13 summoned the elders of the town. Everyone high and low came
running, hardly able to believe that Judith had returned. They
opened the gate and let the two women in; they lit a fire to see by,
14 and gathered round them. Then Judith raised her voice and cried,
'Praise God! O praise him! Praise God, who has not withdrawn
his mercy from the house of Israel, but has crushed our enemies by
15 my hand this very night!' Then she took the head from the bag and
showed it to them. 'Look!' she said. 'The head of Holophernes, the
Assyrian commander-in-chief! And here is the net under which he
lay drunk! The Lord has struck him down by the hand of a woman!
16 And I swear by the Lord who has brought me safely along the way
I have travelled that, though my face lured him to destruction, he
committed no sin with me, and my honour is unblemished.'

17 The people were all astounded; and bowing down in worship to
God, they said with one voice, 'Praise be to thee, O Lord our God,

who hast humiliated the enemies of thy people this day.' And 18
Ozias said to Judith, 'My daughter, the blessing of God Most High
is upon you, you more than all other women on earth; praise be to
the Lord, the God who created heaven and earth, and guided you
when you struck off the head of the enemy commander. The sure 19
hope which inspired you[a] will never fade from men's minds while
they commemorate the power of God. May God make your deed 20
redound to your honour for ever, and shower blessings upon you!
You risked your life for our country when it was faced with humiliation. You went boldly to meet the disaster that threatened us, and
held firmly to God's straight road.' All the people responded:
'Amen! Amen!'

The triumph of Israel

THEN JUDITH SAID to them, 'Listen to me, my friends; take 14
this head and hang it out on the battlements of your wall.
As soon as dawn breaks and the sun rises, take up your weapons, 2
every able-bodied man of you, and march out of the town. You must
set a commander at your head, as if you were going down to the plain
to attack the Assyrian outpost; but do not go down. The Assyrians 3
will take up their weapons and make for their camp, and rouse the
commanders, who will run to Holophernes' tent but will not find him.
They will all be seized with panic and will flee from you; then 4
pursue them, you and all who live within Israel's borders, and cut
them down in their tracks. But first of all summon Achior the 5
Ammonite to me, so that he may see and recognize the man who
treated Israel with contempt and sent him to us as if to his death.'

They summoned Achior from Ozias's house. When he came and 6
saw Holophernes' head held by one of the men in the assembly of the
people, he fainted and fell down. They lifted him up, and he threw 7
himself at Judith's feet and did obeisance to her, and said, 'Your
praises will be sung in every camp in Judah and among all nations.
They will tremble when they hear your name. Tell me now the whole 8
story of what you have done during these days.' Then Judith, in the
hearing of the people, told him everything from the day she left until
that very moment. As she ended her story, the people raised a great 9

[*a*] *Or* which you inspire.

10 shout and made the town ring with their cheers. And when Achior
realized all that the God of Israel had done, he came to full belief in
God, and was circumcised, and admitted as a member of the community of Israel, as his descendants still are.

11 When dawn came they hung Holophernes' head on the wall; then
they all took their weapons and went out in companies into the
12 approaches to the town. When the Assyrians saw them, they sent
word to their leaders, who then went to the generals, captains, and
13 all the other officers. They came to Holophernes' tent and said to his
steward: 'Wake our master. These slaves have had the audacity to
14 offer us battle; they are asking to be utterly wiped out.' Bagoas went
in and knocked at the screen of the inner tent, supposing that Holo-
15 phernes was sleeping with Judith. When there was no reply, he drew
aside the screen, went into the sleeping-apartment, and found the
16 dead body sprawling over a footstool, and the head gone. He gave a
17 great cry, wailing and groaning aloud, and tore his clothes. Then he
went into the tent which Judith had occupied; and not finding her he
18 rushed out to the people shouting, 'The slaves have played us false.
One Hebrew woman has brought shame on Nebuchadnezzar's
kingdom. Look! Holophernes is lying on the ground, and his head
19 is gone!' His words filled the officers of the Assyrian army with
dismay; they tore their clothes, and the camp rang with their shouts
and cries.

15 When the news spread to the men in the camp, they were thrown
2 into consternation at what had happened. In terror and panic they
all scattered at once, with no attempt to keep together, and fled by
3 every path across the plain and the hill-country. Those who were
encamped in the hills round Bethulia also took to flight. Then all the
4 Israelites of military age sallied out after them. Ozias sent men to
Bethomesthaim, Choba, and Chola, and the whole territory of Israel,
to give news of what had happened and to tell them to sally out
5 against the enemy and destroy them. When the news reached them,
every man in Israel joined the attack and cut them down, going as far
as Choba. The men from Jerusalem and all the hill-country also
joined in, for they had been told what had happened in the enemy
camp. The men of Gilead and Galilee outflanked the Assyrians and
inflicted heavy losses on them, continuing beyond Damascus and the
6 district round it. The rest of the inhabitants of Bethulia fell upon the
7 camp and made themselves rich with the spoils. When the Israelites

returned from the slaughter, they took possession of what remained.
The villages and hamlets in the hill-country and in the plain got
masses of booty, for there was a huge quantity of it.
Joakim the high priest and the senate of Israel came from Jeru- 8
salem to see for themselves the great things the Lord had done for
his people, and to meet Judith and wish her well. When they arrived 9
they praised her with one voice and said, 'You are the glory of Jerusalem, the heroine of Israel, the proud boast of our people! With 10
your own hand you have done all this, you have restored the fortunes
of Israel, and God has shown his approval. Blessings on you from
the Lord Almighty, for all time to come!' And all the people
responded, 'Amen!'
The looting of the camp went on for thirty days. They gave Judith 11
Holophernes' tent, with all his silver, and his couches, bowls, and
furniture. She took them and loaded her mule, then got her wagons
ready and piled the goods on them. All the Israelite women came 12
running to see her; they sang her praises, and some of them performed
a dance in her honour. She took garlanded wands in her hands and
gave some also to the women who accompanied her; and she and 13
those who were with her crowned themselves with olive leaves.
Then, at the head of all the people, she led the women in the dance;
and the men of Israel, in full armour and with garlands on their
heads, followed them singing hymns.

IN THE PRESENCE of all Israel, Judith struck up this hymn of 16
praise and thanksgiving, in which all the people joined lustily:

'Strike up a song to my God with tambourines; 2
sing to the Lord with cymbals;
raise a psalm of praise[a] to him;
honour him and invoke his name.
The Lord is a God who stamps out wars; 3
he has brought me safe from my pursuers
into his camp among his people.
The Assyrian came from the mountains of the north; 4
his armies came in such myriads
that his troops choked the valleys,
his cavalry covered the hills.

[a] *Some witnesses read* a new psalm.

5 He threatened to set fire to my land,
put my young men to the sword,
dash my infants to the ground,
take my children as booty,
and my maidens as spoil.
6 The Lord Almighty has thwarted them by a woman's hand.
7 It was no young man that brought their champion low;
no Titan struck him down,
no tall giant set upon him;
but Judith daughter of Merari disarmed him by the beauty of her face.
8 She put off her widow's weeds
to raise up the afflicted in Israel;
she anointed her face with perfume,
and bound her hair with a headband,
and put on a linen gown to beguile him.
9 Her sandal entranced his eye,
her beauty took his heart captive;
and the sword cut through his neck.
10 The Persians shuddered at her daring,
the Medes were daunted by her boldness.
11 Then my oppressed people shouted in triumph, and the enemy were afraid;
my weak ones shouted, and the enemy cowered in fear;
they raised their voices, and the enemy took to flight.
12 The sons of servant girls ran them through,
wounding them like runaway slaves;
they were destroyed by the army of my Lord.

13 'I will sing a new hymn to my God.
O Lord, thou art great and glorious,
thou art marvellous in thy strength, invincible.
14 Let thy whole creation serve thee;
for thou didst speak and all things came to be;
thou didst send out thy spirit and it formed them.
No one can resist thy voice;
15 mountains and seas are stirred to their depths,
rocks melt like wax at thy presence;
but to those who revere thee

thou dost still show mercy.
For no sacrifice is sufficient to please thee with its fragrance, 16
and all the fat in the world is not enough for a burnt-offering,
but he who fears the Lord is always great.
Woe to the nations which rise up against my people! 17
The Lord Almighty will punish them on the day of judgement;
he will consign their bodies to fire and worms;
they will weep in pain for ever.'

When they arrived at Jerusalem they worshipped God. As soon 18
as the people were purified, they offered their burnt-offerings, freewill offerings, and gifts. Judith dedicated to God all Holophernes' 19
possessions, which the people had given to her; and the net, which
she had taken for herself from the sleeping-apartment, she presented
as a votive offering. For three months the people continued their 20
celebrations in Jerusalem in front of the sanctuary; and Judith
remained with them.

At the end of that time they all returned to their own homes. 21
Judith went back to Bethulia and lived on her estate. In her time she
was famous throughout the whole country. She had many suitors; 22
but she remained unmarried all her life after her husband Manasses
died and was gathered to his fathers. Her fame continued to 23
increase; and she lived on in her husband's house until she was a
hundred and five years old. She gave her maid her liberty. She died
in Bethulia and was buried in the same tomb as her husband
Manasses, and Israel observed mourning for her for seven days. 24
Before her death she divided her property among all those who were
most closely related to her husband Manasses, and among her own
nearest relations.

No one dared to threaten the Israelites again in Judith's lifetime, 25
or for a long time after her death.

THE REST OF THE CHAPTERS OF THE BOOK OF

ESTHER

WHICH ARE FOUND NEITHER IN THE HEBREW NOR IN THE SYRIAC

NOTE. The portions of the Book of Esther commonly included in the Apocrypha are extracts from the Greek version of the book, which differs substantially from the Hebrew text (translated in *The New English Bible: Old Testament*). In order that they may be read in their original sequence, the whole of the Greek version is here translated, those portions which are not normally printed in the Apocrypha being enclosed in square brackets, with the chapter and verse numbers in italic figures. The order followed is that of the Greek text, but the chapter and verse numbers are made to conform to those of the Authorized Version. Proper names are given in the form in which they occur in the Greek version.

11 2 IN THE SECOND YEAR of the reign of Artaxerxes the
Great King, on the first day of Nisan, Mardochaeus son of Jairus,
son of Semeius, son of Kisaeus, of the tribe of Benjamin, had a
3 dream. Mardochaeus was a Jew living in the city of Susa, a man of
4 high standing, who was in the royal service; he came of those whom
Nebuchadnezzar king of Babylon had taken into exile from Jeru-
5 salem with Jechonias king of Judah. This was his dream: din and
tumult, peals of thunder and an earthquake, confusion upon the
6 earth. Then appeared two great dragons, ready to grapple with each
7 other, and the noise they made was terrible. Every nation was roused
8 by it to prepare for war, to fight against the righteous nation. It was
a day of darkness and gloom, with distress and anguish, oppression
9 and great confusion upon the earth. And the whole righteous nation
was troubled, dreading the evils in store for them, and they prepared
10 for death. They cried aloud to God; and in answer to their cry there
came as though from a little spring a great river brimming with
11 water. It grew light, and the sun rose; the humble were exalted and
12 they devoured the great. After he had had this dream and had seen

what God had resolved to do, Mardochaeus woke; he kept it before
his mind, seeking in every way to understand it, until nightfall.
Now when Mardochaeus was resting in the royal courtyard with 12
Gabatha and Tharra, the two eunuchs who guarded the courtyard,
he heard them deep in discussion. He listened carefully to discover 2
what was on their minds, and found that they were plotting violence
against King Artaxerxes. He denounced them to the king, who had 3
the two eunuchs interrogated. They confessed and were led away to
execution. Then the king wrote an account of the affair, to have it on 4
record; Mardochaeus also wrote an account of it. The king gave 5
Mardochaeus an appointment at court, and rewarded him for his
services. But Haman, the son of Hamadathus, a Bugaean, who 6
enjoyed the king's favour, sought to injure Mardochaeus and his
people because of the two eunuchs.

A Jewess becomes queen in Persia

[THOSE EVENTS happened in the days of Artaxerxes, the Arta- *1*
xerxes who ruled from India to Ethiopia, a hundred and
twenty-seven provinces. At this time he sat on his royal throne in *2*
the city of Susa. Then in the third year of his reign he gave a *3*
banquet for the King's Friends and persons of various races, the
Persian and Median nobles and the leading provincial governors.
And afterwards, after displaying to them the wealth of his empire *4*
and the splendour of his rich festivities for a hundred and eighty
days, when these days of feasting were over, the king gave a banquet *5*
for all the people of various races present in the city of Susa; it was
held in the court of the king's palace and lasted six days. The court *6*
was decorated with white curtains of linen and cotton stretched on
cords of purple, and these were attached to blocks of gold and silver
resting on stone and marble columns. There were couches of gold
and silver set on a pavement of malachite, marble, and mother-of-
pearl. There were mats of transparent weave elaborately embroidered
with roses arranged in a circle. The cups were of gold and silver, and *7*
there was displayed a miniature cup made of carbuncle worth thirty
thousand talents. The wine was abundant and sweet, from the king's
own cellar. The drinking was not according to a fixed rule, but the *8*

king had laid it down that all the stewards of his palace should respect
9 his will and that of the guests. In addition, Queen Astin gave a
banquet for the women in the same palace where King Artaxerxes
was.
10 On the seventh day, when he was in high good humour, the king
ordered Haman, Mazan, Tharra, Borazes, Zatholtha, Abataza, and
Tharaba, the seven eunuchs who were in attendance on the king's
11 person, to bring the queen before him, so that he might place the
royal diadem on her head and let her display her beauty to the
officers and people of various races; for she was indeed a beautiful
12 woman. But Queen Astin refused to obey him and come with the
eunuchs. This offended the king and made him angry.
13 Then the king said to his courtiers, 'You hear what Astin said.
14 Give your ruling and judgement in the matter.' Then the nobles of
Persia and Media who were closest to the king—Harkesaeus,
Sarsathaeus, and Malesear, who sat next him in the chief seats—
15 approached him and declared what should be done according to the
law to Queen Astin for disobeying the order which the king sent her
16 by the eunuchs. Then Muchaeus said to the king and the nobles:
'Queen Astin has done wrong, and not to the king alone, but to all
17 his nobles and officers as well.' (For he had repeated to them what
18 the queen had said and how she had defied the king.) 'And just as
she defied King Artaxerxes, so now the nobles of Persia and Media
will find that all their ladies are bold enough to treat their husbands
19 with contempt, when they hear what she said to the king. If it please
your majesty, let a royal decree go out from you, and let it be inscribed
among the laws of the Medes and Persians, that Astin shall not again
appear before the king; this is the only course. And let the king give
her place as queen to another woman who is more worthy of it than
20 she. Let whatever law the king makes be proclaimed throughout his
empire, and then all women will give due honour to their husbands,
21 rich and poor alike.' The advice pleased the king and the princes, and
22 the king did as Muchaeus had proposed. Letters were sent to all the
provinces of the empire, to each province in its own language, in
order that every man might be respected in his own house.
2 Later, when the anger of King Artaxerxes had died down, he
remembered Astin and what she had done, and how he had given
2 judgement against her. So the king's attendants said: 'Let beautiful
3 girls of unblemished virtue be sought out for your majesty. Let your

majesty appoint commissioners in all the provinces of the empire to
select these beautiful virgins and bring them to the city of Susa, into
the women's quarters. There let them be committed to the care of
the king's eunuch in charge of the women, and let them be provided
with cosmetics and everything else they need. Then the one who is 4
most acceptable to the king shall become queen in place of Astin.'
The advice pleased the king, and he acted on it.

Now there was a Jew in the city of Susa named Mardochaeus, son 5
of Jairus, son of Semeius, son of Kisaeus, of the tribe of Benjamin;
he had been carried into exile from Jerusalem when it was taken by 6
Nebuchadnezzar king of Babylon. He had a foster-child named 7
Esther, the daughter of his father's brother Aminadab. She had
lost her parents, and he had brought her up to womanhood. She was
a very beautiful girl. When the king's edict was proclaimed, many 8
girls were brought to Susa to be entrusted to Gai, who had charge of
the women, and among them was Esther. She attracted his notice 9
and received his special favour: he readily provided her with her
cosmetics and allowance of food, and also with seven maids assigned
to her from the king's palace. He gave her and her maids honourable
treatment in the women's quarters.

Esther had not disclosed her race or country, because Mardo- 10
chaeus had forbidden her to do so. Every day Mardochaeus passed 11
along by the forecourt of the women's quarters to keep an eye on
Esther and see what would happen to her.

The period after which a girl was to go to the king was twelve 12
months. This was for the completion of the required treatment—six
months with oil and myrrh and six months with perfumes and
cosmetics. Then the girl went to the king. She was handed to the 13
person appointed, and accompanied him from the women's quarters
to the king's palace. She entered the palace in the evening and 14
returned in the morning to Gai, the king's eunuch in charge of the
women, in another part of the women's quarters. She did not go to
the king again unless summoned by name.

When the time came for Esther, daughter of Aminadab the uncle 15
of Mardochaeus, to go to the king, she neglected none of the instructions of Gai the king's eunuch in charge of the women; for Esther
charmed all who saw her. She was taken to King Artaxerxes in the 16
twelfth month, that is, the month Adar, in the seventh year of his
reign. The king fell in love with her, finding her more acceptable 17

than any of the other girls, and crowned her with the queen's diadem.
18 Then the king gave a banquet lasting seven days for all the King's
Friends and the officers, to celebrate Esther's marriage. He also
granted a remission of taxation to all subjects of his empire.
19, 20 Mardochaeus was in attendance in the courtyard. But Esther had
not disclosed her country—such were the instructions of Mardochaeus; but she was to fear God and keep his commandments just as
she had done when she was with him. So Esther made no change in
her way of life.
21 Two of the king's eunuchs, officers of the bodyguard, were
offended at the advancement of Mardochaeus and plotted to kill
22 King Artaxerxes. This became known to Mardochaeus, who told
23 Esther, and she revealed the plot to the king. The king interrogated
the two eunuchs and had them hanged, and he ordered that the
service Mardochaeus had rendered should be recorded in the royal
archives to his honour.

A plot against the Jews

3 AFTER THIS King Artaxerxes promoted Haman son of Hamadathus the Bugaean, advancing him and giving him precedence
2 above all the King's Friends. So all who were at court did obeisance
to Haman, for so the king had commanded; but Mardochaeus did
3 not do obeisance. Then the king's courtiers said to him, 'Mardo-
4 chaeus, why do you flout the king's command?' Day by day they
challenged him, but he refused to listen to them. Then they informed
Haman that Mardochaeus was resisting the king's command.
5 Mardochaeus had told them that he was a Jew. So when Haman
learnt that Mardochaeus was not doing obeisance to him, he was
6 infuriated and plotted to exterminate all the Jews under Artaxerxes'
rule.
7 In the twelfth year of King Artaxerxes he arrived at a decision by
casting lots, taking the days and the months one by one, to decide
on one day for the destruction of the whole race of Mardochaeus.
The lot fell on the thirteenth[a] day of the month Adar.
8 Then Haman said to King Artaxerxes: 'There is a certain nation

[a] *So some witnesses, and compare 8. 12 (page 128); other witnesses read* fourteenth.

dispersed among the other nations of your empire. Their laws are
different from those of every other nation; they do not keep your
majesty's laws. It is not to your majesty's advantage to tolerate
them. If it please your majesty, let an order be made for their 9
destruction; and I will contribute ten thousand talents of silver to
the royal treasury.' So the king took off his signet-ring and gave it to 10
Haman to seal the decree against the Jews. 'Keep the money, and 11
deal with these people as you will', he said.

On the thirteenth day of the first month the king's secretaries were 12
summoned, and in accordance with Haman's instructions, they wrote
in the name of King Artaxerxes to his army commanders and
governors in every province from India to Ethiopia. There were a
hundred and twenty-seven provinces in all, and each was addressed
in its own language. Instructions were dispatched by courier to all 13
the empire of Artaxerxes to exterminate the Jewish race, on a given
day of the twelfth month, Adar, and to plunder their possessions.]

THIS IS a copy of the letter: **13**

Artaxerxes the Great King to the governors of the one hundred and twenty-seven provinces, from India to Ethiopia, and to the subordinate officials.

Ruler as I am over many nations and master of all the world, it is 2
my will—not in the arrogance of power, but because my rule is
mild and equitable—to ensure to my subjects a life permanently
free from disturbance, to pacify my empire and make it safe for
travel to its farthest limits, and to restore the peace that all men
long for. I asked my counsellors how this object might be achieved 3
and received a reply from Haman. Haman is eminent among us
for sound judgement, one whose worth is proved by his constant
goodwill and steadfast loyalty, and who has gained the honour of
the second place at our court. He represented to us that scattered 4
among all the races of the empire is a disaffected people, opposed
in its laws to every nation, and continually ignoring the royal
ordinances, so that our irreproachable plans for the unified
administration of the empire cannot be made effective. We under- 5
stand that this nation stands alone in its continual opposition to all
men, that it evades the laws by its strange manner of life, and in
disloyalty to our government commits grievous offences, thus

6 undermining the security of our empire. We therefore order that
those who are designated to you in the indictments drawn up by
Haman, our vicegerent and second father, shall all, together with
their wives and children, be utterly destroyed by the sword of their
enemies, without mercy or pity, on the thirteenth[a] day of Adar,
7 the twelfth month, of the present year. Those persons who have
long been disaffected shall meet a violent death in one day so that
our government may henceforth be stable and untroubled.

3 14 [Copies of the document were posted up in every province, and all
15 nations of the empire were ordered to be ready by that day. The
matter was expedited also in Susa. While the king and Haman
caroused together, the city of Susa was thrown into confusion.

4 WHEN MARDOCHAEUS learnt all that was being done, he
tore his clothes, put on sackcloth and sprinkled himself with
ashes; and he rushed through the city, crying loudly: 'An innocent
2 nation is being destroyed.' He went as far as the king's gate, and
there he halted, because no one was allowed to enter the courtyard
3 clothed with sackcloth and ashes. In every province where the
king's decree was posted up, there was a great cry of mourning and
lamentation among the Jews, and they put on sackcloth and ashes.
4 When the queen's maids and eunuchs came and told her, she was
distraught at the news, and sent clothes for Mardochaeus, urging
5 him to take off his sackcloth; but he would not consent. Then Esther
summoned Hachrathaeus, the eunuch who waited upon her, and
ordered him to obtain accurate information for her from Mardo-
7 chaeus.[b] So Mardochaeus told him all that had happened, and how
Haman had promised to pay ten thousand talents into the royal
8 treasury to bring about the destruction of the Jews. He also gave
him a copy of the written decree for their destruction which had
been posted up in Susa, to show to Esther; and he gave him a message
for her, that she should go to the king and plead for his favour and
entreat him for her people. 'Remember', he said, 'those days when
you were brought up in my humble home; for Haman, who stands
next to the king, has spoken against us and demanded our death.
Call upon the Lord, and then speak for us to the king and save our

[a] *Gk.* fourteenth; *see note on 3. 7 (page 120).* [b] *Some witnesses add* (6) So he went out to Mardochaeus in the street opposite the city gate.

lives.' Hachrathaeus returned and told her what Mardochaeus had 9
said. She sent him back with this message: 'All nations of the 10, 11
empire know that if any person, man or woman, enters the king's
presence in the inner court unbidden, there is no escape for him.
Only one to whom the king stretches out the golden sceptre is
safe; and it is now thirty days since I myself was called to go to the
king.'

When Hachrathaeus delivered her message, Mardochaeus told 12, 13
him to go back and say: 'Do not imagine, Esther, that you alone of all
the Jews in the empire will escape alive. For if you remain silent at 14
such a time as this, the Jews will somewhere find relief and deliverance, but you and your father's family will perish. Who knows
whether it is not for such a time as this that you have been made a
queen?' Esther gave the messenger this answer to take back to 15
Mardochaeus: 'Go and assemble all the Jews who are in Susa and 16
fast for me; for three days take neither food nor drink, night or day,
and I and my maids will also go without food. Then in defiance of
the law I will enter the king's presence, even if it costs me my life.'
So Mardochaeus went away and did as Esther had bidden him.] 17

AND MARDOCHAEUS prayed to the Lord, calling to mind all the **13** 8
works of the Lord. He said, 'O Lord, Lord and King who rulest 9
over all, because the whole world is under thy authority, and when it
is thy will to save Israel there is no one who can stand against thee:
thou didst make heaven and earth and every wonderful thing under 10
heaven; thou art Lord of all, and there is no one who can resist thee, 11
the Lord. Thou knowest all things; thou knowest, Lord, that it was 12
not from insolence or arrogance or vainglory that I refused to bow
before proud Haman, for I could gladly have kissed the soles of his 13
feet to save Israel; no, I did it so that I might not hold a man in 14
greater honour than God; I will not bow before any but thee, my
Lord, and it is not from arrogance that I refuse this homage.
And now Lord, God and King, God of Abraham, spare thy people; 15
for our enemies are watching us to bring us to ruin, and they have
set their hearts upon the destruction of thy chosen people, thine
from the beginning. Do not disdain thy own possession which 16
thou didst ransom for thyself out of Egypt. Hear my prayer, and 17
have mercy on thy heritage, and turn our mourning into feasting,
that we may live and sing of thy name, Lord; do not put to silence

18 the lips that give thee praise.' And all Israel cried aloud with all their
might, for death stared them in the face.

14 Then Queen Esther, caught up in this deadly conflict,[a] took refuge
2 in the Lord. She stripped off her splendid attire and put on the garb
of mourning and distress. Instead of proud perfumes she strewed
ashes and dung over her head. She abased her body, and every part
that she had delightfully adorned she covered with her dishevelled
3 hair. And so she prayed to the Lord God of Israel:

'O my Lord, thou alone art our king; help me who am alone, with
4, 5 no helper but thee; for I am taking my life in my hands. Ever since
I was born I have been taught by my father's family and tribe that
thou, O Lord, didst choose Israel out of all the nations, and out of all
the founders of our race didst choose our fathers for an everlasting
possession, and that what thou didst promise them, thou didst per-
6 form. But now we have sinned against thee, and thou hast handed us
7 over to our enemies because we honoured their gods; thou art just,
8 O Lord. But they are not content with our bitter servitude; they
9 have now pledged themselves to their idols to annul thy decree and
to destroy thy possession, silencing those who praise thee, extin-
10 guishing the glory of thy house, and casting down thy altar. They
would give the heathen cause to sing the praises of their worthless
gods, and would have a mortal king held in everlasting honour.

11 'Yield not thy sceptre, O Lord, to gods that are nothing; let not
our enemies mock at our ruin, but turn their plot against themselves,
12 and make an example of the man who planned it. Remember us,
O Lord, make thy power known in the time of our distress, and give
13 me courage, O King of gods, almighty Lord. Give me the apt word
to say when I enter the lion's den. Divert his hatred to our enemy,
so that there may be an end of him and his confederates.

14 'Save us by thy power, and help me who am alone and have no
15 helper but thee, Lord. Thou knowest all; thou knowest that I hate
the splendour of the heathen, I abhor the bed of the uncircumcised
16 or of any Gentile. Thou knowest in what straits I am: I loathe that
symbol of pride, the headdress that I wear when I show myself
abroad, I loathe it as one loathes a filthy rag; in private I refuse to
17 wear it. I, thy servant, have not eaten at Haman's table; I have not
graced a banquet of the king or touched the wine of his drink-
18 offerings; I have not known festive joy from the time that I was

[*a*] caught...conflict: *or* seized by mortal anxiety.

brought here until now except in thee, Lord God of Abraham.
O God who dost prevail against all, give heed to the cry of the 19
despairing: rescue us from the power of wicked men, and rescue
me from what I dread.'

ON THE THIRD DAY Esther brought her prayers to an end. She **15**
took off the clothes she had worn while she worshipped and put
on all her splendour. When she was in her royal robes and had 2
invoked the all-seeing God, her preserver, she took two maids with
her; on one she leaned for support, as befitted a fine lady, while the 3, 4
other followed, bearing her train. She was blushing and in the 5
height of her beauty; her face was as cheerful as it was lovely, but her
heart was in the grip of fear. She passed through all the doors and 6
reached the royal presence. The king was seated on his throne, in the
full array of his majesty. He was all gold and precious stones, an
awe-inspiring figure. He looked up, his face glowing with regal 7
dignity, and glanced at her in towering anger. The queen fell, changing colour in a faint, and swooning on the shoulder of the maid who
went before her.

Then God changed the spirit of the king to gentleness, and in deep 8
concern he leapt from his throne and took her in his arms until she
came to herself. He soothed her with reassuring words: 'Esther, 9
what is it? Have no fear of me, your loving husband; you shall not 10
die, for our order is only for our subjects. Come to me.' And the 11
king lifted his golden sceptre and laid it upon her neck; then he kissed 12
her and said, 'You may speak to me.' She answered, 'I saw you, my 13
lord, looking like an angel of God, and I was awestruck at your
glorious appearance; your countenance is so full of grace, my lord, 14
that I look on you in wonder.' But while she was speaking she fell 15
down in a faint; the king was distressed, and all his attendants 16
comforted her.

[Then the king said, 'What is your wish, Queen Esther? What is ***5*** *3*
your request? Up to half my empire, it shall be given you.' 'Today *4*
is a special day for me', said Esther. 'If it please your majesty, will
you come, and Haman with you, to a banquet which I shall give
today?' The king ordered Haman to be sent for in haste, so that *5*
Esther's wish might be fulfilled; and they both went to the banquet
to which Esther had invited them. Over the wine the king said to *6*
her, 'What is it, Queen Esther? Whatever you ask for shall be

7, 8 yours.' Esther said, 'This is my humble request: if I have won your
majesty's favour, will your majesty and Haman come again tomorrow
to the banquet which I shall give for you both, and tomorrow I will
do as I have done today.'

9 So Haman went out from the royal presence in good spirits and
well pleased with himself. But when he saw Mardochaeus the Jew in
10 the king's courtyard, he was filled with rage. He went home, and
11 called for his friends and his wife Zosara, and held forth to them
about his wealth and the honours with which the king had invested
12 him, how he had made him first man in the empire. 'Queen Esther',
he said, 'invited no one but myself to accompany the king to her
13 banquet; and I am invited again for tomorrow. Yet all this is no
pleasure to me so long as I see that Jew Mardochaeus in the court-
14 yard.' Then his wife Zosara and his friends said to him: 'Have a
gallows put up, seventy-five feet[a] high, and in the morning speak to
the king and have Mardochaeus hanged upon it. Then you can go
with the king to the banquet and enjoy yourself.' Haman thought
this an excellent plan, and the gallows was made ready.

The triumph of the Jews

6 THAT NIGHT the Lord kept sleep from the king, so he ordered
his private secretary to bring the court chronicle and read it to
2 him. He found written there the record about Mardochaeus, how he
had given information about the two royal eunuchs who, while they
3 were on guard, had plotted violence against King Artaxerxes. Whereupon the king said, 'What honour or favour did we confer on
Mardochaeus for this?' The king's courtiers who were in attendance
4 replied, 'You have done nothing for him.' While the king was inquir-
ing about the service that Mardochaeus had rendered, Haman
appeared in the courtyard. 'Who is that in the court?' asked the
king. Now Haman had just come in to recommend to the king that
Mardochaeus should be hanged on the gallows which he had pre-
5 pared; so the king's servants said, 'It is Haman standing in the
6 court.' 'Call him', said the king. Then the king said to Haman,
'What shall I do for the man I wish to honour?' Haman said to

[a] *Gk.* fifty cubits.

himself, 'Whom would the king wish to honour but me?' So he said 7
to the king, 'For the man whom the king wishes to honour, let the 8
king's attendants bring a robe of fine linen from the king's own
wardrobe and a horse from the king's own stable. Let both be 9
delivered to one of the king's most honourable Friends, and let him
robe the man whom the king loves and mount him on the horse, and
let him proclaim through the city: "This shall be the lot of any man
whom the king honours."' Then the king said to Haman, 'An 10
excellent suggestion! Do all this for Mardochaeus the Jew who
serves in the courtyard. Let nothing that you have said be omitted.'
So Haman took the robe and put it on Mardochaeus, and mounted 11
him on the horse; then he went through the city, proclaiming: 'This
shall be the lot of any man whom the king wishes to honour.'

Then Mardochaeus returned to the courtyard, and Haman hurried 12
off home with head veiled in mourning. He told his wife Zosara 13
and his friends what had happened to him. They replied, 'If Mardochaeus is a Jew, and you have been humiliated before him, you are a
lost man. You cannot get the better of him, because the living God is
on his side.'

While they were still talking with Haman, the king's eunuchs 14
arrived and hurried him away to the banquet which Esther had
prepared.

So the king and Haman went to the queen's banquet. Again on 7 1, 2
that second day, over the wine, the king said, 'What is it, Queen
Esther? What is your request? What is your petition? You shall have
it, up to half my empire.' Queen Esther answered: 'If I have won 3
your majesty's favour, my request is for my life, my petition is for
my people. For it has come to my ears that we have been sold, I and 4
my people, to be destroyed, plundered, and enslaved, we and our
children, male and female. Our adversary is a disgrace to the king's
court.' The king said, 'Who is it that has dared to do such a thing?' 5
'Our enemy', said Esther, 'is this wicked Haman.' Haman stood 6
dumbfounded before the king and the queen. The king rose from the 7
banquet and went into the garden, and Haman began to plead with
the queen, for he saw that things were going badly for him. When the 8
king returned to the banqueting hall from the garden, Haman in his
entreaties had flung himself across the queen's couch. The king
exclaimed, 'What! You assault the queen in my own house?' At
those words Haman turned away in despair. Then Bugathan, one of 9

the eunuchs, said to the king, 'Look! Haman has even prepared a
gallows for Mardochaeus, the man who reported the plot against the
king, and there it stands, seventy-five feet[a] high, in Haman's com-
10 pound.' 'Have Haman hanged on it', said the king. So Haman was
hanged on the gallows that he himself had prepared for Mardochaeus. After that the king's rage died down.

8 That day King Artaxerxes gave Esther all that had belonged to
Haman the persecutor; and Mardochaeus was called into the king's
presence, for Esther had told him how he was related to her.
2 Then the king took off his signet-ring, which he had taken back from
Haman, and gave it to Mardochaeus. And Esther put Mardochaeus
in charge of Haman's estate.

3 Once again Esther spoke before the king, falling at his feet and
pleading with him to avert the calamity planned by Haman and to
4 frustrate his plot against the Jews. The king stretched out the golden
5 sceptre to Esther, and she rose and stood before the king. 'May it
please your majesty,' she said; 'if I have won your favour, let an
order be issued recalling the letters which Haman sent in pursuance
6 of his plan to destroy the Jews in your empire. How can I bear to see
the downfall of my people? How escape myself when my country is
7 destroyed?' Then the king said to Esther: 'I have given Haman's
property to you, and hanged him on the gallows because he threa-
8 tened the lives of the Jews. If you want anything further, you may
draw up an order in my name, in whatever terms you think fit, and
seal it with my signet. An order written at the king's direction and
sealed with the royal signet cannot be contravened.'

9 And so, on the twenty-third day of the first month, Nisan, in the
same year, the king's secretaries were summoned; and the Jews were
informed in writing of the instructions given to the administrators
and chief governors in the provinces, from India to Ethiopia, a
hundred and twenty-seven provinces, to each province in its own
10 language. The orders were written as from the king and sealed with
11 his signet, and dispatched by courier. By these documents the king
granted permission to the Jews in every city to observe their own
laws and to defend themselves, and to deal as they would with their
12 opponents and enemies, throughout the empire of Artaxerxes, on a
given day, the thirteenth of the twelfth month, Adar.]

[a] *Gk.* fifty cubits.

THE FOLLOWING IS a copy of this letter: 16

Artaxerxes the Great King to the governors of the one hundred
and twenty-seven provinces, from India to Ethiopia, and to those
who are of our allegiance, greeting.
Many who have been honoured only too often by the lavish 2
generosity of their benefactors have grown arrogant and not only 3
attempt to ill-treat our subjects but, unable to carry the favours
heaped upon themselves, even plot mischief against those who
grant them. Not content with destroying gratitude in men, they 4
are carried away by the insolence of those who are strangers to
good breeding; they even suppose that they will escape the justice
of all-seeing God, who is no friend to evil-doers. And often, when 5
the king's business has been entrusted to those he counts his
friends, they have, by their plausibility, made those in supreme
authority partners in shedding innocent blood and involved them
in irreparable misfortunes, for their malevolence with its mislead- 6
ing sophistries has imposed upon the sincere goodwill of their
rulers. The evil brought about by those who wield power un- 7
worthily you can observe, not only in records of tradition and
history but also in your familiar experience, and apply the lesson 8
to the future. Thus we shall peacefully free this realm from disturbance for the benefit of all, making no changes but always 9
deciding matters which come under our notice with firmness and
equity. Now Haman son of Hamadathus, a Macedonian, an alien 10
in fact with no Persian blood, a man with nothing of our kindly
nature,[a] was accepted by us and enjoyed[b] so fully the benevolence 11
with which we treat every nation that he was proclaimed our
Father, and all along received obeisance from everyone as second
only to our royal throne. But this man in his unbridled arrogance 12
planned to deprive us of our empire and our life by using fraud 13
and tortuous cunning to bring about the destruction of Mardochaeus, our constant benefactor who had saved our life, and of
Esther, our blameless consort, together with their whole nation.
For he thought that by these methods he would catch us defence- 14
less and would transfer to the Macedonians the sovereignty now
held by the Persians. But we find that the Jews, whom this triple- 15
dyed villain had consigned to extinction, are no evil-doers; they

[*a*] *Or* a man fallen away greatly from our favour. [*b*] *Or* won.

16 order their lives by the most just of laws, and are children of the
living God, most high, most mighty, who maintains the empire in
most wonderful order, for us as for our ancestors.
17 You will therefore disregard the letters sent by Haman son of
18 Hamadathus, because he, the contriver of all this, has been hanged
aloft at the gate of Susa with his whole household, God who is
Lord of all having speedily brought upon him the punishment
19 that he deserved. Copies of this letter are to be posted up in all
public places. Permit the Jews to live under their own laws,
20 and give them every assistance so that on the thirteenth day of
Adar, the twelfth month, on that very day, they may avenge themselves on those who were ranged against them[a] in the time of their
21 oppression. For God, who has all things in his power, has made
22 this a day not of ruin, but of joy, for his chosen people. Therefore
you also must keep it with all good cheer, as a notable day among
23 your feasts of commemoration, so that henceforth it may be a
standing symbol of deliverance to us and our loyal Persians, but a
24 reminder of destruction to those who plot against us. Any city or
country whatsoever which does not act upon these orders shall
incur our wrath and be wiped out with fire and sword. No man
shall set foot in it and even the beasts and birds shall shun it for
all time.

8 *13* [Let copies be posted up conspicuously throughout the empire,
so that the Jews may be prepared by that day to fight against their
enemies.

14 Mounted messengers set out with all speed to do what the king
commanded; and the decree was posted up also in Susa.
15 Mardochaeus left the king's presence in royal robes, wearing a
golden crown and a turban of fine linen dyed purple, and all in Susa
16, 17 rejoiced to see him. For the Jews there was light and gladness in
every province and every city. Wherever the decree was posted up
there was joy and gladness for the Jews, feasting and merriment.
And many of the Gentiles were circumcised and professed Judaism,
because they were afraid of the Jews.

9 ON THE THIRTEENTH DAY of the twelfth month, Adar, the
decree drawn up by the king arrived. On that very day the

[*a*] *Or* may defend themselves against their assailants.

enemies of the Jews perished. No one offered resistance, because 2
they were afraid of them. The leading provincial governors, the 3
princes, and the royal secretaries paid all respect to the Jews, because
fear of Mardochaeus weighed upon them. For they had received the 4
king's decree that his name should be honoured throughout the
empire.[a][b] In the city itself the Jews slaughtered five hundred men, 6
including Pharsanestan, Delphon, Phasga, Pharadatha, Barsa, 7, 8
Sarbacha, Marmasima, Ruphaeus, Arsaeus, and Zabuthaeus, the ten 9, 10
sons of Haman son of Hamadathus, the Bugaean, the Jews' great
enemy; and that day they took plunder.

When the number of those killed in Susa was reported to the king, 11
he said to Esther, 'In the city of Susa the Jews have killed five 12
hundred men. What do you suppose they have done in the surrounding country? Whatever further request you have will be granted.'
Esther answered him, 'Let the Jews be allowed to do the same to- 13
morrow, and hang up the bodies of Haman's ten sons.' The king 14
consented; he handed over the bodies of Haman's sons to the Jews of
the city to be hung up. The Jews in Susa assembled on the fourteenth 15
day of Adar also, and killed three hundred, but they took no plunder.

The rest of the Jews in the empire rallied together in self-defence, 16–17
and so were quit of their enemies; for they slaughtered fifteen
thousand of them on the thirteenth of Adar; but they took no
plunder. On the fourteenth they rested, and made that day a
day of rest, with rejoicing and merriment. The Jews in the city of 18
Susa had assembled also on the fourteenth day of the month; they
did not rest on that day, but they kept the fifteenth day with rejoicing and merriment. That is why Jews who are dispersed over the 19
remoter parts keep the fourteenth day of Adar as a holiday with
rejoicing and merriment, sending presents of food to one another;
but those who live in the principal cities keep the fifteenth of Adar as
a holiday, sending presents of food to one another.

Then Mardochaeus wrote down the whole story in a book and sent 20
it to all the Jews in the empire of Artaxerxes, far and near, ordering 21
them to establish these holidays, and to keep the fourteenth and
fifteenth of Adar, because these were the days on which the Jews 22
were quit of their enemies, and to keep the whole month of Adar, in

[*a*] For they...empire: *probable reading; Gk. obscure.* [*b*] *Some witnesses add from the Heb.* (5) So the Jews put their enemies to the sword with great slaughter and destruction; they worked their will on those who hated them.

which came the great change from sorrow to joy and from mourning
to holiday, as a time for feasting and merriment, days for sending
presents of food to friends and to the poor.
23 So the Jews formally accepted the account which Mardochaeus
24 wrote: how Haman son of Hamadathus, the Bugaean,[a] fought against
25 them; how he cast lots to decide the date of their destruction; how he
came before the king with a proposal to hang Mardochaeus; and how
all the evils which he had plotted against the Jews recoiled on his
26 own head, and he and his sons were hanged. This is why these days
were named 'Purim', which in the Jews' language means 'lots'.
Because of all that was recorded in this letter—all that they had
experienced, all that had happened—Mardochaeus directed that this
27 festival should be observed, and the Jews undertook, on behalf of
themselves, their descendants, and all who should join them, to do so
28 without fail. These were to be days of commemoration, duly
celebrated age after age in every town, family, and province. These
days of Purim were to be kept for all time, and the commemoration
was never to cease throughout all ages.

29 Queen Esther daughter of Aminadab, and Mardochaeus the Jew,
recorded in writing all that they had done, and confirmed the regula-
30–31 tions for Purim. They made themselves responsible for this decision
32 and staked their life upon the plan.[b] Esther established it for all time
by her decree, and it was put on record.

10 1, 2 The king made decrees for the empire by land and sea. His
strength and courage, his wealth and the splendour of his empire, are
recorded in the annals of the kings of the Persians and Medes.
3 Mardochaeus acted for King Artaxerxes; he was a great man in the
empire and honoured by the Jews. His way of life won him the
affection of his whole nation.**]**

4, 5 MARDOCHAEUS SAID, 'All this is God's doing. For I have been
reminded of the dream I had about these things; not one of the
6 visions I saw proved meaningless. There was the little spring which
became a river, and there was light and sun and water in abundance.
7 The river is Esther, whom the king married and made queen; the
8 two dragons are Haman and myself; the nations are those who
9 gathered to wipe out the Jews; my nation is Israel, which cried aloud

[*a*] *Some witnesses read* the Macedonian. [*b*] They made...plan: *possible meaning; Gk. obscure.*

to God and was delivered. The Lord has delivered his people, he has
rescued us from all these evils. God performed great miracles and
signs such as have not occurred among the nations. He made ready 10
two lots, one for the people of God and one for all the nations; then 11
came the hour and the time for these two lots to be cast, the day of
decision by God before[a] all the nations; he remembered his people 12
and gave the verdict for his heritage.

'So they shall keep these days in the month of Adar, the fourteenth 13
and fifteenth of that month, by gathering with joy and gladness
before God from one generation of his people to another, for ever.'

IN THE FOURTH YEAR of the reign of Ptolemy and Cleopatra, **11** 1
Dositheus, who said that he was a levitical priest, and Ptolemaeus his
son, brought the foregoing letter about Purim, which they said was
authentic and had been translated by Lysimachus son of Ptolemaeus,
a resident in Jerusalem.

[*a*] *Or* the day of judgement by God upon...

THE WISDOM OF SOLOMON

The promise of immortality

1 LOVE JUSTICE, you rulers of the earth; set your mind
upon the Lord, as is your duty, and seek him in simplicity of
2 heart; for he is found by those who trust him without question,
3 and makes himself known to those who never doubt him. Dishonest
thinking cuts men off from God, and if fools will take liberties with
4 his power, he shows them up for what they are. Wisdom will not
enter a shifty soul, nor make her home in a body that is mortgaged to
5 sin. This holy spirit of discipline will have nothing to do with falsehood; she cannot stay in the presence of unreason, and will throw up
6 her case at the approach of injustice. Wisdom is a spirit devoted to
man's good, and she will not hold a blasphemer blameless for his
words, because God is a witness of his inmost being, who sees clear
7 into his heart and hears every word he says. For the spirit of the
Lord fills the whole earth, and that which holds all things together is
8 well aware of what men say. Hence no man can utter injustice and
not be found out, nor will justice overlook him when she passes
9 sentence. The devices of a godless man will be brought to account,
and a report of his words will come before the Lord as proof of his
10, 11 iniquity; no muttered syllable escapes that vigilant ear. Beware,
then, of futile grumbling, and avoid all bitter words; for even a
secret whisper will not go unheeded, and a lying tongue is a man's
12 destruction. Do not stray from the path of life and so court death;
13 do not draw disaster on yourselves by your own actions. For God
did not make death, and takes no pleasure in the destruction of any
14 living thing; he created all things that they might have being. The
creative forces of the world make for life; there is no deadly poison in
15, 16 them. Death is not king on earth, for justice is immortal; but godless
men by their words and deeds have asked death for his company.
Thinking him their friend, they have made a pact with him because
they are fit members of his party; and so they have wasted away.

They said to themselves in their deluded way: 'Our life is short 2
and full of trouble, and when a man comes to his end there is no
remedy; no man was ever known to return from the grave. By mere 2
chance were we born, and afterwards we shall be as though we had
never been, for the breath in our nostrils is but a wisp of smoke; our
reason is a mere spark kept alive by the beating of our hearts, and 3
when that goes out, our body will turn to ashes and the breath of our
life disperse like empty air. Our names will be forgotten with the 4
passing of time, and no one will remember anything we did. Our life
will blow over like the last vestige of a cloud; and as a mist is chased
away by the sun's rays and overborne by its heat, so will it too be dispersed. A passing shadow—such is our life, and there is no post- 5
ponement of our end; man's fate is sealed, and none returns. Come 6
then, let us enjoy the good things while we can, and make full use of
the creation, with all the eagerness of youth. Let us have costly 7
wines and perfumes to our heart's content, and let no flower of
spring escape us. Let us crown ourselves with rosebuds before they 8
can wither. Let none of us miss his share of the good things that are 9
ours; who cares what traces our revelry leaves behind? This is the
life for us; it is our birthright.

'Down with the poor and honest man! Let us tread him under 10
foot; let us show no mercy to the widow and no reverence to the grey
hairs of old age. For us let might be right! Weakness is proved to be 11
good for nothing. Let us lay a trap for the just man; he stands in our 12
way, a check to us at every turn; he girds at us as law-breakers, and
calls us traitors to our upbringing. He knows God, so he says; he 13
styles himself "the servant[a] of the Lord". He is a living condemna- 14
tion of all our ideas. The very sight of him is an affliction to us, 15
because his life is not like other people's, and his ways are different.
He rejects us like base coin, and avoids us and our ways as if we were 16
filth; he says that the just die happy, and boasts that God is his
father. Let us test the truth of his words, let us see what will happen 17
to him in the end; for if the just man is God's son, God will stretch 18
out a hand to him and save him from the clutches of his enemies.
Outrage and torment are the means to try him with, to measure his 19
forbearance and learn how long his patience lasts. Let us condemn 20
him to a shameful death, for on his own showing he will have a
protector.'

[a] *Or* child.

21 So they argued, and very wrong they were; blinded by their own
22 malevolence, they did not understand God's hidden plan; they never
expected that holiness of life would have its recompense; they
23 thought that innocence had no reward. But God created man for
24 immortality, and made him the image of his own eternal self; it was
the devil's spite that brought death into the world, and the experience
of it is reserved for those who take his side.

3 But the souls of the just are in God's hand, and torment shall not
2 touch them. In the eyes of foolish men they seemed to be dead;
3 their departure was reckoned as defeat, and their going from us as
4 disaster. But they are at peace, for though in the sight of men they
5 may be punished, they have a sure hope of immortality; and after a
little chastisement they will receive great blessings, because God has
6 tested them and found them worthy to be his. Like gold in a crucible
he put them to the proof, and found them acceptable like an offering
7 burnt whole upon the altar. In the moment of God's coming to
them they will kindle into flame, like sparks that sweep through
8 stubble; they will be judges and rulers over the nations of the world,
9 and the Lord shall be their king for ever and ever. Those who have
put their trust in him shall understand that he is true, and the faithful shall attend upon him in love; they are his chosen, and grace and
mercy shall be theirs.

10 But the godless shall meet with the punishment their evil thoughts
deserve, because they took no account of justice and rebelled against
11 the Lord. Wretched indeed is he who thinks nothing of wisdom and
discipline; such men's hopes are void, their labours unprofitable,
12 their actions futile; their wives are frivolous, their children criminal,
13 their parenthood is under a curse. No, blessed is the childless
woman if she is innocent, if she has never slept with a man in sin; at
the great assize of souls she shall find a fruitfulness of her own.
14 Blessed is the eunuch, if he has never done anything against the law
and never harboured a wicked thought against the Lord; he shall
receive special favour in return for his faith, and a place in the
15 Lord's temple to delight his heart the more. Honest work bears
glorious fruit, and wisdom grows from roots that are imperishable.
16 But the children of adultery are like fruit that never ripens; they have
17 sprung from a lawless union, and will come to nothing. Even if they
attain length of life, they will be of no account, and at the end their
18 old age will be without honour. If they die young, they will have no

hope, no consolation in the hour of judgement; the unjust generation 19
has a hard fate in store for it.

It is better to be childless, provided one is virtuous; for virtue held 4
in remembrance is a kind of immortality, because it wins recognition
from God, and from men too. They follow the good man's example 2
while it is with them, and when it is gone they mourn its loss; and
through all time virtue makes its triumphal progress, crowned with
victory in the contest for prizes that nothing can tarnish. But the 3
swarming progeny of the wicked will come to no good; none of their
bastard offshoots will strike deep root or take firm hold. For a time 4
their branches may flourish, but as they have no sure footing they
will be shaken by the wind, and by the violence of the winds uprooted. Their boughs will be snapped off half-grown, and their fruit 5
will be worthless, unripe, uneatable, and good for nothing. Children 6
engendered in unlawful union are living evidence of their parents'
sin when God brings them to account.

But the good man, even if he dies an untimely death, will be at rest. 7
For it is not length of life and number of years which bring the 8
honour due to age; if men have understanding, they have grey hairs 9
enough, and an unspotted life is the true ripeness of age. There was 10
once such a man who pleased God, and God accepted him and took
him while still living from among sinful men. He was snatched 11
away before his mind could be perverted by wickedness or his soul
deceived by falsehood (because evil is like witchcraft: it dims the 12
radiance of good, and the waywardness of desire unsettles an
innocent mind); in a short time he came to the perfection of a full 13
span of years. His soul was pleasing to the Lord, who removed him 14
early from a wicked world. The mass of men see this and give it no 15
thought; they do not lay to heart this truth, that those whom God has
chosen enjoy his grace and mercy, and that he comes to the help of
his holy people. Even after his death the just man will shame the 16
godless who are still alive; youth come quickly to perfection will
shame the man grown old in sin. Men will see the wise man's end, 17
without understanding what the Lord had purposed for him and
why he took him into safe keeping; they will see it and make light of 18
him, but it is they whom the Lord will laugh to scorn. In death their
bodies will be dishonoured, and among the dead they will be an
object of contempt for ever; for he shall strike them speechless, fling 19
them headlong, shake them from their foundations, and make an

utter desert of them; they shall be full of anguish, and all memory of
20 them shall perish. So in the day of reckoning for their sins, they will
come cringing, convicted to their face by their lawless doings.
5 Then the just man shall take his stand, full of assurance, to con-
2 front those who oppressed him and made light of all his sufferings; at
the sight of him there will be terror and confusion, and they will be
3 beside themselves to see him so unexpectedly safe home. Filled with
remorse, groaning and gasping for breath, they will say among themselves: 'Was not this the man who was once our butt, a target for our
4 contempt? Fools that we were, we held his way of life to be madness
5 and his end dishonourable. To think that he is now counted one of
the sons of God and assigned a place of his own among God's
6 people! How far we strayed from the road of truth! The lamp of
7 justice never gave us light, the sun never rose upon us. We roamed
to our heart's content along the paths of wickedness and ruin,
wandering through trackless deserts and ignoring the Lord's high-
8 way. What good has our pride done us? What can we show for all
9 our wealth and arrogance? All those things have passed by like a
10 shadow, like a messenger galloping by; like a ship that runs through
the surging sea, and when she has passed, not a trace is to be found,
11 no track of her keel among the waves; or as when a bird flies through
the air, there is no sign of her passing, but with the stroke of her
pinions she lashes the insubstantial breeze and parts it with the whirr
and the rush of her beating wings, and so she passes through it, and
12 thereafter it bears no mark of her assault; or as when an arrow is shot
at a target, the air is parted and instantly closes up again and no one
13 can tell where it passed through. So we too ceased to be, as soon as
we were born; we left no token of virtue behind, and in our wicked-
14 ness we frittered our lives away.' The hope of a godless man is like
down flying on the wind, like spindrift swept before a storm and
smoke which the wind whirls away, or like the memory of a guest
who stayed for one day and passed on.
15 But the just live for ever; their reward is in the Lord's keeping,
16 and the Most High has them in his care. Therefore royal splendour
shall be theirs, and a fair diadem from the Lord himself; he will
17 protect them with his right hand and shield them with his arm. He
will put on from head to foot the armour of his wrath, and make all
18 creation his weapon against his enemies. With the cuirass of justice
19 on his breast, and on his head the helmet of doom inflexible, he will

take holiness for his impenetrable shield and sharpen his relentless 20
anger for a sword; and his whole world shall join him in the fight
against his frenzied foes. The bolts of his lightning shall fly straight 21
on the mark, they shall leap upon the target as if his bow in the
clouds were drawn in its full arc, and the artillery of his resentment 22
shall let fly a fury of hail. The waters of the sea shall rage over them,
and the rivers wash them relentlessly away; a great tempest will arise 23
against them, and blow them away like chaff before a whirlwind. So
lawlessness will make the whole world desolate, and active wickedness will overturn the thrones of princes.

In praise of wisdom

HEAR THEN, YOU KINGS, take this to heart; learn your lesson, 6
lords of the wide world; lend your ears, you rulers of the 2
multitude, whose pride is in the myriads of your people. It is 3
the Lord who gave you your authority; your power comes from the
Most High. He will put your actions to the test and scrutinize your
intentions. Though you are viceroys of his kingly power, you have 4
not been upright judges; you do not stand up for the law or guide
your steps by the will of God. Swiftly and terribly will he descend 5
upon you, for judgement falls relentlessly upon those in high place.
The small man may find pity and forgiveness, but the powerful will 6
be called powerfully to account; for he who is all men's master is 7
obsequious to none, and is not overawed by greatness. Small and
great alike are of his making, and all are under his providence
equally, but it is the powerful for whom he reserves the sternest 8
inquisition. To you then who have absolute power I speak, in hope 9
that you may learn wisdom and not go astray; those who in holiness 10
have kept a holy course, will be accounted holy, and those who have
learnt that lesson will be able to make their defence. Be eager then 11
to hear me, and long for my teaching; so you will learn.

Wisdom shines bright and never fades; she is easily discerned by 12
those who love her, and by those who seek her she is found. She is 13
quick to make herself known to those who desire knowledge of her;
the man who rises early in search of her will not grow weary in the 14
quest, for he will find her seated at his door. To set all one's thoughts 15

on her is prudence in its perfect shape, and to lie wakeful in her cause
16 is the short way to peace of mind. For she herself ranges in search of
those who are worthy of her; on their daily path she appears to them
17 with kindly intent, and in all their purposes meets them half-way. The
true beginning of wisdom is the desire to learn, and a concern for
18 learning means love towards her; the love of her means the keeping
19 of her laws; to keep her laws is a warrant of immortality; and im-
20 mortality brings a man near to God. Thus the desire of wisdom
21 leads to kingly stature. If, therefore, you value your thrones and
your sceptres, you rulers of the nations, you must honour wisdom, so
that you may reign for ever.

22 What wisdom is, and how she came into being, I will tell you;
I will hide no secret from you. From her first beginnings I will trace
out her course, and bring the knowledge of her into the light of day;
23 I will not leave the truth untold. Pale envy shall not travel in my
24 company, for the spiteful man will have no share in wisdom. Wise
men in plenty are the world's salvation, and a prudent king is the
25 sheet-anchor of his people. Learn what I have to teach you, therefore, and it will be for your good.

7 I too am a mortal man like all the rest, descended from the first
2 man, who was made of dust, and in my mother's womb I was
wrought into flesh during a ten-months space, compacted in blood
from the seed of her husband and the pleasure that is joined with
3 sleep. When I was born, I breathed the common air and was laid on
the earth that all men tread; and the first sound I uttered, as all do,
4 was a cry; they wrapped me up and nursed me and cared for me.
5, 6 No king begins life in any other way; for all come into life by a single
path, and by a single path go out again.

7 Therefore I prayed, and prudence was given to me; I called for
8 help, and there came to me a spirit of wisdom. I valued her above
sceptre and throne, and reckoned riches as nothing beside her;
9 I counted no precious stone her equal, because all the gold in the
world compared with her is but a little sand, and silver worth no more
10 than clay. I loved her more than health and beauty; I preferred her
11 to the light of day; for her radiance is unsleeping. So all good things
together came to me with her, and in her hands was wealth past
12 counting; and all was mine to enjoy, for all follows where wisdom
leads, and I was in ignorance before, that she is the beginning of it
13 all. What I learnt with pure intention I now share without grudging,

nor do I hoard for myself the wealth that comes from her. She is an 14
inexhaustible treasure for mankind, and those who profit by it
become God's friends, commended to him by the gifts they derive
from her instruction.
God grant that I may speak according to his will, and that my own 15
thoughts may be worthy of his gifts; for even wisdom is under God's
direction and he corrects the wise; we and our words, prudence and 16
knowledge and craftsmanship, all are in his hand. He himself gave 17
me true understanding of things as they are: a knowledge of the
structure of the world and the operation of the elements; the begin- 18
ning and end of epochs and their middle course; the alternating
solstices and changing seasons; the cycles of the years and the con- 19
stellations; the nature of living creatures and behaviour of wild 20
beasts; the violent force of winds and the thoughts of men; the
varieties of plants and the virtues of roots. I learnt it all, hidden or 21
manifest, for I was taught by her whose skill made all things, wisdom. 22
For in wisdom there is a spirit intelligent and holy, unique in its
kind yet made up of many parts, subtle, free-moving, lucid, spotless,
clear, invulnerable,[a] loving what is good, eager, unhindered, bene-
ficent, kindly towards men, steadfast, unerring, untouched by care, 23
all-powerful, all-surveying, and permeating all intelligent, pure, and
delicate spirits. For wisdom moves more easily than motion itself, 24
she pervades and permeates all things because she is so pure. Like a 25
fine mist she rises from the power of God, a pure effluence from the
glory of the Almighty; so nothing defiled can enter into her by
stealth. She is the brightness that streams from[b] everlasting light, 26
the flawless mirror of the active power of God and the image of his
goodness. She is but one, yet can do everything; herself unchanging, 27
she makes all things new; age after age she enters into holy souls, and
makes them God's friends and prophets, for nothing is acceptable to 28
God but the man who makes his home with wisdom. She is more 29
radiant than the sun, and surpasses every constellation; compared
with the light of day, she is found to excel; for day gives place to 30
night, but against wisdom no evil can prevail. She spans the world **8**
in power from end to end, and orders all things benignly.
Wisdom I loved; I sought her out when I was young and longed to 2
win her for my bride, and I fell in love with her beauty. She adds 3
lustre to her noble birth, because it is given her to live with God,

[*a*] invulnerable: *or* working no harm. [*b*] *Or* She is the reflection of...

4 and the Lord of all things has accepted her. She is initiated into the
knowledge that belongs to God, and she decides for him what he shall
5 do. If riches are a prize to be desired in life, what is richer than
6 wisdom, the active cause of all things? If prudence shows itself in
7 action, who more than wisdom is the artificer of all that is? If virtue
is the object of a man's affections, the fruits of wisdom's labours are
the virtues; temperance and prudence, justice and fortitude, these
are her teaching, and in the life of men there is nothing of more value
8 than these. If a man longs, perhaps, for great experience, she knows
the past, she can infer what is to come; she understands the subtleties
of argument and the solving of problems, she can read signs and
9 portents, and can foretell the outcome of events and periods. So
I determined to bring her home to live with me, knowing that she
would be my counsellor in prosperity and my comfort in anxiety and
10 grief. Through her, I thought, I shall win fame in the eyes of the
11 people and honour among older men, young though I am. When
I sit in judgement, I shall prove myself acute, and the great men will
12 admire me; when I say nothing, they will wait for me to speak;
when I speak they will attend, and though I hold forth at length, they
13 will lay a finger to their lips and listen. Through her I shall have
immortality, and shall leave an undying memory to those who come
14 after me. I shall rule over many peoples, and nations will become my
15 subjects. Grim tyrants will be frightened when they hear of me;
among my own people I shall show myself a good king, and on the
16 battlefield a brave one. When I come home, I shall find rest with her;
for there is no bitterness in her company, no pain in life with her,
only gladness and joy.

17 I thought this over in my mind, and I perceived that in kinship
18 with wisdom lies immortality and in her friendship is pure delight;
that in doing her work is wealth that cannot fail, to be taught in her
school gives understanding, and an honourable name is won by
converse with her. So I went about in search of some way to win her
19 for my own. As a child I was born to excellence, and a noble soul fell
20 to my lot; or rather, I myself was noble, and I entered into an un-
21 blemished body; but I saw that there was no way to gain possession
of her except by gift of God—and it was a mark of understanding to
know from whom that gift must come. So I pleaded with the Lord,
and from the depths of my heart I prayed to him in these words:

9 God of our fathers, merciful Lord, who hast made all things by thy

word, and in thy wisdom hast fashioned man, to be the master of thy 2
whole creation, and to be steward of the world in holiness and 3
righteousness, and to administer justice with an upright heart, give 4
me wisdom, who sits beside thy throne, and do not refuse me a place
among thy servants. I am thy slave, thy slave-girl's son, a weak 5
ephemeral man, too feeble to understand justice and law; for let a 6
man be ever so perfect in the eyes of his fellow-men, if the wisdom
that comes from thee is wanting, he will be of no account. Thou didst 7
choose me to be king of thy own people, and judge over thy sons
and daughters; thou didst tell me to build a temple on thy sacred 8
mountain and an altar in the city which is thy dwelling-place, a copy
of the sacred tabernacle prepared by thee from the beginning. And 9
with thee is wisdom, who is familiar with thy works and was present
at the making of the world by thee, who knows what is acceptable to
thee and in line with thy commandments. Send her forth from the 10
holy heavens, and from thy glorious throne bid her come down, so
that she may labour at my side and I may learn what pleases thee.
For she knows and understands all things, and will guide me 11
prudently in all I do, and guard me in her glory. So shall my life's 12
work be acceptable, and I shall judge thy people justly, and be
worthy of my father's throne. For how can any man learn what is 13
God's plan? How can he apprehend what the Lord's will is? The 14
reasoning of men is feeble, and our plans are fallible; because a 15
perishable body weighs down the soul, and its frame of clay burdens
the mind so full of thoughts. With difficulty we guess even at things 16
on earth, and laboriously find out what lies before our feet; and who
has ever traced out what is in heaven? Who ever learnt to know thy 17
purposes, unless thou hadst given him wisdom and sent thy holy
spirit down from heaven on high? Thus it was that those on earth 18
were set upon the right path, and men were taught what pleases thee;
thus were they preserved by wisdom.

Divine wisdom in history

WISDOM IT WAS who kept guard over the first father of the 10
human race, when he alone had yet been made; she saved him
after his fall, and gave him the strength to master all things. It was 2, 3

because a wicked man forsook her in his anger that he murdered his
4 brother in a fit of rage, and so destroyed himself. Through his fault
the earth was covered with a deluge, and again wisdom came to the
rescue, and taught the one good man to pilot his plain wooden hulk.
5 It was she, when heathen nations leagued in wickedness were thrown
into confusion, who picked out one good man and kept him blameless in the sight of God, giving him strength to resist his pity for his
6 child. She saved a good man from the destruction of the godless,
7 and he escaped the fire that came down on the Five Cities, cities
whose wickedness is still attested by a smoking waste, by plants whose
fruit can never ripen, and a pillar of salt standing there as a memorial
8 of an unbelieving soul. Wisdom they ignored, and they suffered for
it, losing the power to recognize what is good and leaving by their
lives a monument of folly, such that their enormities can never be
9 forgotten. But wisdom brought her servants safely out of their
10 troubles. It was she, when a good man was a fugitive from his
brother's anger, who guided him on the straight path; she showed
him that God is king, and gave him knowledge of his holiness;[a] she
11 prospered his labours and made his toil productive. When men in
their rapacity tried to exploit him, she stood by him and made him
12 rich. She kept him safe from his enemies, and preserved him from
treacherous attacks; she gave him victory after a hard struggle, and
13 taught him that godliness is the greatest power of all. It was she who
refused to desert a good man when he was sold as a slave; she pre-
14 served him from sin and went down into the dungeon with him, nor
did she leave him when he was in chains until she had brought him
sceptre and kingdom and authority over his persecutors; she gave the
15 lie to his accusers, and brought him undying fame. It was she who
rescued a godfearing people, a blameless race, from a nation of
16 oppressors; she inspired a servant of the Lord, and with his signs
17 and wonders he defied formidable kings. She rewarded the labours
of godfearing men, she guided them on a marvellous journey and
became a covering for them by day and a blaze of stars by night.
18 She brought them over the Red Sea and guided them through its
19 deep waters; but their enemies she engulfed, and cast them up again
20 out of the fathomless deep. So good men plundered the ungodly;
they sang the glories of thy holy name, O Lord, and praised with one

[*a*] showed...holiness: *or* gave him a vision of God's realm, and knowledge of his holy angels.

accord thy power, their champion; for wisdom taught the dumb to 21
speak, and made the tongues of infants eloquent.

Wisdom, working through a holy prophet, brought them success **11**
in all they did. They made their way across an unpeopled desert and 2
pitched camp in untrodden wastes; they resisted every enemy, and 3
beat off hostile assaults. When they were thirsty they called upon 4
thee, and water to slake their thirst was given them out of the hard
stone of a rocky cliff. The self-same means by which their oppressors 5
had been punished were used to help them in their hour of need:
those others found their river no unfailing stream of water, but 6
putrid and befouled with blood, in punishment for their order that 7
all the infants should be killed, while to these thou gavest abundant
water unexpectedly. So from the thirst they then endured, they 8
learnt how thou hadst punished their enemies; when they themselves 9
were put to the test, though discipline was tempered with mercy, they
understood the tortures of the godless who were sentenced in anger.
Thy own people thou didst subject to an ordeal, warning them like 10
a father; those others thou didst put to the torture, like a stern king
passing sentence. At home and abroad, they were equally in distress, 11
for a double misery had come upon them, and they groaned as they 12
recalled the past. When they heard that the means of their own 13
punishment had been used to benefit thy people, they saw thy hand
in it, O Lord. The man who long ago had been abandoned and 14
exposed, whom they had rejected with contumely, became in the
event the object of their wonder and admiration; their thirst was such
as the godly never knew.

In return for the insensate imagination of those wicked men, 15
which deluded them into worshipping reptiles devoid of reason, and
mere vermin, thou didst send upon them a swarm of creatures
devoid of reason to chastise them, and to teach them that the instru- 16
ments of a man's sin are the instruments of his punishment. For 17
thy almighty hand, which created the world out of formless matter,
was not without other resource: it could have let loose upon them a
host of bears or ravening lions or unknown ferocious monsters 18
newly created, either breathing out blasts of fire, or roaring and
belching smoke, or flashing terrible sparks like lightning from their
eyes, with power not only to exterminate them by the wounds they 19
inflicted, but by their mere appearance to kill them with fright.
Even without these, a single breath would have sufficed to lay them 20

low, with justice in pursuit and the breath of thy power to blow them
away; but thou hast ordered all things by measure and number and
weight.
21 Great strength is thine to exert at any moment, and the power of
22 thy arm no man can resist, for in thy sight the whole world is like a
grain that just tips the scale or a drop of dew alighting on the ground
23 at dawn. But thou art merciful to all men because thou canst do all
things; thou dost overlook the sins of men to bring them to repen-
24 tance; for all existing things are dear to thee and thou hatest nothing
25 that thou hast created—why else wouldst thou have made it? How
could anything have continued in existence, had it not been thy will?
26 How could it have endured unless called into being by thee? Thou
sparest all things because they are thine, our lord and master who
12 lovest all that lives; for thy imperishable breath is in them all.
2 For this reason thou dost correct offenders little by little, ad-
monishing them and reminding them of their sins, in order that they
3 may leave their evil ways and put their trust, O Lord, in thee. For
4 example, the ancient inhabitants of thy holy land were hateful to thee
5 for their loathsome practices, their sorcery and unholy rites, ruthless
6 murders of children, cannibal feasts of human flesh and blood; they
were initiates of a secret ritual in which parents slaughtered their
defenceless children. Therefore it was thy will to destroy them at the
7 hand of our forefathers, so that the land which is of all lands most
precious in thine eyes could receive in God's children settlers worthy
8 of it. And yet thou didst spare their lives because even they were
men, sending hornets as the advance-guard of thy army to extermi-
9 nate them gradually. It was well within thy power to let the godly
overwhelm the godless in a pitched battle, or to wipe them out in an
10 instant with cruel beasts or by one stern word. But thou didst carry
out their sentence gradually to give them space for repentance,
knowing well enough that they came of evil stock, their wickedness
ingrained, and that their way of thinking would not change to the
11 end of time, for there was a curse on their race from the beginning.
Nor was it out of deference to anyone else that thou gavest them an
12 amnesty for their misdeeds; for to thee no one can say 'What hast
thou done?' or dispute thy verdict. Who shall bring a charge against
thee for destroying nations which were of thy own making? Who
shall appear against thee in court to plead the cause of guilty men?
13 For there is no other god but thee; all the world is thy concern, and

there is none to whom thou must prove the justice of thy sentence.
There is no king or other ruler who can outface thee on behalf of 14
those whom thou hast punished. But thou art just and orderest all 15
things justly, counting it alien to thy power to condemn a man who
ought not to be punished. For thy strength is the source of justice, 16
and it is because thou art master of all that thou sparest all. Thou 17
showest thy strength when men doubt the perfection of thy power;
it is when they know it and yet are insolent that thou dost punish
them. But thou, with strength at thy command, judgest in mercy and 18
rulest us in great forbearance; for the power is thine to use when thou
wilt.

By acts like these thou didst teach thy people that the just man 19
must also be kind-hearted, and thou hast filled thy sons with hope by
the offer of repentance for their sins. If thou didst use such care and 20
such indulgence even in punishing thy children's enemies, who
deserved to die, granting them time and space to get free of their
wickedness, with what discrimination thou didst pass judgement on 21
thy sons, to whose fathers thou hast given sworn covenants full of the
promise of good!

So we are chastened by thee, but our enemies thou dost scourge 22
ten thousand times more, so that we may lay thy goodness to heart
when we sit in judgement, and may hope for mercy when we ourselves are judged. This is why the wicked who had lived their lives in 23
heedless folly were tormented by thee with their own abominations.
They had strayed far down the paths of error, taking for gods the 24
most contemptible and hideous creatures, deluded like thoughtless
children. And so, as though they were mere babes who have not 25
learnt reason, thou didst visit on them a sentence that made them
ridiculous; but those who do not take warning from such derisive 26
correction will experience the full weight of divine judgement. They 27
were indignant at their own sufferings, but finding themselves
chastised through the very creatures they had taken to be gods, they
recognized that the true God was he whom they had long ago refused
to know. Thus the full rigour of condemnation descended on them.

The evils of idolatry

13 WHAT BORN FOOLS all men were who lived in ignorance of
God, who from the good things before their eyes could not
learn to know him who really is, and failed to recognize the artificer
2 though they observed his works! Fire, wind, swift air, the circle of
the starry signs, rushing water, or the great lights in heaven that rule
3 the world—these they accounted gods. If it was through delight in
the beauty of these things that men supposed them gods, they ought
to have understood how much better is the Lord and Master of it all;
for it was by the prime author of all beauty that they were created.
4 If it was through astonishment at their power and influence, men
should have learnt from these how much more powerful is he who
5 made them. For the greatness and beauty of created things give us a
6 corresponding idea of their Creator. Yet these men are not greatly to
be blamed, for when they go astray they may be seeking God and
7 really wishing to find him. Passing their lives among his works and
making a close study of them, they are persuaded by appearances
8 because what they see is so beautiful. Yet even so they do not deserve
9 to be excused, for with enough understanding to speculate about the
universe, why did they not sooner discover the Lord and Master of
it all?

10 The really degraded ones are those whose hopes are set on dead
things, who give the name of gods to the work of human hands, to
gold and silver fashioned by art into images of living creatures, or to
11 a useless stone carved by a craftsman long ago. Suppose some skilled
woodworker fells with his saw a convenient tree and deftly strips off
all the bark, then works it up elegantly into some vessel suitable for
12 everyday use; and the pieces left over from his work he uses to cook
13 his food, and eats his fill. But among the waste there is one useless
piece, crooked and full of knots, and this he takes and carves to
occupy his idle moments, and shapes it with leisurely skill into the
14 image of a human being; or else he gives it the form of some contemptible creature, painting it with vermilion and raddling its surface
15 with red paint, so that every flaw in it is painted over. Then he makes
a suitable shrine for it and fixes it on the wall, securing it with iron
16 nails. It is he who has to take the precautions on its behalf to save it

from falling, for he knows that it cannot fend for itself: it is only an
image, and needs help. Yet he prays to it about his possessions and 17
his wife and children, and feels no shame in addressing this lifeless
object; for health he appeals to a thing that is feeble, for life he prays 18
to a dead thing, for aid he implores something utterly incapable, for a
prosperous journey something that has not even the use of its legs;
in matters of earnings and business and success in handicraft he asks 19
effectual help from a thing whose hands are entirely ineffectual.

The man, again, who gets ready for a voyage, and plans to set his **14**
course through the wild waves, cries to a piece of wood more fragile
than the ship which carries him. Desire for gain invented the ship, 2
and the shipwright with his wisdom built it;[a] but it is thy providence, 3
O Father, that is its pilot, for thou hast given it a pathway through
the sea and a safe course among the waves, showing that thou canst 4
save from every danger, so that even a man without skill can put to
sea. It is thy will that the things made by thy wisdom should not lie 5
idle; and therefore men trust their lives even to the frailest spar, and
passing through the billows on a mere raft come safe to land.
Even in the beginning, when the proud race of giants was being 6
brought to an end, the hope of mankind escaped on a raft and,
piloted by thy hand, bequeathed to the world a new breed of men.
For a blessing is on the wooden vessel through which right has pre- 7
vailed; but the wooden idol made by human hands is accursed, and so 8
is its maker—he because he made it, and the perishable thing because
it was called a god. Equally hateful to God are the godless man and 9
his ungodliness; the doer and the deed shall both be punished. 10

And so retribution shall fall upon the idols of the heathen, because 11
though part of God's creation they have been made into an abomination, to make men stumble and to catch the feet of fools. The 12
invention of idols is the root of immorality; they are a contrivance
which has blighted human life. They did not exist from the begin- 13
ning, nor will they be with us for ever; superstition brought them into 14
the world, and for good reason a short sharp end is in store for them.

Some father, overwhelmed with untimely grief for the child sud- 15
denly taken from him, made an image of the child and honoured
thenceforth as a god what was once a dead human being, handing on
to his household the observance of rites and ceremonies. Then this 16
impious custom, established by the passage of time, was observed as

[a] *Other witnesses read* and wisdom was the shipwright that built it.

a law. Or again graven images came to be worshipped at the com-
17 mand of despotic princes. When men could not do honour to such a
prince before his face because he lived far away, they made a likeness
of that distant face, and produced a visible image of the king they
sought to honour, eager to pay court to the absent prince as though
18 he were present. Then the cult grows in fervour as those to whom the
19 king is unknown are spurred on by ambitious craftsmen. In his
desire, it may be, to please the monarch, a craftsman skilfully distorts
20 the likeness into an ideal form, and the common people, beguiled by
the beauty of the workmanship, take for an object of worship him
21 whom lately they honoured as a man. So this becomes a trap for
living men: enslaved by mischance or misgovernment, men confer
on stocks and stones the name that none may share.

22 Then, not content with gross error in their knowledge of God,
men live in the constant warfare of ignorance and call this monstrous
23 evil peace. They perform ritual murders of children and secret
24 ceremonies and the frenzied orgies of unnatural cults; the purity of
life and marriage is abandoned; and a man treacherously murders his
25 neighbour or corrupts his wife and breaks his heart. All is in chaos—
bloody murder, theft and fraud, corruption, treachery, riot, perjury,
26 honest men driven to distraction; ingratitude, moral corruption,
27 sexual perversion, breakdown of marriage, adultery, debauchery. For
the worship of idols, whose names it is wrong even to mention, is the
28 beginning, cause, and end of every evil. Men either indulge themselves to the point of madness, or produce inspired utterance which is
all lies, or live dishonest lives, or break their oath without scruple.
29 They perjure themselves and expect no harm because the idols they
30 trust in are lifeless. On two counts judgement will overtake them:
because in their devotion to idols they have thought wrongly about
God, and because, in their contempt for religion, they have deliber-
31 ately perjured themselves. It is not any power in what they swear
by, but the nemesis of sin, that always pursues the transgression of
the wicked.

15 But thou, our God, art kind and true and patient, a merciful ruler
2 of all that is. For even if we sin, we are thine; we acknowledge thy
power. But we will not sin, because we know that we are accounted
3 thine. To know thee is the whole of righteousness, and to acknow-
4 ledge thy power is the root of immortality. We have not been led
astray by the perverted inventions of human skill or the barren

labour of painters, by some gaudy painted shape, the sight of which 5
arouses in fools a passionate desire for a mere image without life or
breath. They are in love with evil and deserve to trust in nothing 6
better, those who do these evil things or hanker after them or
worship them.

For a potter kneading his clay laboriously moulds every vessel for 7
our use, but out of the self-same clay he fashions without distinction
the pots that are to serve for honourable uses and the opposite; and
what the purpose of each one is to be, the moulder of the clay
decides. And then with ill-directed toil he makes a false god out of 8
the same clay, this man who not long before was himself fashioned
out of earth and soon returns to the place whence he was taken, when
the living soul that was lent to him must be repaid. His concern is 9
not that he must one day fall sick or that his span of life is short; but
he must vie with goldsmiths and silversmiths and copy the bronze-
workers, and he thinks it does him credit to make counterfeits. His 10
heart is ashes, his hope worth less than common earth, and his life
cheaper than his own clay, because he did not recognize by whom he 11
himself was moulded, or who it was that inspired him with an active
soul and breathed into him the breath of life. No, he reckons our life 12
a game, and our existence a market where money can be made; 'one
must get a living', he says, 'by fair means or foul'. But this man 13
knows better than anyone that he is doing wrong, this maker of
fragile pots and idols from the same earthy stuff.

The greatest fools of all, and worse than infantile, were the enemies 14
and oppressors of thy people, for they supposed all their heathen 15
idols to be gods, although they have eyes that cannot see, nostrils that
cannot draw breath, ears that cannot hear, fingers that cannot feel,
and feet that are useless for walking. It was a man who made them; 16
one who draws borrowed breath gave them their shape. But no
human being has the power to shape a god like himself: he is only 17
mortal, but what he makes with his impious hands is dead; and so he
is better than the objects of his worship, for he is at least alive—they
never can be.

Moreover, these men worship animals, the most revolting animals. 18
Compared with the rest of the brute creation, their divinities are the
least intelligent. Even as animals they have no beauty to make them 19
desirable; when God approved and blessed his work, they were left
out.

The pattern of divine justice

16 AND SO THE OPPRESSORS were fittingly chastised by creatures
2 like these: they were tormented by swarms of vermin. But while
they were punished, thou didst make provision for thy people, sending quails for them to eat, an unwonted food to satisfy their hunger;
3 for thy purpose was that whereas those others, hungry as they were,
should turn in loathing even from necessary food because the
creatures sent upon them were so disgusting, thy people after a short
4 spell of scarcity should enjoy unwonted delicacies. It was right that
the scarcity falling on the oppressors should be inexorable, and that
thy people should learn by brief experience how their enemies were
5 tormented. Even when fierce and furious snakes attacked thy people
and the bites of writhing serpents were spreading death, thy anger
6 did not continue to the bitter end; their short trouble was sent them
as a lesson, and they were given a symbol[a] of salvation to remind
7 them of the requirements of thy law. For any man who turned towards it was saved, not by the thing he looked upon but by thee, the
8 saviour of all. In this way thou didst convince our enemies that thou
9 art the deliverer from every evil. Those other men died from the bite
of locusts and flies, and no remedy was found to save their lives,
because it was fitting for them to be chastised by such creatures.
10 But thy sons did not succumb to the fangs of snakes, however
11 venomous, because thy mercy came to their aid and healed them. It
was to remind them of thy utterances that they were bitten and
quickly recovered; it was for fear they might fall into deep forgetful-
12 ness and become unresponsive to thy kindness. For it was neither
herb nor poultice that cured them, but thy all-healing word,
13 O Lord. Thou hast the power of life and death, thou bringest a man
14 down to the gates of death and up again. Man in his wickedness may
kill, but he cannot bring back the breath of life that has gone forth
nor release a soul that death has arrested.

15, 16 But from thy hand there is no escape; for godless men who refused
to acknowledge thee were scourged by thy mighty arm, pursued by
extraordinary storms of rain and hail in relentless torrents, and
17 utterly destroyed by fire. Strangest of all, in water, that quenches

[a] *Or* pledge.

everything, the fire burned more fiercely; creation itself fights to
defend the godly. At one time the flame was moderated, so that it 18
should not burn up the living creatures inflicted on the godless, who
were to learn from this that it was by God's justice that they were
pursued; at another time it blazed even under water with more than 19
the natural power of fire, to destroy the produce of a sinful land.
By contrast, thy own people were given angels' food, and thou didst 20
send them from heaven, without labour of their own, bread ready to
eat, rich in delight of every kind and suited to every taste. The 21
sustenance thou didst supply showed thy sweetness towards thy
children, and the bread, serving the desire of each man who ate it,
was changed into what he wished. Its snow and ice resisted fire and 22
did not melt, to teach them that whereas their enemies' crops had
been destroyed by fire that blazed in the hail and flashed through the
teeming rain, that same fire had now forgotten its own power, in 23
order that the godly might be fed.

For creation, serving thee its maker, exerts its power to punish the 24
godless and relaxes into benevolence towards those who trust in thee.
And so it was at that time too: it adapted itself endlessly in the 25
service of thy universal bounty, according to the desire of thy sup-
pliants. So thy sons, O Lord, whom thou hast chosen, were to learn 26
that it is not the growing of crops by which mankind is nourished,
but it is thy word that sustains those who trust in thee. That sub- 27
stance, which fire did not destroy, simply melted away when warmed
by the sun's first rays, to teach us that we must rise before the sun to 28
give thee thanks and pray to thee as daylight dawns. The hope of an 29
ungrateful man will melt like the hoar-frost of winter, and drain
away like water that runs to waste.

Great are thy judgements and hard to expound; and thus it was **17**
that uninstructed souls went astray. Thus heathen men imagined 2
that they could lord it over thy holy people; but, prisoners of darkness and captives of unending night, they lay each immured under
his own roof, fugitives from eternal providence. Thinking that their 3
secret sins might escape detection beneath a dark pall of oblivion,
they lay in disorder, dreadfully afraid, terrified by apparitions.
For the dark corner that held them offered no refuge from fear, but 4
loud unnerving noises roared around them, and phantoms with
downcast unsmiling faces passed before their eyes. No fire, however 5
great, had force enough to give them light, nor had the brilliant

6 flaming stars strength to illuminate that hideous darkness. There
shone upon them only a blaze, of no man's making, that terrified
them, and in their panic they thought the real world even worse than
7 that imaginary sight. The tricks of the sorcerers' art failed, and all
8 their boasted wisdom was exposed and put to shame; for the very
men who profess to drive away fear and trouble from sick souls were
9 themselves sick with dread that made them ridiculous. Even if
nothing frightful was there to terrify them, yet having once been
10 scared by the advancing vermin and the hissing serpents, they collapsed in terror, refusing even to look upon the air from which there
11 can be no escape.[a] For wickedness proves a cowardly thing when
condemned by an inner witness, and in the grip of conscience gives
12 way to forebodings of disaster. Fear is nothing but an abandonment
13 of the aid that comes from reason; and hope, defeated by this inward
weakness, capitulates before ignorance of the cause by which the
torment comes.

14 So all that night, which really had no power against them because
it came upon them from the powerless depths of hell, they slept the
15 same haunted sleep, now harried by portentous spectres, now paralysed by the treachery of their own souls; sudden and unforeseen,
16 fear came upon them. Thus a man would fall down where he stood
17 and be held in durance, locked in a prison that had no bars. Farmer
or shepherd or labourer toiling in the wilds, he was caught, and
awaited the inescapable doom; the same chain of darkness bound all
18 alike. The whispering breeze, the sweet melody of birds in spreading
19 branches, the steady beat of water that rushes by, the headlong crash
of rocks falling, the racing of creatures as they bound along unseen,
the roar of fierce wild beasts, or echo reverberating from hollows in
20 the hills—all these sounds paralysed them with fear. The whole
world was bathed in the bright light of day, and went about its tasks
21 unhindered; those men alone were overspread with heavy night, fit
image of the darkness that awaited them; and heavier than the darkness was the burden each was to himself.

18 But for thy holy ones there shone a great light. And so their
enemies, hearing their voices but not seeing them, counted them
2 happy because they had not suffered like themselves, gave thanks for
their forbearance under provocation, and begged as a favour that
3 they should part company. Accordingly, thy gift was a pillar of fire

[*a*] *Or* there is no need to escape.

to be the guide of their uncharted journey, a sun that would not
scorch them on their glorious expedition. Their enemies did indeed 4
deserve to lose the light of day and be kept prisoners in darkness, for
they had kept in durance thy sons, through whom the imperishable
light of the law was to be given to the world.

They planned to kill the infant children of thy holy people, but 5
when one child had been exposed to death and rescued, thou didst
deprive them of all their children in requital, and drown them all
together in the swelling waves. Of that night our forefathers were 6
given warning in advance, so that, having sure knowledge, they
might be heartened by the promises which they trusted. Thy people 7
were looking for the deliverance of the godly and the destruction of
their enemies; for thou didst use the same means to punish our 8
enemies and to make us glorious when we heard thy call. The devout 9
children of a virtuous race were offering sacrifices in secret, and
covenanted with one consent to keep the law of God and to share
alike in the same blessings and the same dangers, and they were
already singing their sacred ancestral songs of praise. In discordant 10
contrast there came an outcry from their enemies, as piteous lamentation for their children spread abroad. Master and slave were 11
punished together with the same penalty; king and common man
suffered the same fate. All alike had their dead, past counting, 12
struck down by one common form of death; there were not enough
living even to bury the dead; at one stroke the most precious of their
offspring had perished. Relying on their magic arts, they had scouted 13
all warnings; but when they saw their first-born dead, they confessed
that thy people have God as their father.

All things were lying in peace and silence, and night in her swift 14
course was half spent, when thy almighty Word leapt from thy 15
royal throne in heaven into the midst of that doomed land like a
relentless warrior, bearing the sharp sword of thy inflexible decree, 16
and stood and filled it all with death, his head touching the heavens,
his feet on earth. At once nightmare phantoms appalled them, and 17
unlooked-for fears set upon them; and as they flung themselves to 18
the ground half dead, one here, one there, they confessed the reason
for their deaths; for the dreams that tormented them had taught 19
them before they died, so that they should not die ignorant of the
reason why they suffered.

The godly also had a taste of death when a multitude were struck 20

down in the wilderness; but the divine wrath did not long continue.
21 A blameless man was quick to be their champion, bearing the
weapons of his priestly ministry, prayer and the incense that pro-
pitiates; he withstood the divine anger and set a limit to the disaster,
22 thus showing that he was thy servant. He overcame the avenging
fury not by bodily strength or force of arms; by words he subdued
the avenger, appealing to the sworn covenants made with our fore-
23 fathers. When the dead had already fallen in heaps one on another, he
interposed himself and beat back the divine wrath, barring its line of
24 attack upon the living. On his long-skirted robe the whole world
was represented; the glories of the fathers were engraved on his four
rows of precious stones; and thy majesty was in the diadem upon his
25 head. To these the destroyer yielded, for these made him afraid;
only to taste his wrath had been enough.

19 But the godless were pursued by pitiless anger to the bitter end,
2 for God knew their future also: how after allowing thy people to
depart, and even urging their departure, they would change their
3 minds and set out in pursuit. While they were still mourning, still
lamenting at the graves of their dead, they rushed into another
foolish decision, and pursued as fugitives those whom they had
4 begged to leave. For the fate they had merited was drawing them on
to this conclusion and made them forget what had happened, so
that they might suffer the torments still needed to complete their
5 punishment, and that thy people might achieve an incredible journey,
and that their enemies might meet an outlandish death.

6 The whole creation, with all its elements, was refashioned in sub-
servience to thy commands, so that thy servants might be preserved
7 unscathed. Men gazed at the cloud that overshadowed the camp, at
dry land emerging where before was only water, at an open road
leading out of the Red Sea, and a grassy plain in place of stormy
8 waves, across which the whole nation passed, under the shelter of thy
9 hand, after all the marvels they had seen. They were like horses at
pasture, like skipping lambs, as they praised thee, O Lord, by whom
10 they were rescued. For they still remembered their life in a foreign
land: how instead of cattle the earth bred lice, and instead of fish
11 the river spewed up swarms of frogs; and how, after that, they had
seen a new sort of bird when, driven by greed, they had begged for
12 delicacies to eat, and for their relief quails came up from the sea.

13 So punishment came upon those sinners, not unheralded by violent

thunderbolts. They suffered justly for their own wickedness, for they
had raised bitter hatred of strangers to a new pitch. There had been 14
others who refused to welcome strangers when they came to them,
but these made slaves of guests who were their benefactors. There is 15
indeed a judgement awaiting those who treated foreigners as enemies;
but these, after a festal welcome, oppressed with hard labour men 16
who had earlier shared their rights. They were struck with blindness 17
also, like the men at the door of the one good man, when yawning
darkness fell upon them and each went groping for his own doorway.

For as the notes of a lute can make various tunes with different 18
names though each retains its own pitch, so the elements combined
among themselves in different ways, as can be accurately inferred
from the observation of what happened. Land animals took to the 19
water and things that swim migrated to dry land; fire retained its 20
normal power even in water, and water forgot its quenching properties. Flames on the other hand failed to consume the flesh of 21
perishable creatures that walked in them, and the substance of
heavenly food, like ice and prone to melt, no longer melted.

In everything, O Lord, thou hast made thy people great and 22
glorious, and hast not neglected in every time and place to be their
helper.

ECCLESIASTICUS

OR
THE WISDOM OF JESUS
SON OF SIRACH

Preface

A LEGACY of great value has come to us through the law, the prophets, and the writers who followed in their steps, and for this Israel's traditions of discipline and wisdom deserve recognition. It is the duty of those who study the scriptures not only to become expert themselves, but also to use their scholarship for the benefit of the outside world through both the spoken and the written word. So my grandfather Jesus, who had applied himself industriously to the study of the law, the prophets, and the other writings of our ancestors, and had gained a considerable proficiency in them, was moved to compile a book of his own on the themes of discipline and wisdom, so that, with this further help, scholars might make greater progress in their studies by living as the law directs.

You are asked then to read with sympathetic attention, and make allowances if, in spite of all the devoted work I have put into the translation, some of the expressions appear inadequate. For it is impossible for a translator to find precise equivalents for the original Hebrew in another language. Not only with this book, but with the law, the prophets, and the rest of the writings, it makes no small difference to read them in the original.

When I came to Egypt and settled there in the thirty-eighth year of[a] the reign of King Euergetes, I found great scope for education; and I thought it very necessary to spend some energy and labour on the translation of this book. Ever since then I have been applying my skill night and day to complete it, and to publish it for the use of those who have made their home in a foreign land, and wish to become scholars by training themselves to live according to the law.

[*a*] *Or* there at the age of thirty-eight in...

The ways of wisdom

All wisdom is from the Lord; 1
wisdom is with him for ever.
Who can count the sand of the sea, 2
the drops of rain, or the days of unending time?
Who can measure the height of the sky, 3
the breadth of the earth, or the depth of the abyss[a]?
Wisdom was first of all created things; 4
intelligent purpose has been there from the beginning.[b]
Who has laid bare the root of wisdom? 6
Who has understood her subtlety?[c]
One alone is wise, the Lord most terrible, 8
seated upon his throne.
It is he who created her, surveyed and measured her, 9
and infused her into all his works.
To all mankind he has given her in some measure, 10
but in plenty to those who love him.

The fear of the Lord brings honour and pride, 11
cheerfulness and a garland of joy.
The fear of the Lord gladdens the heart; 12
it brings cheerfulness and joy and long life.
Whoever fears the Lord will be prosperous at the last; 13
blessings will be his on the day of his death.
The essence of wisdom is the fear of the Lord; 14
she is created with the faithful in their mother's womb,
she has built an everlasting home among men, 15
and will keep faith with their descendants.
Those who fear the Lord have their fill of wisdom; 16
she gives them deep draughts of her wine.
She stocks her home with all that the heart can desire 17
and her storehouses with her produce.

[*a*] *Some witnesses add* or wisdom. [*b*] *Some witnesses add* (5) The fountain of wisdom is God's word on high, and her ways are the eternal commandments. [*c*] *Some witnesses add* (7) Who has discovered all that wisdom knows, or understood her wealth of experience?

18 Wisdom's garland is the fear of the Lord,
flowering with peace and health.
19 She showers down knowledge and ability,
and bestows high honour on those who hold fast to her.
20 Wisdom is rooted in the fear of the Lord,
and long life grows on her branches.[a]

22 Unjust rage can never be excused;
when anger tips the scale it is a man's downfall.
23 Until the right time comes, a patient man restrains himself,
and afterwards cheerfulness breaks through again;
24 until the right moment he keeps his thoughts to himself,
and later his good sense is on everyone's lips.
25 In wisdom's store are wise proverbs,
but godliness is detestable to a sinner.
26 If you long for wisdom, keep the commandments,
and the Lord will give it you in plenty.
27 For the fear of the Lord is wisdom and discipline;
fidelity and gentleness are his delight.
28 Do not disregard the fear of the Lord
or approach him without sincerity.
29 Do not act a part before the eyes of the world;
keep guard over your lips.
30 Never be arrogant, for fear you fall
and bring disgrace on yourself;
the Lord will reveal your secrets
and humble you before the assembly,
because it was not the fear of the Lord that prompted you,[b]
but your heart was full of hypocrisy.

2 MY SON, IF YOU ASPIRE to be a servant of the Lord,
prepare yourself for testing.
2 Set a straight course, be resolute,
and do not lose your head in time of disaster.
3 Hold fast to him, never desert him,
if you would end your days in prosperity.

[*a*] *Some witnesses add* (21) The fear of the Lord drives away sins, and wherever it dwells it averts his anger. [*b*] *Or* because you had no concern for the fear of the Lord.

Bear every hardship that is sent you; 4
be patient under humiliation, whatever the cost.
For gold is assayed by fire, 5
and the Lord proves men in the furnace of humiliation.
Trust him and he will help you; 6
steer a straight course and set your hope on him.

You who fear the Lord, wait for his mercy; 7
do not stray or you will fall.
You who fear the Lord, trust in him, 8
and you shall not miss your reward.
You who fear the Lord, expect prosperity, 9
lasting happiness and favour.
Consider the past generations and see: 10
was anyone who trusted the Lord ever disappointed?
was anyone who stood firm in the fear of him ever deserted?
did he ever neglect anyone who prayed to him?
For the Lord is compassionate and merciful; 11
he forgives sins and comes to the rescue in time of trouble.

Woe to faint hearts and nerveless hands 12
and to the sinner who leads a double life!
Woe to the feeble-hearted! they have no faith, 13
and therefore shall go unprotected.
Woe to you who have given up the struggle! 14
What will you do when the Lord's reckoning comes?

Those who fear the Lord never disobey his words; 15
and all who love him keep to his ways.
Those who fear the Lord try to do his will; 16
and all who love him steep themselves in the law.
Those who fear the Lord are always prepared; 17
they humble themselves before him and say:
'We will fall into the hands of the Lord, not into the hands of men, 18
for his majesty is equalled by his mercy.'

CHILDREN, LISTEN TO ME, for I am your father; 3
do what I tell you, if you wish to be safe.

2 It is the Lord's will that a father should be honoured by his children,
and a mother's rights recognized by her sons.
3 Respect for a father atones for sins,
4 and to honour your mother is to lay up a fortune.
5 A son who respects his father will be made happy by his own children;
when he prays, he will be heard.
6 He who honours his father will have a long life,
and he who obeys the Lord comforts his mother;
7 he obeys his parents as though he were their slave.
8 My son, honour your father by word and deed,
so that you may receive his blessing.
9 For a father's blessing strengthens his children's houses,
but a mother's curse uproots their foundations.
10 Never seek honour at the cost of discredit to your father;
how can his discredit bring honour to you?
11 A man is honoured if his father is honoured,
and neglect of a mother is a disgrace to children.
12 My son, look after your father in his old age;
do nothing to vex him as long as he lives.
13 Even if his mind fails, make allowances for him,
and do not despise him because you are in your prime.
14 If you support your father it will never be forgotten,
but be put to your credit against your sins;
15 when you are in trouble, it will be remembered in your favour,
and your sins will melt away like frost in the sunshine.
16 To leave your father in the lurch is like blasphemy,
and to provoke your mother's anger is to call down the Lord's curse.

17 My son, be unassuming in all you do,
and those the Lord approves will love you.
18 The greater you are, the humbler you must be,
and the Lord will show you favour.[a]
20 For his power is great,
and he is honoured by the humble.
21 Do not pry into things too hard for you
or examine what is beyond your reach.
22 Meditate on the commandments you have been given;

[a] *Some witnesses add* (19) Many are high and mighty; but he reveals his secrets to the modest.

what the Lord keeps secret is no concern of yours.
Do not busy yourself with matters that are beyond you; 23
even what has been shown you is above man's grasp.
Many have been led astray by their speculations, 24
and false conjectures have impaired their judgement.[a]

Stubbornness will come to a bad end, 26
and the man who flirts with danger will lose his life.
Stubbornness brings a load of troubles; 27
the sinner piles sin on sin.
When calamity befalls the arrogant, there is no cure; 28
wickedness is too deeply rooted in him.

A sensible man will take a proverb to heart; 29
an attentive ear is the desire of the wise.
As water quenches a blazing fire, 30
so almsgiving atones for sin.
He who repays a good turn is mindful of the future; 31
when he falls he will find support.

My son, do not cheat a poor man of his livelihood 4
or keep him waiting with hungry eyes.
Do not tantalize a starving man 2
or drive him to desperation in his need.
If a man is desperate, do not add to his troubles 3
or keep him waiting for the charity he asks.
Do not reject the appeal of a man in distress 4
or turn your back on the poor;
when he begs for alms, do not look the other way 5
and so give him reason to curse you,
for if he curses you in his bitterness, 6
his Maker will listen to his prayer.
Make yourself popular in the assembly, 7
and show deference to the great.
When a poor man speaks to you, give him your attention 8
and answer his greeting politely.
Rescue the downtrodden from the oppressor, 9

[*a*] *Some witnesses add* (25) Without eyes you will be deprived of light; if you have no knowledge, do not lay claim to it.

and be firm when giving a verdict.
10 Be a father to orphans
and like a husband to their mother;
then the Most High will call you his son,
and his love for you will be greater than a mother's.

11 WISDOM RAISES HER SONS to greatness
and cares for those who seek her.
12 To love her is to love life;
to rise early for her sake is to be filled with joy.
13 The man who attains her will win recognition;
the Lord's blessing rests upon every place she enters.
14 To serve her is to serve the Holy One,
and the Lord loves those who love her.
15 Her dutiful servant will give laws to the heathen,
and because he listens to her, his home will be secure.
16 If he trusts her, he will possess her
and bequeath her to his descendants.
17 At first she will lead him by devious ways,
filling him with craven fears.
Her discipline will be a torment to him,
and her decrees a hard test
until he trusts her with all his heart.[a]
18 Then she will come straight back to him again and gladden him,
and reveal her secrets to him.
19 But if he strays from her, she will desert him
and abandon him to his fate.

20 WATCH YOUR CHANCE and defend yourself against wrong,
and do not be over-modest in your own cause;
21 for there is a modesty that leads to sin,
as well as a modesty that brings honour and favour.
22 Do not be untrue to yourself in deference to another,
or so diffident that you fail in your duty.
23 Never remain silent when a word might put things right,
24 for wisdom shows itself by speech,

[a] *Or* until she can trust him.

and a man's education must find expression in words.
Do not argue against the truth, 25
but have a proper sense of your own ignorance.
Never be ashamed to admit your mistakes, 26
nor try to swim against the current.
Do not let yourself be a doormat to a fool 27
or curry favour with the powerful.
Fight to the death for truth, 28
and the Lord God will fight on your side.

Do not be forward in your speech 29
but slack and neglectful in your work.
Do not play the lion in your home 30
or swagger[a] among your servants.
Do not keep your hand open to receive 31
and close it when it is your turn to give.

Do not rely upon your money **5**
and say, 'I am independent.'
Do not yield to every impulse you can gratify 2
or follow the desires of your heart.
Do not say, 'I am my own master'; 3
you may be sure the Lord will call you to account.
Do not say, 'I sinned, yet nothing happened to me'; 4
it is only that the Lord is very patient.
Do not be so confident of pardon 5
that you sin again and again.
Do not say, 'His mercy is so great, 6
he will pardon my sins, however many.'
To him belong both mercy and wrath,
and sinners feel the weight of his retribution.
Come back to the Lord without delay; 7
do not put it off from one day to the next,
or suddenly the Lord's wrath will be upon you,
and you will perish at the time of reckoning.

Do not rely upon ill-gotten gains, 8
for they will not avail in time of calamity.

[*a*] *Possible meaning; Gk. obscure.*

9 Do not winnow in every wind
or walk along every path.[a]
10 Stand firmly by what you know
and be consistent in what you say.
11 Be quick to listen,
but take time over your answer.
12 Answer a man if you know what to say,
but if not, hold your tongue.
13 Honour or shame can come through speaking,
and a man's tongue may be his downfall.
14 Do not get a name for being a gossip
or lay traps with your tongue;
for as there is shame in store for the thief,
so there is harsh censure for duplicity.
15 Avoid the little faults as well as the great.
6 Do not change from a friend into an enemy,
for a bad name brings shame and disgrace,
and this is the mark of duplicity.

2 Never be roused by violent passions;
they will tear you apart like a bull,[b]
3 they will eat up your leaves, destroy your fruit,
and leave you a withered tree.
4 Evil passion ruins the man who harbours it,
to the delight of his gloating enemies.
5 Pleasant words win many friends,
and an affable manner makes acquaintance easy.
6 Accept a greeting from everyone,
but advice from only one in a thousand.
7 When you make a friend, begin by testing him,
and be in no hurry to trust him.
8 Some friends are loyal when it suits them
but desert you in time of trouble.
9 Some friends turn into enemies
and shame you by making the quarrel public.
10 Another sits at your table,
but is nowhere to be found in time of trouble;

[*a*] *Gk. adds* this is the mark of duplicity (*from 6. 1*). [*b*] they...bull: *probable meaning; Gk. and Heb. both obscure.*

when you are prosperous, he will be your second self 11
and make free with your servants,
but if you come down in the world, he will turn against you 12
and you will not see him again.
Hold your enemies at a distance, 13
and keep a wary eye on your friends.
A faithful friend is a secure shelter; 14
whoever finds one has found a treasure.
A faithful friend is beyond price; 15
his worth is more than money can buy.
A faithful friend is an elixir of life, 16
found only by those who fear the Lord.
The man who fears the Lord keeps his friendships in repair, 17
for he treats his neighbour as himself.

MY SON, SEEK WISDOM'S DISCIPLINE while you are young, 18
and when your hair is white, you will find her still.
Come to her like a farmer ploughing and sowing; 19
then wait for her plentiful harvest.
If you cultivate her, you will labour for a little while,
but soon you will be eating her crops.
How harsh she seems to the undisciplined! 20
The fool cannot abide her;
like a stone she is a burden that tests his strength, 21
but he is quick to toss her aside.
Wisdom well deserves her name, 22
for she is not accessible to many.

Listen, my son, accept my judgement; 23
do not reject my advice.
Put your feet in wisdom's fetters 24
and your neck into her collar.
Stoop to carry her on your shoulders 25
and do not chafe at her bonds.
Come to her whole-heartedly, 26
and keep to her ways with all your might.
Follow her track, and she will make herself known to you; 27
once you have grasped her, never let her go.

28 In the end you will find the relief she offers;
she will transform herself into joy for you.
29 Her fetters will become your strong defence
and her collar a gorgeous robe.
30 Her yoke[a] is a golden ornament
and her bonds a purple cord.
31 You shall put her on like a gorgeous robe
and wear her like a splendid crown.

32 If it is your wish, my son, you can be trained;
if you give your mind to it, you can become clever;
33 if you enjoy listening, you will learn;
if you are attentive, you will grow wise.
34 When you stand among your elders,
decide who is wise and join him.
35 Listen gladly to every godly argument
and see that no wise proverb escapes you.
36 If you discover a wise man, rise early to visit him;
let your feet wear out his doorstep.
37 Ponder the decrees of the Lord
and study his commandments at all times.
He will strengthen your mind
and grant your desire for wisdom.
7 Do no evil, and evil will not come upon you;
2 turn away from wrong, and it will avoid you.
3 Do not sow in the furrows of injustice,
for fear of reaping a sevenfold crop.

4 Do not ask the Lord for high office
or the king for preferment.
5 Do not pose as a righteous man before the Lord
or play the sage in the king's presence.
6 Do not aspire to be a judge,
unless you have the strength to put an end to injustice;
for you may be intimidated by a man of rank
and so compromise your integrity.
7 Do not commit an offence against the community
and so incur a public disgrace.

[a] *So Heb.; Gk.* Upon her.

Do not pile sin upon sin, 8
for even one is enough to make you guilty.
Do not say, 'My liberality will be taken into account; 9
when I make an offering to God Most High he will accept it.'
Do not grow weary of praying 10
or neglect the giving of charity.
Never laugh at a man in his bitter humiliation, 11
for there is One who both humbles and exalts.
Do not plot to deceive your brother 12
or pay back a friend in his own coin.
Refuse ever to tell a lie; 13
it is a habit from which no good comes.
Never be garrulous among your elders 14
or repeat yourself when you pray.
Do not resent manual labour or farm-work, 15
for it was ordained by the Most High.
Do not enlist in the ranks of sinners; 16
remember that retribution will not delay.
Humble yourself to the uttermost, 17
for the doom of the impious is fire and worms.

Do not part with a friend for gain,[a] 18
or a true brother for all the gold of Ophir.
Do not lose the chance of a wise and good wife, 19
for her attractions are worth more than gold.
Do not ill-treat a slave who works honestly 20
or a hired servant whose heart is in his work.
Love a good slave from the bottom of your heart 21
and do not grudge him his freedom.
Have you cattle? Take care of them, 22
and if they bring you profit, keep them.
Have you sons? Discipline them 23
and break them in from their earliest years.
Have you daughters? See that they are chaste, 24
and do not be too lenient with them.
Marry your daughter, and a great load will be off your 25
hands;
but give her to a sensible husband.

[a] *Probable reading (compare 27. 1), supported by Vss.; Gk.* for a trifle.

26 If you have a wife after your own heart, do not divorce her;
but do not trust yourself to one you cannot love.
27 Honour your father with all your heart
and do not forget your mother's birth-pangs;
28 remember that your parents brought you into the world;
how can you repay what they have done for you?

29 Fear the Lord with all your heart
and reverence his priests.
30 Love your Maker with all your might
and do not leave his ministers without support.
31 Fear the Lord and honour the priest
and give him his dues, as you have been commanded,
the firstfruits, the guilt-offering, and the shoulder of the victim,
the dedication sacrifice, and the firstfruits of holy things.
32 Be open-handed also with the poor,
so that your own well-being may be complete.
33 Every living man appreciates generosity;
do not withhold your kindness even when a man is dead.
34 Do not turn your back on those who weep,
but mourn with those who mourn.
35 Do not hesitate to visit the sick,
for by such visits you will win their affection.
36 Whatever you are doing, remember the end that awaits you;
then all your life you will never go wrong.

8 Do not pit yourself against a great man,
for fear of falling into his power.
2 Do not quarrel with a rich man;
you may be sure he will outbid you.
For money has been the ruin of many
and has misled the minds of kings.
3 Do not argue with a long-winded man,
and so add fuel to his fire.
4 Never make fun of an ill-mannered man,
or you may hear your ancestors insulted.
5 Do not rebuke a man who is already penitent;
remember that we are all guilty.

Despise no man for being old; 6
some of us are growing old as well.
Do not be smug over another man's death; 7
remember that we must all die.

Do not neglect the studies of the learned, 8
but apply yourself to their maxims;
from these you will learn discipline,
and how to be the servant of princes.
Do not ignore the discourse of your elders, 9
for they themselves learned from their fathers;
they can teach you to understand
and to have an answer ready in time of need.

Do not kindle a sinner's coals, 10
for fear of being burnt in the flames of his fire.
Do not let a man's insolence bring you to your feet; 11
he will only sit waiting to trap you with your own words.
Do not lend to a man with more influence than yourself, 12
or, if you do, write off the loan as a loss.
Do not stand surety beyond your means, 13
and, when you do stand surety, be prepared to pay.

Do not go to law with a judge, 14
for in deference to his position they will give him the verdict.
Do not go travelling with a reckless man: 15
you may find him a burden on you.
He will do as he fancies,
and his folly will bring death on you as well.
Do not fall out with a hot-tempered man 16
or walk with him in unfrequented places;
he thinks nothing of bloodshed,
and where no help is at hand he will set upon you.
Never discuss your plans with a fool, 17
for he cannot keep a secret.
Do nothing private in the presence of a stranger; 18
you do not know what use he will make of it.
Do not tell what is in your mind to all comers 19
or accept favours from them.

9 Do not be jealous over the wife you cherish,
and so put into her head the idea of wronging you.
2 Do not surrender yourself to a woman
and let her trample down your strength.
3 Do not go near a loose woman,
for fear of falling into her snares.
4 Do not keep company with a dancing-girl,
or you may be caught by her tricks.
5 Do not let your mind dwell on a virgin,
or you may be trapped into paying damages for her.
6 Never surrender yourself to prostitutes,
for fear of losing all you possess,
7 nor gaze about you in the city streets
or saunter in deserted corners.
8 Do not let your eye linger on a woman's figure
or your thoughts dwell on beauty not yours to possess.
Many have been seduced by the beauty of a woman,
which kindles passion like fire.
9 Never sit at table with another man's wife
or join her in a drinking party,
for fear of succumbing to her charms
and slipping into fatal disaster.

10 Do not desert an old friend;
a new one is not worth as much.
A new friend is like new wine;
you do not enjoy drinking it until it has matured.
11 Do not envy a bad man his success;
you do not know what fate is in store for him.
12 Take no pleasure in the pleasures of the wicked;
remember that they will not go scot-free all their lives.
13 Keep clear of a man who has power to kill,
and you will not be haunted by the fear of death.
If you do approach him, make no false step
or you will risk losing your life.
Tell yourself that you are making your way among pitfalls,
or walking on the battlements of the city.
14 Take the measure of your neighbours as best you can,
and accept advice from those who are wise.

Let your discussion be with intelligent men 15
and all your talk about the law of the Most High.
Choose the company of good men at table, 16
and take pride in fearing the Lord.

A craftsman is recognized by his skilful hand 17
and a councillor by his words of wisdom.
A gossip is the terror of his town, 18
detested for his unguarded talk.
A wise ruler trains his people, **10**
and gives them sound and orderly government.
Like ruler, like ministers; 2
like sovereign, like subjects;
a king untutored is the people's ruin, 3
but wise rulers make a city fit to live in.

Man's life under divine providence

THE GOVERNMENT of the world is in the hand of the Lord; 4
at the right time he appoints the right man to rule it.
In the Lord's hand is all human success; 5
it is he who confers honour on the legislator.

Do not nurse a grievance against your neighbour for every offence, 6
and do not resort to acts of insolence.
Arrogance is hateful to God and man, 7
and injustice is offensive to both.
Empire passes from nation to nation 8
because of injustice, insolence, and greed.
What has man to be so proud of? He is only dust and ashes, 9
subject even in life to bodily decay.[a]
A long illness mocks the doctor's skill; 10
today's king is tomorrow's corpse.
When a man dies, he comes into an inheritance 11
of maggots and vermin and worms.
The origin of pride is to forsake the Lord, 12

[*a*] subject...decay: *probable meaning, based on Heb.; Gk. obscure.*

man's heart revolting against his Maker;
13 as its origin is sin,
so persistence in it brings on a deluge of depravity.
Therefore the Lord sends upon them signal punishments
and brings them to utter disaster.

14 The Lord overturns the thrones of princes
and enthrones the gentle in their place.
15 The Lord pulls up nations by the roots
and plants the humble instead.
16 The Lord lays waste the territory of nations,
destroying them to the very foundations of the earth.
17 Some he shrivels away to nothing,
so that all memory of them vanishes from the earth.
18 Pride was not the Creator's design for man
nor violent anger for those born of woman.

19 What creature is worthy of honour? Man.
What men? Those who fear the Lord.
What creature is worthy of contempt? Man.
What men? Those who break the commandments.
20 As the members of the family honour their head,
so the Lord honours those who fear him.[a]
22 The rich, the famous, and the poor—
their only boast is the fear of the Lord.
23 It is unjust to despise a poor man who is intelligent,
and wrong to honour a man who is a sinner.
24 The prince, the judge, and the ruler win high honours,
but none of them is as great as the godfearing man.
25 The wise slave will have free men to wait on him,
and a man of sense will not grumble at it.

26 DO NOT BE TOO CLEVER to do a day's work
or boast when you have nothing to live on.
27 It is better to work and have more than enough
than to boast and go hungry.
28 My son, in all modesty, keep your self-respect

[*a*] *Some witnesses add* (21) Fear the Lord, and you will be accepted; be obstinate and proud, and you will be rejected.

and value yourself at your true worth.
Who will speak up for a man who is his own enemy, 29
or respect one who disparages himself?
A poor man may be honoured for his wisdom, 30
a rich man for his wealth;
if a man is honoured in poverty, how much more in wealth! 31
And if he is despised in wealth, how much more in poverty!
A poor man with wisdom can hold his head high **11**
and take his seat among the great.

Do not overrate one man for his good looks 2
or be repelled by another man's appearance.
The bee is small among winged creatures, 3
yet her produce takes first place for sweetness.
Do not pride yourself on your fine clothes 4
or be haughty when honours come to you;
for the Lord can perform marvels
which are hidden from the eyes of men.
Many kings have been reduced to sitting on the ground, 5
while a mere nobody has worn the crown.
Many rulers have been stripped of their honours, 6
and great men have found themselves at the mercy of others.

Do not find fault before examining the evidence; 7
think first, and criticize afterwards.
Do not answer without first listening, 8
and do not interrupt when another is speaking.
Never take sides in a quarrel not your own 9
or become involved in the disputes of rascals.

My son, do not engage in too many transactions; 10
if you attempt too much, you will come to grief.
When you are in pursuit, you will not overtake;
when you are in flight, you will not escape.
One man slaves and strains and hurries 11
and is all the farther behind.
Another is slow-witted and in need of help, 12
lacking in strength and abounding in poverty;
but the Lord turns a kindly eye upon him

and lifts him up out of his miserable plight.
13 He raises him to dignity
to the amazement of all.

14 Good fortune and bad, life and death,
poverty and wealth, all come from the Lord.[a]
17 His gifts to the devout are lasting;
his approval brings unending success.
18 A man may grow rich by stinting and sparing,
but what does he get for his pains?
19 When he says, 'I have earned my rest,
now I can live on my savings',
he does not know how long it will be
before he must die and leave his wealth to others.

20 Stand by your contract and give your mind to it;
grow old at your work.
21 Do not envy a rogue his success;
trust the Lord and stick to your job.
It is no difficult thing for the Lord
to make a poor man rich in a moment.
22 The Lord's blessing is the reward of piety,
which blossoms in one short hour.
23 Do not say, 'What use am I?
What good[b] can the future hold for me?'
24 And do not say, 'I am independent;
nothing can ever go wrong for me.'
25 Hardship is forgotten in time of success,
and success in time of hardship.
26 Even on the day a man dies it is easy for the Lord
to give him his deserts.
27 One hour's misery wipes out all memory of delight,
and a man's end reveals his true character.
28 Call no man happy before he dies,
for not until death is a man known for what he is.[c]

[*a*] *Some witnesses add* (15) From the Lord come wisdom, understanding, and love, knowledge of the law, and the doing of good works. (16) Error and darkness have been with sinners from their birth, and evil grows old along with those who take delight in it. [*b*] *Or* 'What more do I need? What greater success... [*c*] not...he is: *so Heb.; Gk.* a man is known by his children.

DO NOT INVITE ALL COMERS into your home; 29
dishonesty has many disguises.
A proud man's mind is like a decoy-partridge in its cage, 30
or like a spy watching for a false step.
He waits for a chance to twist good into evil 31
or to cast blame on innocent actions.
A small spark kindles many coals, 32
and the insinuations of a bad man end in bloodshed.
Beware of a scoundrel and his evil plots, 33
or he may ruin your reputation for ever.
Admit a stranger to your home and he will stir up trouble for you 34
and make you a stranger to your own flesh and blood.

If you do a good deed, make sure to whom you are doing it; 12
then you will have credit for your kindness.
A good turn done to a godfearing man will be rewarded, 2
if not by him, then by the Most High.
No good comes to the persistent wrong-doer 3
or to the man who never gives alms;[a]
refuse him bread; give him nothing at all; 5
he will only use your gifts to get the better of you,
and you will suffer a double wrong
in return for the favours you have done him.
The Most High himself hates sinners 6
and sends bad men what they deserve.
Give to a good man, but never help a sinner; 7
keep your good works for the humble, not the insolent.[b]

Prosperity does not reveal your friends; 8
adversity does not conceal your enemies.
When all goes well a man's enemies are friendly,[c] 9
but in hard times even his friend will desert him.
Never trust your enemy; 10
he will turn vicious as sure as metal rusts.
If he appears humble and obsequious, 11
take care! Be on your guard against him!

[*a*] *The order of the following verses has been disturbed in all versions; Gk. reads*...gives alms; (4) give to a godfearing man, but never help a sinner; (5) keep your good works for the humble, not the insolent; refuse him... (*compare verse 7*). [*b*] keep...insolent: *this is the beginning of verse 5 in Gk.* [*c*] *So Heb.; Gk.* grieve.

Behave towards him like a man who polishes a mirror
to make sure that it does not corrode away.
12 Do not have him at your side,
or he will trip you up and supplant you.
Do not let him sit at your right hand,
or he will soon be wanting your own seat;
and in the end you will see the force of my words
and recall my warning with regret.
13 Who sympathizes with a snake-charmer when he is bitten,
or with a tamer of wild animals?
14 No more does anyone pity the man who keeps bad company
and involves himself in another's wickedness.
15 He may stand by you for a while,
but, if you falter, his friendship will not last.

16 An enemy has honey on his lips,
but in his heart he plans to trip you into the ditch.
He may have tears in his eyes,
but give him a chance and he will not stop at bloodshed.
17 If disaster overtakes you, you will find him there ahead of you,
ready, with a pretence of help, to pull your feet from under you.
18 Then he will nod his head and rub his hands
and spread gossip, showing his true colours.
13 Handle pitch and it will make you dirty;
keep company with an arrogant man and you will grow like him.

2 Do not lift a weight too heavy for you,
keeping company with a man greater and richer than yourself.
How can a jug be friends with a kettle?
If they knock together, the one will be smashed.
3 A rich man does wrong, and adds insult to injury;
a poor man is wronged, and must apologize into the bargain.
4 If you can serve his turn, a rich man will exploit you,
but if you are in need, he will leave you alone.
5 If you are in funds, he will be your constant companion,
and drain you dry without a twinge of remorse.
6 He may need you; and then he will deceive you,
and will be all smiles and encouragement,
paying you compliments and asking, 'What can I do for you?',

embarrassing you with his hospitality, 7
until he has drained you two or three times over;
but in the end he will laugh at you.
Afterwards, when he sees you, he will pass you by,
nodding his head over you.

Take care not to be led astray 8
and humiliated when you are enjoying yourself.
If a great man invites you, be slow to accept, 9
and he will be the more pressing in his invitation.
Do not be forward, for fear of a rebuff, 10
but do not keep aloof, or you may be forgotten.
Do not presume to converse with him as an equal 11
or be over-confident if he holds you long in talk.
The more he speaks, the more he is testing you,
examining you even while he smiles.
The man who cannot keep your secrets is without compunction 12
and will not spare you harm or imprisonment;
so keep your secrets to yourself and be very careful, 13
for you are walking on the brink of ruin.[a]

Every animal loves its like, 15
and every man his neighbour.
All creatures flock together with their kind, 16
and men form attachments with their own sort.
What has a wolf in common with a lamb, 17
or a sinner with a man of piety?
What peace can there be between hyena and dog, 18
what peace between rich man and pauper?
As lions prey on the wild asses of the desert, 19
so the rich batten on the poor.
As humility disgusts the proud, 20
so is the rich man disgusted by the poor.

If a rich man staggers, he is held up by his friends; 21
a poor man falls, and his friends disown him as well.
When a rich man slips, many come to his rescue; 22

[*a*] *Some witnesses add* When you hear this in your sleep, wake up. (14) Love the Lord all your life and appeal to him for salvation.

if he says something outrageous, they make excuses for him.
A poor man makes a slip, and they all criticize him;
even if he talks sense, he is not given a hearing.
23 A rich man speaks, and all are silent;
then they praise his speech to the skies.
A poor man speaks, and they say, 'Who is this?',
and if he stumbles, they give him an extra push.

24 WEALTH IS GOOD, if sin has not tainted it;
poverty is a crime only to the ungodly.
25 It is a man's heart that changes the look on his face
either for better or worse.
26 The sign of a happy heart is a cheerful face,
but the invention of proverbs involves wearisome thought.
14 Happy the man who has never let slip a careless word,
who has never felt the sting of remorse!
2 Happy the man whose conscience does not accuse him,
whose hope has never been disappointed!

3 It is not proper for a mean man to be rich:
what use is money to a miser?
4 He deprives himself only to hoard for other men;
others will live in luxury on his riches.
5 How can a man be hard on himself and kind to others?
His possessions bring him no enjoyment.
6 No one is worse than the man who is grudging to himself:
his niggardliness is its own punishment.
7 If ever he does good, it is by mistake,
and then in the end he reveals his meanness.
8 It is a hard man who has a grudging eye;
he turns his back on need and looks the other way.
9 A covetous man's eye is not satisfied with his share;
greedy injustice shrivels the soul.
10 A miser grudges bread
and keeps an empty table.

11 My son, if you can afford it, do yourself well,
always offering to the Lord the sacrifice due to him.
12 Remember that death is not to be postponed;

the hour of your appointment with the grave is undisclosed.
Before you die, do good to your friend; 13
reach out as far as you can to help him.
Do not miss a day's enjoyment 14
or forgo your share of innocent pleasure.
Are you to leave to others all you have laboured for 15
and let them draw lots for your hard-earned wealth?
Give and receive; indulge yourself; 16
you need not expect luxuries in the grave.
Man's body wears out like a garment; 17
for the ancient sentence stands: You shall die.
In the thick foliage of a growing tree 18
one crop of leaves falls and another grows instead;
so the generations of flesh and blood pass
with the death of one and the birth of another.
All man's works decay and vanish, 19
and the workman follows them into oblivion.

HAPPY THE MAN WHO fixes his thoughts on wisdom 20
and uses his brains to think,
the man who contemplates her ways 21
and ponders her secrets.
Stalk her like a hunter 22
and lie in wait beside her path!
The man who peers in at her windows 23
and listens at her keyhole,
who camps beside her house, 24
driving his tent-peg into her wall,
who pitches his tent close by her, 25
where it is best for men to live—
he will put his children in her shade 26
and camp beneath her branches,
sheltered by her from the heat, 27
and dwelling in the light of her presence.

The man who fears the Lord will do all this, **15**
and if he masters the law, wisdom will be his.
She will come out to meet him like a mother; 2

she will receive him like a young bride.
3 For food she will give him the bread of understanding
and for drink the water of knowledge.
4 He will lean on her and not fall;
he will rely on her to save him from disgrace.
5 She will promote him above his neighbours,
and find words for him when he speaks in the assembly.
6 He shall be crowned with joy and exultation;
lasting honour shall be his heritage.
7 Fools shall never possess wisdom;
sinners shall catch no glimpse of her.
8 She holds aloof from arrogance,
far from the thoughts of liars.

9 Worship is out of place on the lips of a sinner,
unprompted as he is by the Lord.
10 Worship is the outward expression of wisdom,
and the Lord himself inspires it.

11 Do not say, 'The Lord is to blame for my failure';
it is for you to avoid doing what he hates.
12 Do not say, 'It was he who led me astray';
he has no use for sinful men.
13 The Lord hates every kind of vice;
you cannot love it and still fear him.
14 When he made man in the beginning,
he left him free to take his own decisions;
15 if you choose, you can keep the commandments;
whether or not you keep faith is yours to decide.
16 He has set before you fire and water;
reach out and take which you choose;
17 before man lie life and death,
and whichever he prefers is his.
18 For in his great wisdom and mighty power
the Lord sees everything.
19 He keeps watch over those who fear him;
no human act escapes his notice.
20 But he has commanded no man to be wicked,
nor has he given licence to commit sin.

DO NOT SET YOUR HEART on a large family of ne'er-do-wells **16**
or be content if your sons are godless.
However many they are, do not think yourself happy, 2
unless the fear of the Lord is in them.
Do not count on their living to be old 3
or rely on their numbers;
for one son can be better than a thousand;
better indeed to die childless than to have godless children.
Thanks to one man of good sense a city may be populous, 4
while a tribe of lawless men becomes a desert.
Many a time have I seen this with my own eyes, 5
and still weightier examples have come to my ears.

Where sinners gather, the fire breaks out; 6
retribution blazes up in a rebellious nation.
There was no pardon for the giants of old, 7
who revolted in all their strength.
There was no reprieve for Lot's adopted home, 8
abhorrent in its arrogance.
There was no mercy for the doomed nation, 9
exterminated for their sins—
those six hundred thousand warriors 10
marshalled in stubborn defiance.
Even if only one man were obstinate, 11
it would be a miracle for him to escape punishment.
For mercy and anger belong to the Lord;
he shows his power in forgiveness, or in the flood of his wrath.
His mercy is great, but great also is his condemnation; 12
he judges a man by what he has done.
He does not let the sinner escape with his loot 13
or try the patience of the godly too long.
He opens a way for every work of mercy, 14
and everyone is treated according to his own deserts.[a]

Do not say, 'I am hidden from the Lord; 17
who is there in heaven to give a thought to me?

[*a*] *Some witnesses add* (15) The Lord made Pharaoh too stubborn to acknowledge him, so that his deeds might be published to the world. (16) He displays his mercy to the whole creation, and has separated light from darkness with a plumb-line.

Among so many I shall not be noticed;
what is my life compared with the measureless creation?
18 Heaven itself, the highest heaven,
the abyss and the earth are shaken at his coming;
19 the very mountains and the foundations of the world
tremble when he looks upon them.
20 What human mind can grasp this,
or comprehend his ways?
21 As a squall takes men unawares,
so most of his works are done in secret.
22 Who is to declare his acts of justice
or wait for his remote decree?'
23 These are the thoughts of a small mind,
the absurdities of a senseless and misguided man.

24 LISTEN TO ME, MY SON, and learn sense;
pay close attention to what I say;
25 I will show you exact discipline
and teach you accurate knowledge.
26 When the Lord created his works in the beginning,
and after making them defined[a] their boundaries,
27 he disposed them in an eternal order
and fixed their influences for all time.
They do not grow hungry or weary,
or abandon their tasks;
28 one does not jostle another;
they never disobey his word.
29 The Lord then looked at the earth
and filled it with his good things.
30 With every kind of living creature he covered the ground,
into which they must all return.

17 The Lord created man from the earth
and sent him back to it again.
2 He set a fixed span of life for men
and granted them authority over everything on earth.

[a] When...defined: *probable reading, based on Heb.; Gk.* The works of the Lord have been under his judgement from the beginning,...he defined...

He clothed them with strength like his own,[a] 3
forming them in his own image.
He put the fear of man into all creatures 4
and gave him lordship over beasts and birds.[b]
He gave men tongue and eyes and ears, 6
the power of choice and a mind for thinking.
He filled them with discernment 7
and showed them good and evil.
He kept watch over their hearts, 8
to display to them the majesty of his works.[c]
They shall praise his holy name, 10
proclaiming the grandeur of his works.
He gave them knowledge as well 11
and endowed them with the life-giving law.
He established a perpetual covenant with them 12
and revealed to them his decrees.
Their eyes saw his glorious majesty, 13
and their ears heard the glory of his voice.
He said to them, 'Guard against all wrongdoing', 14
and taught each man his duty towards his neighbour.

Their conduct always lies open before him, 15
never hidden from his scrutiny.[d]
For every nation he appointed a ruler, 17
but chose Israel to be his own possession.[e]
So whatever they do is clear to him as daylight; 19
he keeps constant watch over their lives.
Their wrongdoing is not hidden from the Lord; 20
he observes all their sins.[f]
A man's good deeds he treasures like a signet-ring, 22
and his kindness like the apple of his eye.

[*a*] *So one Vs.; Gk.* their own. [*b*] *Some witnesses add* (5) The Lord gave them the use of the five faculties; as a sixth gift he distributed to them mind, and as a seventh, reason, the interpreter of those faculties. [*c*] *Some witnesses add* (9) He has given them the right to boast for ever of his marvels. [*d*] *Some witnesses read* ...scrutiny. (16) Every man from his youth tended towards evil; they could not make themselves hearts of flesh in place of their hearts of stone. (17) When he distributed the nations over all the earth, for every... [*e*] *Some witnesses add* (18) He rears them with discipline as his first-born, imparting to them the light of love and never neglecting them. [*f*] *Some witnesses add* (21) The Lord who is gracious and knows what they are made of has neither rejected nor deserted them, but spared them.

23 In the end he will rise up and give the wicked their deserts,
bringing down their recompense on their own heads.
24 Yet he leaves a way open for the penitent to return to him,
and gives the waverer strength to endure.

25 Turn to the Lord and have done with sin;
make your prayer in his presence, and so lessen your offence.
26 Come back to the Most High, renounce wrongdoing,
and hate intensely what he abhors.
27 Who will praise the Most High in the grave
in place of the living who give him thanks?
28 When a man is dead and ceases to be, his gratitude dies with him;
it is when he is alive and well that he praises the Lord.
29 How great is the Lord's mercy
and his pardon to those who turn to him!
30 Not everything is within man's reach,
for the human race is not immortal.
31 Is anything brighter than the sun? Yet the sun suffers eclipse.
So flesh and blood have evil thoughts.
32 The Lord marshals the armies of high heaven,
but all men are dust and ashes.

18 He who lives for ever is the Creator of the whole universe;
2 right belongs to the Lord alone.[a]
4 To no man is it given to unfold the story of his works;
who can trace his marvels to their source?
5 No one can measure his majestic power,
still less, tell the full tale of all his mercies.
6 Man can neither increase nor diminish them,
nor fathom the wonders of the Lord.
7 When a man comes to the end of them he is still at the beginning,
and when he has finished he will still be perplexed.

8 What is man and what use is he?
What do his good or evil deeds signify?
9 His span of life is at the most a hundred years;

[*a*] *Some witnesses add* and there is none beside him, (3) who can steer the world with his little finger, so that all things obey his will; as king of the universe, he has power to fix the bounds between what is holy and what is profane.

compared with endless time, his few years 10
are like one drop of sea-water or a single grain of sand.
This is why the Lord is patient with them, 11
lavishing his mercy upon them.
He sees and knows the harsh fate in store for them, 12
and therefore gives full play to his forgiveness.
Man's compassion is only for his neighbour, 13
but the Lord's compassion is for every living thing.
He corrects and trains and teaches
and brings them back as a shepherd his flock.
He has compassion on those who accept discipline 14
and are eager to obey his decrees.

My son, do good without scolding; 15
do not spoil your generosity with hard words.
Does not the dew give respite from the sweltering heat? 16
So a word can do more than a gift.
A kind word counts for more than a rich present; 17
with a gracious man you will find both.
A fool cannot refrain from tactless criticism, 18
and a grudging giver makes no eyes sparkle.

Before you speak, learn; 19
and before you fall sick, consult a doctor.
Before judgement comes, examine yourself, 20
and you will find pardon in the hour of scrutiny.
Before you fall ill, humble yourself; 21
show your penitence as soon as you sin.
Let nothing hinder the prompt discharge of your vows; 22
do not wait till death to be absolved.
Before you make a vow, give it due thought; 23
do not be like those who try the Lord's patience.
Think of the wrath you must face in the hour of death, 24
when the time of reckoning comes, and he turns away his face.
In time of plenty remember the time of famine, 25
poverty and need in days of wealth.
Between dawn and dusk times may alter; 26
all change comes quickly, when the Lord wills it.
A wise man is always on his guard; 27

when sin is rife, he will beware of negligence.
28 Every man of sense makes acquaintance with wisdom,
and to him who finds her she gives cause for thankfulness.
29 Skilled speakers display their special wisdom
by a flow of apt proverbs.

Maxims of prudence and self-discipline

30 DO NOT LET your passions be your guide,
but restrain your desires.
31 If you indulge yourself with all that passion fancies,
it will make you the butt of your enemies.
32 Do not revel in great luxury,
or the expense of it may ruin you.
33 Do not beggar yourself by feasting on borrowed money,
when there is nothing in your purse.
19 A drunken workman never grows rich;
carelessness in small things leads little by little to ruin.
2 Wine and women rob the wise of their wits,
and a frequenter of prostitutes becomes more and more reckless,
3 till sores[a] and worms take possession of him,
and his recklessness becomes his undoing.

4 To trust a man hastily shows a shallow mind,
and to sin is to do an injury to yourself.
5 To delight in wickedness is to court condemnation,
6 but evil loses its hold on the man who hates gossip.
7 Never repeat what you hear,
and you will never be the loser.
8 Tell no tales about friend or foe;
unless silence makes you an accomplice, never betray a man's secret.
9 Suppose he has heard you and learnt to distrust you,
he will seize the first chance to show his hatred.
10 Have you heard a rumour? Let it die with you.
Never fear, it will not make you burst.
11 A fool with a secret goes through agony

[*a*] *Or* decay.

like a woman in childbirth.
As painful as an arrow through the thigh 12
is a rumour in the heart of a fool.
Confront your friend with the gossip about him; he may not have 13
done it;
or if he did it, he will know not to do it again.
Confront your neighbour; he may not have said it; 14
or if he did say it, he will know not to say it again.
Confront your friend; it will often turn out to be slander; 15
do not believe everything you hear.
A man may let slip more than he intends; 16
whose tongue is always free from guilt?
Confront your neighbour before you threaten him, 17
and let the law of the Most High take its course.[a]

All wisdom is the fear of the Lord 20
and includes the fulfilling of the law.[b]
The knowledge of wickedness is not wisdom, 22
nor is there good sense in the advice of sinners.
There is a cleverness that is loathsome, 23
and some fools are merely ignorant.
Better to be godfearing and lack brains 24
than to have great intelligence and break the law.
A meticulous cleverness may lead to injustice, 25
and a man may make himself offensive in order that right may
prevail.
There is a scoundrel who stoops and wears mourning, 26
but who is a fraud at heart.
He covers his face and pretends to be deaf, 27
but when nobody is looking, he will steal a march on you;
and if lack of strength prevents him from doing wrong, 28
he will still harm you at the first opportunity.
Yet you can tell a man by his looks 29
and recognize good sense at first sight.

[*a*] *Some witnesses add* without giving way to anger. (18) The fear of the Lord is the way towards acceptance, and wisdom wins love from him. (19) The knowledge of the Lord's commandments is life-giving discipline, and those who do what pleases him eat from the tree of immortality. [*b*] *Some witnesses add* and a knowledge of his omnipotence. (21) A servant who says, 'I will not do as you wish', even if he does it later, angers the man who feeds him.

30 A man's clothes, and the way he laughs,
and his gait, reveal his character.

20 A reproof may be untimely,
and silence may show a man's good sense.
2 Yet how much better it is to complain than to nurse a grudge,
and confession saves a man from disgrace.[a]
4 Like a eunuch longing to seduce a girl
is the man who tries to do right by violence.
5 One man is silent and is found to be wise;
another is hated for his endless chatter.
6 One man is silent, at a loss for an answer;
another is silent, biding his time.
7 The wise man is silent until the right moment,
but a swaggering fool is always speaking out of turn.
8 A garrulous man makes himself detested,
and one who abuses his position arouses hatred.

9 A MAN SOMETIMES FINDS profit in adversity,
and a windfall may result in loss.
10 Sometimes liberality does not benefit the giver,
sometimes it brings a double return.
11 The quest for honour may lead to disgrace,
but there are those who have risen from obscurity to eminence.
12 A man may make a good bargain,
but pay for it seven times over.
13 A wise man endears himself when he speaks,
but fools scatter compliments in vain.
14 A gift from a fool will bring you no benefit;
it looks bigger to him than it does to you.
15 He gives small gifts accompanied by long lectures,
and opens his mouth as wide as the town crier.
He gives a loan today and asks it back tomorrow,
obnoxious fellow that he is!
16 The fool says, 'I have no friends,
I get no thanks for my kindnesses;

[*a*] *Some witnesses add* (3) How good it is to respond to reproof with repentance, and so escape deliberate sin!

though they eat my bread, they speak ill of me.'
How everyone will laugh at him—and how often! 17

Better a slip on the stone floor than a slip of the tongue; 18
and the fall of the wicked comes just as suddenly.
An ill-mannered man is like an unseasonable story, 19
continually on the lips of the ill-bred.
A proverb will fall flat when uttered by a fool, 20
for he will produce it at the wrong time.

Poverty may keep a man from doing wrong; 21
when the day's work is over, conscience will not trouble him.
A man's diffidence may be his undoing, 22
or the foolish figure he cuts in the eyes of the world.
A man may be shamed into making promises to a friend 23
and needlessly turn him into an enemy.

A lie is an ugly blot on a man's name, 24
and is continually on the lips of those who know no better.
It is better to be a thief than a habitual liar, 25
but both will come to the same bad end.
A lying disposition brings disgrace; 26
the shame of it can never be shaken off.

A wise man advances himself when he speaks, 27
and a man of sense makes himself pleasant to the great.
The man who tills his land heaps up a harvest, 28
and he who pleases the great reaps pardon for his wrongdoing.
Hospitality and presents make wise men blind; 29
like a gag in the mouth they silence criticism.
Hidden wisdom and buried treasure, 30
what use is there in either?
Better a man who hides his folly 31
than one who hides his wisdom![a]

Have you done wrong, my son? Do it no more, **21**
but ask pardon for your past wrongdoing.

[*a*] *Some witnesses add* (32) Better to seek the Lord with unremitting patience than to be the masterless charioteer of one's own life.

2 Avoid wrong as you would a viper,
for if you go near, it will bite you;
its teeth are like a lion's teeth
and can destroy the lives of men.
3 Every breach of the law is like a two-edged sword;
it inflicts an incurable wound.
4 By intimidation and insolence a man forfeits his wealth;
thus a proud man will be stripped of his possessions.
5 The Lord listens to the poor man's appeal,
and his verdict follows without delay.
6 To hate reproof is to go the way of sinners,
but whoever fears the Lord will repent whole-heartedly.
7 A great talker is known far and wide,
but a sensible man is aware of his failings.
8 To build a house with borrowed money
is like collecting stones for your own tomb.[a]
9 A gathering of lawless men is like a bundle of tow,
which ends by going up in flames.
10 The road of sinners is smoothly paved,
but it leads straight down to the grave.
11 Whoever keeps the law keeps his thoughts under control;
the fear of the Lord has its outcome in wisdom.

12 A MAN WHO IS NOT CLEVER cannot be taught,
but there is a cleverness which only breeds bitterness.
13 A wise man's knowledge is like a river in full spate,
and his advice is a life-giving spring.
14 A fool's mind is a leaky bucket:
it cannot hold anything it learns.
15 If an instructed man hears a wise saying,
he applauds it and improves on it.
If a rake hears it, he is annoyed
and throws it behind his back.
16 Listening to a fool is like travelling with a heavy pack,
but there is delight to be found in intelligent conversation.
17 The assembly welcomes a word from the wise man,
and thinks over what he says.

[a] *Some witnesses read* like harvesting stones against the winter.

A fool's wisdom is like a tumbledown house; 18
his knowledge is a string of ill-digested sayings.
To fools education is like fetters, 19
like a handcuff on the wrist.
To the wise education is a golden ornament 21
like a bracelet on the arm.
A fool laughs out loud; 20
a clever man smiles quietly, if at all.

A fool rushes into a house, 22
while a man of experience hangs back politely.
A boor peers into the house from the doorstep, 23
while a well-bred man stands outside.
It is bad manners to listen at doors; 24
a man of sense would think it a crushing disgrace.
The glib only repeat what others have said, 25
but the wise weigh every word.
Fools speak before they think; 26
wise men think first and speak afterwards.
When a bad man curses his adversary,[a] 27
he is cursing himself.
A tale-bearer blackens his own character 28
and makes himself hated throughout the neighbourhood.

An idler is like a filthy stone; **22**
everyone jeers at his disgrace.
An idler is like a lump of dung; 2
whoever picks it up shakes it off his hand.

There is shame in being father to a spoilt son, 3
and the birth of a daughter means loss.
A sensible daughter wins a husband, 4
but an immodest one is a grief to her father.
A brazen daughter disgraces both father and husband 5
and is despised by both.
Unseasonable talk is like music in time of mourning, 6
but the lash of wisdom's discipline is always in season.

[*a*] *Or* curses Satan.

7 Teaching a fool is like mending pottery with glue,
or like rousing a sleeper from heavy sleep.
8 As well reason with a drowsy man as with a fool;
when you have finished, he will say, 'What was that?'[a]
11 Mourn over the dead for the eclipse of his light;
mourn over the fool for the eclipse of his wits.
Mourn less bitterly for the dead, for he is at rest;
but the fool's life is worse than death.
12 Mourning for the dead lasts seven days,
but for a godless fool it lasts all his life.
13 Do not talk long with a fool
or visit a stupid man.
Beware of him, or you may be in trouble
and find yourself bespattered when he shakes himself.
Avoid him, if you are looking for peace,
and you will not be worn out by his folly.
14 What is heavier than lead?
What is its name but 'Fool'?
15 Sand, salt, and a lump of iron
are less of a burden than a stupid man.

16 A tie-beam fixed firmly into a building
is not shaken loose by an earthquake;
so a mind kept firm by intelligent advice
will not be daunted in a crisis.
17 A mind solidly backed by intelligent thought
is like the stucco that decorates a smooth wall.
18 As a fence set on a hill-top
cannot stand against the wind,
so a mind made timid by foolish fancies
is not proof against any terror.

19 Hurt the eye and tears will flow;
hurt the mind and you will find it sensitive.
20 Throw a stone at the birds and you scare them away;
abuse a friend and you break off your friendship.
21 If you have drawn your sword on a friend,

[*a*] *Some witnesses add* (9) Children well brought up reveal no trace of any humble origin. (10) But those who run riot, haughty and undisciplined, sully the nobility of their parentage.

do not give up hope, there is still a way back.
If you have quarrelled with your friend, 22
never fear, there can still be a reconciliation.
But abuse, scorn, a secret betrayed, a stab in the back—
these will make any friend keep his distance.
Win your neighbour's confidence while he is poor, 23
and you will share the joy of his prosperity;
stand by him in time of trouble,
and you will be his partner when he comes into a fortune.
As furnace-fumes and smoke come before the flame, 24
so insults come before bloodshed.
I will not be afraid to protect my friend 25
nor will I turn my back on him.
If harm should befall me on his account, 26
everyone who hears of it will beware of him.

OH FOR A SENTRY to guard my mouth 27
and a seal of discretion to close my lips,
to keep them from being my downfall,
and to keep my tongue from causing my ruin!
Lord, Father, and Ruler of my life, **23**
do not abandon me to the tongue's control
or allow me to fall on its account.
Oh for wisdom's lash to curb my thoughts 2
and to discipline my mind,
without overlooking my mistakes
or condoning my sins!
Then my mistakes would not multiply 3
nor my sins increase,
humiliating me before my opponents
and giving my enemy cause to gloat.
Lord, Father, and God of my life, 4
do not let me have a supercilious eye.
Protect me from the onslaught of desire; 5
let neither gluttony nor lust take hold of me, 6
nor give me over to the power of shameless passion.

Hear, my sons, how to discipline the mouth, 7
take warning, and you will never be caught out.

8 It is by his own words that the sinner is ensnared;
he is tripped up by his own scurrility and pride.
9 Do not inure your mouth to oaths
or make a habit of naming the Holy One.
10 As a slave constantly under the lash
is never free from weals,
so the man who has oaths and the sacred name for ever on his lips
will never be clear of guilt.
11 A man given to swearing is lawless to the core;
the scourge will never be far from his house.
If he goes back on his word, he must bear the blame;
if he wilfully neglects it, he sins twice over;
if his oath itself was insincere, he cannot be acquitted;
his house will be filled with trouble.

12 There is a kind of speech that is the counterpart of death;
may it never be found among Jacob's descendants!
The pious keep clear of such conduct
and do not wallow in sin.
13 Do not make a habit of coarse, vulgar talk,
or you will be bound to say something sinful.
14 Remember your father and mother
when you take your seat among the great,
or you may forget yourself in their presence
and make a fool of yourself through bad habit;
then you will wish you had never been born,
and curse the day of your birth.
15 A man addicted to scurrilous talk
will never learn better as long as he lives.

16 TWO KINDS OF MEN add sin to sin,
and a third brings retribution on himself.
Hot lust that blazes like a fire
can never be quenched till life is destroyed.
A man whose whole body is given to sensuality
never stops till the fire consumes him.
17 To a seducer every loaf is as sweet as the last,
and he does not weary until he dies.
18 The man who strays from his own bed

says to himself, 'Who can see me?
All around is dark and the walls hide me;
nobody can see me, why need I worry?
The Most High will not take note of my sins.'
The eyes of men are all he fears; 19
he forgets that the eyes of the Lord
are ten thousand times brighter than the sun,
observing every step men take
and penetrating every secret.
Before the universe was created, it was known to him, 20
and so it is since its completion.
This man will pay the penalty in the public street, 21
caught where he least expected it.
So too with the woman who is unfaithful to her husband, 22
presenting him with an heir by a different father:
first, she disobeys the law of the Most High; 23
secondly, she commits an offence against her husband;
thirdly, she has prostituted herself
by bearing bastard children.
She shall be disgraced before the assembly, 24
and the consequences will fall on her children.
Her children will not take root, 25
nor will fruit grow on her branches.
A curse will rest on her memory, 26
and her shame will never be blotted out.
All who survive her will learn 27
that nothing is better than the fear of the Lord
or sweeter than obeying his commandments.[a]

The praise of wisdom

HEAR THE PRAISE of wisdom from her own mouth, **24**
as she speaks with pride among her people,
before the assembly of the Most High 2
and in the presence of the heavenly host:

[*a*] *Some witnesses add* (28) To follow God brings great honour; to win his approval means long life.

3 'I am the word which was spoken by the Most High;
it was I who covered the earth like a mist.
4 My dwelling-place was in high heaven;
my throne was in a pillar of cloud.
5 Alone I made a circuit of the sky
and traversed the depth of the abyss.
6 The waves of the sea, the whole earth,
every people and nation were under my sway.
7 Among them all I looked for a home:
in whose territory was I to settle?
8 Then the Creator of the universe laid a command upon me;
my Creator decreed where I should dwell.
He said, "Make your home in Jacob;
find your heritage in Israel."
9 Before time began he created me,
and I shall remain for ever.
10 In the sacred tent I ministered in his presence,
and so I came to be established in Zion.
11 Thus he settled me in the city he loved
and gave me authority in Jerusalem.
12 I took root among the people whom the Lord had honoured
by choosing them to be his special possession.

13 'There I grew like a cedar of Lebanon,
like a cypress on the slopes of Hermon,
14 like a date-palm at Engedi,
like roses at Jericho.
I grew like a fair olive-tree in the vale,
or like a plane-tree planted beside the water.
15 Like cassia or camel-thorn I was redolent of spices;
I spread my fragrance like choice myrrh,
like galban, aromatic shell, and gum resin;
I was like the smoke of incense in the sacred tent.
16 Like a terebinth I spread out my branches,
laden with honour and grace.
17 I put forth lovely shoots like the vine,
and my blossoms were a harvest of wealth and honour.[a]

[*a*] *Some witnesses add* (18) I give birth to noble love, reverence, knowledge, and holy hope; and I give all these my eternal progeny to God's elect (*probable meaning; Gk. obscure*).

'Come to me, you who desire me, 19
and eat your fill of my fruit.
The memory of me is sweeter than syrup, 20
the possession of me sweeter than honey dripping from the comb.
Whoever feeds on me will be hungry for more, 21
and whoever drinks from me will thirst for more.
To obey me is to be safe from disgrace; 22
those who work in wisdom will not go astray.'

All this is the covenant-book of God Most High, 23
the law which Moses enacted to be the heritage of the assemblies of
Jacob.[a]
He sends out wisdom in full flood like the river Pishon 25
or like the Tigris at the time of firstfruits;
he overflows with understanding like the Euphrates 26
or like Jordan at the time of harvest.
He pours forth instruction like the Nile,[b] 27
like the Gihon at the time of vintage.
No man has ever fully known wisdom; 28
from first to last no one has fathomed her;
for her thoughts are vaster than the ocean 29
and her purpose deeper than the great abyss.

As for me, I was like a canal leading from a river, 30
a watercourse into a pleasure-garden.
I said, 'I will water my garden, 31
drenching its flower-beds';
and at once my canal became a river
and my river a sea.
I will again make discipline shine like the dawn, 32
so that its light may be seen from afar.
I will again pour out doctrine like prophecy 33
and bequeath it to future generations.
Truly, my labour has not been for myself alone 34
but for all seekers of wisdom.

[*a*] *Some witnesses add* (24) Never fail to be strong in the Lord; hold fast to him, so that he may strengthen you; the Lord Almighty is God alone; beside him there is no saviour.
[*b*] *So one Vs.; Gk.* He makes instruction shine like light.

25 THERE ARE THREE SIGHTS which warm my heart[a]
and are beautiful in the eyes of the Lord and of men:
concord among brothers, friendship among neighbours,
and a man and wife who are inseparable.
2 There are three kinds of men who arouse my hatred,
who disgust me by their manner of life:
a poor man who boasts, a rich man who lies,
and an old fool who commits adultery.

3 If you have not gathered wisdom in your youth,
how will you find it when you are old?
4 Sound judgement sits well on grey hairs
and wise advice comes well from older men.
5 Wisdom is fitting in the aged,
and ripe counsel in men of eminence.
6 Long experience is the old man's crown,
and his pride is the fear of the Lord.

7 I can think of nine men I count happy,
and I can tell you of a tenth:
a man who can take delight in his children,
and one who lives to see his enemy's downfall;
8 happy the husband of a sensible wife,
the farmer who does not plough with ox and ass together,[b]
the man whose tongue never betrays him,
and the servant who has never worked for an inferior!
9 Happy the man who has found a friend,[c]
and the speaker who has an attentive audience!
10 How great is the man who finds wisdom!
But no greater than he who fears the Lord.
11 The fear of the Lord excels all other gifts;
to what can we compare the man who has it?[d]

[*a*] *So Vss.; Gk.* which make me beautiful. [*b*] the farmer...together: *so Heb.; Gk. omits.* [*c*] *So Vss.; Gk.* found good sense. [*d*] *Some witnesses add* (12) The fear of the Lord is the source of love for him, and faith is the source of loyalty to him.

Counsels upon social behaviour

ANY WOUND BUT a wound in the heart! 13
Any spite but a woman's!
Any disaster but one caused by hate! 14
Any vengeance but the vengeance of an enemy!
There is no venom[a] worse than a snake's, 15
and no anger worse than an enemy's.

I would sooner share a home with a lion or a snake 16
than keep house with a spiteful wife.
Her spite changes her expression, 17
making her look as surly as a bear.
Her husband goes to a neighbour for his meals 18
and cannot repress a bitter sigh.

There is nothing so bad as a bad wife; 19
may the fate of the wicked overtake her![b]
It is as easy for an old man to climb a sand-dune 20
as for a quiet husband to live with a nagging wife.
Do not be enticed by a woman's beauty 21
or set your heart on possessing her.
If a man is supported by his wife 22
he must expect tantrums, shamelessness, and outrage.
A bad wife brings humiliation, 23
downcast looks, and a wounded heart.
Slack of hand and weak of knee
is the man whose wife fails to make him happy.
Woman is the origin of sin, 24
and it is through her that we all die.
Do not leave a leaky cistern to drip 25
or allow a bad wife to say what she likes.
If she does not accept your control, 26
divorce her and send her away.

[*a*] *Probable meaning, based on one Vs.; Gk.* head. [*b*] *Or* may it fall to her lot to marry a scoundrel!

26 A good wife makes a happy husband;
she doubles the length of his life.
2 A staunch wife is her husband's joy;
he will live out his days in peace.
3 A good wife means a good life;
she is one of the Lord's gifts to those who fear him.
4 Rich or poor, they are light-hearted,
and always have a smile on their faces.

5 Three things there are that alarm me,
and a fourth I am afraid to face:
the scandal of the town, the gathering of a mob,
and calumny—all harder to bear than death;
6 but it is heart-ache and grief when a wife is jealous of a rival,
and everyone alike feels the lash of her tongue.
7 A bad wife is a chafing yoke;
controlling her is like clutching a scorpion.
8 A drunken wife is a great provocation;
she cannot keep her excesses secret.

9 A loose woman betrays herself by her bold looks;
you can tell her by her glance.
10 Keep close watch over a headstrong daughter;
if she finds you off your guard, she will take her chance.
11 Beware of her impudent looks
and do not be surprised if she disobeys you.
12 As a parched traveller with his tongue hanging out
drinks from any spring that offers,
she will open her arms to every embrace,
and her quiver to the arrow.

13 A wife's charm is the delight of her husband,
and her womanly skill puts flesh on his bones.
14 A silent wife is a gift from the Lord;
her restraint is more than money can buy.
15 A modest wife has charm upon charm;
no scales can weigh the worth of her chastity.
16 As beautiful as the sunrise in the Lord's heaven
is a good wife in a well-ordered home.

As bright as the light on the sacred lamp-stand 17
is a beautiful face in the settled prime of life.
Like a golden pillar on a silver base 18
is a shapely leg with a firm foot.[a b]

Two things grieve my heart, 28
and a third excites my anger:
a soldier in distress through poverty,
wise men treated with contempt,
and a man deserting right conduct for wrong—
the Lord will bring him to the scaffold.

How hard it is for a merchant to keep clear of wrong 29
or for a shopkeeper to be innocent of dishonesty!
Many have cheated for gain;[c] **27**
a money-grubber will always turn a blind eye.
As a peg is held fast in the joint between stones, 2
so dishonesty squeezes in between selling and buying.
Unless a man holds resolutely to the fear of the Lord, 3
his house will soon be in ruins.

[*a*] is...foot: *probable meaning; Gk. obscure.* [*b*] *Some witnesses add*

My son, guard your health in the bloom of your youth, 19
and do not waste your vigour on what belongs to others.
Search the whole plain for a fertile plot; 20
sow your own seed, trusting in your pedigree.
Then the children you leave behind 21
will prosper, confident in their parentage.
A woman of the streets counts as mere spittle, 22
a married woman as a mortuary for her lovers.
A godless woman is a good match for a lawless husband, 23
a pious one for a man who fears the Lord.
A brazen woman courts disgrace, 24
but a virtuous one is modest even before her husband.
A wilful woman is a shameless bitch, 25
but a modest one fears the Lord.
A woman who honours her husband is accounted wise by all, 26
but if she despises him, all know her as proud and godless.
A good wife makes a happy husband;
she doubles the length of his life.
A strident, garrulous wife is like a trumpet sounding the charge; 27
in a home like hers a man lives in the tumult of war.

[*c*] *Some witnesses read* for a trifle.

4 Shake a sieve, and the rubbish remains;
start an argument, and discover a man's faults.
5 As the work of a potter is tested in the furnace,
so a man is tried in debate.
6 As the fruit of the tree reveals the skill of its grower,
so the expression of a man's thought reveals his character.
7 Do not praise a man till you hear him in discussion,
for this is the test.

8 If justice is what you seek, you will succeed,
and wear it like a splendid robe.
9 Birds of a feather roost together,
and honesty comes home to those who practise it.
10 A lion lies in wait for its prey,
and so do sins for those who do wrong.

11 The conversation of the pious is constantly wise,
but a fool is as changeable as the moon.
12 Grudge every minute spent among fools,
but linger among the thoughtful.
13 The conversation of fools is repulsive;
they make a joke of unbridled vice.
14 Their cursing and swearing make the hair stand on end;
when such men quarrel, others stop their ears.
15 The quarrels of the proud lead to bloodshed;
their abuse offends the ear.

16 The betrayer of secrets loses his credit
and can never find an intimate friend.
17 Love your friend and keep faith with him,
but if you betray his secrets, keep out of his way;
18 as a man kills his enemy,
so you have killed your neighbour's friendship.
19 As a bird that is allowed to escape your hand,
your neighbour, once lost, will not be caught again.
20 He has gone too far for you to pursue him,
and escaped like a gazelle from a trap.
21 A wound may be bandaged, an insult pardoned,
but the betrayer of secrets has nothing to hope for.

A man who winks is plotting mischief; 22
those who know him will keep their distance.
He speaks sweetly enough to your face 23
and admires whatever you say,
but later he will change his tune
and use your own words to trip you.
There are many things I hate, but him above all; 24
the Lord will hate him too.

Whoever throws a stone up in the air is throwing it at his own head, 25
and a treacherous blow means wounds all round.
Dig a pit and you will fall into it; 26
set a trap and you will be caught by it.
The wrong a man does recoils on him, 27
and he does not know where it has come from.
An arrogant man deals in mockery and insults, 28
but retribution lies in wait for him like a lion.
Those who rejoice at the downfall of good men will be trapped 29
and consumed with pain before they die.

Rage and anger, these also I abhor, 30
but a sinner has them ready at hand.
The vengeful man will face the vengeance of the Lord, **28**
who keeps strict account of his sins.
Forgive your neighbour his wrongdoing; 2
then, when you pray, your sins will be forgiven.
If a man harbours a grudge against another, 3
is he to expect healing from the Lord?
If he has no mercy on his fellow-man, 4
is he still to ask forgiveness for his own sins?
If a mere mortal cherishes rage, 5
where is he to look for pardon?
Think of the end that awaits you, and have done with hate; 6
think of mortality and death, and be true to the commandments;
think of the commandments, and do not be enraged at your neighbour; 7
think of the covenant of the Most High, and overlook faults.

8 To avoid a quarrel is a setback for sin,
for it is a hot temper that kindles quarrels.
9 A sinner sows trouble between friends
and spreads scandal where before there was peace.
10 A fire is kept hot by stoking
and a quarrel by persistence.
A man's rage is in proportion to his strength,
and his anger in proportion to his wealth.
11 A hasty argument kindles a fire,
and a hasty quarrel leads to bloodshed.
12 Blow on a spark to make it glow, or spit on it to put it out;
both results come from the one mouth.

13 Curses on the gossip and the tale-bearer!
For they have been the ruin of many peaceable men.
14 The talk of a third party has wrecked the lives of many
and driven them from country to country;
it has destroyed fortified towns
and demolished the houses of the great.
15 The talk of a third party has brought divorce on staunch wives
and deprived them of all they have laboured for.
16 Whoever pays heed to it will never again find rest
or live in peace of mind.
17 The lash of a whip raises weals,
but the lash of a tongue breaks bones.
18 Many have been killed by the sword,
but not so many as by the tongue.
19 Happy the man who is sheltered from its onslaught,
who has not been exposed to its fury,
who has not borne its yoke,
or been chained with its fetters!
20 For its yoke is of iron,
its fetters of bronze.
21 The death it brings is an evil death;
better the grave than the tongue!
22 But it has no power over the godfearing;
they cannot be burned in its flames.
23 Those who desert the Lord fall victim to it;
among them it will burn like fire and not be quenched.

It will launch itself against them like a lion
and tear them like a leopard.
As you enclose your garden with a thorn hedge, 24
and lock up your silver and gold,
so weigh your words and measure them, 25
and make a door and a bolt for your mouth.
Beware of being tripped by your tongue 26
and falling into the power of a lurking enemy.

A DEVOUT MAN LENDS to his neighbour; **29**
by supporting him he keeps the commandments.
Lend to your neighbour in his time of need; 2
repay your neighbour punctually.
Be as good as your word and keep faith with him, 3
and your needs will always be met.
Many treat a loan as a windfall 4
and bring trouble on those who helped them.
Until he gets a loan, a man kisses his neighbour's hand 5
and talks with bated breath about his money;
but when it is time to repay, he postpones it,
pays back only perfunctory promises,
and alleges that the time is too short.[a]
If he can pay, his creditor will scarcely get back half, 6
and will count himself lucky at that;
if he cannot pay, he has defrauded the other of his money,
and gratuitously made an enemy of him;[b]
he will pay him back in curses and insults
and with shame instead of honour.
Because of such dishonesty many refuse to lend, 7
for fear of being needlessly defrauded.

Nevertheless be patient with the penniless, 8
and do not keep him waiting for your charity;
for the commandment's sake help the poor, 9
and in his need do not send him away empty-handed.
Be ready to lose money for a brother or a friend; 10

[*a*] *Or* that times are hard. [*b*] and...him: *some witnesses read* and the other has won himself an enemy at his own expense.

do not leave it to rust away under a stone.
11 Store up for yourself the treasure which the Most High has commanded,
and it will benefit you more than gold.
12 Let almsgiving be the treasure in your strong-room,
and it will rescue you from every misfortune.
13 It will arm you against the enemy
better than stout shield or strong spear.

14 A good man will stand surety for his neighbour;
only a man who has lost all sense of shame will fail him.
15 If a man stands surety for you, do not forget his kindness,
for he has staked his very self for you.
16 A sinner wastes the property of his surety,
17 and an ungrateful man fails his rescuer.
18 Suretyship has ruined the prosperity of many
and wrecked them like a storm at sea;
it has driven men of influence into exile,
and set them wandering in foreign countries.
19 When a sinner commits himself to suretyship,
his pursuit of gain will involve him in lawsuits.
20 Help your neighbour to the best of your ability,
but beware of becoming too deeply involved.

21 The necessities of life are water, bread, and clothes,
and a home with its decent privacy;
22 better the life of a poor man in his own hut
than a sumptuous banquet in another man's house.
23 Be content with whatever you have,
and do not get a name for living on hospitality.[a]
24 It is a poor life going from house to house,
keeping your mouth shut because you are a visitor.
25 You receive the guests and hand the drinks without being thanked for it,
and into the bargain must listen to words that rankle:
26 'Come here, stranger, and lay the table;
whatever you have there, hand it to me.'
27 'Be off, stranger! Make way for a more important guest;

[*a*] *Reading based on one Vs.; Gk.* and do not hear reproaches from your family.

my brother has come to stay, and I need the guest-room.'
How hard it is for a sensible man to bear 28
criticism from the household or abuse from his creditor!

A MAN WHO LOVES HIS SON will whip him often **30**
so that when he grows up he may be a joy to him.
He who disciplines his son will find profit in him 2
and take pride in him among his acquaintances.
He who gives his son a good education will make his enemy jealous 3
and will boast of him among his friends.
When the father dies, it is as if he were still alive, 4
for he has left a copy of himself behind him.
While he lived he saw and rejoiced, 5
and when he died he had no regrets.
He has left an heir to take vengeance on his enemies 6
and to repay the kindness of his friends.

A man who spoils his son will bandage every wound 7
and will be on tenterhooks at every cry.
An unbroken horse turns out stubborn, 8
and an unchecked son turns out headstrong.
Pamper a boy and he will shock you; 9
play with him and he will grieve you.
Do not share his laughter, for fear of sharing his pain; 10
you will only end by grinding your teeth.
Do not give him freedom while he is young 11
or overlook his errors.
Break him in while he is young, 12
beat him soundly while he is still a child,
or he may grow stubborn and disobey you
and cause you vexation.
Discipline your son and take pains with him 13
or he may offend you by some disgraceful act.

BETTER A POOR MAN who is healthy and fit 14
than a rich man racked by disease.
Health and fitness are better than any gold, 15

and bodily vigour than boundless prosperity.
16 There is no wealth to compare with health of body,
no festivity to equal a joyful heart.
17 Better death than a life of misery,
eternal rest than a long illness.
18 Good things spread before a man without appetite
are like offerings of food placed on a tomb.
19 What use is a sacrifice to an idol
which can neither taste nor smell?
So it is with the man afflicted by the Lord.
20 He gazes at the food before him and sighs
as a eunuch sighs when he embraces a girl.

21 Do not give yourself over to sorrow
or distress yourself deliberately.
22 A merry heart keeps a man alive,
and joy lengthens his span of days.
23 Indulge yourself, take comfort,
and banish sorrow;
for sorrow has been the death of many,
and no advantage ever came of it.
24 Envy and anger shorten a man's life,
and anxiety brings premature old age.
25 A man with a gay heart has a good appetite
and relishes the food he eats.

31 A rich man loses weight by wakeful nights,
when the cares of wealth drive sleep away;
2 sleepless worry keeps him wide awake,
just as serious illness banishes[a] sleep.
3 A rich man toils to amass a fortune,
and when he relaxes he enjoys every luxury.
4 A poor man toils to make a slender living,
and when he relaxes he finds himself in need.

5 Passion for gold can never be right;
the pursuit of money leads a man astray.[b]

[*a*] banishes: *probable meaning, based on Heb.; Gk. obscure.* [*b*] the pursuit...astray: *so Heb.; Gk.* the man who pursues destruction shall have his fill of it.

Many a man has come to ruin for the sake of gold 6
and found disaster staring him in the face.
Gold is a pitfall to those who are infatuated with it, 7
and every fool is caught by it.
Happy the rich man who has remained free of its taint 8
and has not made gold his aim!
Show us that man, and we will congratulate him; 9
he has performed a miracle among his people.
Has anyone ever come through this test unscathed? 10
Then he has good cause to be proud.
Has anyone ever had it in his power to sin and refrained,
or to do wrong and has not done it?
Then he shall be confirmed in his prosperity, 11
and the whole people will hail him as a benefactor.

IF YOU ARE SITTING at a grand table, 12
do not lick your lips and exclaim, 'What a spread!'
Remember, it is a vice to have a greedy eye. 13
There is no greater evil in creation than the eye;
that is why it must shed tears at every turn.
Do not reach for everything you see, 14
or jostle your fellow-guest at the dish;
judge his feelings by your own 15
and always behave considerately.
Eat what is set before you like a gentleman; 16
do not munch and make yourself objectionable.
Be the first to stop for good manners' sake 17
and do not be insatiable, or you will give offence.
If you are dining in a large company, 18
do not reach out your hand before others.
A man of good upbringing is content with little, 19
and he is not short of breath when he goes to bed.
The moderate eater enjoys healthy sleep; 20
he rises early, feeling refreshed.
But sleeplessness, indigestion, and colic
are the lot of the glutton.
If you cannot avoid overeating at a feast, 21
leave the table and find relief by vomiting.

22 Listen to me, my son; do not disregard me,
and in the end my words will come home to you.
Whatever you do, do it shrewdly,
and no illness will come your way.
23 Everyone has a good word for a liberal host,
and the evidence of his generosity is convincing.
24 The whole town grumbles at a mean host,
and there is precise evidence of his meanness.

25 Do not try to prove your manhood by drinking,
for wine has been the ruin of many.
26 As the furnace tests iron when it is being tempered,
so wine tests character when boastful men are wrangling.
27 Wine puts life into a man,
if he drinks it in moderation.
What is life to a man deprived of wine?
Was it not created to warm men's hearts?
28 Wine brings gaiety and high spirits,
if a man knows when to drink and when to stop;
29 but wine in excess makes for bitter feelings
and leads to offence and retaliation.
30 Drunkenness inflames a fool's anger to his own hurt;
it saps his strength and exposes him to injury.
31 At a banquet do not rebuke your fellow-guest
or make him feel small while he is enjoying himself.
This is no time to take up a quarrel with him
or pester him to pay his debts.

32 If they choose you to preside at a feast, do not put on airs;
behave to them as one of themselves.
Look after the others before you sit down;
2 do not take your place until you have discharged all your duties.
Let their enjoyment be your pleasure,
and you will win the prize for good manners.

3 Speak, if you are old—it is your privilege—
but come to the point and do not interrupt the music.
4 Where entertainment is provided, do not keep up a stream of talk;
it is the wrong time to show off your wisdom.

Like a signet of ruby in a gold ring 5
is a concert of music at a banquet.
Like a signet of emerald in a gold setting 6
is tuneful music with good wine.

Speak, if you are young, when the need arises, 7
but twice at the most, and only when asked.
Be brief, say much in few words, 8
like a man who knows and can still hold his tongue.
Among the great do not act as their equal 9
or go on chattering when another is speaking.
As lightning travels ahead of thunder, 10
so popularity goes before a modest man.
Leave in good time and do not be the last to go; 11
go straight home without lingering.
There you may amuse yourself to your heart's content, 12
and run no risk of arrogant talk.
And one thing more: give praise to your Maker, 13
who has filled your cup with his blessings.

THE MAN WHO FEARS THE LORD will accept his discipline, 14
and the diligent will receive his approval.
The genuine student will find satisfaction in the law, 15
but it will prove a stumbling-block to the insincere.
Those who fear the Lord will discover what is right, 16
and will make his decrees[a] shine out like a lamp.
A sinner will not accept criticism; 17
he will find precedents to justify his choice.

A sensible man can always take a hint; 18
but an arrogant heathen does not know the meaning of diffidence.
Never do anything without deliberation, 19
and afterwards you will have no regrets.[b]
Do not travel by a road full of obstacles 20
and stumble along through its boulders.
Do not be careless on a clear road 21

[*a*] *Or* their good conduct. [*b*] you...regrets: *or* do not change your mind.

22 but watch where you are going.[a]
23 Whatever you are doing, rely on yourself,
for this too is a way of keeping the commandments.
24 To rely on the law is to heed its commandments,
and to trust the Lord is to want for nothing.

33 Disaster never comes the way of the man who fears the Lord:
in times of trial he will be rescued again and again.
2 A wise man never hates the law,
but the man who is insincere about it is like a boat in a squall.
3 A sensible man trusts the law
and finds it as reliable as the divine oracle.

4 Prepare what you have to say, if you want a hearing;
marshal your learning and then give your answer.
5 The feelings of a fool turn like a cart-wheel,
and his thoughts spin like an axle.
6 A sarcastic friend is like a stallion
which neighs no matter who is on its back.

7 Why is one day more important than another,
when every day in the year has its light from the sun?
8 It was by the Lord's decision that they were distinguished;
he appointed the various seasons and festivals:
9 some days he made high and holy,
and others he assigned to the common run of days.
10 All men alike come from the ground;
Adam was created out of earth.
11 Yet in his great wisdom the Lord distinguished them
and made them go various ways:
12 some he blessed and lifted high,
some he hallowed and brought near to himself,
some he cursed and humbled
and removed from their place.
13 As clay is in the potter's hands,
to be moulded just as he chooses,
so are men in the hands of their Maker,
to be dealt with as he decides.

[*a*] but...going: *so Heb.; Gk.* and keep an eye on your children.

Good is the opposite of evil, and life of death; 14
yes, and the sinner is the opposite of the godly.
Look at all the works of the Most High: 15
they go in pairs, one the opposite of the other.

I was the last to wake up, 16
I was like a gleaner following the grape-pickers;
by the Lord's blessing I arrived in time
to fill my winepress as full as any of them.
Remember that I did not toil for myself alone, 17
but for all who seek learning.
Listen to me, you dignitaries; 18
leaders of the assembly, give me your attention.

As long as you live, give no one power over yourself— 19
son or wife, brother or friend.
Do not give your property to another,
in case you change your mind and want it back.
As long as you have life and breath, 20
never change places with anyone.
It is better for your children to ask from you 21
than for you to be dependent on them.
Whatever you are doing, keep the upper hand, 22
and allow no blot on your reputation.
Let your life run its full course, 23
and then, at the hour of death, distribute your estate.

Fodder, and stick, and burdens for the donkey; 24
bread, and discipline, and work for the servant!
Make your slave work, if you want rest for yourself; 25
if you leave him idle, he will be looking for his liberty.
The ox is tamed by yoke and harness, 26
the bad servant by racks and tortures.
Put him to work to keep him from being idle, 27
for idleness is a great teacher of mischief.
Set him to work, for that is what he is for, 28
and if he disobeys you, load him with fetters.

29 Do not be too exacting towards anyone
or do anything contrary to justice.
30 If you have a servant, treat him as an equal,
because you bought him with blood.
31 If you have a servant, treat him like a brother;
you will need him as much as you need yourself.
If you ill-treat him and he takes to his heels,
where will you go to look for him?

34 Vain hopes delude the senseless,
and dreams give wings to a fool's fancy.
2 It is like clutching a shadow, or chasing the wind,
to take notice of dreams.
3 What you see in a dream is nothing but a reflection,
like the image of a face in a mirror.
4 Purity cannot come out of filth;
how then can truth issue from falsehood?
5 Divination, omens, and dreams are all futile,
mere fantasies, like those of a woman in labour.
6 Unless they are sent by intervention from the Most High,
pay no attention to them.
7 Dreams have led many astray
and ruined those who built their hopes on them.
8 Such delusions can add nothing to the completeness of the law;
the wisdom spoken by the faithful is complete in itself.

9 An educated man knows many things,
and a man of experience understands what he is talking about.
10 An inexperienced man knows little,
but a man who travels grows in ability.
11 I have seen many things in the course of my travels,
and understand more than I can tell.
12 I have often been in deadly danger
and escaped, thanks to the experience I had gained.

True piety and the mercy of God

THOSE WHO FEAR the Lord shall live, 13
for their trust is in one who can keep them safe.
The man who fears the Lord will have nothing else to fear; 14
he will never be a coward, because his trust is in the Lord.
How blest is the man who fears the Lord! 15
He knows where to look for support.
The Lord keeps watch over those who love him, 16
their strong shield and firm support,
a shelter from scorching wind and midday heat,
a safeguard against stumbles and falls.
He raises the spirits and makes the eyes sparkle, 17
giving health, and life, and blessing.

A sacrifice derived from ill-gotten gains is contaminated, 18
a lawless mockery that cannot win approval.
The Most High is not pleased with the offering of the godless, 19
nor do endless sacrifices win his forgiveness.
To offer a sacrifice from the possessions of the poor 20
is like killing a son before his father's eyes.
Bread is life to the destitute, 21
and it is murder to deprive them of it.
To rob your neighbour of his livelihood is to kill him, 22
and the man who cheats a worker of his wages sheds blood.
When one builds and another pulls down, 23
what have they gained except hard work?
When one prays and another curses, 24
which is the Lord to listen to?
Wash after touching a corpse and then touch it again, 25
and what have you gained by your washing?
So it is with the man who fasts for his sins 26
and goes and does the same again;
who will listen to his prayer?
what has he gained by his penance?

35 Keeping the law is worth many offerings;
to heed the commandments is to sacrifice a thank-offering.
2 A kindness repaid is an offering of flour,
and to give alms is a praise-offering.
3 The way to please the Lord is to renounce evil;
and to renounce wrongdoing is to make atonement.
4 Yet do not appear before the Lord empty-handed;
5 perform these sacrifices because they are commanded.
6 When the just man brings his offering of fat to the altar,
its fragrance rises to the presence of the Most High.
7 The just man's sacrifice is acceptable;
it will never be forgotten.
8 Be generous in your worship of the Lord
and present the firstfruits of your labour in full measure.
9 Give all your gifts cheerfully
and be glad to dedicate your tithe.
10 Give to the Most High as he has given to you,
as generously as you can afford.
11 For the Lord always repays;
you will be repaid seven times over.

12 Do not offer him a bribe, for he will not accept it,
and do not rely on a dishonest sacrifice;
for the Lord is a judge
who knows no partiality.
13 He has no favourites at the poor man's expense,
but listens to his prayer when he is wronged.
14 He never ignores the appeal of the orphan
or the widow when she pours out her complaint.
15 How the tears run down the widow's cheeks,
and her cries accuse the man who caused them!
16 To be accepted a man must serve the Lord as he requires,
and then his prayer will reach the clouds.
17 The prayer of the humble pierces the clouds,
but he is not consoled until it reaches its destination.
He does not desist until the Most High intervenes,
gives the just their rights, and sees justice done.
18 The Lord will not be slow,
neither will he be patient with the wicked,

until he crushes the sinews of the merciless
and sends retribution on the heathen;
until he blots out the insolent, one and all,
and breaks the power of the unjust;
until he gives all men their deserts, 19
judging their actions by their intentions;
until he gives his people their rights
and gladdens them with his mercy.
His mercy is as timely in days of trouble 20
as rain-clouds in days of drought.

HAVE PITY ON US, O LORD, thou God of all; look down, **36**
and send thy terror upon all nations. 2
Raise thy hand against the heathen, 3
and let them see thy power.
As they have seen thy holiness displayed among us, 4
so let us see thy greatness displayed among them.
Let them learn, as we also have learned, 5
that there is no God but only thou, O Lord.
Renew thy signs, repeat thy miracles, 6
win glory for thy hand, for thy right arm.
Rouse thy wrath, pour out thy fury, 7
destroy the adversary, wipe out the enemy.
Remember the day thou hast appointed and hasten it,[a] 8
and give men cause to recount thy wonders.
Let fiery anger devour the survivors, 9
and let the oppressors of thy people meet their doom.
Crush the heads of hostile princes, 10
who say, 'There is no one to match us.'
Gather all the tribes of Jacob, 11
and grant them their inheritance,[b] as thou didst long ago.
Have pity, O Lord, on the people called by thy name, 12
Israel, whom thou hast named thy first-born.
Show mercy to the city of thy sanctuary, 13
Jerusalem, the city of thy rest.
Fill Zion with the praise of thy triumph; 14

[*a*] Remember...it: *some witnesses read* Hasten the day and remember thy oath.
[*b*] *Or* and take them to be thy own.

fill thy people with thy glory.
15 Thou didst create them at the beginning; acknowledge them now
and fulfil the prophecies spoken in thy name.
16 Reward those who wait for thee;
prove thy prophets trustworthy.
17 Listen, O Lord, to the prayer of thy servants,
who claim Aaron's blessing upon thy people.
Let all who live on earth acknowledge
that thou art the Lord, the eternal God.

Man in society

18 ALL IS FOOD for the stomach,
but one food is better than another.
19 As the palate identifies game by its taste,
so the discerning mind detects lies.
20 A warped mind makes trouble,
but a man of experience can pay it back.

21 A woman will take any man for husband,
but a man may prefer one girl to another.
22 A woman's beauty makes a man happy,
and there is nothing he desires more.
23 If she has a kind and gentle tongue,
then her husband is luckier than most men.
24 The man who wins a wife has the beginnings of a fortune,
a helper to match his needs and a pillar to support him.
25 Where there is no hedge, property is plundered;
and where there is no wife, the wanderer sighs for a home.
26 Does anyone trust a roving bandit
who swoops on town after town?
No more will they trust a homeless man
who lodges wherever night overtakes him.

37 Every friend says, 'I too am your friend';
but some are friends in name only.
2 What a mortal grief it is
when a dear friend turns into an enemy!

Oh this propensity to evil, how did it creep in 3
to cover the earth with treachery?
A friend may be all smiles when you are happy, 4
but turn against you when trouble comes.
Another shares your toil for the sake of a meal, 5
and yet may protect you against an enemy.
Never forget a friend 6
or neglect him when prosperity comes your way.

Every counsellor says his own advice is best, 7
but some have their own advantage in view.
Beware of the man who offers advice, 8
and find out beforehand where his interest lies.
His advice will be weighted in his own favour
and may tip the scales against you.
He may say, 'Your road is clear', 9
and stand aside to see what happens.
Do not consult a man who is suspicious of you 10
or reveal your intentions to those who envy you.
Never consult a woman about her rival 11
or a coward about war,
a merchant about a bargain
or a buyer about a sale,
a skinflint about gratitude
or a hard-hearted man about a kind action,
an idler about work of any sort,
a casual labourer about finishing the job,
or a lazy servant about an exacting task—
do not turn to them for any advice.
Rely rather on a godfearing man 12
whom you know to be a keeper of the commandments,
whose interests are like your own,
who will sympathize if you have a setback.
But also trust your own judgement, 13
for it is your most reliable counsellor.
A man's own mind has sometimes a way of telling him more 14
than seven watchmen posted high on a tower.
But above all pray to the Most High 15
to keep you on the straight road of truth.

16 Every undertaking begins in discussion,
and consultation precedes every action.
17 Here you can trace the mind's variety.
18 Four kinds of destiny are offered to men,
good and evil, life and death;
and always it is the tongue that decides the issue.
19 A man may be clever enough to teach others
and yet be useless to himself.
20 A brilliant speaker may make enemies
and end by dying of hunger,
21 if the Lord has withheld the gift of popular appeal,
because he is devoid of wisdom.
22 If a man is wise in the conduct of his own life,
his good sense can be trusted when he speaks.
23 If a man is wise and instructs his people,
then his good sense can be trusted.
24 A wise man will have praise heaped on him,
and all who see him will count him happy.
25 The days of a man's life can be numbered,
but the days of Israel are countless.
26 A wise man will possess the confidence of his people,
and his name will live for ever.

27 MY SON, TEST YOURSELF all your life long;
take note of what is bad for you and do not indulge in it.
28 For not everything is good for everyone;
we do not all enjoy the same things.
29 Do not be greedy for every delicacy
or eat without restraint.
30 For illness is a sure result of overeating,
and gluttony is next door to colic.
31 Gluttony has been the death of many;
be on your guard and prolong your life.

38 Honour the doctor for his services,
for the Lord created him.
2 His skill comes from the Most High,
and he is rewarded by kings.

The doctor's knowledge gives him high standing 3
and wins him the admiration of the great.
The Lord has created medicines from the earth, 4
and a sensible man will not disparage them.
Was it not a tree that sweetened water 5
and so disclosed its properties[a]?
The Lord has imparted knowledge to men, 6
that by their use of his marvels he may win praise;
by using them the doctor[b] relieves pain 7
and from them the pharmacist makes up his mixture. 8
There is no end to the works of the Lord,
who spreads health over the whole world.

My son, if you have an illness, do not neglect it, 9
but pray to the Lord, and he will heal you.
Renounce your faults, amend your ways, 10
and cleanse your heart from all sin.
Bring a savoury offering and bring flour for a token 11
and pour oil on the sacrifice; be as generous as you can.[c]
Then call in the doctor, for the Lord created him; 12
do not let him leave you, for you need him.
There may come a time when your recovery is in their hands; 13
then they too will pray to the Lord 14
to give them success in relieving pain
and finding a cure to save their patient's life.
When a man has sinned against his Maker, 15
let him put himself in the doctor's hands.

My son, shed tears for the dead; 16
raise a lament for your grievous loss.
Shroud his body with proper ceremony,
and do not neglect his burial.
With bitter weeping and passionate lament 17
make your mourning worthy of him.
Mourn for a few days as propriety demands,
and then take comfort for your grief.
For grief may lead to death, 18

[*a*] *Or* and revealed the power of the Lord. [*b*] the doctor: *so Heb.; Gk.* he heals and...
[*c*] be...can: *so Heb.; Gk. obscure.*

and a sorrowful heart saps the strength.
19 When a man is taken away, suffering is over,
but to live on in poverty goes against the grain.
20 Do not abandon yourself to grief;
put it from you and think of your own end.
21 Never forget! there is no return;
you cannot help him and can only injure yourself.
22 Remember that his fate will also be yours:
'Mine today and yours tomorrow.'
23 When the dead is at rest, let his memory rest too;
take comfort as soon as he has breathed his last.

24 A SCHOLAR'S WISDOM COMES of ample leisure;
if a man is to be wise he must be relieved of other tasks.
25 How can a man become wise who guides the plough,
whose pride is in wielding his goad,
who is absorbed in the task of driving oxen,
and talks only about cattle?
26 He concentrates on ploughing his furrows,
and works late to give the heifers their fodder.
27 So it is with every craftsman or designer
who works by night as well as by day,
such as those who make engravings on signets,
and patiently vary the design;
they concentrate on making an exact representation,
and sit up late to finish their task.
28 So it is with the smith, sitting by his anvil,
intent on his iron-work.
The smoke of the fire shrivels his flesh,
as he wrestles in the heat of the furnace.
The hammer rings again and again in his ears,
and his eyes are on the pattern he is copying.
He concentrates on completing the task,
and stays up late to give it a perfect finish.
29 So it is with the potter, sitting at his work,
turning the wheel with his feet,
always engrossed in the task
of making up his tally;

he moulds the clay with his arm, 30
crouching forward to apply his strength.
He concentrates on finishing the glazing,
and stays awake to clean out the furnace.

All these rely on their hands, 31
and each is skilful at his own craft.
Without them a city would have no inhabitants; 32
no settlers or travellers would come to it.
Yet they are not in demand at public discussions 33
or prominent in the assembly.
They do not sit on the judge's bench
or understand the decisions of the courts.
They cannot expound moral or legal principles
and are not ready with maxims.
But they maintain the fabric of this world, 34
and their prayers are about their daily work.[a]

How different it is with the man who devotes himself **39**
to studying the law of the Most High,
who investigates all the wisdom of the past,
and spends his time studying the prophecies!
He preserves the sayings of famous men 2
and penetrates the intricacies of parables.
He investigates the hidden meaning of proverbs 3
and knows his way among riddles.
The great avail themselves of his services, 4
and he is seen in the presence of rulers.
He travels in foreign countries
and learns at first hand the good or evil of man's lot.
He makes a point of rising early 5
to pray to the Lord, his Maker,
and prays aloud to the Most High,
asking pardon for his sins.
If it is the will of the great Lord, 6
he will be filled with a spirit of intelligence;
then he will pour forth wise sayings of his own
and give thanks to the Lord in prayer.

[*a*] *Or* and their daily work is their prayer.

7 He will have sound advice and knowledge to offer,
and his thoughts will dwell on the mysteries he has studied.
8 He will disclose what he has learnt from his own education,
and will take pride in the law of the Lord's covenant.
9 Many will praise his intelligence;
it will never sink into oblivion.
The memory of him will not die
but will live on from generation to generation;
10 the nations will talk of his wisdom,
and his praises will be sung in the assembly.
11 If he lives long, he will leave a name in a thousand,
and if he goes to his rest, his reputation is secure.[a]

12 I HAVE STILL MORE in my mind to express;
I am full like the moon at mid-month.
13 Listen to me, my devout sons, and blossom
like a rose planted by a stream.
14 Spread your fragrance like incense,
and bloom like a lily.
Scatter your fragrance; lift your voices in song,
praising the Lord for all his works.
15 Ascribe majesty to his name
and give thanks to him with praise,
with songs on your lips, and with harps;
let these be your words of thanksgiving:
16 'All that the Lord has made is very good;
all that he commands will happen in due time.'
17 No one should ask, 'What is this?' or 'Why is that?'
At the proper time all such questions will be answered.
When he spoke the water stood up like a heap,
and his word created reservoirs for it.
18 When he commands, his purpose is fulfilled,
and no one can thwart his saving power.
19 He sees the deeds of all mankind;
there is no hiding from his gaze.
20 From the beginning to the end of time he keeps watch,
and nothing is too marvellous for him.

[*a*] his reputation is secure: *possible reading; Gk. obscure.*

No one should ask, 'What is this?' or 'Why is that?' 21
Everything has been created for its own purpose.
His blessing is like a river in flood 22
which inundates the parched ground.
But the doom he assigns the heathen is his wrath, 23
as when he turned a watered plain into a salt desert.
For the devout his paths are straight, 24
but full of pitfalls for the wicked.
From the beginning good things were created for the good, 25
and evils for sinners.
The chief necessities of human life 26
are water, fire, iron, and salt,
flour, honey, and milk,
the juice of the grape, oil, and clothing.
All these are good for the godfearing, 27
but turn to evil for sinners.

There are winds created to be agents of retribution, 28
with great whips to give play to their fury;
on the day of reckoning, they exert their force
and give full vent to the anger of their Maker.
Fire and hail, famine and deadly disease, 29
all these were created for retribution;
beasts of prey, scorpions and vipers, 30
and the avenging sword that destroys the wicked.
They delight in carrying out his orders, 31
always standing ready for his service on the earth;
and when their time comes, they never disobey.

I have been convinced of all this from the beginning; 32
I have thought it over and left it in writing:
all the works of the Lord are good, 33
and he supplies every need as it occurs.
No one should say, 'This is less good than that', 34
for all things prove good at their proper time.
Come then, sing with heart and voice, 35
and praise the name of the Lord.

40 HARD WORK IS THE LOT of every man,
and a heavy yoke is laid on the sons of Adam,
from the day when they come from their mothers' womb
until the day of their return to the mother of all;
2 troubled thoughts and fears are theirs,
and anxious expectation of the day of their death.
3 Whether a man sits in royal splendour on a throne
or grovels in dust and ashes,
4 whether he wears the purple and a crown
or is clothed in sackcloth,
5 his life is nothing but anger and jealousy, worry and perplexity,
fear of death, and guilt, and rivalry.
Even when he goes to bed at night,
sleep only brings to mind the same things in a new form.
6 His rest is little or nothing;
he begins to struggle as hard in his sleep as in the day.[a]
Disturbed by nightmares,
he fancies himself a fugitive from the battlefield;
7 and at the moment when he reaches safety, he wakes up,
astonished to find his fears groundless.

8 To all living creatures, man and beast—
and seven times over to sinners—
9 come death and bloodshed, quarrel and sword,
disaster, famine, ruin, and plague.
10 All these were created for the wicked,
and on their account the flood happened.
11 All that is of earth returns to earth again,
and all that is of water finds its way back to the sea.

12 Bribery and injustice will all vanish,
but good faith will last for ever.
13 The wealth of the wicked will dry up like a torrent
and die away like a great roll of thunder in a storm.
14 As a generous man will have cause for rejoicing,
so law-breakers will come to utter ruin.
15 The shoots of an impious stock put out few branches;
their tainted roots are planted on sheer rock.

[*a*] he begins...day: *possible meaning; Gk. obscure.*

The rush that grows on every river-bank 16
is pulled up before any other grass,
but kindness is like a luxuriant garden, 17
and almsgiving lasts for ever.

To be employed and to be one's own master, both are sweet, 18
but it is better still to find a treasure.
Offspring and the founding of a city perpetuate a man's name, 19
but better still is a perfect wife.
Wine and music gladden the heart, 20
but better still is the love of wisdom.
Flute and harp make pleasant melody, 21
but better still is a pleasant voice.
A man likes to see grace and beauty, 22
but better still the green shoots in a cornfield.
A friend or companion is always welcome, 23
but better still to be man and wife.
Brothers and helpers are a stand-by in time of trouble, 24
but better still is almsgiving.
Gold and silver make a man stand firm, 25
but better still is good advice.
Wealth and strength make for confidence, 26
but better still is the fear of the Lord.
To fear the Lord is to lack nothing
and never to be in need of support.
The fear of the Lord is like a luxuriant garden; 27
it shelters a man better than any riches.

My son, do not live the life of a beggar; 28
it is better to die than to beg.
When a man starts looking to another man's table, 29
his existence is not worth calling life.
It is demoralizing to live on another man's food,
and a wise, well-disciplined man will guard against it.
When a man has lost all shame, he speaks as if begging were sweet, 30
but inside him there is a blazing fire.

Death, how bitter is the thought of you **41**
to a man living at ease among his possessions,

free from anxiety, prosperous in all things,
and still vigorous enough to enjoy a good meal!
2 Death, how welcome is your sentence
to a destitute man whose strength is failing,
worn down by age and endless anxiety,
resentful and at the end of his patience!
3 Do not be afraid of death's summons;
remember those who have gone before you, and those who will come after.
4 This is the Lord's decree for all living men;
why try to argue with the will of the Most High?
Whether life lasts ten years, or a hundred, or a thousand,
there will be no questions asked in the grave.

5 What a loathsome brood are the children of sinners,
brought up in haunts of vice!
6 Their inheritance dwindles away,
and their descendants suffer a lasting disgrace.
7 A godless father is blamed by his children
for the disgrace they endure on his account.
8 Woe to you, godless men
who have abandoned the law of God Most High!
9 When you are born, you are born to a curse,
and when you die, a curse is your lot.
10 Whatever comes from earth returns to earth;
so too the godless go from curse to ruin.
11 Men grieve over the death of the body,
but sinners have no good name to survive them.
12 Take thought for your name, for it will outlive you
longer than a thousand hoards of gold.
13 The days of a good life are numbered,
but a good name lasts for ever.

14 MY CHILDREN, BE TRUE to your training and live in peace.
Wisdom concealed and treasure hidden—
what is the use of either?
15 Better a man who hides his folly
than one who hides his wisdom!

Show deference then to my teaching: 16
shame is not always to be encouraged,
or given unqualified approval in all circumstances.
Be ashamed to be found guilty of fornication by your parents, 17
or of lies by a ruler or prince;
of crime by a judge or magistrate, 18
or of a breach of the law by the assembly and people;
of dishonesty by a partner or friend,
or of theft by the neighbourhood; 19
be ashamed before the truth of God and his covenant.
Be ashamed of bad manners at table,
of giving or receiving with a sneer,
of refusing to return a greeting, 20
or of ogling a prostitute.
Be ashamed of turning away a relative, 21
of robbing someone of his rightful share,
or of eyeing another man's wife.
Be ashamed of meddling with his slave-girl, 22
and keep away from her bed.
Be ashamed of reproaching your friends,
or following up your charity with a lecture.
Be ashamed of repeating what you have heard 23
and of betraying a secret.
Then you will be showing a proper shame 24
and will be popular with everyone.

But at other times you must not be ashamed, **42**
or you will do wrong out of deference to others.
Do not be ashamed of the law and covenant of the Most High, 2
or of justice, for fear you acquit the guilty;
of settling accounts with a partner or a travelling-companion, 3
or of sharing an inheritance with the other heirs;
of using accurate weights and measures, 4
or of business dealings, large or small,
and making a profit out of trade; 5
of frequent disciplining of children,
or of drawing blood from the back of a worthless servant.
If your wife is untrustworthy, or where many hands are at work, 6
it is well to keep things under lock and key.

7 When you make a deposit, see that it is counted and weighed,
and when you give or receive, have it all in writing.
8 Do not be ashamed to correct the ignorant and foolish,
or a greybeard guilty of fornication.
Then you will be showing your sound upbringing
and will win everyone's approval.

9 A daughter is a secret anxiety to her father,
and the worry of her keeps him awake at night;
when she is young, for fear she may grow too old to marry,
and when she is married, for fear she may lose her husband's love;
10 when she is a virgin, for fear she may be seduced
and become pregnant in her father's house,
when she has a husband, for fear she may misbehave,
and after marriage, for fear she may be barren.
11 Keep close watch over a headstrong daughter,
or she may give your enemies cause to gloat,
making you the talk of the town and a byword[a] among the people,
and shaming you in the eyes of the world.
12 Do not let her display her beauty to any man,
or gossip in the women's quarters.[b]
13 For out of clothes comes the moth,
and out of woman comes woman's wickedness.
14 Better a man's wickedness than a woman's goodness;
it is woman who brings shame and disgrace.

The wonders of creation

15 NOW I WILL CALL to mind the works of the Lord
and describe what I have seen;
by the words of the Lord his works are made.
16 As the sun in its brilliance looks down on everything,
so the glory of the Lord fills his creation.
17 Even to his angels the Lord has not given the power
to tell the full story of his marvels,
which the Lord Almighty has established

[*a*] a byword: *so Heb.; Gk. obscure.* [*b*] Do not...quarters: *so Heb.; Gk. obscure.*

so that the universe may stand firm in his glory.
He fathoms the abyss and the heart of man, 18
he is versed in their intricate secrets;
for the Lord possesses all knowledge
and observes the signs of all time.
He discloses the past and the future, 19
and uncovers the traces of the world's mysteries.
No thought escapes his notice, 20
and not a word is hidden from him.
He has set in order the masterpieces of his wisdom, 21
he who is from eternity to eternity;
nothing can be added, nothing taken away,
and he needs no one to give him advice.
How beautiful is all that he has made, 22
down to the smallest spark that can be seen!
His works endure, all of them active for ever 23
and all responsive to their various purposes.
All things go in pairs, one the opposite of the other; 24
he has made nothing incomplete.
One thing supplements the virtues of another. 25
Who could ever contemplate his glory enough?

What a masterpiece is the clear vault of the sky! **43**
How glorious is the spectacle of the heavens!
The sun comes into view proclaiming as it rises 2
how marvellous a thing it is, made by the Most High.
At noon it parches the earth, 3
and no one can endure its blazing heat.
The stoker of a furnace works in the heat,
but three times as hot is the sun scorching the hills.
It breathes out fiery vapours,
and its glare blinds the eyes.
Great is the Lord who made it, 5
whose word speeds it on its course.

He made the moon also to serve in its turn, 6
a perpetual sign to mark the divisions of time.
From the moon, feast-days are reckoned; 7
it is a light that wanes as it completes its course.

8 The moon gives its name to the month;
it waxes marvellously as its phases change,
a beacon to the armies of heaven,
shining in the vault of the sky.

9 The brilliant stars are the beauty of the sky,
a glittering array in the heights of the Lord.
10 At the command of the Holy One they stand in their appointed place;
they never default at their post.

11 Look at the rainbow and praise its Maker;
it shines with a supreme beauty,
12 rounding the sky with its gleaming arc,
a bow bent by the hands of the Most High.

13 His command speeds the snow-storm
and sends the swift lightning to execute his sentence.
14 To that end the storehouses are opened,
and the clouds fly out like birds.
15 By his mighty power the clouds are piled up
and the hailstones broken small.
16–17 The crash of his thunder makes the earth writhe,
and, when he appears, an earthquake shakes the hills.
At his will the south wind blows,
the squall from the north and the hurricane.
He scatters the snow-flakes like birds alighting;
they settle like a swarm of locusts.
18 The eye is dazzled by their beautiful whiteness,
and as they fall the mind is entranced.
19 He spreads frost on the earth like salt,
and icicles form like pointed stakes.
20 A cold blast from the north,
and ice grows hard on the water,
settling on every pool,
as though the water were putting on a breastplate.
21 He consumes the hills, scorches the wilderness,
and withers the grass like fire.
22 Cloudy weather quickly puts all to rights,
and dew brings welcome relief after heat.

By the power of his thought he tamed the deep 23
and planted it with islands.
Those who sail the sea tell stories of its dangers, 24
which astonish all who hear them;
in it are strange and wonderful creatures, 25
all kinds of living things and huge sea-monsters.
By his own action he achieves his end, 26
and by his word all things are held together.

However much we say, we cannot exhaust our theme; 27
to put it in a word: he is all.
Where can we find the skill to sing his praises? 28
For he is greater than all his works.
The Lord is terrible and very great, 29
and marvellous is his power.
Honour the Lord to the best of your ability, 30
and he will still be high above all praise.
Summon all your strength to declare his greatness,
and be untiring, for the most you can do will fall short.
Has anyone ever seen him, to be able to describe him? 31
Can anyone praise him as he truly is?
We have seen but a small part of his works, 32
and there remain many mysteries greater still.
The Lord has made everything 33
and has given wisdom to the godly.

Heroes of Israel's past

LET US NOW SING the praises of famous men, **44**
the heroes of our nation's history,
through whom the Lord established his renown, 2
and revealed his majesty in each succeeding age.
Some held sway over kingdoms 3
and made themselves a name by their exploits.
Others were sage counsellors,
who spoke out with prophetic power.
Some led the people by their counsels 4

and by their knowledge of the nation's law;
out of their fund of wisdom they gave instruction.
5 Some were composers of music or writers of poetry.
6 Others were endowed with wealth and strength,
living peacefully in their homes.
7 All these won fame in their own generation
and were the pride of their times.
8 Some there are who have left a name behind them
to be commemorated in story.
9 There are others who are unremembered;
they are dead, and it is as though they had never existed,
as though they had never been born
or left children to succeed them.
10 Not so our forefathers; they were men of loyalty,
whose good deeds have never been forgotten.
11 Their prosperity is handed on to their descendants,
and their inheritance to future generations.[a]
12 Thanks to them their children are within the covenants—
the whole race of their descendants.
13 Their line will endure for all time,
and their fame will never be blotted out.
14 Their bodies are buried in peace,
but their name lives for ever.
15 Nations will recount their wisdom,
and God's people will sing their praises.

16 Enoch pleased the Lord and was carried off to heaven,
an example of repentance to future generations.
17 Noah was found perfect and righteous,
and thus he made amends in the time of retribution;
therefore a remnant survived on the earth,
when the flood came.
18 A perpetual covenant was established with him,
that never again should all life be swept away by a flood.

19 Great Abraham was the father of many nations;
no one has ever been found to equal him in fame.
20 He kept the law of the Most High;

[*a*] Their prosperity...generations: *probable meaning, based on other Vss.; Gk. obscure.*

he entered into covenant with him,
setting upon his body the mark of the covenant;
and, when he was tested, he proved faithful.
Therefore the Lord swore an oath to him, 21
that nations should find blessing through his descendants,
that his family should be countless as the dust of the earth
and be raised as high as the stars,
and that their possessions should reach from sea to sea,
from the Great River to the ends of the earth.

To Isaac he made the same promise 22
for the sake of his father Abraham,
a blessing for all mankind and a covenant;
and so he transmitted them to Jacob. 23
He confirmed him in the blessings he had received
and gave him the land he was to inherit,
dividing it into portions,
which he allotted to the twelve tribes.

From Jacob's stock the Lord raised up a loyal servant, **45**
who won the approval of all mankind,
beloved by God and men,
Moses of blessed memory.
The Lord made him equal in glory to the angels 2
and gave him power to strike terror into his enemies.
At his request he put an end to the portents, 3
and enhanced his reputation with kings.
He gave him commandments for his people
and showed him a vision of his own glory.
For his loyalty and humility he consecrated him, 4
choosing him out of all mankind.
He let him hear his voice 5
and led him into the dark cloud.
Face to face, he gave him the commandments,
a law that brings life and knowledge,
so that he might teach Jacob the covenant
and Israel his decrees.

6 He raised to a like holy office
Moses' brother Aaron from the tribe of Levi.
7 He made a perpetual covenant with him,
conferring on him the priesthood of the nation.
He honoured him with splendid ornaments
and clothed him in gorgeous vestments.
8 He robed him in perfect splendour
and armed him with the emblems of power,
the breeches, the mantle, and the tunic.
9 Round his robe he placed pomegranates
and a circle of many golden bells,
to make music as he walked,
ringing aloud throughout the temple
as a reminder to his people.
10 He gave him the sacred vestment adorned by an embroiderer
with gold and violet and purple;
the oracle of judgement with the tokens of truth;[a]
11 the scarlet thread spun with a craftsman's art;
the precious stones, engraved like seals,
and placed by the jeweller in a gold setting,
with inscriptions to serve as reminders,
one for each of the tribes of Israel;
12 the gold crown upon his turban,
engraved like a seal with 'Holy to the Lord'.[b]
What rich adornments to feast the eyes!
What a miracle of art! What a proud honour!
13 Before him no such splendour existed,
and no one outside his family has ever put them on,
no one except his sons
and his descendants in perpetuity.
14 Twice every day without fail
they present his sacrifice of a whole-offering.

15 It was Moses who ordained him
and anointed him with sacred oil,
in token of the perpetual covenant made with him

[*a*] the oracle...truth: *or* the breast-piece of judgement with the Urim and Thummim (*Exodus 28. 30*). [*b*] *Compare Exodus 28. 36; literally* a seal of holiness.

and with his descendants as long as the heavens endure,
that he should be the Lord's minister in the priestly office
and bless his people in his name.
He chose him out of all mankind 16
to bring offerings to the Lord,
incense and the fragrance of memorial sacrifice,
to make atonement for the people.
He entrusted to him his commandments, 17
with authority to pronounce legal decisions,
to teach Jacob his decrees
and enlighten Israel about his law.

Upstarts grew jealous of him 18
and conspired against him in the desert,
Dathan and Abiram with their supporters
and Korah's band in their violent anger.
The Lord saw and refused his sanction; 19
he destroyed them in the heat of his wrath,
and worked a miracle against them
by consuming them in a blazing fire.
But he added fresh honours to Aaron 20
and gave him a special privilege,
allotting to the priests the choicest firstfruits,
to ensure that they above all should have bread in plenty.
For they eat the sacrifices of the Lord, 21
which he gave to Aaron and his descendants.
But he was to have no inheritance in the land of his people, 22
no portion allotted to him among them;
for the Lord himself is his portion, his inheritance.

Phinehas son of Eleazar ranks third in renown 23
for being zealous in his reverence for the Lord,
and for standing firm with noble courage,
when the people were in revolt;
by so doing he made atonement for Israel.
Therefore a covenant was established with him, 24
assuring him command of the sanctuary and of the nation,
conferring on him and his descendants
the high-priesthood for ever.

25 Just as a covenant was made with David son of Jesse of the tribe of Judah,
that the royal succession should always pass from father to son,
so the succession was to pass from Aaron to his descendants.
26 May the Lord grant you a wise mind
to judge his people with justice,
so that their prosperity may never vanish
and their glory may be handed on to future generations!

46 Joshua son of Nun was a mighty warrior,
who succeeded Moses in the prophetic office.
He lived up to his name
as a great liberator of the Lord's chosen people,
able to take reprisals on the enemies who attacked them,
and to put Israel in possession of their territory.
2 How glorious he was when he raised his hand
and brandished his sword against cities!
3 Never before had a man made such a stand,
for he was fighting the Lord's battles.
4 Was it not through him that the sun stood still
and made one day as long as two?
5 He called on the Most High, the Mighty One,
when the enemy was pressing him on every side,
and the great Lord answered his prayer
6 with a violent storm of hail.
He overwhelmed that nation in battle
and crushed his assailants as they fled down the pass,
to make the nations recognize his strength in arms
and teach them that he fought under the very eyes of the Lord,
for he followed the lead of the Mighty One.

7 In the time of Moses he had proved his loyalty,
he and Caleb son of Jephunneh:
they stood their ground against the whole assembly,
restrained the people from sin,
and silenced their wicked grumbling.
8 Out of six hundred thousand warriors
these two alone escaped with their lives
to enter the land and take possession of it,

the land flowing with milk and honey.
The Lord gave Caleb strength, 9
which still remained with him in his old age,
so that he was able to invade the hill-country
and win possession of it for his descendants.
So all Israel could see 10
how good it is to be a loyal follower of the Lord.

Then there are the judges, name after famous name, 11
all of them men who rejected idolatry
and never rebelled against the Lord:
blessings be on their memory!
May their bones send forth new life from the ground where they lie! 12
May the fame of the honoured dead be matched by their sons!

Samuel was beloved by his Lord; 13
as prophet of the Lord he established the monarchy
and anointed rulers over his people.
As long as he dispensed justice according to the law of the Lord, 14
the Lord kept watch over Jacob.
Because of his fidelity he proved to be an accurate prophet; 15
the truth of his vision was shown by his utterances.
He called on the Mighty Lord, 16
when enemies were pressing him on every side,
and offered a sucking-lamb in sacrifice;
then the Lord thundered from heaven, 17
making his voice heard in a mighty crash,
and routed the leaders of the enemy,[a] 18
all the rulers of the Philistines.
Before the time came for his eternal sleep, 19
Samuel called the Lord and his anointed to witness:
'I never took any man's property,
not so much as a pair of shoes';
and no man accused him.
Even after he had gone to his rest he prophesied 20
and foretold to the king his death,
lifting up his voice in prophecy from the ground
to wipe out the people's guilt.

[*a*] the enemy: *so Heb.; Gk.* Tyre.

47 After him Nathan came forward
to be prophet in the reign of David.
2 As the fat is separated from the sacrifice,
so David was chosen out of all Israel.
3 He played with lions as though they were kids,
with bears as though they were lambs.
4 In his youth did he not kill a giant
and restore the honour of his people,
when he whirled his sling with its stone
and brought down boastful Goliath?
5 For he called on the Lord Most High,
who gave strength to his right arm
to strike down that mighty warrior
and win victory for his people.
6 So they hailed him as conqueror of tens of thousands,
they sang his praises for the blessings bestowed by the Lord,
when he was offered the royal diadem.
7 For he subdued their enemies on every side
and crushed the resistance of the Philistines,
whose power remains broken to this day.
8 In all he did he gave thanks,
ascribing glory to the Holy One, the Most High.
With his whole heart he sang hymns of praise,
to show his love for his Maker.
9 He appointed musicians to stand before the altar
and sing sweet music to the harp.
10 So he gave splendour to the festivals
and fixed for all time the round of sacred seasons,
when men praise the holy name of the Lord
and the sanctuary resounds from morning to night.
11 The Lord pardoned his sins
and endowed him with great power for ever:
he gave him a covenant of kingship
and the glorious throne of Israel.

12 He was succeeded by a wise son, Solomon,
who, thanks to his father David, lived in spacious days.
13 He reigned in an age of peace,
because God made all his frontiers quiet,

and so he was able to build a house in God's honour,
a sanctuary founded to last for ever.
How wise you were, Solomon, in your youth! 14
Your mind was like a brimming river;
your influence spread throughout the world, 15
which you filled with your proverbs and riddles.
Your fame reached to distant islands, 16
and you were beloved for your peaceful reign.
Your songs, your proverbs, your parables, 17
and the answers you gave were the admiration of the world.
In the name of the Lord God, 18
who is known as the God of Israel,
you amassed gold and silver
as though they were tin and lead.
But you took women to lie at your side 19
and gave yourself up to their control.
You stained your reputation 20
and tainted your line.
You brought retribution on your children
and made them grieve over your folly,
because it divided the sovereignty 21
and produced out of Ephraim a rebel kingdom.
But the Lord never ceases to be merciful; 22
he does not destroy what he himself has made;
he will not wipe out the children of his chosen servant
or cut short the line of the man who has loved him.
So he granted a remnant to Jacob
and let one scion of David survive.

So Solomon died like his forefathers 23
and left one of his sons to succeed him,
a man of weak intelligence, the fool of the nation,
Rehoboam, whose policy drove the people to revolt.
Then Jeroboam son of Nebat led Israel into sin
and started Ephraim on its wicked course.
Their sins increased beyond measure, 24
until they were driven into exile from their native land;
for they had explored every kind of wickedness, 25
until retribution came upon them.

48 Then Elijah appeared, a prophet like fire,
whose word flamed like a torch.
2 He brought famine upon them,
and his zeal made their numbers small.
3 By the word of the Lord he shut up the sky
and three times called down fire.
4 How glorious you were, Elijah, in your miracles!
Who else can boast such deeds?
5 You raised a corpse from death
and from the grave, by the word of the Most High.
6 You sent kings and famous men
from their sick-beds down to their deaths.
7 You heard a denunciation at Sinai,
a sentence of doom at Horeb.
8 So you anointed kings for vengeance,
and prophets to succeed you.
9 You were taken up to heaven in a fiery whirlwind,
in a chariot drawn by horses of fire.
10 It is written that you are to come at the appointed time with warnings,
to allay the divine wrath before its final fury,
to reconcile father and son,
and to restore the tribes of Jacob.
11 Happy are those who saw you
and were honoured with your love! [a]

12 When Elijah had vanished in a whirlwind,
Elisha was filled with his spirit.
Throughout his life no ruler made him tremble;
no one could make him subservient.
13 Nothing was too difficult for him;
even in the grave his body kept its prophetic power.
14 In life he worked miracles,
and in death his deeds were marvellous.

15 In spite of all this the people did not repent
or renounce their sins,
until they were carried off as plunder from their land
and scattered over the whole earth.

[*a*] honoured...love: *probable meaning; Gk. adds* for we also shall certainly live.

Only a tiny nation was left,
with a ruler from the house of David;
and of these some did what was pleasing to the Lord, 16
but others heaped sin upon sin.

Hezekiah fortified his city, 17
bringing water within its walls;
he drilled through the rock with tools of iron
and made cisterns for the water.
In his reign Sennacherib invaded the country. 18
He sent Rab-shakeh from Lachish,[a]
who made threats against Zion
and grew arrogant in his boasting.
Then they were unnerved in heart and hand; 19
they suffered the anguish of a woman in labour.
So they called on the merciful Lord, 20
spreading out their hands in supplication to him.
The Holy One quickly answered their prayer from heaven
by sending Isaiah to the rescue;
he struck down the Assyrian camp, 21
and his angel wiped them out.
For Hezekiah did what was pleasing to the Lord, 22
and kept firmly to the ways of his ancestor David,
as he was instructed by Isaiah,
the great prophet whose vision could be trusted.
In his time the sun went back, 23
and he added many years to the king's life.
With inspired power he saw the future 24
and comforted the mourners in Zion.
He revealed things to come before they happened, 25
the secrets of the future to the end of time.

The memory of Josiah is fragrant as incense **49**
blended by the skill of the perfumer,
sweet as honey to every palate
or as music at a banquet.
He did what was right: he reformed the nation 2
and rooted out their loathsome and lawless practices.

[*a*] from Lachish: *other witnesses read* and went away.

3 He was whole-heartedly loyal to the Lord
and in lawless times made godliness prevail.

4 Except David, Hezekiah, and Josiah,
all were guilty of wrongdoing,
for they deserted the law of the Most High;
and so the royal line of Judah came to an end.
5 They surrendered their power to others
and their glory to a foreign nation,
6 who set fire to the chosen city, the city of the sanctuary,
and left its streets deserted, as Jeremiah prophesied;
7 for they had ill-treated him,
a prophet consecrated even before his birth
to uproot, to destroy, and to demolish,
but also to build and to plant.

8 Ezekiel had a vision of the Glory,
which was revealed enthroned on the chariot of the cherubim.
9 The Lord remembered his enemies and sent a storm,
but he did good to those who kept to the straight path.
10 May the bones of the twelve prophets also
send forth new life from the ground where they lie!
For they put new heart into Jacob,
and rescued the people by their confident hope.

11 How can we tell the greatness of Zerubbabel,
who was like a signet-ring on the Lord's right hand?
12 With him was Joshua son of Jehozadak;
in their days they built the house,
raising a holy temple to the Lord,
destined for eternal glory.
13 Great is the memory of Nehemiah,
who raised our fallen walls,
constructed gates and bars,
and rebuilt our ruined homes.

14 No one on earth has been created to equal Enoch,
for he was taken up from the earth.
15 No man has been born to be Joseph's peer,

the ruler of his brothers and the strength of his people;
and the Lord kept watch over his body.
Shem and Seth were given distinction among men, 16
but Adam holds pre-eminence over all creation.

It was the high priest Simon son of Onias **50**
in whose lifetime the house was repaired,
in whose days the temple was fortified.
He laid the foundation for the high double wall, 2
the high retaining wall of the temple precinct.
In his day they dug[a] the reservoir, 3
a cistern broad as the sea.
He applied his mind to protecting his people from ruin 4
and strengthened the city against siege.
How glorious he was, surrounded by the people, 5
when he came from behind the temple curtain!
He was like the morning star appearing through the clouds 6
or the moon at the full;
like the sun shining on the temple of the Most High 7
or the light of the rainbow on the gleaming clouds;
like a rose in spring 8
or lilies by a fountain of water;
like a green shoot upon Lebanon on a summer's day
or burning incense in the censer; 9
like a cup of beaten gold,
decorated with every kind of precious stone;
like an olive-tree laden with fruit 10
or a cypress with its top in the clouds.
When he put on his gorgeous vestments, 11
robed himself in perfect splendour,
and went up to the holy altar,
he added lustre to the court of the sanctuary.
When the priests were handing him the portions of the sacrifice, 12
as he stood by the altar hearth
with his brothers round him like a garland,
he was like a young cedar of Lebanon
in the midst of a circle of palms.
All the sons of Aaron in their magnificence 13

[a] they dug: *so Heb.; Gk. obscure.*

stood with the Lord's offering in their hands
before the whole congregation of Israel.
14 To complete the ceremonies at the altar
and adorn the offering of the Most High, the Almighty,
15 he held out his hand for the libation cup
and poured out the blood of the grape,
poured its fragrance at the foot of the altar
to the Most High, the King of all.
16 Then the sons of Aaron shouted
and blew their trumpets of beaten silver;
they sounded a mighty fanfare
as a reminder before the Lord.
17 Instantly the people as one man fell on their faces
to worship the Lord their God, the Almighty, the Most High.
18 Then the choir broke into praise,
in the full sweet strains of resounding song,
19 while the people of the Most High
were making their petitions to the merciful Lord,
until the liturgy of the Lord was finished
and the ritual complete.
20 Then Simon came down and raised his hands
over the whole congregation of Israel,
to pronounce the Lord's blessing,
proud to take his name on his lips;
21 and a second time they bowed in worship
to receive the blessing from the Most High.

22 COME THEN, PRAISE the God of the universe,
who everywhere works great wonders,
who from our birth ennobles our life[a]
and deals with us in mercy.
23 May he grant us a joyful heart,
and in our time send Israel lasting peace.
24 May he confirm his mercy towards us,
and in his own good time grant us deliverance.

[*a*] ennobles our life: *or* brings us up.

Two nations I detest, 25
and a third is no nation at all:
the inhabitants of Mount Seir,[a] the Philistines, 26
and the senseless folk that live at Shechem.

In this book I have written 27
lessons of good sense and understanding,
I, Jesus son of Sirach,[b] of Jerusalem,
whose mind was a fountain of wisdom.
Happy the man who occupies himself with these lessons, 28
who lays them to heart and grows wise!
If he lives by them, he will be equal to anything, 29
with the light of the Lord shining on his path.

Epilogue

I THANK THEE, my Lord and King, **51**
I praise thee, my God and Saviour,
I give thee thanks,
because thou hast been my protector and helper, 2
rescuing me from death,
from the trap laid by a slanderous tongue
and from lips that utter lies.
In the face of my assailants thou didst come to my help;
in the fullness of thy mercy and glory thou didst rescue me 3
from grinding teeth which waited to devour me,
from hands that threatened my life,
from the many troubles I endured,
from the choking fire around me, 4
from the flames I had not kindled,
from the deep recesses of the grave, 5
from the foul tongue and its lies—
a wicked slander spoken in the king's presence. 6
I came near to death;
I was on the brink of the grave.

[*a*] Mount Seir: *so Heb.; Gk.* the mountain of Samaria. [*b*] Sirach: *some witnesses read* Sirach Eleazar.

7 They surrounded me on every side,
and there was no one to help me.
I looked for human aid and there was none.
8 Then I remembered thy mercy, Lord,
thy deeds in bygone days;
thou dost deliver those who patiently trust thee
and free them from the power of their enemies.
9 So I sent up a prayer from the earth
and begged for rescue from death.
10 I cried, 'Lord, thou art my Father;[a]
do not desert me in time of trouble,
when I am helpless in the face of arrogance.
11 I will praise thee continually,
I will sing hymns of thanksgiving.'
And my prayer was granted;
12 for thou didst save me from death
and rescue me from my desperate plight.
Therefore I will thank thee and praise thee
and bless thee, O Lord.

13 When I was still young, before I set out on my travels,
I asked openly for wisdom in my prayers.
14 In the forecourt of the sanctuary I laid claim to her,
and I shall seek her out to the end.
15 From the first blossom to the ripening of the grape
she has been the delight of my heart.
From my youth my steps have followed her without swerving.
16 I had hardly begun to listen when I was rewarded,
and I gained for myself much instruction.
17 I made progress in my studies;
all honour to him who gives me wisdom!
18 I determined to practise what I had learnt;
I pursued goodness, and shall never regret it.
19 I strove for wisdom with all my might,
and was scrupulous in whatever I did.
I spread out my hands to heaven above,
deploring my ignorance;
20 I set my heart on possessing wisdom,

[*a*] thou...Father: *so Heb.; Gk.* Father of my lord.

and by keeping myself pure I found her.
With her I gained understanding from the first;
therefore I shall never be at a loss.
Because I passionately yearned to discover her, 21
I won a noble prize.
The Lord gave me eloquence as my reward, 22
and with it I will praise him.

Come to me, you who need instruction, 23
and lodge in my house of learning.
Why do you admit to a lack of these things, 24
yet leave your great thirst unslaked?
I have made my proclamation: 25
'Buy for yourselves without money,
bend your neck to the yoke, 26
be ready to accept discipline;
you need not go far to find it.'
See for yourselves how little were my labours 27
compared with the great peace I have found.
Your share of instruction may cost you a large sum of silver, 28
but it will bring you a large return in gold.
May you take delight in the Lord's mercy 29
and never be ashamed of praising him.
Do your duty in good time, 30
and in his own time he will reward you.

BARUCH

A message to a conquered people

1 THIS IS THE BOOK of Baruch, son of Neriah, son of
Mahseiah, son of Zedekiah, son of Hasadiah, son of Hilkiah,
2 written in Babylon, on the seventh day of the month, in the
fifth year after the Chaldaeans had captured and burnt Jerusalem.
3 Baruch read the book aloud to Jeconiah son of Jehoiakim, king of
4 Judah, and to all the people who had assembled to hear it: the nobles,
the princes of the royal blood, the elders, and the whole community,
high and low—in short, all who lived in Babylon, by the river Soud.
5, 6 Then they prayed to the Lord with tears and fasting; and each of
7 them collected as much money as he could, and they sent it to Jerusalem,
to Jehoiakim the high priest, son of Hilkiah, son of Shallum,
8 and to the priests and all the people who were with him. This was
the time when he took the vessels belonging to the house of the Lord
which had been looted from the temple, and returned them to the
land of Judah, on the tenth of the month Sivan. These were the silver
9 vessels made by Zedekiah son of Josiah, king of Judah, after Nebuchadnezzar
king of Babylon had deported Jeconiah, the rulers, the
captives, the nobles, and the common people from Jerusalem and
taken them to Babylon.

10 They said: We are sending you money to buy whole-offerings,
sin-offerings, and incense; provide a grain-offering, and offer them
11 all upon the altar of the Lord our God; and pray for Nebuchadnezzar
king of Babylon, and for his son Belshazzar, that their life on earth
12 may last as long as the heavens. So the Lord will give us strength,
and light to walk by, and we shall live under the protection of Nebuchadnezzar
king of Babylon, and of Belshazzar his son; we shall give
13 them long service and gain their favour. Pray also for us to the Lord
our God, because we have sinned against him, and to this day the
Lord's anger and wrath have not been averted from us.

14 You are to read this book that we are sending you, and make your
confession in the house of the Lord on the feast day and during the
15 festal season, and say: The Lord our God is in the right; but on us
the shame rests to this very day—on the men of Judah, the citizens of

Jerusalem, on our kings and rulers, on our priests and prophets, and 16
on our fathers. We have sinned against the Lord and disobeyed him; 17, 18
we did not listen to the Lord our God or follow the precepts he gave
us. From the day when the Lord brought our fathers out of Egypt 19
until now, we have been disobedient to the Lord our God and have
heedlessly disregarded his voice. So here we are today in the grip of 20
adversity, suffering under the curse which the Lord commanded his
servant Moses to pronounce, when he led our fathers out of Egypt to
give us a land flowing with milk and honey. Moreover we refused to 21
hear the Lord our God speaking in all the words of the prophets he
sent us; we went our own way, each following the promptings of his 22
own wicked heart, serving other gods, doing what was evil in the
sight of the Lord our God.

So the Lord made good the warning he had given to us, to our 2
magistrates in Israel, our kings and our rulers, and the men of Israel
and Judah. Nowhere under heaven have such deeds been done as 2
were done in Jerusalem, thus fulfilling what was foretold in the law of
Moses, that we should eat the flesh of our children, one his own son 3
and another his own daughter. The Lord made our nation subject to 4
all the kingdoms round us, our land a waste, our name a byword to
all the nations among whom he had scattered our people. Instead of 5
rising to the top, they sank to the bottom, because we sinned against
the Lord our God and did not listen to his voice. The Lord our God 6
is in the right; but on us and our fathers the shame rests to this very
day. All these evils of which the Lord warned us have come about. 7
Yet we did not entreat the Lord that we might all turn away from the 8
thoughts of our wicked hearts. The Lord kept strict watch and 9
brought these evils on our heads, because he is just; he laid all these
commandments upon us, but we did not listen to his voice or follow 10
the precepts which he gave us.

And now, Lord God of Israel, who didst bring thy people out of 11
Egypt with a mighty hand, with signs and portents, with great power
and arm uplifted, winning for thyself a renown that lives on to this
day: by our sin, our godlessness, and our injustice we have broken all 12
thy commandments, O Lord our God. Be angry with us no longer, 13
for we are left a mere handful among the heathen where thou hast
scattered us. Listen, O Lord, to our prayer and our entreaty, deliver 14
us for thy own sake, and grant us favour with those who have
taken us into exile, so that the whole earth may know that thou art 15

the Lord our God, who hast named Israel and his posterity as thy
own.
16 O Lord, look down from thy holy dwelling and think of us. Turn
17 thy ear to us, Lord, and hear us; open thine eyes and see. The dead
are in their graves, the breath is gone from their bodies; it is not they
18 who can sing the Lord's praises or applaud his justice; it is living
men, mourning their fall from greatness, walking the earth bent and
feeble, blind and famished—it is these who will sing thy praises,
O Lord, and applaud thy justice.
19 Not for any just deeds of our fathers and our kings do we lay
20 before thee our plea for pity, O Lord our God. Thou hast vented
upon us that wrath and anger of which thou didst warn us through
21 thy servants the prophets who said: 'These are the words of the
Lord: Bow your shoulders and serve the king of Babylon and you
22 shall remain in the land that I gave to your fathers; but if you do not
23 listen to the Lord and serve the king of Babylon, then I will banish
from Jerusalem and the cities of Judah all sounds of joy and merriment, the voice of bride and bridegroom; the whole land shall lie
24 waste and uninhabited.' But we did not obey thy command to serve
the king of Babylon. And so thou didst make good the warning given
through thy servants the prophets: the bones of our kings and of our
25 fathers have been taken from their resting-place; and there they lie,
exposed to the heat by day and the frost by night. They died a painful
26 death by famine, sword, and disease.[a] And because of the wickedness
of Israel and Judah the house that was named as thine has become
what it is today.
27 Yet thou hast shown us, O Lord our God, all thy wonted for-
28 bearance and great mercy. For this is what thou didst promise
through thy servant Moses, on the day thou didst command him to
29 write thy law in the presence of the Israelites: 'If you will not listen
to my voice, this great swarming multitude will be reduced to a tiny
30 remnant among the heathen where I will scatter them. I know they
will not hear me, this stubborn people, but in the land of their exile
31 they will come to their senses and know that I am the Lord their
32 God. I will give them a mind to understand and ears to hear. Then
they will praise me in the land of their exile and will turn their
33 thoughts to me; they will repent of their stubbornness and their
wicked deeds, for they will recall how their fathers sinned against the

[a] disease: *probable meaning (compare Jeremiah 32. 36); Gk. obscure.*

Lord. Then I will restore them to the land that I swore to give to 34
their forefathers, Abraham, Isaac, and Jacob, and they shall rule over
it. And I will increase their number: they shall never dwindle away.
I will enter into an eternal covenant with them, that I will become 35
their God and they shall become my people. Never again will I
remove my people Israel from the land that I have given them.'

O Lord Almighty, God of Israel, the soul in anguish and the **3**
fainting spirit cry out to thee. Listen, Lord, and have mercy, for we 2
have sinned against thee. Thou art enthroned for ever; we are for 3
ever passing away. Now, Almighty Lord, God of Israel, hear the 4
prayer of Israel's dead and of the sons of those who sinned against
thee. They did not heed the voice of their God, and so we are in the
grip of adversity. Do not recall the misdeeds of our fathers, but 5
remember now thy power and thy name, for thou art the Lord our 6
God, and we will praise thee, O Lord. It is for this that thou hast put 7
the fear of thee in our hearts, to make us call upon thy name. And
we will praise thee in our exile, for we have put away from us all the
wrongdoing of our fathers who sinned against thee. Today we are in 8
exile; thou hast scattered us and made us a byword and a curse, to be
punished for all the sins of our fathers, who rebelled against the
Lord our God.

LISTEN, ISRAEL, to the commandments of life; hear, and learn 9
wisdom. Why is it, Israel, that you are in your enemies' country, 10
that you have grown old in an alien land? Why have you shared the
defilement of the dead and been numbered with those that lie in the 11
grave? It is because you have forsaken the fountain of wisdom. If 12, 13
you had walked in the way of God, you would have lived in peace for
ever. Where is understanding, where is strength, where is intelli- 14
gence? Learn that, and then you will know where to find life and light
to walk by, long life and peace. Has any man discovered the dwelling- 15
place of wisdom or entered her storehouse? Where are the rulers of 16
the nations now? Where are those who have hunted wild beasts or 17
the birds of the air for sport? Where are those who have hoarded the
silver and gold men trust in, never satisfied with their gains? Where 18
are the silversmiths with their patient skill and the secrets of their
craft? They have all vanished and gone down to the grave, and others 19
have risen to take their place. A younger generation saw the light 20
of day and dwelt in the land. But they did not learn the way of

21 knowledge, or discover its paths; they did not lay hold of it; their
22 sons went far astray. Wisdom was not heard of in Canaan, nor seen
23 in Teman. The sons of Hagar who sought for understanding on
earth, the merchants of Merran and Teman, the myth-makers, the
seekers after knowledge, none of them discovered the way of wisdom,
or remembered her paths.

24 How great, O Israel, is God's dwelling-place, how vast the extent
25 of his domain! Great it is, and boundless, lofty, and immeasurable.
26 There in ancient time the giants were born, a famous race, great in
27 stature, skilled in war. But these men were not chosen by God, nor
28 shown the way of knowledge. So their race died out because they
29 had no understanding; they lacked the wit to survive. Has any man
gone up to heaven to gain wisdom and brought her down from the
30 clouds? Has any man crossed the sea to find her or bought her for
31 fine gold? No one can know the path or conceive the way that will
32 lead to her. Only the One who knows all things knows her: his
understanding discovered her. He who established the earth for all
33 time filled it with four-footed beasts. He sends forth the light, and it
34 goes on its way; he called it, it feared him and obeyed. The stars
shone at their appointed stations and rejoiced; he called them and
they answered, 'We are here!' Joyfully they shone for their Maker.
35, 36 This is our God; there is none to compare with him. The whole way
of knowledge he found out and gave to Jacob his servant, and to
37 Israel, whom he loved. Thereupon wisdom appeared on earth and
4 lived among men. She is the book of the commandments of God, the
law that stands for ever. All who hold fast to her shall live, but those
2 who forsake her shall die. Return, Jacob, and lay hold of her; set
3 your course towards her radiance, and face her beacon light. Do not
give up your glory to another or your privileges to an alien people.
4 Happy are we, Israel, because we know what is pleasing to God!

5, 6 Take heart, my people, you who keep Israel's name alive. You
were sold to the heathen, but not to be destroyed; it was because you
7 roused God's anger that you were handed over to your enemies. You
provoked your Maker by sacrificing to demons and to that which is
8 not God. You forgot the Everlasting God who nurtured you, and you
9 grieved Jerusalem who fostered you; for she saw how God's anger
had come upon you, and she said: Listen, you neighbours of Zion,
10 God has brought great grief upon me. I have seen the captivity of
my sons and daughters which the Everlasting has inflicted upon

them; I nursed them in delight, but with tears and mourning I saw 11
them go. Let no one exult over me in my widowhood, bereaved of so 12
many. I have been left desolate through the sins of my children,
through their turning away from the law of God. They would not 13
learn his statutes, or follow his commandments, or let God guide and
train them in his righteousness.

Come then, neighbours of Zion, remember the captivity of my 14
sons and daughters which the Everlasting has inflicted upon them.
For he brought down on them a nation from far away, a ruthless 15
nation speaking a strange language and without reverence for age or
pity for children. They carried off the widow's beloved sons, and left 16
her in loneliness, deprived of her daughters. But I, how can I help 17
you? Only the One who brought these evils upon you can deliver 18
you from your enemies. Go your way, my children, go, for I am left 19
desolate. I have put off the robes of peaceful days, and put on the 20
sackcloth of a suppliant. I will cry out to the Everlasting as long as
I live.

Take heart, my children! Cry out to God, and he will rescue you 21
from tyranny and from the power of your enemies. For I have set my 22
hope of your deliverance on the Everlasting; the Holy One, your
everlasting saviour, has filled me with joy over the mercy soon to be
granted you. I saw you go with mourning and tears, but God will 23
give you back to me with joy and gladness for ever. For as the 24
neighbours of Zion have now seen your captivity, so they will soon
see your deliverance coming upon you from your God with the great
glory and splendour of the Everlasting. My children, endure in 25
patience the wrath God has brought upon you; your enemy has
hunted you down, but soon you will see him destroyed, and will put
your foot upon his neck. My pampered children have trodden rough 26
paths; they have been carried off like a flock seized by raiders.

Take heart, my children! Cry out to God, for he who afflicted you 27
will not forget you. You once resolved to go astray from God; now 28
with tenfold zeal you must turn about and seek him. He who 29
brought these calamities upon you will bring you everlasting joy
when he delivers you.

Take heart, Jerusalem! He who called you by name will comfort 30
you. Wretched shall they be who despoiled you and gloated over 31
your fall; wretched the cities where your children were slaves; 32
wretched the city that received your sons! The same city that rejoiced 33

at your downfall and made merry over your ruin shall grieve over her
34 own desolation. I will strip her of the multitudes that were her boast,
35 and turn her pride to mourning. Fire from the Everlasting shall be
her doom for many a day, and long shall she be a haunt of demons.
36 Jerusalem, look eastwards and see the joy that is coming to you
37 from God. They come, the sons from whom you parted, they come,
gathered together at the word of the Holy One from east to west,
rejoicing in the glory of God.

5 Jerusalem, strip off the garment of your sorrow and affliction,
and put on for ever the glorious majesty that is the gift of God.
2 Wrap about you his robe of righteousness; set on your head for
3 diadem the splendour of the Everlasting; for God will show your
4 radiance to every land under heaven. You shall receive from God for
ever the name Righteous Peace, Godly Splendour.
5 Jerusalem, arise and stand upon the height; look eastwards and
see from west to east your children gathered together at the word of
6 the Holy One, rejoicing that God has remembered them. They went
away from you on foot, led off by their enemies, but God is bringing
them home to you borne aloft in glory, like a king on his throne.
7 For God has commanded every high mountain and the everlasting
hills to be made low, and the valleys to be filled and levelled, so that
8 Israel may walk safely in the glory of God. And woods and every
9 fragrant tree shall give Israel shade by God's command. For God
shall lead Israel with joy in the light of his glory, granting them his
mercy and his righteousness.

A LETTER OF JEREMIAH

The folly of idolatry

A COPY OF A LETTER sent by Jeremiah to the captives 6[a]
who were to be taken to Babylon by the king of Babylon,
conveying a message entrusted to him by God.
The sins you have committed in the sight of God are the cause of 2
your being led away captive to Babylon by Nebuchadnezzar king of
Babylon. Once you are in Babylon, your stay there will be long; it 3
will last for many years, up to seven generations; but afterwards I will
lead you out in peace and prosperity.

Now in Babylon you will see carried on men's shoulders gods 4
made of silver, gold, and wood, which fill the heathen with awe.
Be careful, then, never to imitate these Gentiles; do not be overawed 5
by their gods when you see them in the midst of a procession of
worshippers. But say in your hearts, 'To thee alone, Lord, is worship 6
due.' For my angel is with you; your lives are in his care. 7

The idols are plated with gold and silver, they have tongues 8
fashioned by a craftsman, but they are a fraud and cannot speak.
And the people take gold and make crowns for the heads of their 9
gods, as one might for a girl fond of finery. Sometimes also the 10
priests filch gold and silver from their gods and spend it on themselves; they will even give some of it to the prostitutes in the inner 11
chamber. They dress up the idols in clothes like human beings, these
gods of silver, gold, and wood. But the gods, decked in purple 12
though they are, cannot protect themselves against rust and moth.
The dust in the temple, too, lies thick upon them, so that their faces 13
have to be wiped clean. Like a human judge the god holds a sceptre, 14
yet he cannot put to death anyone who offends him. In his right 15
hand he has a dagger and an axe, yet he cannot deliver himself from
war and pillage. This shows they are not gods, so have no fear of 16
them.

[a] *The chapter and verse numbering is that of the Authorized Version, in which this forms chapter 6 of Baruch.*

17 Their gods are no more use than a broken tool, sitting there in
their temples. Their eyes get filled with dust from the feet of those
18 who come in. And just as the palace-court is barricaded to secure a
traitor awaiting execution, so the priests secure their temples with
doors and bolts and bars to guard against plundering by robbers.
19 They light lamps, more than they need for themselves—yet the idols
20–21 can see none of them. They are like one of the beams of the temple;
their hearts are eaten out, as the saying is, for creatures crawl out of
the ground and devour them and their clothing. When their faces are
blackened by the smoke of the temple they are quite unaware of it.
22 Bats and swallows and birds of all kinds perch on their heads and
23 bodies, and cats do the same. From all this you may be sure that
they are not gods, so have no fear of them.

24 Though plated with gold for ornament, the idols will not shine,
unless someone rubs off the tarnish. Even when they were being cast
25 they did not feel it. They were bought at great cost, but there is no
26 breath in them. As they have no real feet they are carried on men's
27 shoulders, which shows how worthless they are. Even those who
serve them are ashamed, because if ever an idol falls on the ground,
it does not get up by itself; nor, if anyone sets it up again, can it move
by its own effort, and if it is tilted it cannot straighten itself. To set
28 offerings before them is like setting them before the dead. The
sacrifices made to gods are sold by the priests, who spend the proceeds
on themselves. Their wives are no better; they take portions of these
sacrifices and cure the meat, and give no share to the poor or helpless.
29 Their offerings are touched by women who are menstruating or by
mothers fresh from childbed. Be assured by all this that they are not
gods, and have no fear of them.

30 Why should they be called gods? These gods of silver, gold, and
31 wood have food served to them by women. In their temples the
priests sit shaven and shorn, with their clothes rent, and their heads
32 uncovered. They shout and howl before these gods of theirs, like
33 mourners at a funeral feast. The priests strip vestments from the
34 gods to clothe their own wives and children. Should anyone do these
gods either injury or service they will not be able to repay it. They
35 cannot set up or depose a king. So also they are incapable of bestow-
ing wealth or money; if someone makes a vow to them and does not
36 honour it, they will never exact payment. They will never save any
37 man from death, never rescue the weak from the strong. They cannot

restore the blind man's sight or give relief to the needy. They do not 38
pity the widow or befriend the orphan. They are like blocks from the 39
quarry, these wooden things plated with gold and silver, and their
worshippers will be humiliated. How then can anyone suppose 40
them to be gods or call them so?

Besides, even the Chaldaeans themselves bring these idols of
theirs into disrepute; for, when they see a dumb man without the 41
power of articulate speech, they bring him into the temple and make
him call upon Bel, as if Bel could understand him. They cannot see 42
the folly of it and abandon the idols, because they themselves have no
understanding. The women too sit in the street with cords round 43
them, burning bran for incense. And when a passer-by has pulled
one of them to him and she has lain with him, she taunts her neighbour, because she has not been thought as attractive as herself and
her cord has not been broken. Everything to do with these idols is 44
fraud and delusion. How then can anyone suppose them to be gods
or call them so?

They are things manufactured by carpenters and goldsmiths; they 45
can be nothing but what the craftsmen wish them to be. Even their 46
makers' lives cannot be prolonged; what, then, can the things they
make expect? It is simply a scandalous fraud that they have be- 47
queathed to posterity. When war and disasters befall the gods, it is 48
the priests who discuss amongst themselves where they and their
gods can hide. How then can men fail to see that these are not gods, 49
when they cannot save themselves from war and disaster? Since 50
they are nothing but wood plated with gold and silver, they will in
time be recognized for the frauds they are. All the heathen and their 51
kings will plainly see that they are not gods but the work of men's
hands, with no divine power in them at all. Can there still be anyone 52
who does not realize that they are not gods?

They cannot set up a king over a country, and they cannot give men 53
rain. They cannot decide a case or redress a wrong.[a] They are as 54
helpless as crows tossed about in mid air. When fire breaks out in a 55
temple belonging to those wooden gods all gilded and silvered, their
priests will run away to safety, but the gods will be burnt up in the
flames like timbers. They cannot resist king or enemy. How then 56
can anyone allow or believe that they are gods?

They cannot save themselves from thieves and robbers, these 57

[a] *Some witnesses read* cannot judge in their own cause, or redress a wrong done them.

58 wooden gods, plated with silver and gold. Anyone who can will strip
away their gold and silver and make off with the clothing they wear,
59 and the gods can do nothing to help themselves. It is better to be a
king who proves his courage than such a sham god, better a household
vessel that serves its owner's purpose, better even the door of a
60 house that keeps the contents safe, or a wooden pillar in a palace. Sun
and moon and the stars that shine so brightly are sent to serve a
61 purpose, and they obey. So too, when the lightning flashes, it is seen
far and wide. It is the same with the wind; it blows in every land.
62 And when God orders the clouds to travel over all the world they
63 carry out their task, and so does fire when it is sent down from above
to consume mountains and forests. But idols are not to be compared
64 with any of these, in appearance or in power. It follows that they are
not to be considered gods or called by that name, seeing that they
are incapable of pronouncing judgement or of conferring benefits on
65 mankind. Recognize, therefore, that they are not gods, and have no
fear of them.

66 They wield no power over kings, either to curse them or to bless
67 them; and they cannot provide heavenly signs for the nations, either
68 by shining like the sun or by giving light like the moon. They are
more helpless than wild beasts, which can at least save themselves by
69 taking cover. There is no evidence at all that they are gods, so have no
fear of them.

70 These wooden gods of theirs, plated with gold and silver, give no
71 better protection than a scarecrow in a plot of cucumbers. They are
like a thorn-bush in a garden, a perch for every bird, like a corpse
cast out in the dark. Such are their wooden gods, with their plating
72 of gold and silver. The purple and fine linen[a] rotting on them proves
that they are not gods; in the end they will themselves be eaten
away, held in contempt throughout the land.

73 Better, then, is an upright man who has no idols; he will be in no
danger of contempt.

[*a*] fine linen: *probable meaning; Gk.* marble.

THE SONG OF THE THREE

AN ADDITION IN THE GREEK VERSION OF DANIEL BETWEEN 3.23 AND 3.24

THEY WALKED in the heart of the fire, praising God and 1
blessing the Lord. Azariah stood still among the flames and 2
began to pray aloud: 'Blessed art thou, O Lord, the God of 3
our fathers, thy name is worthy of praise and glorious for ever:
thou art just in all thy deeds and true in all thy works; straight are 4
thy paths, and all thy judgements just. Just sentence hast thou passed 5
in all that thou hast brought upon us and upon Jerusalem the holy
city of our fathers: yes, just sentence thou hast passed upon our sins.
For indeed we sinned and broke thy law in rebellion against thee, in 6, 7
all we did we sinned; we did not heed thy commandments, we did
not keep them, we did not do what thou hadst commanded us for
our good. In all the punishments thou hast sent upon us thy judge- 8
ments have been just. Thou hast handed us over to our bitterest 9
enemies, rebels against thy law, and to a wicked king, the vilest in the
world. And so now we are speechless for shame: contempt has fallen 10
on thy servants and thy worshippers. For thy honour's sake do not 11
abandon us for ever; do not annul thy covenant. Do not withdraw 12
thy mercy from us, for the sake of Abraham, thy beloved, for the
sake of Isaac, thy servant, and Israel, thy holy one. Thou didst 13
promise to multiply their descendants as the stars in the sky and the
sand on the sea-shore. But now, Lord, we have been made the smal- 14
lest of all nations; for our sins we are today the most abject in the
world. We have no ruler, no prophet, no leader now; there is no 15
burnt-offering, no sacrifice, no oblation, no incense, no place to
make an offering before thee and find mercy. But because we come 16
with contrite heart and humbled spirit, accept us. As though we 17
came with burnt-offerings of rams and bullocks and with thousands
of fat lambs, so let our sacrifice be made before thee this day. Accept

our pledge of loyalty to thee,[a] for no shame shall come to those who
18 put their trust in thee. Now we will follow thee with our whole heart
19 and fear thee. We seek thy presence; do not put us to shame, but
deal with us in thy forbearance and in the greatness of thy mercy.
20 Grant us again thy marvellous deliverance, and win glory for thy
21 name, O Lord. Let all who do thy servants harm be humbled; may
they be put to shame and stripped of all their power, and may their
22 strength be crushed; let them know that thou alone art the Lord
God, and glorious over all the world.'
23 The servants of the king who threw them in kept on feeding the
24 furnace with naphtha, pitch, tow, and faggots, and the flames poured
25 out above it to a height of seventy-five feet.[b] They spread out and
26 burnt those Chaldaeans who were caught near the furnace. But the
angel of the Lord came down into the furnace to join Azariah and his
27 companions; he scattered the flames out of the furnace and made the
heart of it as if a moist wind were whistling through. The fire did not
touch them at all and neither hurt nor distressed them.

The praises of creation

28 THEN THE THREE with one voice praised and glorified and blessed God in the furnace:

29 'Blessed art thou, O Lord, the God of our fathers;
worthy of praise, highly exalted for ever.
30 Blessed is thy holy and glorious name;
highly to be praised, highly exalted for ever.
31 Blessed art thou in thy holy and glorious temple;
most worthy to be hymned and glorified for ever.
32 Blessed art thou who dost behold the depths from thy seat upon the cherubim;
worthy of praise, highly exalted for ever.
33 Blessed art thou on thy royal throne;
most worthy to be hymned, highly exalted for ever.
34 Blessed art thou in the dome of heaven;
worthy to be hymned and glorified for ever.

[*a*] Accept our...thee: *possible meaning; Gk. obscure.*
[*b*] *Gk.* forty-nine cubits.

'Let the whole creation bless the Lord, 35
sing his praise and exalt him for ever.
Bless the Lord, you heavens; 36
sing his praise and exalt him for ever.
Bless the Lord, you angels of the Lord; 37
sing his praise and exalt him for ever.
Bless the Lord, all you waters above the heavens; 38
sing his praise and exalt him for ever.
Bless the Lord, all you his hosts; 39
sing his praise and exalt him for ever.
Bless the Lord, sun and moon; 40
sing his praise and exalt him for ever.
Bless the Lord, stars of heaven; 41
sing his praise and exalt him for ever.
Bless the Lord, all rain and dew; 42
sing his praise and exalt him for ever.
Bless the Lord, all winds that blow; 43
sing his praise and exalt him for ever.
Bless the Lord, fire and heat; 44
sing his praise and exalt him for ever.
Bless the Lord, scorching blast and bitter cold; 45
sing his praise and exalt him for ever.
Bless the Lord, dews and falling snow; 46
sing his praise and exalt him for ever.
Bless the Lord, nights and days; 47
sing his praise and exalt him for ever.
Bless the Lord, light and darkness; 48
sing his praise and exalt him for ever.
Bless the Lord, frost and cold; 49
sing his praise and exalt him for ever.
Bless the Lord, rime and snow; 50
sing his praise and exalt him for ever.
Bless the Lord, lightnings and clouds; 51
sing his praise and exalt him for ever.

'O earth, bless the Lord; 52
sing his praise and exalt him for ever.
Bless the Lord, mountains and hills; 53
sing his praise and exalt him for ever.

54 Bless the Lord, all that grows in the ground;
sing his praise and exalt him for ever.
56 Bless the Lord, seas and rivers;
sing his praise and exalt him for ever.
55 Bless the Lord, you springs;
sing his praise and exalt him for ever.
57 Bless the Lord, you whales and all that swim in the waters;
sing his praise and exalt him for ever.
58 Bless the Lord, all birds of the air;
sing his praise and exalt him for ever.
59 Bless the Lord, you cattle and wild beasts;
sing his praise and exalt him for ever.

60 'All men on earth, bless the Lord;
sing his praise and exalt him for ever.
61 Bless the Lord, O Israel;
sing his praise and exalt him for ever.
62 Bless the Lord, you priests of the Lord;
sing his praise and exalt him for ever.
63 Bless the Lord, you servants of the Lord;
sing his praise and exalt him for ever.
64 Bless the Lord, all men of upright spirit;
sing his praise and exalt him for ever.
65 Bless the Lord, you that are holy and humble in heart;
sing his praise and exalt him for ever.
66 Bless the Lord, Hananiah, Azariah, and Mishael;
sing his praise and exalt him for ever.
For he has rescued us from the grave and from the power of death:
he has saved us from the furnace of burning flame;
he has rescued us from the heart of the fire.
67 Give thanks to the Lord, for he is good;
for his mercy endures for ever.
68 All who worship the Lord, bless the God of gods;
sing his praise and give him thanks,
for his mercy endures for ever.'

DANIEL AND SUSANNA

Innocence vindicated

THERE ONCE LIVED in Babylon a man named Joakim. 1
He married Susanna daughter of Hilkiah, a very beautiful 2
and devout woman. Her parents, religious people, had 3
brought up their daughter according to the law of Moses. Joakim 4
was very rich and his house had a fine garden adjoining it, which was
a regular meeting-place for the Jews, because he was the man of
greatest distinction among them.

Now two elders of the community were appointed that year as 5
judges. It was of them that the Lord had said, 'Wickedness came
forth from Babylon from elders who were judges and were supposed
to govern my people.' These men were constantly at Joakim's house, 6
and everyone who had a case to be tried came to them there.

When the people went away at noon, Susanna used to go and walk 7
in her husband's garden. Every day the two elders saw her entering 8
the garden and taking her walk, and they were obsessed with lust for
her. They no longer prayed to God, but let their thoughts stray from 9
him and forgot the claims of morality. They were both infatuated 10
with her; but they did not tell each other what pangs they suffered,
because they were ashamed to confess that they wanted to seduce 11
her. Day after day they watched eagerly to see her. 12

One day they said, 'Let us go home; it is time for lunch.' So they 13, 14
went off in different directions, but soon retraced their steps and
found themselves face to face. When they questioned one another,
each confessed his passion. Then they agreed on a time when they
might find her alone.

And while they were watching for an opportune day, she went into 15
the garden as usual with only her two maids; it was very hot, and she
wished to bathe there. No one else was in the garden except the two 16
elders, who had hidden and were spying on her. She said to her 17
maids, 'Bring me soap and olive oil, and shut the garden doors so

18 that I can bathe.' They did as she told them: they closed the garden
doors and went out by the side door to fetch the things they had been
ordered to bring; they did not see the elders because they were
19 hiding. As soon as the maids had gone, the two elders started up and
20 ran to Susanna. 'Look!' they said, 'the garden doors are shut, and no
one can see us. We are burning with desire for you, so consent and
21 yield to us. If you refuse, we shall give evidence against you that
there was a young man with you and that was why you sent your
22 maids away.' Susanna groaned and said: 'I see no way out. If I do
this thing, the penalty is death; if I do not, you will have me at your
23 mercy. My choice is made: I will not do it. It is better to be at
your mercy than to sin against the Lord.'
24 With that Susanna gave a loud shout, but the two elders shouted
25, 26 her down. One of them ran and opened the garden door. The
household, hearing the uproar in the garden, rushed in through the
27 side door to see what had happened to her. And when the elders had
told their story, the servants were deeply shocked, for no such allega-
tion had ever been made against Susanna.
28 Next day, when the people gathered at her husband Joakim's house,
the two elders came, full of their criminal design to put Susanna to
29 death. In the presence of the people they said, 'Send for Susanna
30 daughter of Hilkiah, Joakim's wife.' So they sent for her, and she
31 came with her parents and children and all her relatives. Now
32 Susanna was a woman of great beauty and delicate feeling. She was
closely veiled, but those scoundrels ordered her to be unveiled so
33 that they might feast their eyes on her beauty. Her family and all
34 who saw her were in tears. Then the two elders stood up before the
35 people and put their hands on her head. She looked up to heaven
36 through her tears, for she trusted in the Lord. The elders said: 'As
we were walking alone in the garden, this woman came in with two
37 maids. She shut the garden doors and dismissed her maids. Then a
38 young man, who had been in hiding, came and lay down with her. We
were in a corner of the garden, and when we saw this wickedness we
39 ran up to them. Though we saw them in the act, we could not hold the
man; he was too strong for us, and he opened the door and forced his
40 way out. We seized the woman and asked who the young man was,
but she would not tell us. That is our evidence.'
41 As they were elders of the people and judges, the assembly believed
42 them and condemned her to death. Then Susanna cried out loudly:

'Eternal God, who dost know all secrets and foresee all things, thou 43
knowest that their evidence against me was false. And now I am to
die, guiltless though I am of all the wicked things these men have
said against me.'

The Lord heard her cry. Just as she was being led off to execution, 44, 45
God inspired a devout young man named Daniel to protest, and he 46
shouted out, 'I will not have this woman's blood on my head.' All 47
the people turned and asked him, 'What do you mean by that?' He 48
came forward and said: 'Are you such fools, you Israelites, as to
condemn a woman of Israel, without making careful inquiry and
finding out the truth? Re-open the trial; the evidence these men 49
have brought against her is false.'

So the people all hurried back, and the rest of the elders said to 50
him, 'Come, take your place among us and state your case, for God
has given you the standing of an elder.' Daniel said to them, 51
'Separate these men and keep them at a distance from each other,
and I will examine them.' When they had been separated Daniel 52
summoned one of them. 'You hardened sinner,' he said, 'the sins of
your past have now come home to you. You gave unjust decisions, 53
condemning the innocent, and acquitting the guilty, although the
Lord has said, "You shall not put to death an innocent and guiltless
man." Now then, if you saw this woman, tell us, under what tree did 54
you see them together?' He answered, 'Under a clove-tree.'[a] Then 55
Daniel retorted, 'Very good: this lie has cost you your life, for already
God's angel has received your sentence from God, and he will
cleave[b] you in two.' And he told him to stand aside, and ordered 56
them to bring in the other.

He said to him: 'Spawn of Canaan, no son of Judah, beauty has
been your undoing, and lust has corrupted your heart! Now we 57
know how you have been treating the women of Israel, frightening
them into consorting with you; but here is a woman of Judah who
would not submit to your villainy. Now then, tell me, under what 58
tree did you surprise them together?' 'Under a yew-tree',[c] he
replied. Daniel said to him, 'Very good: this lie has cost you your 59
life, for the angel of God is waiting with his sword to hew[d] you down
and destroy you both.'

Then the whole assembly gave a great shout and praised God, the 60

[a] clove: *literally* mastic. [b] clove...cleave: *there is a play on words in the Gk.*
[c] yew: *literally* oak. [d] yew...hew: *there is a play on words in the Gk.*

61 saviour of those who trust in him. They turned on the two elders, for
out of their own mouths Daniel had convicted them of giving false
62 evidence; they dealt with them according to the law of Moses, and
put them to death, as they in their wickedness had tried to do to their
63 neighbour. And so an innocent life was saved that day. Then
Hilkiah and his wife gave praise for their daughter Susanna, because
she was found innocent of a shameful deed, and so did her husband
64 Joakim and all her relatives. And from that day forward Daniel was
a great man among his people.

DANIEL, BEL, AND THE SNAKE

The destruction of Bel

1 WHEN KING ASTYAGES was gathered to his
fathers he was succeeded on the throne by Cyrus the
2 Persian. Daniel was a confidant of the king, the most
honoured of all the King's Friends.

3 Now the Babylonians had an idol called Bel, for which they provided every day twelve bushels of fine flour, forty sheep, and fifty
4 gallons of wine. The king held it to be divine and went daily to
worship it, but Daniel worshipped his God. So the king said to him,
5 'Why do you not worship Bel?' He replied, 'Because I do not
believe in man-made idols, but in the living God who created heaven
6 and earth and is sovereign over all mankind.' The king said, 'Do you
think that Bel is not a living god? Do you not see how much he eats
7 and drinks each day?' Daniel laughed and said, 'Do not be deceived,
your majesty; this Bel of yours is only clay inside and bronze outside,
and has never eaten anything.'

8 Then the king was angry, and summoned the priests of Bel and

said to them, 'If you cannot tell me who it is that eats up all these
provisions, you shall die; but if you can show that it is Bel that eats 9
them, then Daniel shall die for blasphemy against Bel.' Daniel said
to the king, 'Let it be as you command.' (There were seventy priests 10
of Bel, not counting their wives and children.) Then the king went
with Daniel into the temple of Bel. The priests said, 'We are now 11
going outside; set out the food yourself, your majesty, and mix the
wine; then shut the door and seal it with your signet. When you 12
come back in the morning, if you do not find that Bel has eaten it all,
let us be put to death; but if Daniel's charges against us turn out to
be false, then he shall die.' They treated the whole affair with con- 13
tempt, because they had made a hidden entrance under the table,
and they regularly went in by it and ate everything up.

So when the priests had gone, the king set out the food for Bel; 14
and Daniel ordered his servants to bring ashes and sift them over the
whole temple in the presence of the king alone. Then they left the
temple, closed the door, sealed it with the king's signet, and went
away. During the night the priests, with their wives and children, 15
came as usual and ate and drank everything. Early in the morning 16
the king came, and Daniel with him. The king said, 'Are the seals 17
intact, Daniel?' He answered, 'They are intact, your majesty.' As 18
soon as he opened the door, the king looked at the table and cried
aloud, 'Great art thou, O Bel! In thee there is no deceit at all.' But 19
Daniel laughed and held back the king from going in. 'Just look at
the floor,' he said, 'and judge whose footprints these are.' The king 20
said, 'I see the footprints of men, women, and children.' In a rage he 21
put the priests under arrest, with their wives and children. Then they
showed him the secret doors through which they used to go in and
consume what was on the table. So the king put them to death, and 22
handed Bel over to Daniel, who destroyed the idol and its temple.

The destruction of the snake

NOW THERE WAS a huge snake, which the Babylonians held to 23
be divine. The king said to Daniel, 'You cannot say that this is 24
not a living god; so worship him.' Daniel answered, 'I will worship 25
the Lord my God, for he is the living God. But give me authority, 26

your majesty, and without sword or staff I will kill the snake.'
27 'I give it you', said the king. So Daniel took pitch and fat and hair,
boiled them together, and made them into cakes, which he put into
the mouth of the snake. When the snake ate them, it burst. Then
28 Daniel said, 'See what things you worship!' When the Babylonians
heard of this they gathered in an angry crowd to oppose the king.
'The king has turned Jew!' they cried. 'He has pulled down Bel,
29 killed the snake, and put the priests to the sword.' So they went to
the king and said, 'Hand Daniel over to us, or else we will kill you
30 and your family.' The king, finding himself hard pressed, was com-
31 pelled to give Daniel up to them. They threw him into the lion-pit,
32 and he was there for six days. There were seven lions in the pit, and
every day two men and two sheep were fed to them; but now they
were given nothing, to make sure that they would devour Daniel.

33 Now the prophet Habakkuk was in Judaea; he had made a stew
and crumbled bread into the bowl, and he was on the way to his field,
34 carrying it to the reapers, when an angel of the Lord said, 'Habakkuk,
carry the meal you have with you to Babylon, for Daniel, who is in
35 the lion-pit.' Habakkuk said, 'My lord, I have never been to Baby-
36 lon. I do not know where the lion-pit is.' Then the angel took the
prophet by the crown of his head, and carrying him by his hair, he
swept him to Babylon with the blast of his breath and put him down
37 above the pit. Habakkuk called out, 'Daniel, Daniel, take the meal
38 that God has sent you!' Daniel said, 'O God, thou dost indeed
39 remember me; thou dost never forsake those who love thee.' Then
he got up and ate; and God's angel returned Habakkuk at once to his
40 home. On the seventh day the king went to mourn for Daniel, but
41 when he arrived at the pit and looked in, there sat Daniel! Then the
king cried aloud, 'Great art thou, O Lord, the God of Daniel, and
42 there is no God but thou alone.' So the king drew Daniel up; and the
men who had planned to destroy him he flung into the pit, and then
and there they were eaten up before his eyes.

THE PRAYER OF MANASSEH

Repentance

LORD ALMIGHTY, 1
God of our fathers,
of Abraham, Isaac, and Jacob,
and of their righteous offspring;
who hast made heaven and earth in their manifold array; 2
who hast confined the ocean by thy word of command, 3
who hast shut up the abyss and sealed it with thy fearful and glorious name;
all things tremble and quake in the face of thy power. 4
For the majesty of thy glory is more than man can bear, 5
and none can endure thy menacing wrath against sinners;
the mercy in thy promise is beyond measure: none can fathom it. 6
For thou art Lord Most High, 7
compassionate, patient, and of great mercy,
relenting when men suffer for their sins.
For out of thy great goodness thou, O God,
hast promised repentance and remission to those who sin against thee,
and in thy boundless mercy thou hast appointed repentance for sinners as the way to salvation.[a]
So thou, Lord God of the righteous, 8
didst not appoint repentance for Abraham, Isaac, and Jacob,
who were righteous and did not sin against thee,
but for me, a sinner,
whose sins are more in number than the sands of the sea. 9
My transgressions abound, O Lord, my transgressions abound,
and I am not worthy to look up and gaze at the height of heaven
because of the number of my wrongdoings.
Bowed down with a heavy chain of iron, 10

[a] *Some witnesses omit* For out of...salvation.

I grieve over my sins and find no relief,
because I have provoked thy anger
and done what is evil in thine eyes,
setting up idols and so piling sin on sin.
11 Now I humble my heart, imploring thy great goodness.
12 I have sinned, O Lord, I have sinned,
and I acknowledge my transgressions.
13 I pray and beseech thee,
spare me, O Lord, spare me,
destroy me not with my transgressions on my head,
do not be angry with me for ever, nor store up evil for me.
Do not condemn me to the grave,
for thou, Lord, art the God of the penitent.
14 Thou wilt show thy goodness towards me,
for unworthy as I am thou wilt save me in thy great mercy;
15 And so I shall praise thee continually all the days of my life.
For all the host of heaven sings thy praise,
and thy glory is for ever and ever. Amen.

THE FIRST BOOK OF THE
MACCABEES

Antiochus and the Jewish revolt

ALEXANDER of Macedon, the son of Philip, marched 1
from the land of Kittim, defeated Darius, king of Persia and
Media, and seized his throne, being already king of Greece.[a]
In the course of many campaigns he captured fortified towns, 2
slaughtered kings, traversed the earth to its remotest bounds, and 3
plundered innumerable nations. When at last the world lay quiet
under his rule, his pride knew no limits; he built up an extremely 4
powerful army, and ruled over countries, nations, and dominions; all
paid him tribute.

The time came when he fell ill, and, knowing that he was dying, 5
he summoned his generals, nobles who had been brought up with 6
him from childhood, and divided his empire among them while he
was still alive. Alexander had reigned twelve years when he died. 7
His generals took over the government, each in his own province. On 8, 9
his death they were all crowned as kings, and their descendants succeeded them for many years. They brought untold miseries upon
the world.

A scion of this stock was that wicked man, Antiochus Epiphanes, 10
son of King Antiochus. He had been a hostage in Rome before he
succeeded to the throne in the year 137 of the Greek era.[b]

At that time there appeared in Israel a group of renegade Jews, 11
who incited the people. 'Let us enter into a covenant with the
Gentiles round about,' they said, 'because disaster upon disaster has
overtaken us since we segregated ourselves from them.' The people 12
thought this a good argument, and some of them in their enthusiasm 13
went to the king and received authority to introduce non-Jewish
laws and customs. They built a sports-stadium in the gentile style in 14
Jerusalem. They removed their marks of circumcision and repudiated 15
the holy covenant. They intermarried with Gentiles, and abandoned
themselves to evil ways.

[a] being...Greece: *probable meaning; Gk. obscure.* [b] *That is* 175 B.C.

16 When he was firmly established on his throne, Antiochus made up
his mind to become king of Egypt and so to rule over both kingdoms.
17 He assembled a powerful force of chariots, elephants, and cavalry,
18 and a great fleet, and invaded Egypt. When battle was joined,
Ptolemy king of Egypt was seized with panic and took to flight,
19 leaving many dead. The fortified towns were captured and the land
pillaged.

20 On his return from the conquest of Egypt, in the year 143,[a]
Antiochus marched with a strong force against Israel and Jerusalem.
21 In his arrogance he entered the temple and carried off the golden
22 altar, the lamp-stand with all its equipment, the table for the Bread
of the Presence, the sacred cups and bowls, the golden censers, the
curtain, and the crowns. He stripped off all the gold plating from
23 the temple front. He seized the silver, gold, and precious vessels,
24 and whatever secret treasures he found, and took them all with him
when he left for his own country. He had caused much bloodshed,
and he gloated over all he had done.

25 Great was the lamentation throughout Israel;
26 rulers and elders groaned in bitter grief.
Girls and young men languished;
the beauty of our women was disfigured.
27 Every bridegroom took up the lament,
and every bride sat grieving in her chamber.
28 The land trembled for its inhabitants,
and all the house of Jacob was wrapped in shame.

29 Two years later, the king sent to the towns of Judaea a high
revenue official, who arrived at Jerusalem with a powerful force.
30 His language was friendly, but full of guile. For, once he had gained
the city's confidence, he suddenly attacked it. He dealt it a heavy
31 blow, and killed many Israelites, plundering the city and setting it
32 ablaze. He pulled down houses and walls on every side; women and
children were made prisoners, and the cattle seized.

33 The city of David was turned into a citadel, enclosed by a high,
34 stout wall with strong towers, and garrisoned by impious foreigners
35 and renegades. Having made themselves secure, they accumulated
arms and provisions, and deposited there the massed plunder of

[*a*] *That is* 169 B.C.

Jerusalem. There they lay in ambush, a lurking threat to the temple 36
and a perpetual menace to Israel.

They shed the blood of the innocent round the temple; 37
they defiled the holy place.
The citizens of Jerusalem fled for fear of them; 38
she became the abode of aliens,
and alien herself to her offspring:
her children deserted her.
Her temple lay desolate as a wilderness; 39
her feasts were turned to mourning,
her sabbaths to a reproach,
her honour to contempt.
The shame of her fall matched the greatness of her renown, 40
and her pride was bowed low in grief.

The king then issued a decree throughout his empire: his subjects 41
were all to become one people and abandon their own laws and 42
religion. The nations everywhere complied with the royal command,
and many in Israel accepted the foreign worship, sacrificing to idols 43
and profaning the sabbath. Moreover, the king sent agents with 44
written orders to Jerusalem and the towns of Judaea. Ways and
customs foreign to the country were to be introduced. Burnt- 45
offerings, sacrifices, and libations in the temple were forbidden;
sabbaths and feast-days were to be profaned; the temple and its 46
ministers to be defiled. Altars, idols, and sacred precincts were to be 47
established; swine and other unclean beasts to be offered in sacrifice.
They must leave their sons uncircumcised; they must make them- 48
selves in every way abominable, unclean, and profane, and so forget 49
the law and change all their statutes. The penalty for disobedience 50
was death.

Such was the decree which the king issued to all his subjects. He 51
appointed superintendents over all the people, and instructed the
towns of Judaea to offer sacrifice, town by town. People thronged to 52
their side in large numbers, every one of them a traitor to the law.
Their wicked conduct throughout the land drove Israel into hiding 53
in every possible place of refuge.

On the fifteenth day of the month Kislev in the year 145,[a] 'the 54

[a] *That is* 167 B.C.

abomination of desolation' was set up on the altar. Pagan altars were
55 built throughout the towns of Judaea; incense was offered at the
56 doors of houses and in the streets. All scrolls of the law which were
57 found were torn up and burnt. Anyone discovered in possession of a
Book of the Covenant, or conforming to the law, was put to death by
58 the king's sentence. Thus month after month these wicked men used
their power against the Israelites whom they found in their towns.
59 On the twenty-fifth day of the month they offered sacrifice on the
60 pagan altar which was on top of the altar of the Lord. In accordance
with the royal decree, they put to death women who had had their
61 children circumcised. Their babies, their families, and those who had
62 circumcised them, they hanged by the neck. Yet many in Israel found
strength to resist, taking a determined stand against eating any un-
63 clean food. They welcomed death rather than defile themselves and
64 profane the holy covenant, and so they died. The divine wrath raged
against Israel.[a]

2 AT THIS TIME a certain Mattathias, son of John, son of Symeon,
appeared on the scene. He was a priest of the Joarib family from
2 Jerusalem, who had settled at Modin. Mattathias had five sons, John
3, 4 called Gaddis, Simon called Thassis, Judas called Maccabaeus,
5 Eleazar called Avaran, and Jonathan called Apphus.
6 When Mattathias saw the sacrilegious acts committed in Judaea
7 and Jerusalem, he said:

'Oh! Why was I born to see this,
the crushing of my people, the ruin of the holy city?
They sat idly by when it was surrendered,
when the holy place was given up to the alien.
8 Her temple is like a man robbed of honour;
9 its glorious vessels are carried off as spoil.
Her infants are slain in the street,
her young men by the sword of the foe.
10 Is there a nation that has not usurped her sovereignty,[b]
a people that has not plundered her?
11 She has been stripped of all her adornment,
no longer free, but a slave.

[*a*] The divine...Israel: *or* Israel lived under a reign of terror. [*b*] *Or* occupied her palaces.

Now that we have seen our temple with all its beauty and splendour 12
laid waste and profaned by the Gentiles, why should we live any 13
longer?' So Mattathias and his sons tore their garments, put on 14
sackcloth, and mourned bitterly.

The king's officers who were enforcing apostasy came to the town 15
of Modin to see that sacrifice was offered, and many Israelites went 16
over to them. Mattathias and his sons stood in a group. The king's 17
officers spoke to Mattathias: 'You are a leader here,' they said, 'a
man of mark and influence in this town, with your sons and brothers
at your back. You be the first now to come forward and carry out the 18
king's order. All the nations have done so, as well as the leading men
in Judaea and the people left in Jerusalem. Then you and your sons
will be enrolled among the King's Friends; you will all receive high
honours, rich rewards of silver and gold, and many further benefits.'

To this Mattathias replied in a ringing voice: 'Though all the 19
nations within the king's dominions obey him and forsake their
ancestral worship, though they have chosen to submit to his commands, yet I and my sons and brothers will follow the covenant of 20
our fathers. Heaven forbid we should ever abandon the law and its 21
statutes. We will not obey the command of the king, nor will we 22
deviate one step from our forms of worship.'

As soon as he had finished, a Jew stepped forward in full view of all 23
to offer sacrifice on the pagan altar at Modin, in obedience to the
royal command. The sight stirred Mattathias to indignation; he 24
shook with passion, and in a fury of righteous anger rushed forward
and slaughtered the traitor on the very altar. At the same time he 25
killed the officer sent by the king to enforce sacrifice, and pulled the
pagan altar down. Thus Mattathias showed his fervent zeal for the 26
law, just as Phinehas had done by killing Zimri son of Salu.
'Follow me,' he shouted through the town, 'every one of you who is 27
zealous for the law and strives to maintain the covenant.' He and his 28
sons took to the hills, leaving all their belongings behind in the town.

At that time many who wanted to maintain their religion and law 29
went down to the wilds to live there. They took their sons, their 30
wives, and their cattle with them, for their miseries were more than
they could bear. Word soon reached the king's officers and the forces 31
in Jerusalem, the city of David, that men who had defied the king's
order had gone down into hiding-places in the wilds. A large body of 32
men went quickly after them, came up with them, and occupied

positions opposite. They prepared to attack them on the sabbath.
33 'There is still time,' they shouted; 'come out, obey the king's com-
34 mand, and your lives will be spared.' 'We will not come out,' the
Jews replied; 'we will not obey the king's command or profane
35, 36 the sabbath.' Without more ado the attack was launched; but the
Israelites did nothing in reply; they neither hurled stones, nor
37 barricaded their caves. 'Let us all meet death with a clear conscience,'
they said; 'we call heaven and earth to testify that there is no justice
38 in this slaughter.' So they were attacked and massacred on the
sabbath, men, women, and children, up to a thousand in all, and
their cattle with them.

39 Great was the grief of Mattathias and his friends when they heard
40 the news. They said to one another, 'If we all do as our brothers have
done, if we refuse to fight the Gentiles for our lives as well as for our
laws and customs, then they will soon wipe us off the face of the
41 earth.' That day they decided that, if anyone came to fight against
them on the sabbath, they would fight back, rather than all die as
their brothers in the caves had done.

42 It was then that they were joined by a company of Hasidaeans,
stalwarts of Israel, every one of them a volunteer in the cause of
43 the law; and all who were refugees from the troubles came to swell
44 their numbers, and so add to their strength. Now that they had an
organized force, they turned their wrath on the guilty men and
renegades. Those who escaped their fierce attacks took refuge with
the Gentiles.

45 Mattathias and his friends then swept through the country,
46 pulling down the pagan altars, and forcibly circumcising all the
47 uncircumcised boys found within the frontiers of Israel. They hunted
down their arrogant enemies, and the cause prospered in their hands.
48 Thus they saved the law from the Gentiles and their kings, and broke
the power of the tyrant.

49 The time came for Mattathias to die, and he said to his sons:
'Arrogance now stands secure and gives judgement against us; it is a
50 time of calamity and raging fury. But now, my sons, be zealous for
51 the law, and give your lives for the covenant of your fathers. Remember the deeds they did in their generations, and great glory and
52 eternal fame shall be yours. Did not Abraham prove steadfast under
53 trial, and so gain credit as a righteous man? Joseph kept the commandments, hard-pressed though he was, and became lord of Egypt.

Phinehas, our father, never flagged in his zeal, and his was the 54
covenant of an everlasting priesthood. Joshua kept the law, and he 55
became a judge in Israel. Caleb bore witness before the congrega- 56
tion, and a share in the land was his reward. David was a man of 57
loyalty, and he was granted the throne of an everlasting kingdom.
Elijah never flagged in his zeal for the law, and he was taken up to 58
heaven. Hananiah, Azariah, and Mishael had faith, and they were 59
saved from the blazing furnace. Daniel was a man of integrity, and he 60
was rescued from the lions' jaws. As generation succeeds generation, 61
follow their example; for no one who trusts in Heaven shall ever lack
strength. Do not fear a wicked man's words; all his success will end 62
in filth and worms. Today he may be high in honour, but tomorrow 63
there will be no trace of him, because he will have returned to the dust
and all his schemes come to nothing. But you, my sons, draw your 64
courage and strength from the law, for by it you will win great glory.

'Now here is Symeon, your brother; I know him to be wise in 65
counsel: always listen to him, for he shall be a father to you. Judas 66
Maccabaeus has been strong and brave from boyhood; he shall be
your commander in the field, and fight his people's battles. Gather 67
to your side all who observe the law, and avenge your people's
wrongs. Repay the Gentiles in their own coin, and always heed the 68
law's commands.'

Then Mattathias blessed them, and was gathered to his fathers. 69
He died in the year 146,[a] and was buried by his sons in the family 70
tomb at Modin. All Israel raised a loud lament for him.

The war under Judas and Jonathan

THEN JUDAS MACCABAEUS came forward in his father's place. 3
He had the support of all his brothers and his father's followers, 2
and they carried on the fight for Israel with zest.

> He enhanced his people's glory. 3
> He put on his breastplate like a giant,
> and girt himself with weapons of war.
> He fought battle on battle;

[a] *That is* 166 B.C.

he guarded his army with his sword.
4 He was like a lion in his exploits,
like a lion's whelp roaring for prey.
5 He hunted and tracked down the lawless;
he blasted the troublers of his people.
6 The lawless cowered in fear of him;
all evil-doers were confounded.
The cause of freedom prospered in his hands;
7 he provoked many kings to anger.
But he made Jacob glad by his deeds;
he is remembered for ever in blessing.
8 He passed through the towns of Judaea;
he destroyed the godless there.
He turned wrath away from Israel;
9 his fame spread to the ends of the earth,
and he rallied a people near to destruction.

10 Apollonius now collected a gentile force and a large contingent
11 from Samaria, to fight against Israel. When Judas heard of it, he
marched out to meet him, and defeated and killed him. Many of the
12 Gentiles fell, and the rest took to flight. From the arms they captured,
Judas took the sword of Apollonius, and used it in his campaigns for
the rest of his life.
13 When Seron, who commanded the army in Syria, heard that Judas
had mustered a large force, consisting of all his loyal followers of
14 military age, he said to himself, 'I will win a glorious reputation in
the empire by making war on Judas and his followers, who defy the
15 royal edict.' Seron was reinforced by a strong contingent of renegade Jews, who marched up to help him take vengeance on Israel.
16 When he reached the pass of Beth-horon, Judas advanced to meet
17 him with a handful of men. When his followers saw the host coming
against them, they said to Judas, 'How can so few of us fight against
so many? Besides, we have had nothing to eat all day, and we are
exhausted.'
18 Judas replied: 'Many can easily be overpowered by a few; it makes
19 no difference to Heaven to save by many or by few. Victory does not
20 depend on numbers; strength comes from Heaven alone. Our
enemies come filled with insolence and lawlessness to plunder and to
21 kill us and our wives and children. But we are fighting for our lives

and our religion. Heaven will crush them before our eyes. You need 22
not be afraid of them.'

When he had finished speaking, he launched a sudden attack, 23
and Seron and his army broke before him. They pursued them 24
down the pass of Beth-horon as far as the plain; some eight hundred
of the enemy fell, and the rest fled to Philistia.

Thus Judas and his brothers began to be feared, and alarm spread 25
to the Gentiles all round. His fame reached the ears of the king, and 26
the story of his battles was told in every nation. When King Antio- 27
chus heard this news, he flew into a rage and ordered all the forces of
his empire to be assembled, an immensely powerful army. He 28
opened his treasury and gave a year's pay to his troops, ordering
them to be prepared for any duty. But he found that his resources 29
were running low; his tribute, too, had dwindled as a result of the
disaffection and violence he had brought upon the world by abolish-
ing traditional laws and customs. He now saw with alarm that he 30
might be short of money, as had happened once or twice before,
both for his normal expenses and for the gifts he had been accustomed
to distribute with an even more lavish hand than any of his predecessors on the throne.

For a time he was much perplexed; then he decided to go to Persia, 31
collect the tribute due from the provinces, and raise a large sum of
ready money. He left Lysias, a distinguished member of the royal 32
family, as viceroy of the territories between the Euphrates and the
Egyptian frontier. He also appointed him guardian of his son 33
Antiochus until his return. He transferred to Lysias half the armed 34
forces, together with the elephants, and told him all that he wanted
done, especially to the population of Judaea and Jerusalem. Against 35
these Lysias was to send a force, and break and destroy the strength
of Israel and those who were left in Jerusalem, to blot out all
memory of them from the place. He was to settle foreigners in all 36
their territory, and allot the land to the settlers. The other half of the 37
forces the king took with him, and set out from Antioch, his capital,
in the year 147.[a] He crossed the Euphrates and marched through
the upper provinces.

Lysias chose Ptolemaeus son of Dorymenes, with Nicanor and 38
Gorgias, all three powerful members of the order of King's Friends,
and sent with them forty thousand infantry and seven thousand 39

[*a*] *That is* 165 B.C.

cavalry to invade Judaea and devastate the country as the king had
40 commanded. They set out with all their forces and encamped near
41 Emmaus in the lowlands. The merchants of the region, impressed by
what they heard of the army, took a large quantity of silver and gold,
with a supply of fetters, and came into the camp to buy the Israelites
for slaves. The army was also reinforced by troops from Syria and
Philistia.

42 Judas and his brothers saw that their plight had become grave,
with the enemy encamped inside their frontiers. They learnt, too, of
the commands which the king had given for the complete destruction
43 of the nation. So they said to one another, 'Let us restore the shattered fortunes of our nation; let us fight for our nation and for the
44 holy place.' They gathered in full assembly to prepare for battle, and
to pray and seek divine mercy and compassion.

45 Jerusalem lay deserted like a wilderness;
none of her children went in or out.
Her holy place was trampled down;
aliens and heathen lodged in her citadel.
Joy had been banished from Jacob;
and flute and harp were dumb.

46 They assembled at Mizpah, opposite Jerusalem, for in former
47 times Israel had a place of worship at Mizpah. That day they fasted,
put on sackcloth, sprinkled ashes on their heads, and tore their
48 garments. They unrolled the scroll of the law, seeking the guidance
49 which Gentiles seek from the images of their gods. They brought the
priestly vestments, the firstfruits, and the tithes; they presented
50 Nazirites who had completed their vows, and they cried to Heaven:
'What shall we do with these Nazirites, and where shall we take them?
51 Thy holy place is trodden down and defiled, and sorrow and humilia-
52 tion have come upon thy priests. And see, the Gentiles have gathered
against us to destroy us. Thou knowest the fate they plan for us;
53, 54 how can we withstand them unless thou help us?' Then the trumpets
sounded, and a great shout went up.

55 Judas then appointed leaders of the people, officers over thousands,
56 hundreds, fifties, and tens. As the law commands, he ordered back
to their homes those who were building their houses or were newly
wed or who were planting vineyards, or who were faint-hearted.
57 Thereupon the army moved and took up their positions to the south

of Emmaus, where Judas thus addressed them: 'Prepare for action 58
and show yourselves men. Be ready at dawn to fight these Gentiles
who are massed against us to destroy us and our holy place. Better 59
die fighting than look on while calamity overwhelms our people and
the holy place. But it will be as Heaven wills.' 60

Gorgias, taking a detachment of five thousand men and a thousand 4
picked cavalry, set out by night to attack the Jewish army and fall 2
upon them unawares; his guides were men from the citadel. But 3
Judas had word of this, and he and his soldiers moved out to attack
the king's army in Emmaus, while its forces were still divided. 4
Gorgias reached the camp of Judas during the night, but found no 5
one there. He set out to search for them in the hills, thinking, 'These
Jews are running away from us.'

At daybreak, there was Judas in the plain with three thousand 6
men, though they had not all the armour and the swords they
wanted. They saw the Gentiles' camp strongly fortified with breast- 7
works, while mounted guards, seasoned troops, patrolled round it.

Judas said to his men: 'Do not be afraid of their great numbers or 8
panic when they charge. Remember how our fathers were saved at the 9
Red Sea, when Pharaoh and his army were pursuing them. Let us cry 10
now to Heaven to favour our cause, to remember the covenant made
with our fathers, and to crush this army before us today. Then all the 11
Gentiles will know that there is One who saves and liberates Israel.'

When the foreigners looked up and saw them advancing to the 12
attack, they marched out of their camp to give battle. Judas and his 13
men sounded their trumpets and closed with them. The Gentiles 14
broke, and fled to the plain. All the rearmost fell by the sword. The 15
pursuit was pressed as far as Gazara and the lowlands of Idumaea,
Azotus and Jamnia; about three thousand of the enemy were killed.

Judas and his force then broke off the pursuit and returned. He 16, 17
said to the people: 'Curb your greed for spoil; there is more fighting
before us; Gorgias and his force are in the hills near by. Stand firm 18
now against our enemies and fight; after that, plunder as you please.'

Before Judas had finished speaking, an enemy patrol appeared, 19
reconnoitring from the hills. They saw that their army was in flight, 20
and that their camp was being set on fire; the smoke that met their
gaze showed what had happened. They were filled with panic as they 21
took in the scene, and when they saw the army of Judas in the plain,
ready for battle, they all fled to Philistia. 22

23 Then Judas turned back to plunder the camp, and there they got
much gold and silver, violet and purple stuffs, and great riches.
24 On their return they sang songs of thanksgiving and praised Heaven,
25 'for it is right, because his mercy endures for ever'. That day saw a
great deliverance for Israel.

26 Those of the Gentiles who escaped with their lives went and
27 reported to Lysias all that had happened. On hearing the news he
was overwhelmed with disappointment, because Israel had not
suffered the disaster he had hoped for, and the issue was not what the
king had ordered.

28 In the following year he gathered sixty thousand picked infantry
29 and five thousand cavalry to make war on the Jews. They marched
into Idumaea, and encamped at Bethsura, where Judas met them
30 with ten thousand men. When he saw the strength of the enemy's
army, he prayed: 'All praise to thee, the Saviour of Israel, who didst
break the attack of the giant by thy servant David. Thou didst
deliver the army of the Philistines into the power of Saul's son,
31 Jonathan, and of his armour-bearer. In like manner put this army
into the power of thy people Israel. Humble their pride in their
32 forces and their mounted men. Strike them with panic, turn their
insolent strength to water, make them reel under a crushing defeat.
33 Overthrow them by the sword of those who love thee, and let all who
know thy name praise thee with songs of thanksgiving.'

34 So they joined battle, and Lysias lost about five thousand men in
35 the close fighting. When he saw his own army routed and Judas's
army full of daring, ready to live or die nobly, he departed for
Antioch, and there collected a force of mercenaries, in order to
return to Judaea with a much larger army than before.[a]

36 But Judas and his brothers said: 'Now that our enemies have been
crushed, let us go up to Jerusalem to cleanse the temple and re-
37 dedicate it.' So the whole army was assembled and went up to
38 Mount Zion. There they found the temple laid waste, the altar
profaned, the gates burnt down, the courts overgrown like a thicket
39 or wooded hill-side, and the priests' rooms in ruin. They tore their
40 garments, wailed loudly, put ashes on their heads, and fell on their
faces to the ground. They sounded the ceremonial trumpets, and
cried aloud to Heaven.

41 Then Judas detailed troops to engage the garrison of the citadel

[a] in order...before: *probable meaning; Gk. obscure.*

while he cleansed the temple. He selected priests without blemish, 42
devoted to the law, and they purified the temple, removing to an 43
unclean place the stones which defiled it. They discussed what to do 44
with the altar of burnt-offering, which was profaned, and rightly 45
decided to demolish it, for fear it might become a standing reproach
to them because it had been defiled by the Gentiles. They therefore
pulled down the altar, and stored away the stones in a fitting place on 46
the temple hill, until a prophet should arise who could be consulted
about them. They took unhewn stones, as the law commands, and 47
built a new altar on the model of the previous one. They rebuilt the 48
temple and restored its interior, and consecrated the temple courts.
They renewed the sacred vessels and the lamp-stand, and brought 49
the altar of incense and the table into the temple. They burnt incense 50
on the altar and lit the lamps on the lamp-stand to shine within the
temple. When they had put the Bread of the Presence on the table 51
and hung the curtains, all their work was completed.

Then, early on the twenty-fifth day of the ninth month, the month 52
Kislev, in the year 148,[a] sacrifice was offered as the law commands 53
on the newly made altar of burnt-offering. On the anniversary of the 54
day when the Gentiles had profaned it, on that very day, it was rededicated, with hymns of thanksgiving, to the music of harps and
lutes and cymbals. All the people prostrated themselves, worship- 55
ping and praising Heaven that their cause had prospered.

They celebrated the rededication of the altar for eight days; there 56
was great rejoicing as they brought burnt-offerings and sacrificed
peace-offerings and thank-offerings. They decorated the front of the 57
temple with golden wreaths and ornamental shields. They renewed
the gates and the priests' rooms, and fitted them with doors. There 58
was great merry-making among the people, and the disgrace brought
on them by the Gentiles was removed.

Then Judas, his brothers, and the whole congregation of Israel 59
decreed that the rededication of the altar should be observed with
joy and gladness at the same season each year, for eight days,
beginning on the twenty-fifth of Kislev.

At that time they encircled Mount Zion with high walls and strong 60
towers to prevent the Gentiles from coming and trampling it down
as they had done before. Judas set a garrison there; he also fortified 61
Bethsura, so that the people should have a fortress facing Idumaea.

[a] *That is* 164 B.C.

5 WHEN THE GENTILES round about heard that the altar had
2 been rebuilt and the temple rededicated, they were furious, and
determined to wipe out all those of the race of Jacob who lived
among them. Thus began the work of massacre and extermination
among the people.

3 Judas then made war on the descendants of Esau in Idumaea and
attacked Acrabattene, because they had hemmed Israel in. There he
inflicted on them a severe and humiliating defeat, and took spoils
4 from them. He remembered also the wrong done by the Baeanites,
who with their traps and road-blocks were continually ambushing
5 the Israelites. He first confined them to their forts and took up
positions against them; then he solemnly committed them to destruc-
6 tion and set the forts ablaze with all their occupants. He crossed
over to the Ammonites, and came upon a strong and numerous force
7 under the command of a certain Timotheus. He fought many battles
8 with them, and they broke before him and were crushed. After
capturing Jazer and its dependent villages, he returned to Judaea.

9 Then the Gentiles in Gilead gathered against the Israelites within
their territory, intending to destroy them; but they took refuge in the
10 fortress of Dathema, and sent this letter to Judas and his brothers:

11 The Gentiles round us have gathered to wipe us out. They are
preparing to come and seize the fortress where we have taken
12 refuge; Timotheus is in command of their army. So come at once
and rescue us from their clutches, for many of our number have
13 already fallen. All our fellow-Jews in the region of Tubias have
been massacred, their wives and their children taken captive, and
their property carried off. About a thousand men there have lost
their lives.

14 While the letter was being read, other messengers with their
15 garments torn arrived from Galilee. 'Ptolemais, Tyre and Sidon,'
they said, 'and all heathen Galilee have mustered their forces to
make an end of us.'

16 When Judas and the people heard this, a full assembly was called
to decide what they should do for their fellow-countrymen in distress
17 and under enemy attack. Judas said to Simon his brother, 'Choose
your men, and go and rescue your countrymen in Galilee, while
18 I and my brother Jonathan march into Gilead.' The rest of his forces

he left for the defences of Judaea, with Josephus son of Zacharias,
and Azarias, leading citizens, and gave them this order: 'Take 19
charge of the people of Jerusalem, but on no account join battle with
the Gentiles until we return.' Simon was allotted three thousand 20
men for the march on Galilee, and Judas eight thousand for the
march on Gilead.

Simon invaded Galilee and, after many battles, broke the resis- 21
tance of the Gentiles. He pursued them as far as the gate of Ptole- 22
mais, killed nearly three thousand of them, and stripped their
corpses. He took back with him the Jews from Galilee and Arbatta, 23
their wives and children, and all their property, and brought them to
Judaea with great jubilation.

Meanwhile Judas Maccabaeus and his brother Jonathan crossed 24
the Jordan and made a three days' march through the desert. They 25
came upon some Nabataeans, who met them peacefully, and gave
them an account of all that had happened to their fellow-Jews in
Gilead: many of them were held prisoner in Bozrah and Bezer, in 26
Alema, Casphor, Maked, and Carnaim—all large fortified towns;
some in the other towns of Gilead. 'Your enemies', they told them, 27
'are marshalling their forces to storm your fortresses tomorrow so as
to capture them and destroy all the Jews in them in a single day.'

Then Judas and his army suddenly turned aside to Bozrah by way 28
of the desert, captured the town, and put all the males to the sword.
He plundered all their property and set fire to the town. From there 29
he made a night-march and came within reach of the fortress of
Dathema. When dawn broke they saw in front of them an innumer- 30
able host, bringing up scaling-ladders and siege-engines and en-
gaging the defenders, to capture the fortress. Judas saw that battle 31
was already joined, and a cry went up to heaven from the town, with
trumpeting and loud shouting. Judas said to his men: 'Now is the 32
time to fight for our brothers.'

They marched out in three columns to take the enemy in the rear. 33
Then they sounded the trumpets and cried aloud in prayer, and the 34
army of Timotheus recognized that it was Maccabaeus and took to
flight before him. He inflicted a severe defeat on them, and nearly
eight thousand of the enemy fell that day.

Judas then turned aside to Alema,[a] attacked and captured it, and 35
killed all the males. He plundered the town and set it on fire. From 36

[a] *Some witnesses read* Maapha.

there he moved on and occupied Casphor, Maked, Bezer, and the
other towns of Gilead.

37 After these events, Timotheus gathered another army, and took
38 up position opposite Raphon, on the other side of the ravine. Judas
sent spies to their camp, and they reported that all the Gentiles in the
39 neighbourhood had rallied in very great strength to Timotheus, who
had also hired Arab mercenaries to help them; they were encamped
on the far side of the ravine, ready to engage him in battle. So Judas
marched to meet them.

40 As Judas and his army were approaching the flooded ravine,
Timotheus said to his officers: 'If Judas crosses over to our side first,
we shall not be able to stand up to him; he will certainly get the
41 better of us. If, however, his courage fails him and he takes up a
position on the other side of the river, then we will cross over and get
42 the better of him.' When Judas reached the ravine, he stationed the
officers of the muster on its bank, with instructions that no one
should be allowed to take up a fixed position, but that all should
43 advance to battle. Thus Judas forestalled the enemy by crossing to
attack them, with all his people following. The Gentiles broke before
him; they all threw away their arms and took refuge in the temple at
44 Carnaim. Judas captured the town and burnt the temple together
with all its occupants: Carnaim was completely subdued and could
no longer withstand him.

45 Then Judas gathered together all the Israelites in Gilead to escort
them to Judaea. They amounted to an immense host, small and
46 great, women and children, with their property. They came as far as
Ephron, a large and strongly fortified town on the road: it was impossible to pass by it on either side; the only route was through the
47 town. But the townsmen kept them out, barricading their gates with
48 boulders. Judas sent them a conciliatory message: 'We have to pass
through your territory to reach our own. No one shall do you any
harm: we shall only march through.' But they refused to open their
gates to him.

49 Judas issued orders to the whole host for everyone to halt where he
50 was. Then the fighting men took up battle positions and attacked the
town all that day and all the night, until it fell into their hands.
51 They put every male to the sword, razed the town to the ground and
plundered it, and then marched through it over the bodies of the
52 dead. They crossed the Jordan to the great plain opposite Bethshan,

while Judas brought up the stragglers and encouraged the people all 53
along the road till he arrived in Judaea. They went up to Mount Zion 54
with gladness and jubilation, and offered burnt-offerings, because
they had returned in safety without the loss of a single man.

Now while Judas and Jonathan were in Gilead, and Simon their 55
brother in Galilee was besieging Ptolemais, the two commanders, 56
Josephus son of Zacharias, and Azarias, heard of their exploits in
battle. 'We too', they said, 'must make a name for ourselves: let us go 57
and fight the Gentiles in our neighbourhood.' So they gave orders to 58
their forces and marched against Jamnia. Gorgias came out of the 59
town with his men to meet them in battle; and Josephus and Azarias 60
were routed and pursued to the frontier of Judaea. Some two
thousand of the people fell that day. So the Israelites suffered a 61
heavy defeat, because their commanders, thinking to play the hero
themselves, had not obeyed Judas and his brothers. They were not, 62
however, of that family to whom it was granted to bring deliverance
to Israel.

Judas and his brothers won a great reputation in all Israel and 63
among the Gentiles, wherever their fame was heard, and crowds 64
flocked to acclaim them.

After this, Judas marched out with his brothers and made war on 65
the descendants of Esau to the south. He struck at Hebron and its
villages, demolished its fortifications, and burnt down its forts on all
sides. He then set out to invade Philistine territory, marching 66
through Marisa. On that day several priests, who had ill-advisedly 67
gone into action wishing to distinguish themselves, fell in battle.
Then Judas turned aside to Azotus in Philistia. He pulled down their 68
altars, burnt the images of their gods, carried off the spoil from their
towns, and returned to Judaea.

As King Antiochus marched through the upper provinces he heard **6**
that there was a city in Persia called Elymais, famous for its wealth
in silver and gold. Its temple was very rich, full of gold shields, coats 2
of mail, and arms, left there by Alexander son of Philip, king of
Macedon and the first to be king over the Greeks. Antiochus came 3
and tried to capture and plunder the city, but failed because his plan
had become known to the citizens. They gave battle and put him to 4
flight, and he withdrew to Babylon in bitter disappointment.

A messenger met him in Persia with the news that the armies which 5
had invaded Judaea were in full retreat. Lysias had marched up with 6

an exceptionally strong force, only to be flung back before the enemy,
and the strength of the Jews had grown by the capture of arms,
equipment, and spoils from the Syrian armies they had defeated.
7 They had pulled down the abomination he had built on the altar in
Jerusalem, and surrounded their temple with high walls as before,
and had even fortified Bethsura.

8 When the king heard this news, he was thrown into such deep
dismay that he took to his bed, ill with grief at the miscarriage of his
9 plans. There he lay for many days, his bitter grief breaking out again
10 and again, and he realized that he was dying. So he summoned all
his Friends and said to them: 'Sleep has deserted me; the weight
11 of care has broken my heart. At first I said to myself, "Why am
I overwhelmed by this flood of trouble, I who was kind and well-
12 loved in the day of my power?" But now I remember the wrong
I did in Jerusalem, when I took all her vessels of silver and gold, and
when I made an unjustified attempt to wipe out the inhabitants of
13 Judaea. It is for this, I know, that these misfortunes have come upon
me; and here I am, dying of grief in a foreign land.'

14 He summoned Philip, one of his Friends, and appointed him
15 regent over his whole empire, giving him the crown, the royal robe,
and the signet-ring, with authority to take his son Antiochus and
16 bring him up to be king. King Antiochus died there in the year 149.[a]
17 When Lysias learnt that the king was dead, he placed the young
Antiochus, whom he had brought up from boyhood, on the throne in
succession to his father, and gave him the name of Eupator.

18 MEANWHILE the garrison of the citadel were confining the
Israelites to the neighbourhood of the temple, and giving continual
19 support to the Gentiles by their harassing tactics. Judas therefore
determined to make an end of them. He gathered all the people
20 together to lay siege to the citadel in the year 150,[b] erecting emplacements and siege-engines against the enemy.

21 Now some of the besieged garrison escaped and were joined by a
22 number of renegade Israelites. They went to the king and said:
'How long must we wait for you to do justice and avenge our com-
23 rades? We were willing to serve your father, to follow his instructions
24 and to obey his decrees, and what was the result? Our own countrymen became our enemies. They actually killed as many of us as they

[a] *That is* 163 B.C. [b] *That is* 162 B.C.

could find, and robbed us of our property. Nor are we the only ones 25
to suffer at their hands. They have attacked all their neighbours as
well. At this very moment they are besieging the citadel in Jeru- 26
salem and mean to capture it; and they have fortified both the temple
and Bethsura. Unless your majesty quickly overpowers them they 27
will go to yet greater lengths, and you will not be able to keep them in
check.'

When the king heard this he was furious. He assembled all his 28
Friends, the commanders of his army, and his cavalry officers. He 29
was joined by mercenary troops from other kingdoms and from the
islands. His forces numbered one hundred thousand infantry, 30
twenty thousand cavalry, and thirty-two war-elephants. They passed 31
through Idumaea and laid siege to Bethsura. They kept up the attack
for a long time and erected siege-engines, but the defenders made a
sortie and set fire to them, and fought back manfully.

Judas now withdrew from the citadel and encamped at Beth- 32
zacharia, opposite the camp of the king. Early next morning the king 33
broke camp and rushed his army along the road to Bethzacharia;
there his forces were drawn up for battle and the trumpets were
sounded. The elephants were roused for battle with the juice of 34
grapes and of mulberries. The great beasts were distributed among 35
the phalanxes; by each were stationed a thousand men, equipped
with coats of chain-mail and bronze helmets. Five hundred picked
horsemen were also assigned to each animal. These had been 36
stationed beforehand where the beast was; and wherever it went, they
went with it, never leaving it. Each animal had a strong wooden tur- 37
ret fastened on its back with a special harness, by way of protection,
and carried four[a] fighting men as well as an Indian driver. The rest of 38
the cavalry Lysias stationed on either flank of the army, to harass the
enemy while themselves protected by the phalanxes. When the sun 39
shone on the gold and bronze shields, they lit up the hills, which
flashed like torches.

Part of the king's army was deployed over the heights, and part 40
over the low ground. They advanced confidently and in good order.
All who heard the din of this marching multitude and its clashing 41
arms shook with fear. It was a very great and powerful array
indeed.

Judas advanced with his army and gave battle, and six hundred of 42

[a] *Probable reading; Gk.* thirty-two (*compare verse 30*).

43 the king's men were killed. Eleazar Avaran, seeing that one of the
elephants wore royal armour and stood out above all the rest, thought
44 that the king was riding on it. So he gave his life to save his people
45 and win everlasting renown for himself. He ran boldly towards it,
into the middle of the phalanx, dealing death right and left, while
46 they fell back on either side before him. He got in underneath the
elephant, and thrust at it from below and killed it. It fell to the
ground on top of him, and there he died.

47 When the Jews saw the strength and impetus of the imperial
48 forces, they fell back before them. Part of the king's army marched
up to Jerusalem to renew the engagement, and the king put Judaea
49 and Mount Zion into a state of siege. He made peace with the people
of Bethsura, who abandoned the town, having no more food there to
withstand a siege, as it was a sabbatical year when the land was left
50 fallow. Thus the king occupied Bethsura and detailed a garrison to
hold it.

51 He then attacked the temple and subjected it to a long siege; he set
up emplacements and siege-engines, with flame-throwers, catapults
52 for discharging stones and barbed missiles, and slings. But the
defenders too constructed engines to counter his engines, and put up
53 a prolonged resistance. There was no food, however, in the stores[a]
because of the sabbatical year; those who from time to time had
arrived in Judaea as refugees from the Gentiles had eaten up all that
54 remained of the provisions. There were only a few men left in the
temple, because the famine had been too severe for them, and they
had scattered to their own homes.

55 Lysias heard that Philip, whom King Antiochus had appointed
56 before he died to educate his son Antiochus for the kingship, had
returned from Persia and Media with the late king's expeditionary
57 force, and that he was seeking to take over the government. So he
hastily gave orders for departure, saying to the king, his commanders, and his troops: 'Every day we are growing weaker, provisions are low, the place we are besieging is strong, and the affairs of
58 the empire are pressing. So let us offer these men terms and make
59 peace with them and their whole nation. Let us guarantee their right
to follow their laws and customs as they used to do, for it was our
abolition of these very customs and laws that roused their resentment,
and produced all these consequences.'

[a] *Some witnesses read* in the temple.

The proposal met with the approval of the king and the com- 60
manders, and an offer of peace was sent and accepted. The king and 61
his commanders bound themselves by oath, and on the agreed terms
the besieged emerged from their stronghold. But when the king 62
entered Mount Zion and saw how strongly the place was fortified, he
went back on the oath he had sworn, and gave orders for the surrounding wall to be demolished. He then set off at top speed for 63
Antioch, where he found Philip in possession; a battle ensued, and
the city was taken by storm.

IN THE YEAR 151,[a] Demetrius son of Seleucus left Rome, landed 7
with a handful of men at a town on the coast, and there made
himself king. While he was travelling to the royal seat of his ancestors, 2
the army seized Antiochus and Lysias, intending to hand them over
to him. When this was reported to him, he said, 'Do not let me set 3
eyes on them.' The soldiers accordingly put them to death, and 4
Demetrius ascended the throne.

All the godless renegades from Israel, led by Alcimus, who aspired 5
to be high priest, came to the king and brought charges against their 6
people. They said to him: 'Judas and his brothers have killed all
your supporters, and have driven us from our country. Be pleased 7
now to send a man whom you trust, to go and see what devastation
they have brought upon us and upon the king's territory, and to
punish them and all their supporters.' The king chose Bacchides, one 8
of the royal Friends, who was governor beyond the Euphrates, a man
of high standing in the empire and loyal to the king. He sent him 9
and the godless Alcimus, on whom he had conferred the high-
priesthood, with orders to take vengeance on Israel.

They set out with a large army and entered Judaea. Bacchides 10
sent envoys to Judas and his brothers to make false offers of friendship; but when they saw what a large force he had brought with him, 11
they took no notice of these offers.

A deputation of doctors of the law came before Alcimus and 12
Bacchides, asking for justice. The Hasidaeans were in fact the first 13
group in Israel to make overtures to them; for they said to them- 14
selves, 'A priest of the family of Aaron has come with their forces, and
he will do us no harm.' The language of Alcimus was conciliatory; he 15
assured them on oath that no harm was intended to them or their

[a] *That is* 161 B.C.

16 friends. But once he had gained their confidence, he arrested sixty of
them and put them to death in a single day; as Scripture says:

17 'The bodies of thy saints were scattered,
their blood was shed round Jerusalem,
and there was none to bury them.'

18 This put all the people in fear and terror of them, and they said to
each other, 'There is neither truth nor justice among them; they
19 have broken their pledge and the oath they swore.' Then Bacchides
left Jerusalem and camped in Bethzaith; and he ordered the arrest of
many of those who had deserted to him, together with some of the
20 people, and had them slaughtered and thrown into a great pit. He
assigned the whole district to Alcimus, detailed some troops to assist
him, and returned to the king.

21, 22 Alcimus fought hard for his high-priesthood. All the trouble-
makers rallied to him; they gained control over Judaea, and did ter-
23 rible damage in Israel. When Judas saw all the mischief which
Alcimus and his followers had brought upon the Israelites, far worse
24 than anything the Gentiles had done, he marched through all the
territory of Judaea and its environs, punishing deserters and debar-
25 ring them from access to the country districts. When Alcimus saw
that Judas and his band had grown powerful, and recognized that he
was unable to withstand them, he returned to the king and accused
them of atrocities.

26 Then the king sent Nicanor, one of his distinguished commanders
27 and a bitter enemy of Israel, with orders to wipe them out. Nicanor
arrived at Jerusalem with a large force, and sent envoys to Judas and
28 his brothers to make false offers of friendship: 'Let there be no
quarrel between us,' he said; 'I propose to come with a few men for a
friendly personal meeting.'

29 He came to Judas and they greeted one another as friends, yet the
30 enemy were preparing to kidnap Judas. When Judas discovered that
Nicanor's visit was a trick, he took alarm and refused to meet him
31 again. Nicanor, realizing that his plan had been detected, marched
32 out to engage Judas near Capharsalama. About five hundred of
Nicanor's army were killed, and the rest escaped to the city of
David.

33 After these events, Nicanor went up to Mount Zion, and some of
the priests and members of the senate came out from the temple to

give him a friendly welcome, and to show him the burnt-offering
which was being sacrificed for the king. But he mocked them, jeered 34
at them, and spat on them,[a] boasting and swearing angrily: 'Unless 35
Judas and his army are surrendered to me at once, when I return
victorious I will burn down this house.' And he went off in a rage.
Thereupon the priests went in, and stood facing the altar and the 36
temple. They wept and said: 'Thou didst choose this house to bear 37
thy name, to be a house of prayer and supplication for thy people;
take vengeance on this man and his army, and make them fall by the 38
sword. Remember all their blasphemy, and grant them no reprieve.'

Nicanor moved from Jerusalem and encamped at Beth-horon, 39
where he was joined by an army from Syria. Judas encamped at 40
Adasa with three thousand men; there he prayed in these words:
'There was a king whose followers blasphemed, and thy angel 41
came forth and struck down one hundred and eighty-five thousand of
them. So do thou crush this army before us today, and let all men 42
know that Nicanor has reviled thy holy place; judge him as his
wickedness deserves.'

The armies joined battle on the thirteenth of the month Adar, and 43
the army of Nicanor suffered a crushing defeat, he himself being the
first to fall in the battle. When his army saw that Nicanor had fallen, 44
they threw away their arms and took to flight. The Jews, sounding the 45
signal trumpets in the enemy's rear, pursued them as far as Gazara, a
day's journey from Adasa. From all the villages of Judaea round 46
about, the inhabitants came out and attacked their flanks, forcing
them back upon their pursuers. They all fell by the sword; there were
no survivors. The Jews seized spoil and booty; they cut off Nicanor's 47
head and that right hand which he had stretched out so arrogantly,
and brought them to be displayed at Jerusalem. There was great 48
public rejoicing and that day was kept as a special day of jubilation.
It was ordained that the day should be observed annually, on the 49
thirteenth of Adar. Thus Judaea entered upon a short period of 50
peace.

NOW JUDAS had heard about the Romans: they were renowned **8**
for their military power and for the welcome they gave to those
who became their allies; any who joined them could be sure of their
firm friendship. He was told about the wars they had fought, and 2

[a] *Literally* and polluted them.

the valour they had shown in their conquest of the Gauls, whom
3 they had laid under tribute. He heard of their successes in Spain,
4 where they had seized silver-mines and gold-mines, maintaining
their hold on the entire country—distant as it was from their own
land—by their patience and good judgement. There were kings from
far and near who had marched against them, but they had been
beaten off after crushing defeats; others paid them annual tribute.
5 They had crushed in battle and conquered Philip, and Perseus
6 king of Kittim, and all who had attacked them. Antiochus the Great,
king of Asia, had marched against them with one hundred and
twenty elephants, with cavalry and chariots and an immense force,
7 but they had totally defeated him. They had taken the king alive, and
had required that he and his successors should pay them a large
8 annual tribute, give hostages, and cede the territories of India,
Media, and Lydia, together with some of their finest provinces.
These they had taken from him and given to King Eumenes.
9, 10 When the Greeks planned to attack and destroy them, they heard
of it and sent a single general against them. Battle was joined, and
many of the Greeks fell; the Romans took their women and children
prisoner, plundered their territory and annexed it, razed their
11 fortifications, and made them slaves, as they are to this day. The
remaining kingdoms, the islands, and all who had ever opposed
12 them, they destroyed or reduced to slavery. With their friends,
however, and all who put themselves under their protection, they
maintained firm friendship. They thus conquered kings near and far,
13 and all who heard their fame went in fear of them. Those whom they
wished to help and to appoint as kings, became kings, and those
they wished to depose, they deposed; and thus they rose to great
14 heights of power. For all this, not one of them made any personal
15 claim to greatness by wearing the crown or donning the purple. They
had established a senate where three hundred and twenty senators
met daily to deliberate, giving constant thought to the proper
16 ordering of the affairs of the common people. They entrusted their
government and the ruling of all their territory to one of their
number every year, all obeying this one man without envy or jealousy
among themselves.
17 Judas accordingly chose Eupolemus son of John son of Accos, and
Jason son of Eleazar, and sent them to Rome to conclude a treaty
18 of friendship and alliance, so that the Romans might rid them of

tyranny, for it was clear that the Greek empire was reducing Israel to
slavery. They made the long journey to Rome and entered the 19
Senate, where they spoke as follows: 'Judas, known as Maccabaeus, 20
his brothers, and the Jewish people have sent us to you to conclude a
treaty of friendly alliance with you, so that we may be enrolled as
your allies and friends.' The Romans found the proposal acceptable, 21
and the following is a copy of the reply which they inscribed on 22
tablets of bronze and sent to Jerusalem, so that the Jews there might
have a record of the treaty of alliance:

Success to the Romans and the Jewish nation by sea and land for 23
ever! May sword and foe be far from them! But if war breaks out 24
first against Rome or any of her allies throughout her dominion,
then the Jewish nation shall support them whole-heartedly as 25
occasion may require. To the enemies of Rome or of her allies the 26
Jews shall neither give nor supply provisions, arms, money, or
ships; so Rome has decided; and they shall observe their commit-
ments, without compensation.

Similarly, if war breaks out first against the Jewish nation, then 27
the Romans shall give them hearty support as occasion may
require. To their enemies there shall be given neither provisions, 28
arms, money, nor ships; so Rome has decided. These commit-
ments shall be kept without breach of faith.

These are the terms of the agreement which the Romans have 29
made with the Jewish people. But if, hereafter, both parties shall 30
agree to add or to rescind anything, then they shall do as they
decide; any such addition or rescindment shall be valid.

To this the Romans added: As for the misdeeds which King 31
Demetrius is perpetrating against the Jews, we have written to him as
follows: 'Why have you oppressed our friends and allies the Jews so
harshly? If they make any further complaint against you, then we 32
will see that justice is done them, and will make war upon you by sea
and by land.'

When Demetrius heard that Nicanor and his forces had fallen in 9
battle, he sent Bacchides and Alcimus a second time into Judaea,
with the right wing of his army. They marched along the Gilgal 2
road, laid siege to Messaloth in Arbela, and captured it, inflicting
heavy loss of life.

3 In the first month of the year 152,[a] they moved camp to Jeru-
4 salem. From there they marched to Berea with twenty thousand
5 infantry and two thousand cavalry. Now Judas was in camp at
6 Alasa, with three thousand picked men. But when they saw the size
of the enemy forces, their courage failed, and many deserted, leaving
a mere eight hundred men in the field.

7 When Judas saw that with the campaign going against him his
army had melted away, his heart sank, for there was no time to rally
8 them. Though much discouraged, he said to those who were left,
9 'Let us move to the attack and see if we can defeat them.' But his
men tried to dissuade him: 'Impossible!' they said. 'No; let us save
our lives now and come back later with our comrades to fight them.
10 Now we are too few.' But Judas replied: 'Heaven forbid that
I should do such a thing as run away! If our time is come, let us die
bravely for our fellow-countrymen, and leave no stain on our
honour.'

11 The Syrian army left its camp and took up position to meet the
Jews. The cavalry[b] was divided into two detachments; the slingers
and the archers went ahead of the main force, and the picked troops
12 were in the front line. Bacchides was on the right. The phalanx came
13 on in two divisions with trumpets sounding; Judas's men also
sounded their trumpets. The earth shook at the din of the armies
as battle was joined, and they fought from dawn until evening.

14 When Judas saw that Bacchides and the main strength of his army
was on the right flank, all his stout-hearted men rallied to him,
15 and they broke the Syrian right; then he pursued them as far as
16 Mount Azotus. When the Syrians on the left wing saw that their
right had been broken, they turned about and followed on the heels of
17 Judas and his men, attacking them in the rear. The fighting became
18 very heavy, and many fell on both sides. Judas himself fell, and the
19 rest of the Jews took to flight. Jonathan and Simon carried off Judas
20 their brother; they buried him in the family tomb at Modin, and
wept over him. Great was the grief in Israel, and they mourned him
for many days, saying,

21 'How is our champion fallen,
the saviour of Israel!'

[*a*] *That is* 160 B.C. [*b*] The Syrian army...cavalry: *or* The Jewish army left its camp and stood to meet the enemy. The Syrian cavalry...

The rest of the history of Judas, his wars, exploits, and achievements 22
—all these were so numerous that they have not been written down.

AFTER THE DEATH of Judas the renegades raised their heads in 23
every part of Israel, and all the evil-doers reappeared. In those 24
days a terrible famine broke out, and the country went over to their
side. Bacchides chose apostates to be in control of the country. 25
These men set inquiries on foot, and tracked down the friends of 26
Judas and brought them before Bacchides, who took vengeance on
them, loading them with indignities. It was a time of great affliction 27
for Israel, worse than any since the day when prophets ceased to
appear among them. Then all the friends of Judas assembled and 28
said to Jonathan: 'Since your brother Judas died, there has not been 29
a man like him to take the lead against our enemies, Bacchides and
those of our own nation who are hostile to us. Today, therefore, we 30
choose you to succeed him as our ruler and leader and to fight our
battles.' So Jonathan took over the leadership at that time in place of 31
his brother Judas.

The news reached Bacchides, and he set himself to kill Jonathan. 32
When Jonathan and his brother Simon and all their men learnt of 33
this, they took refuge in the desert of Tekoa, encamping by the pool
of Asphar. Bacchides discovered this on the sabbath, and crossed the 34
Jordan with his whole army. So Jonathan sent his brother John to 35
take the camp followers and appeal to his friends the Nabataeans to
look after their baggage train, which was of some size. But the 36
Jambrites appeared from Medaba and kidnapped John; they seized
the baggage and made off with it. Some time afterwards, news was 37
brought to Jonathan and his brother Simon that the Jambrites were
celebrating an important wedding, and bringing the bride, the
daughter of one of the great nobles of Canaan, from Nadabath with
a large retinue. Remembering how their brother John had been 38
killed, Jonathan and his men set out and hid themselves under cover
of a hill. They looked out and there they saw the bridegroom, in the 39
middle of a bustling crowd and a train of baggage, coming to meet
the bridal party, escorted by his friends and kinsmen fully armed, to
the sound of drums and instruments of music. Emerging from 40
ambush, Jonathan attacked and cut them down; many fell, while
others made off into the hills and the Jews took all their goods as
spoil. So the wedding was turned into mourning, and the sound of 41

42 music to lamentation. The blood of their brother was fully avenged,
and Jonathan returned to the marshes of Jordan.
43 Bacchides heard this and came to the banks of Jordan on the
44 sabbath with a powerful force. Jonathan said to his men: 'Now is
the time to fight for our lives; we are today in worse plight than ever:
45 the enemy in front, the water of Jordan behind, to right and left
46 marsh and thicket; there is no escape. Cry to Heaven to save you
47 from the hands of the enemy.' Battle was joined, and Jonathan had
raised his hand to strike down Bacchides, when he fell back and
48 evaded him. Then Jonathan and his men leapt into the Jordan and
swam over to the other side; but the enemy did not cross the river in
49 pursuit. The army of Bacchides lost about a thousand men that day.
50 Bacchides returned to Jerusalem and fortified with high walls,
gates, and bars a number of places in Judaea: the fortress at Jericho,
Emmaus and Beth-horon, Bethel, Timnath-pharathon, and Tephon;
51, 52 in all of these he placed garrisons to harass Israel. He fortified the
towns of Bethsura and Gazara and the citadel, placing forces and
53 stores of provisions there. He took the sons of the leading men of the
country as hostages and put them under guard in the citadel at
Jerusalem.
54 In the second month of the year 153,[a] Alcimus gave orders for the
wall of the inner court of the temple to be demolished, thereby
55 destroying the work of the prophets. But at the moment when he
began demolition, Alcimus had a stroke, which put a stop to his
activities. Paralysed and with his speech impaired, he could not
56 utter a word or give final instructions about his property. Thus
57 he died in great torment. On learning that Alcimus was dead,
Bacchides returned to the king, and for two years Judaea had peace.
58 Then the renegades put their heads together: 'Look!' they said,
'Jonathan and his people are living in peace and security. Let us
bring Bacchides here; he will capture them all in a single night.'
59, 60 They went and conferred with Bacchides, and he set out with a large
force, sending letters secretly to all his supporters in Judaea, with
instructions to seize Jonathan and his men. But they were unable to
61 do so, because their plan leaked out. About fifty of the ringleaders
62 of this villainy in Judaea were seized and put to death. Jonathan,
Simon, and their men then made their way out to Bethbasi in the
63 desert, built up its ruined fortifications, and strengthened it. When

[a] *That is* 159 B.C.

Bacchides learnt of this, he gathered together all his army and sent
word to those in Judaea. He came and took up position against 64
Bethbasi, and attacked it for a long time, erecting siege-engines.
Jonathan left his brother Simon in the town and slipped out into the 65
country with a few men. He attacked Odomera and his people and 66
the Phasirites in their encampment; he began to get the better of 67
them and to advance towards Bethbasi with his forces.

Simon and his men made a sally out of the town and set fire to the
siege-engines. They fought Bacchides and defeated him. They kept 68
up heavy pressure upon him, and so his plan and his expedition
proved fruitless. There was great anger against the renegades at 69
whose instance he had invaded the land, and many of them were put
to death. Bacchides then decided to return to his own country.

When Jonathan learnt of this, he sent envoys to Bacchides to 70
arrange terms of peace with him and a return of the Jewish prisoners.
Bacchides agreed and did as Jonathan proposed, swearing to do him 71
no harm for the rest of his life. He sent him back the prisoners he 72
had taken previously from Judaea, and returned to his own country;
never again did he enter their territory. So the war came to an end in 73
Israel. Jonathan took up residence in Michmash and began to
govern the people, rooting the godless out of Israel.

Jonathan rules the nation

IN THE YEAR 160,[a] Alexander Epiphanes son of Antiochus came and **10**
took possession of Ptolemais, where he was welcomed and proclaimed king. When King Demetrius heard of this, he raised a huge 2
army and marched out to meet him in battle. At the same time 3
Demetrius sent Jonathan a letter in friendly and flattering terms; for 4
he said to himself, 'Let us forestall Alexander by making peace with
the Jews before Jonathan comes to terms with him against us, for he 5
will remember all the harm we have done him by our treatment of his
brothers and of his nation.' He gave Jonathan authority to collect 6
and equip an army, conferred on him the title of ally, and ordered the
hostages in the citadel to be handed over to him. Jonathan came to 7
Jerusalem and read the letter aloud before all the people and the

[*a*] *That is* 152 B.C.

8 garrison of the citadel, who were filled with apprehension when they
heard that the king had given Jonathan authority to raise an army.
9 They surrendered the hostages to him, and he restored them to their
parents.

10 Jonathan took up his quarters in Jerusalem and began to repair
11 and rebuild the city. He gave orders to those engaged on the work to
build the walls and surround Mount Zion with a fortification of
12 squared stones, and this was done. The foreigners in the strongholds
13 which Bacchides had built made their escape, each man leaving his
14 post and returning to his own country; however, in Bethsura there
were still left some of those who had abandoned the law and
ordinances, and had found asylum there.

15 King Alexander heard of the promises which Demetrius had sent
to Jonathan, and was told of the battles and heroic deeds of Jonathan
16 and his brothers, and the hardships they had endured. 'Where shall
we ever find another man like this?' he exclaimed. 'Let us make him
17 our friend and ally.' He therefore wrote a letter to Jonathan to this
effect:

18 King Alexander to his brother Jonathan, greeting.

19 We have heard about you, what a valiant man you are and how
20 fit to be our friend. Now therefore we do appoint you this day to
be High Priest of your nation with the title of King's Friend, to
support our cause and to keep friendship with us.

He sent him a purple robe and a gold crown.

21 Jonathan assumed the vestments of the high priest in the seventh
month of the year 160[a] at the Feast of Tabernacles, and he gathered
an army together and prepared a large supply of arms.

22, 23 When this news reached Demetrius he was mortified. 'How did
we come to let Alexander forestall us', he asked, 'in gaining the
24 friendship and support of the Jews? I too will send them cordial
25 messages and offer honours and gifts to keep them on my side.' So
he sent a message to the Jews to this effect:

King Demetrius to the Jewish nation, greeting.

26 We have heard with great pleasure that you have kept your
agreements and remained in friendship with us and have not gone
27 over to our enemies. Continue, then, to keep faith with us, and we

[a] *That is* 152 B.C.

shall reward you well for all that you do in our cause, both by 28
granting you numerous exemptions and making you gifts.
I hereby release and exempt you and all Jews whatsoever from 29
tribute, from the tax on salt, and from the crown-money. From 30
today and hereafter I release you from the one-third of the grain-
harvest and the half of the fruit-harvest due to me. From today
and for all time, I will no longer exact them from Judaea or from
the three administrative districts, formerly part of Samaria and
Galilee, which I now attach to Judaea. Jerusalem and its environs, 31
with its tithes and tolls, shall be sacred and tax free. I also sur- 32
render authority over the citadel in Jerusalem and grant the High
Priest the right to garrison it with men of his own choice. All 33
Jewish prisoners of war taken from Judaea into any part of my
kingdom, I set at liberty without ransom. No man shall exact any
levy whatsoever on the cattle of the Jews. All their festivals, 34
sabbaths, new moons, and appointed days, and three days preced-
ing and following each festival, shall be days of exemption and
release for all the Jews in my kingdom; no one shall have authority 35
to impose any exaction or burden on a Jew in any respect.
Jews shall be enlisted in the forces of the King to the number 36
of thirty thousand men; they shall receive the usual army pay.
Some of them shall be stationed in the great royal fortresses, others 37
put in positions of trust in the kingdom. Their commanders and
officers shall be of their own race, and they shall follow their own
customs, just as the King has ordered for Judaea.
The three districts added to Judaea from the territory of Samaria 38
shall be attached to Judaea so as to be under one authority, and
subject to the High Priest alone.
Ptolemais and the lands belonging to it I make over to the temple 39
in Jerusalem, to meet the expenses proper to it. I give fifteen 40
thousand silver shekels annually, charged on my own royal
accounts, to be drawn from such places as may prove convenient.
And the arrears of the subsidy, in so far as it has not been paid by 41
the revenue officials, as it formerly was, shall henceforth be paid in
for the needs of the temple. In addition, the five thousand silver 42
shekels which used to be taken from the annual income of the
temple are also released, because they belong to the ministering
priests. Whoever shall take sanctuary in the temple at Jerusalem, 43
or in any part of its precincts, because of a debt to the crown or

any other debt, shall be free from distraint on his person or on his
44 property within my kingdom. The cost of the rebuilding and
45 repair of the temple shall be borne by the royal revenue; also the
repair of the walls of Jerusalem and its surrounding fortification, as
well as of the fortresses in Judaea, shall be at the expense of the
royal revenue.

46 When Jonathan and the people heard these proposals, they did not
believe or accept them, for they recalled the terrible calamity the
47 king had brought upon Israel, and his harsh oppression. They
favoured Alexander, because it was he who had been the initiator of
peaceful overtures; so they remained his allies to the end.

48 King Alexander mustered powerful forces and took up position
49 against Demetrius, and the two kings joined battle. The army of
Alexander took to flight, and Demetrius pursued him and got the
50 better of them. He fought hard till sunset, but on that day Demetrius
fell.

51 Thereupon Alexander sent ambassadors to Ptolemy king of
52 Egypt, with a message to this effect: 'I have returned to my kingdom
and sit on the throne of my ancestors. I have assumed the government, defeated Demetrius, and made myself master of our country;
53 for I gave him battle, and he and his army were crushed by us, and we
54 sit on the throne of his kingdom. Let us now form an alliance; make
me your son-in-law by giving me your daughter in marriage, and
I will give presents to you and her worthy of your royal state.'

55 King Ptolemy replied: 'It was a happy day when you returned to
the land of your ancestors and ascended the throne of their realm.
56 I will now do as you ask; only come to Ptolemais so that we may meet,
and I will become your father-in-law as you propose.'

57 In the year 162,[a] Ptolemy set out from Egypt, with his daughter
58 Cleopatra, and arrived at Ptolemais, where King Alexander met him,
and Ptolemy gave him his daughter in marriage. The wedding was
celebrated in royal style, with great pomp.

59, 60 King Alexander wrote to Jonathan to come and meet him. Jonathan went in state to Ptolemais, where he met the two kings; he gave
them silver and gold, and also made many gifts to their Friends; and
so he won their favour.

61 There were some scoundrelly Jewish renegades who conspired to

[a] *That is* 150 B.C.

lodge complaints against Jonathan. The king, however, paid no
attention to them, but gave orders for Jonathan to be divested of the 62
garment he wore and robed in purple, and this was done. The king 63
made him sit at his side, and told his officers to go with Jonathan into
the centre of the city and proclaim that no one should bring any
complaint against him or make trouble for him for any reason whatsoever. When this proclamation was made and those who planned to 64
lodge complaints saw Jonathan's splendour, and the purple robe he
wore, they all made off. Thus the king honoured him, enrolling him 65
in the first class of the order of King's Friends, and making him a
general and a provincial governor. Jonathan returned to Jerusalem 66
well pleased with his success.

IN THE YEAR 165,[a] Demetrius, the son of King Demetrius, arrived 67
in the land of his fathers from Crete. King Alexander was greatly 68
upset by this news, and returned to Antioch. Demetrius appointed 69
as his commander Apollonius the governor of Coele-syria, who raised
a powerful force and encamped at Jamnia. From there he sent this
message to Jonathan the high priest: 'You are all alone in resisting 70
us, and you are making me look ridiculous and absurd. Why do you
defy us up there in the hills? If you have confidence in your forces, 71
come down to meet us on the plain, and let us try conclusions with
each other there, for I have the power of cities behind me. Make 72
inquiries; find out who I am and who are our allies; you will be told
that you cannot stand your ground against us, for your predecessors
have twice been routed in their own territory, and now you will not 73
be able to resist my cavalry, and such a force as mine, on the plain,
where there is not so much as a stone or a pebble to give you cover,
or any place to which you can escape.'

Jonathan was provoked by this message from Apollonius. He took 74
ten thousand men and marched out from Jerusalem, and was joined
by his brother Simon with reinforcements. He laid siege to Joppa, 75
whose gates the citizens had closed against him because Apollonius
had a garrison there. But when fighting started, the citizens took 76
fright and opened the gates; thus Jonathan became master of Joppa.
When Apollonius heard of it he took three thousand cavalry and a 77
large force of infantry, and marched to Azotus as if to pass through it,
but at the same time, relying on his numerous cavalry, he advanced

[a] *That is* 147 B.C.

78 into the plain. Jonathan went in pursuit as far as Azotus, where the
79 armies joined battle. But Apollonius had left a thousand cavalry in
80 hiding in their rear, and Jonathan discovered that there was an
ambush behind him. The enemy surrounded his army, showering
81 arrows on our people from dawn till dusk. But they stood fast as
82 Jonathan had ordered them, and the enemy cavalry grew weary. At
that point Simon led out his troops and joined battle with the enemy
phalanx, now that the cavalry was exhausted. They were routed by
him and took to flight.

83 The horsemen scattered across the plain and took refuge in
Azotus, where they sought asylum in the temple of Dagon their idol.
84 But Jonathan set fire to Azotus and its surrounding villages, and
plundered them; the temple of Dagon, and those who had taken
85 refuge there, he destroyed with fire. The numbers of those who fell
by the sword, together with those who lost their lives in the fire,
86 reached eight thousand. Jonathan marched away from Azotus, and
encamped at Ascalon, where the citizens came out to meet him with
87 great pomp. Then he and his men returned to Jerusalem loaded with
spoil.

88 When King Alexander heard of all this, he did Jonathan still
89 greater honour, sending him the gold clasp which it is the custom to
give to the King's Kinsmen. He also presented him with Accaron
and all its districts.

11 The king of Egypt collected a huge army, countless as the sand on
the sea-shore, and a great fleet of ships, meaning to make himself
master of Alexander's kingdom by treachery and add it to his own.
2 He set out for Syria with professions of peace, and the people of the
towns proceeded to open their gates to him and went to meet him;
King Alexander had ordered them to do this, because Ptolemy was
his father-in-law.

3 As he went on his progress from town to town, Ptolemy left a
4 detachment of troops in each of them as a garrison. When he reached
Azotus, he was shown the burnt-out temple of Dagon, the city itself
and its ruined suburbs strewn with corpses, and, piled up along his
way, the bodies of those who had been burned in the course of the
5 fighting. They told the king that it was Jonathan's doing, hoping that
6 he would reprimand him; but the king said nothing. Jonathan met
him in state at Joppa, where they exchanged greetings and passed the
7 night. Jonathan accompanied the king as far as the river Eleutherus

and then returned to Jerusalem. King Ptolemy made himself master 8
of the coast towns as far as Seleucia-by-the-sea. He was harbouring
malicious designs against Alexander.

He sent ambassadors to King Demetrius with the following 9
message: 'I propose that you and I should make a pact: I will give
you my daughter, now Alexander's wife, and you shall reign over the
kingdom of your father. I now regret having given my daughter to 10
him, for he has tried to kill me.'

He maligned Alexander in this way because he coveted his king- 11
dom, and he took his daughter away and gave her to Demetrius. 12
This led to a breach between him and Alexander, and to open
enmity.

Ptolemy now entered Antioch, where he assumed the crown of 13
Asia; thus he wore two crowns, that of Egypt and that of Asia.

King Alexander was at this time in Cilicia, because the inhabitants 14
of that region were in revolt. But when he heard the news he 15
marched against Ptolemy, who came to meet him with a powerful
army and routed him. Alexander fled to Arabia for protection, and 16
King Ptolemy was triumphant. Zabdiel the Arab chieftain cut off 17
Alexander's head and sent it to Ptolemy. But two days later King 18
Ptolemy died, and his garrisons in the fortresses were killed by the
inhabitants. So in the year 167[a] Demetrius became king. 19

At this time Jonathan gathered together the Judaeans to assault the 20
citadel in Jerusalem, and they brought up many siege-engines against
it. But a number of renegades, enemies of their own people, went to 21
the king and reported that Jonathan was besieging the citadel. The 22
king was furious at the news and immediately moved his quarters to
Ptolemais. He wrote to Jonathan ordering him to raise the siege, and
to meet him for conference at Ptolemais with all speed.

When Jonathan received this letter, he gave orders for the siege to 23
be continued. Then, selecting elders of Israel and priests to accompany him, he set out on his dangerous mission. He took with him 24
silver and gold, and robes, and many other gifts, and went to meet
the king at Ptolemais.

He won the favour of Demetrius, although some renegade Jews 25
tried to lodge complaints against him. But the king treated him just 26
as his predecessors had done, honouring him in the presence of all
his Friends. He confirmed him in the high-priesthood and in all his 27

[*a*] *That is* 145 B.C.

former dignities, and appointed him head of the first class of the
King's Friends.

28 Jonathan requested the king to exempt Judaea and the three
Samaritan districts[a] from tribute, promising him in return three
29 hundred talents. King Demetrius consented, writing to Jonathan on
all these affairs as follows:

30 King Demetrius to his brother Jonathan, and to the Jewish
nation, greeting.
31 This is a copy of our letter written to our kinsman Lasthenes
about you, which we have had made for your information:
32 'King Demetrius to his respected kinsman Lasthenes, greeting.
33 'Because our friends the Jewish nation show us goodwill, and
observe their obligations to us, we are resolved to become their
34 benefactor. We have therefore settled on them the lands of Judaea
and the three districts, Apherema, Lydda, and Ramathaim, which
are now transferred from Samaria to Judaea, together with all the
lands adjacent thereto, for the benefit of the priesthood at Jerusalem. This is a transfer of the annual dues which the King
formerly received from these territories, from the produce of the
35 soil and of the orchards. Other of our revenues, the tithes and tolls
now pertaining to us, the salt-pans, and the crown-money, all these
36 we shall cede to them. These provisions are irrevocable from now
37 for all future time. See to it then that you make a copy of them to
be given to Jonathan and set by him in a conspicuous position on
the holy mountain.'

38 When King Demetrius saw that the country was quiet under his
rule and resistance was at an end, he disbanded all his forces, sending
every man home, with the exception of the foreign mercenaries he
had hired from the islands of the Gentiles. Then all the troops enlisted
39 under his predecessors turned against the king. A certain Trypho,
formerly of the party of Alexander, aware of the disaffection of all the
forces towards Demetrius, went to Imalcue, the Arab chieftain, who
40 had charge of the child Antiochus, Alexander's son, and kept pressing
him to hand the boy over to him to be made king in succession to his
father. He also informed Imalcue of all the measures Demetrius was
taking and of his unpopularity with his troops. There he remained
for some time.

[*a*] three...districts: *probable reading; Gk.* three districts and Samaria.

Meanwhile Jonathan sent to King Demetrius requesting him to 41
withdraw, from the citadel in Jerusalem and from the fortresses, the
garrisons which were constantly harassing Israel. Demetrius sent 42
Jonathan this reply: 'I will not only meet your request, but when
opportunity arises I will do you and your people the highest honour.
And now be so good as to send men to support me, for all my troops 43
are in revolt.'

Jonathan dispatched three thousand fighting men to Antioch, and 44
the king was much relieved at their arrival. The citizens poured into 45
the centre of the city, a hundred and twenty thousand strong, bent on
killing the king. He took refuge in the palace, while the citizens 46
seized control of the streets and fighting broke out. King Demetrius 47
called the Jews to his assistance, and they rallied to him at once.
They then dispersed all over the city and slaughtered that day as
many as a hundred thousand, setting the city on fire and taking much 48
booty. And thus they saved the king's life.

When the citizens saw that the Jews had the city completely at 49
their mercy, their courage failed them and they clamoured to the
king to accept their surrender and to stop the Jews fighting against 50
them and the city. They threw down their arms and made peace; and 51
the Jews, now in high repute with the king and all his subjects,
returned to Jerusalem loaded with booty. But when King Demetrius 52
was secure upon his throne, with the country quiet under him,
he went back on all his promises and broke off relations with 53
Jonathan; instead of repaying the benefits he had received, he put
severe pressure upon him.

After this, Trypho returned, and with him Antiochus, a mere lad. 54
Antiochus was crowned, and all the forces Demetrius had so con- 55
temptuously discharged rallied to the king. These fought against
Demetrius, and he was utterly routed. Trypho brought up his 56
elephants and made himself master of Antioch. The young Antiochus 57
wrote to Jonathan confirming him in the high-priesthood, with
authority over the four districts, and making him one of the King's
Friends. He also sent him a service of gold plate, and gave him the 58
right to drink from a gold cup, to be robed in purple, and to wear
the gold clasp. He appointed Jonathan's brother Simon as officer 59
commanding the area from the Ladder of Tyre to the borders of
Egypt.

Jonathan made a tour through the country on the far side of the 60

river and the towns there; and all the forces of Syria gathered to his
support.
He went to Ascalon, where he was received with great honour by
61 the citizens. From there he went on to Gaza, but the inhabitants
closed the gates against him; so he blockaded the city, set fire to its
62 suburbs, and plundered them. The citizens of Gaza then sought
peace, and he made terms with them, taking the sons of their
magistrates as hostages and sending them off to Jerusalem; he himself continued his progress through the country in the direction of
Damascus.
63 Jonathan heard that Demetrius's officers had arrived at Kedesh-in-
Galilee with a large force to prevent him from reaching his objective.
64 He went to meet them, leaving his brother Simon in Judaea.
65 Simon took up position against Bethsura and, after prolonged fight-
66 ing, blockaded it. Finally the citizens sued for terms of peace and
Simon consented; he evicted them, took over the town, and installed
a garrison there.
67 Jonathan, who had encamped with his army by the Lake of
Gennesaret, marched out early in the morning into the plain of Asor.
68 There in the plain the gentile army was advancing to meet him; they
had set an ambush for him in the hills, while they themselves con-
69 fronted him. When the men from the ambush emerged and joined in
70 the fighting, all Jonathan's men took to flight; not one remained
except Mattathias son of Absalom, and Judas son of Chalphi, officers
71 in the army. Jonathan tore his clothes, put dust upon his head, and
72 prayed. Then he turned upon the enemy and routed them in head-
73 long flight. When the fugitives of Jonathan's army saw this, they
rallied to him and joined in the pursuit as far as the enemy base at
74 Kedesh; there they encamped. That day about three thousand of the
Gentiles fell. Jonathan then returned to Jerusalem.

12 JONATHAN NOW SAW his opportunity and sent picked men on a
mission to Rome to confirm and renew the treaty of friendship
2 with that city. He sent letters to the same effect to Sparta and to
3 other places. The envoys travelled to Rome and went to the Senate
House to deliver their message: 'Jonathan the High Priest and the
Jewish people have sent us to renew their former pact of friendship
4 and alliance.' The Romans gave them letters requiring the authorities
in each place to give them safe conduct to Judaea.

Here follows a transcript of the letter which Jonathan wrote to the 5
Spartans:

Jonathan the High Priest, the Senate of the Jews, the priests, 6
and the rest of the Jewish people, to our brothers of Sparta,
greeting.
On a previous occasion a letter was sent to Onias the High 7
Priest from Arius your king, acknowledging our kinship; a copy is
given below. Onias welcomed your envoy with full honours and 8
received the letter in which the terms of the alliance and friendship
were set forth. We do not regard ourselves as needing such alliances, 9
since our support is the holy books in our possession. Neverthe- 10
less, we now venture to send and renew our pact of brotherhood
and friendship with you, so that we may not become estranged, for
it is many years since you wrote to us. We never lose any oppor- 11
tunity, on festal and other appropriate days, of remembering you
at our sacrifices and in our prayers, as it is right and proper to
remember kinsmen; and we rejoice at your fame. We ourselves 12, 13
have been under the pressure of hostile attacks on every side; all
the surrounding kings have made war upon us. In the course of 14
these wars we had no wish to trouble you or the rest of our allies
and friends: we have the aid of Heaven to support us, and so we 15
have been saved from our enemies, and they have been humbled.
Accordingly, we chose Numenius son of Antiochus, and Antipater 16
son of Jason, and have sent them to the Romans to renew our
former friendship and alliance with them. We instructed them to 17
go to you also with our greetings, and to deliver this letter about
the renewal of our pact of brotherhood. And now we pray you to 18
send us a reply to this letter.

This is a copy of the letter sent by the Spartans to Onias: 19

Arius, King of Sparta, to Onias the High Priest, greeting. 20
A document has come to light which shows that Spartans and 21
Jews are kinsmen, descended alike from Abraham. Now that we 22
have learnt this, we beg you to write and tell us how your affairs
prosper. The message we return to you is, 'What is yours, your 23
cattle and every kind of property, is ours, and what is ours is
yours', and we have therefore instructed our envoys to report to
you in these terms.

24 Jonathan heard that Demetrius's generals had returned to attack
25 him with larger forces than before. He marched from Jerusalem and
met them in the region of Hamath, giving them no chance to set foot
26 in his territory. He sent spies to their camp, who on their return
27 reported that preparations were being made for a night attack. At
sunset Jonathan gave orders to his men to stay awake and stand to
arms all night, ready for battle; and he stationed outposts all round
28 the camp. When the enemy heard that Jonathan and his men were
ready for battle, they were alarmed; their courage failed, and they
29 withdrew, first lighting watch-fires in their camp. Jonathan and his
men, seeing the watch-fires burning, did not realize what had hap-
30 pened until morning. Then Jonathan set out in pursuit, but failed to
31 overtake them, for they had crossed the river Eleutherus. So Jonathan
turned aside against the Arabs called Zabadaeans, and he dealt them
32 a severe blow and plundered them. He struck camp and came to
Damascus, and then made a march through the whole country.

33–34 Simon set out and marched as far as Ascalon and the neighbouring
fortresses. He then turned towards Joppa; he had heard that the
citizens intended to hand it over to the supporters of Demetrius, but
before they could do so, he occupied the town and placed a garrison
there to defend it.

35 When Jonathan returned he convened the senate. With their
36 agreement he decided to build fortresses in Judaea, to heighten the
walls of Jerusalem, and to erect a high barrier to separate the citadel
from the city and so to isolate it that the garrison could not buy or
37 sell. They assembled to rebuild the city, for the wall along the ravine
to the east had partly collapsed, and he repaired the section of the
38 wall called Chaphenatha. Simon also rebuilt and fortified Adida in
the Shephelah, erecting gates and bars.

39 Trypho now aspired to be king of Asia; he meant to rebel against
40 King Antiochus and assume the crown himself. But he was afraid
that Jonathan would fight to prevent this, so he cast about for some
means of capturing and killing him. He set off and reached Bethshan.
41 Jonathan marched out to meet him with forty thousand picked troops,
42 and he also reached Bethshan. Trypho, seeing that Jonathan had a
43 large force with him, was afraid to attack. So he received him
honourably and commended him to all his Friends, gave him
presents, and ordered his Friends and his troops to obey Jonathan as
44 they would himself. He said to Jonathan: 'Why have you put all

these men to so much trouble, when we are not at war? Send them 45
home now and choose a few to accompany you, and come with me
to Ptolemais. I will hand it over to you with all the other fortresses,
the rest of the troops, and all the officials, and then I will leave the
country. This is the only purpose of my coming.' Jonathan took him 46
at his word and did as he said: he dismissed his forces and they
returned to Judaea. He kept back three thousand men, of whom he 47
left two thousand in Galilee, while a thousand accompanied him. But 48
when Jonathan entered Ptolemais, the citizens closed the gates,
seized him, and put to the sword all who had entered with him.

Trypho sent a force of infantry and cavalry into Galilee to the 49
great plain, to wipe out all Jonathan's men. They now learnt that 50
Jonathan had been seized and was lost, along with his escort, but
they put heart into one another and marched in close formation,
ready for battle. When their pursuers saw that they would fight to 51
the death, they turned back. So all came safely home to Judaea, 52
mourning for Jonathan and his followers, and filled with alarm. All
Israel was plunged in grief. The surrounding Gentiles were now 53
bent on destroying them root and branch, saying to themselves, 'The
Jews have no leader or champion, so now is the time to attack, and
we shall blot out all memory of them among men.'

The high-priesthood of Simon

THE NEWS REACHED Simon that Trypho had mustered a large 13
force for the invasion and destruction of Judaea, and it threw the 2
people into a state of panic. When Simon saw this, he went up to
Jerusalem, called an assembly, and encouraged them in these words: 3
'I need not remind you of all that my brothers and I and my father's
house have done for the laws and the holy place, what battles we
have fought, what hardships we have endured. My brothers have all 4
fallen in this cause, fighting for Israel, and I am the only one left.
Now Heaven forbid that I should grudge my own life in any moment 5
of danger, for I am not worth more than my brothers. No! I will 6
take up the cause of my nation and the holy place, of your wives and
children, since all the Gentiles in their hatred have gathered to
destroy us.' At these words the people plucked up courage, and they 7, 8

shouted in answer: 'You shall be our leader in place of Judas and
9 your brother Jonathan. Fight our battles, and we will do whatever
10 you tell us.' So Simon mustered all the fighting men and hurried on
the completion of the walls of Jerusalem until it was fortified on all
11 sides. He sent Jonathan son of Absalom with a considerable force to
Joppa; he expelled its inhabitants and remained in possession of the
town.
12 Trypho marched out from Ptolemais with a large force to invade
13 Judaea, taking Jonathan with him as a prisoner. Simon encamped at
14 Adida on the edge of the plain. When Trypho learnt that Simon
had come forward to take the place of his brother Jonathan, and that
he was about to join battle with him, he sent envoys to Simon with
15 the following message: 'We are detaining your brother Jonathan
because of certain monies which he owed to the royal treasury in
16 connection with the offices he held. To ensure that he will not again
revolt if we release him, send one hundred talents of silver and two of
17 his sons as hostages, and we will let him go.' Simon himself realized
that this was a trick, but he had the money and the children brought
to him, fearing that otherwise he might arouse deep animosity among
18 the people, who would say, 'It was because you did not send the
19 money and the children that Jonathan lost his life.' So he sent the
children and the hundred talents, but Trypho broke his word and
did not release Jonathan.
20 After this, Trypho set out to invade the country and ravage it,
taking a roundabout way through Adora. Simon and his army
21 marched parallel with him everywhere he went. Meanwhile the
garrison of the citadel were sending emissaries to Trypho, urging him
to come to them by way of the desert, and to send them provisions.
22 Trypho prepared to send all his cavalry, but that night there was a
severe snow-storm, which prevented their arrival; so he withdrew
23 into Gilead. When he reached Bascama, he had Jonathan put to
24 death, and there he was buried. Trypho then turned and went back
to his own country.
25 Simon had the body of his brother Jonathan brought to Modin,
26 and buried in the town of their fathers; and all Israel made a great
27 lamentation and mourned him for many days. Simon built a high
monument over the tomb of his father and his brothers, visible at a
28 great distance, faced back and front with polished stone. He erected
seven pyramids, those for his father and mother and his four brothers

arranged in pairs. For the pyramids he contrived an elaborate 29
setting: he surrounded them with great columns surmounted with
trophies of armour for a perpetual memorial, and between the
trophies carved ships, plainly visible to all at sea. This mausoleum 30
which he made at Modin stands to this day.

Trypho now plotted against the young King Antiochus and 31
murdered him. He usurped his throne and assumed the crown of 32
Asia. This was a disaster for the country.

Simon rebuilt the fortresses of Judaea, furnishing them with high 33
towers and great walls with gates and bars; he also provisioned the
fortresses. He sent representatives to King Demetrius to negotiate a 34
remission of taxes for the country, on the ground that all Trypho's
exactions had been exorbitant. Demetrius replied favourably to 35
this request and wrote him a letter in the following terms:

> King Demetrius to Simon the High Priest and friend of kings, 36
> and to the Senate and nation of the Jews, greeting.
>
> We have received the golden crown and the palm branch which 37
> you sent, and we are ready to make a lasting peace with you and
> to instruct the revenue officers to grant you immunities. All our 38
> agreements with you stand, and the strongholds which you built
> shall remain yours. We give a free pardon for any errors of omis- 39
> sion or commission, to take effect from the date of this letter. We
> remit the crown-money which you owed us, and every other tax
> formerly exacted in Jerusalem is henceforth cancelled. All those 40
> of you who are suitable for enrolment in our retinue shall be so
> enrolled. Let there be peace between us.

In the year 170,[a] Israel was released from the gentile yoke. The 41, 42
people began to write on their contracts and agreements, 'In the first
year of Simon, the great high priest, general and leader of the Jews'.

Then Simon invested Gazara,[b] and surrounded it with his forces. 43
He constructed a siege-engine and brought it up to the town, made
a breach in one of the towers and captured it. The men on the siege- 44
engine leapt out of it into the town, and there was a great com-
motion. The townspeople and their wives and children climbed up 45
on to the city wall with their garments torn, clamouring to Simon to
offer them terms. 'Do not treat us as our wickedness deserves,' they 46
cried, 'but as your mercy prompts you.' Simon came to terms with 47

[*a*] *That is* 142 B.C. [*b*] *Probable reading; Gk.* Gaza.

them, and brought the war to an end. But he expelled them from
the town, and after purifying the houses in which the idols stood, he
48 made his entry with songs of thanksgiving and praise. He removed
every pollution from it and settled men in it who would keep the law.
He strengthened its fortifications and built a residence there for
himself.

49 The men in the citadel in Jerusalem were prevented from going in
and out to buy and sell in the country; famine set in and many of
50 them died of starvation. They clamoured to Simon to accept their
surrender, and he agreed: he expelled them from the citadel and
51 cleansed it from its pollutions. It was on the twenty-third day of the
second month in the year 171[a] that he made his entry, with a chorus
of praise and the waving of palm branches, with lutes, cymbals, and
zithers, with hymns and songs, to celebrate Israel's final riddance of a
52 formidable enemy. Simon decreed that this day should be observed
as an annual festival. He fortified the temple hill opposite the citadel,
53 and he and his men took up residence there. When Simon saw that
his son John had become a man, he made him commander of all
the forces, with Gazara as his headquarters.

14 In the year 172,[b] King Demetrius mustered his army and went
into Media to recruit additional forces for his war against Trypho.
2 When Arsakes king of Persia and Media heard that Demetrius had
entered his territories, he sent one of his generals to capture him alive.
3 The general marched out and defeated Demetrius, captured him and
brought him to Arsakes, who put him in prison.

4 As long as Simon lived, Judaea was at peace. He promoted his
people's welfare, and they lived happily all through the glorious days
5 of his reign. Among other notable achievements he captured the
6 port of Joppa to secure his communications overseas. He extended
his nation's territories and made himself master of the whole land.
7 He repatriated a large number of prisoners of war. Without meeting
any resistance he gained control over Gazara and Bethsura and over
the citadel, and removed their pollution.

8 They farmed their land in peace, and the land produced its crops,
9 and the trees in the plains their fruit. Old men sat in the streets,
talking together of their blessings; and the young men dressed
10 themselves in splendid military style. Simon supplied the towns
with food in plenty and equipped them with weapons for defence.

[*a*] *That is* 141 B.C. [*b*] *That is* 140 B.C.

His renown reached the ends of the earth. He restored peace to the 11
land, and there were great rejoicings throughout Israel. Each man 12
sat under his own vine and fig-tree, and they had no one to fear. Those 13
were days when every enemy vanished from the land and every hostile
king was crushed. Simon gave his protection to the poor among the 14
people; he paid close attention to the law and rid the country of
lawless and wicked men. He gave new splendour to the temple and 15
furnished it with a wealth of sacred vessels.

THE REPORT OF Jonathan's death reached Rome, and Sparta too, 16
and they were deeply grieved. When they heard, however, that 17
his brother Simon had become high priest in his place, and was in
firm control of the country and the towns in it, they inscribed on 18
bronze tablets a renewal of the treaty of friendship and alliance
which they had established with his brothers Judas and Jonathan.
This was read before the assembly in Jerusalem. The following is a 19, 20
copy of the letter from Sparta:

The rulers and city of Sparta to the High Priest Simon, to the Senate, the priests, and the rest of the Jewish people, our brothers, greeting.

The envoys you sent to our people have told us about your fame 21
and honour; their visit has given us great pleasure. We have 22
entered a transcript of the message they brought in the minutes of
the public assembly: 'Numenius son of Antiochus, and Antipater
son of Jason, envoys of the Jews, visited us to renew their treaty of
friendship with us. It was resolved by the public assembly to 23
receive these men with honour and to place a copy of their address
in the public archives, so that the Spartans might have it on
permanent record. A copy of this document has been made for
Simon the High Priest.'

After this, Simon sent Numenius to Rome with a large gold shield, 24
worth a thousand minas, to confirm the alliance with the Romans.

When the people heard of these events they asked themselves how 25
they could show their gratitude to Simon and his sons. For he, with 26
his brothers and his father's family, had stood firm, fought off the
enemies of Israel, and ensured his nation's freedom. So an inscrip- 27
tion was engraved on tablets of bronze and placed on a monument on
Mount Zion. A copy of the inscription follows:

On the eighteenth day of the month Elul, in the year 172,[a] the
28 third year of Simon's high-priesthood, at Asaramel, in a large
assembly of priests, people, rulers of the nation, and elders of the
29 land, the following facts were placed on record. Whereas our land
had been subject to frequent wars, Simon son of Mattathias, a
priest of the Joarib family, and his brothers, risked their lives in
resisting the enemies of their people, in order that the temple and
law might be preserved, and they brought great glory to their
30 nation. Jonathan rallied the nation, became their high priest, and
31 then was gathered to his fathers. Their enemies resolved to invade
32 their land and destroy it, and to attack the temple. Then Simon came
forward and fought for his nation. He spent large sums of his own
money to arm the soldiers of his nation and to provide their pay.
33 He fortified the towns of Judaea, and Bethsura on the boundaries
of Judaea, formerly an enemy arsenal, and stationed a garrison
34 of Jews there. He fortified Joppa by the sea, and Gazara near
Azotus, formerly occupied by the enemy. There he settled Jews,
and provided these towns with everything needful for their welfare.
35 When the people saw Simon's patriotism and his resolution to win
fame for his nation, they made him their leader and high priest, in
recognition of all that he had done, of his just conduct, his loyalty
36 to his nation, and his constant efforts to enhance its renown. His
leadership was crowned with success, and the Gentiles were
expelled from the land, as were also the troops in Jerusalem who
had built themselves a citadel in the city of David, from which
they sallied forth to bring defilement upon the whole precinct
37 of the temple and do violence to its purity. He settled Jews in
it and fortified it for the security of the land and of the city, and
38 he raised the height of the walls of Jerusalem. King Demetrius
39 confirmed him in the office of high priest, made him one of his
40 Friends, and granted him the highest honours; for he had heard
that the Romans were naming the Jews friends, allies, and brothers,
and had gone in state to meet Simon's envoys.

41 The Jews and their priests confirmed Simon as their leader and
high priest in perpetuity until a true prophet should appear.
42 He was to be their general, and to have full charge of the temple;
and in addition to this the supervision of their labour, of the
country, and of the arms and fortifications was to be entrusted to

[a] *That is* 140 B.C.

him. He was to be obeyed by all; all contracts in the country were 43
to be drawn up in his name. He was to wear the purple robe and
the gold clasp.
None of the people or the priests shall have authority to abrogate 44
any of these decrees, to oppose commands issued by Simon or
convene any assembly in the land without his consent, to be robed
in purple, or to wear the gold clasp. Whoever shall contravene these 45
provisions or neglect any of them shall be liable to punishment.
It is the unanimous decision of the people that Simon shall 46
officiate in the ways here laid down. Simon has agreed and con- 47
sented to be high priest, general and ethnarch of the Jews and the
priests, and to be the protector of them all.

This inscription, it was declared, should be engraved on bronze 48
tablets and set up within the precincts of the temple in a conspicuous position, and copies should be placed in the treasury, in the 49
keeping of Simon and his sons.
Antiochus son of King Demetrius sent a letter from overseas to **15**
Simon the high priest and ethnarch of the Jews, and to the whole
nation. The contents were as follows: 2

King Antiochus to Simon, High Priest and Ethnarch, and to the Jewish nation, greeting.

Whereas certain traitors have seized my ancestral kingdom, 3
I have now decided to assert my claim to it, so that I may restore it
to its former condition. I have raised a large body of mercenaries
and fitted out ships of war. I intend to land in my country and to 4
attack those who have ravaged my kingdom and destroyed many of
its cities. Now therefore I confirm all the tax remissions which my 5
royal predecessors granted you, and all their other remissions of
tribute. I permit you to mint your own coinage as currency for 6
your country. Jerusalem and the temple shall be free. All the 7
arms you have prepared, and the fortifications which you have
built and now hold, shall remain yours. All debts now owing to 8
the royal treasury and all future liabilities thereto shall be cancelled
from this time on for ever. When we have re-established our 9
kingdom, we shall confer the highest honours upon you, your
nation and temple, to make your country's greatness apparent to
the whole world.

10 In the year 174,[a] Antiochus marched into his ancestral domain, and
all the armed forces came over to him, leaving very few with
11 Trypho. Antiochus pursued him, and Trypho came as a fugitive to
12 Dor by the sea. He knew that his position was desperate now that all
13 his troops had deserted. Antiochus, at the head of a hundred and
twenty thousand trained soldiers and eight thousand horsemen, laid
14 siege to Dor. He encircled the town, and his ships joined in the
blockade from the sea. He thus exerted heavy pressure on it from
both land and sea, and prevented anyone from leaving or entering.

15 NUMENIUS AND HIS PARTY arrived from Rome with a letter
to the various kings and countries, which read as follows:

16 Lucius, Consul of the Romans, to King Ptolemy, greeting.
17 Envoys have come to us from our friends and allies the Jews,
sent by Simon the High Priest and the Jewish people, to renew
18 their original treaty of friendship and alliance. They brought a
19 gold shield worth a thousand minas. We have decided, therefore,
to write to the kings and countries, requiring them to do no harm
to the Jews, nor make war on them or their cities or their country,
20 nor ally themselves with those who so make war. And we have
21 decided to accept the shield from them. If therefore any traitors
have escaped from their country to you, hand them over to Simon
the High Priest to be punished by him according to the law of
the Jews.

22 The same message was sent to King Demetrius, to Attalus,
23 Ariarathes, Arsakes, Sampsakes, and the Spartans, and also to the
following places: Delos, Myndos, Sicyon, Caria, Samos, Pamphylia,
Lycia, Halicarnassus, Rhodes, Phaselis, Cos, Sidé, Aradus, Gortyna,
24 Cnidus, Cyprus, and Cyrene. A copy was sent to Simon the high
priest.

25 KING ANTIOCHUS laid siege to Dor for the second time,[b] and
launched repeated attacks against it; he had siege-engines constructed, and blockaded Trypho, preventing all movement in or out
of the town.
26 Simon sent Antiochus two thousand picked men to assist him,
27 with silver and gold and much equipment; but he refused the offer.

[*a*] *That is* 138 B.C. [*b*] *Some witnesses read* on the second day.

He repudiated all his previous agreements with Simon and broke off
relations. He sent Athenobius, one of the Friends, to parley with 28
him. This was his message: 'You are occupying Joppa and Gazara
and the citadel in Jerusalem, cities that belong to my kingdom.
You have laid waste their territories, and done great damage to the 29
country, and have made yourselves masters of many places in my
kingdom. I demand the return of the cities you have captured and 30
the surrender of the tribute exacted from places beyond the frontiers
of Judaea over which you have assumed control. Otherwise, you 31
must pay five hundred talents of silver on their account, and another
five hundred as compensation for the destruction you have caused
and for the loss of tribute from the cities. Failing this, we shall go to
war with you.'

Athenobius, the King's Friend, came to Jerusalem, and when he 32
saw the splendour of Simon's establishment, the gold and silver
vessels on his sideboard, and his display of wealth, he was amazed.
He delivered the king's message, to which Simon replied: 'We have 33
not occupied other people's land or taken other people's property,
but only the inheritance of our ancestors, unjustly seized for a time
by our enemies. We have grasped our opportunity and have claimed 34
our patrimony. With regard to Joppa and Gazara, which you demand, 35
these towns were doing a great deal of damage among our people and
in our land. For these we offer one hundred talents.'

Athenobius answered not a word, but went off in a rage to the 36
king; he reported what Simon had said, and described Simon's
splendour and all the things he had seen. The king was furious.

Meanwhile Trypho boarded a ship and made good his escape to 37
Orthosia. The king appointed Kendebaeus as commander-in-chief 38
of the coastal zone, and gave him infantry and cavalry. He instructed 39
him to blockade Judaea, to rebuild Kedron and strengthen its gates,
and to make war on our people, while he himself continued the
pursuit of Trypho. Kendebaeus arrived in Jamnia and began to 40
harass our people by invading Judaea, and by capturing and killing
the inhabitants. He rebuilt Kedron, stationing cavalry and troops 41
there to sally out and patrol the roads of Judaea, in accordance with
the king's instructions.

John came from Gazara and reported to his father Simon the **16**
results of Kendebaeus's campaign. Simon summoned his two eldest 2
sons Judas and John, and said to them: 'My brothers and I and my

father's family have fought Israel's battles from our youth until this
day, and many a time we have been successful in rescuing Israel.
3 Now I am old, but mercifully you are in the prime of life. Take my
place and my brother's and go out and fight for our nation. And may
help from on high be with you.'
4 He then levied from the country twenty thousand picked warriors
and cavalry, and they marched against Kendebaeus. After passing
5 the night at Modin they rose early and proceeded to the plain, where
a large force of infantry and cavalry stood ready to meet them on the
6 far side of a gully. When his army had taken up a position opposite,
John saw that his men were afraid to cross the gully. So he crossed
7 first himself; his men saw him and followed. John drew up his army
with the cavalry in the centre of the infantry, for the enemy cavalry
8 were very numerous. The trumpets were sounded, and Kendebaeus
and his army were routed; many of them fell, and the remainder took
9 refuge in the fortress. It was in this engagement that John's brother
Judas was wounded. John kept up the pursuit until Kendebaeus
10 reached Kedron, which he had rebuilt. The enemy took refuge in the
towers in the open country round Azotus, whereupon John set fire to
Azotus. Some two thousand of the enemy fell in the fighting, and
John returned to Judaea in safety.
11 Now Ptolemaeus son of Abubus had been appointed commander
12 for the plain of Jericho. He had great wealth, for he was the high
13 priest's son-in-law. But he became over-ambitious; he proposed to
make himself master of the country and plotted to put Simon and his
14 sons out of the way. In the course of a tour to inspect the towns in
that region and to attend to their needs, Simon came to Jericho with
his sons Mattathias and Judas in the year 177,[a] in the eleventh
15 month, the month of Shebat. The son of Abubus, with treachery in
his heart, received them at the small fort called Dok which he had
built, and entertained them lavishly. But he had men in conceal-
16 ment there, and when Simon and his sons had drunk freely, Ptolemaeus and his accomplices jumped up, seized their weapons, and
rushed in to the banquet. They attacked Simon and killed him, along
17 with his two sons and some of his servants. It was an act of base
treachery in which evil was returned for good.
18 Ptolemaeus sent news of this in a dispatch to the king, asking him
to send troops to his assistance and to give him authority over the

[a] *That is* 134 B.C.

country and its towns. He sent some of his men to Gazara to kill 19
John, and wrote to the army officers urging them to join him, and
offering them silver and gold and presents. Other troops he sent to 20
take Jerusalem and the temple hill. But someone ran ahead and 21
reported to John at Gazara that his father and brothers had been
murdered, and that Ptolemaeus had sent men to kill him as well.
When John heard this he was beside himself; he arrested the men 22
who came to kill him, and put them to death, because he had discovered their plot against his life.

The rest of the story of John, his wars and the deeds of valour he 23
performed, the walls he built, and his exploits, are written in the 24
annals of his high-priesthood from the time when he succeeded his
father.

THE SECOND BOOK OF THE
MACCABEES

Foreword: letters to the Jews in Egypt

1 TO THEIR JEWISH KINSMEN in Egypt, the Jews
who are in Jerusalem and those in the country of Judaea
send brotherly greeting.
2 May God give you peace and prosperity and remember his
covenant with Abraham, Isaac, and Jacob, his faithful servants.
3 May he give to you all a will to worship him, to fulfil his purposes
4 eagerly with heart and soul. May he give you a mind open to his law
5 and precepts. May he make peace and answer your prayers, and be
6 reconciled to you and not forsake you in an evil hour. Here and now
we are praying for you.
7 In the reign of Demetrius, in the year 169,[a] we the Jews wrote to
you during the persecution and the crisis that came upon us in those
years since the time when Jason and his partisans revolted from the
8 holy land and the kingdom. They set the porch of the temple on fire
and shed innocent blood. Then we prayed to the Lord and were
answered. We offered a sacrifice and fine flour, we lit the lamps, and
9 set out the Bread of the Presence. And now, you are to observe the
celebration of a Feast of Tabernacles in the month Kislev.
10 Written in the year 188.[b]

FROM THE PEOPLE of Jerusalem and Judaea, from the Senate,
and from Judas, to Aristobulus, the teacher of King Ptolemy and
a member of the high-priestly family, and to the Jews in Egypt,
greeting and good health.
11 We have been saved by God from great dangers, and give him all
12 thanks, as men standing ready to resist the king. It was God who
drove out the enemy force in the holy city.
13 For when the king went into Persia with an army that seemed
invincible, they were cut to pieces in the temple of Nanaea through a
14 stratagem employed by Nanaea's priests. Antiochus, along with his

[*a*] *That is* 143 B.C. [*b*] *That is* 124 B.C.

Companions, arrived at the temple to marry the goddess, in order to
secure the considerable treasure by way of dowry. After this had 15
been laid out by the priests, he went into the temple precinct with a
small retinue. When Antiochus entered, the priests shut the sanctuary, opened a secret door in the panelling, and hurled stones at 16
them. The king fell, as if struck by a thunderbolt. They hacked off
limbs and heads and threw them to those outside. Blessed in all 17
things be our God, who handed over the evil-doers to death!

We are about to celebrate the purification of the temple on the 18
twenty-fifth of Kislev, and think it right to inform you, so that you
also for your part may celebrate a Feast of Tabernacles, in honour of
the fire which appeared when Nehemiah offered sacrifices, after he
had built the temple and the altar. When our fathers were carried off 19
to Persia, the pious priests of those days secretly took fire from the
altar and concealed it in a dry well. It proved a safe hiding-place and
remained undiscovered. After many years had passed, in God's 20
good time, Nehemiah was sent back by the king of Persia. He then
dispatched the descendants of the priests who had hidden it to get
the fire, and they informed our people that they found, not fire, but a
thick liquid. Nehemiah ordered them to draw some out and bring it 21
to him. When the materials of the sacrifice had been presented, he
ordered the priests to sprinkle this liquid over the wood and the
things laid upon it, and this was done. Some time passed; then 22
the sun, which earlier had been hidden by clouds, shone out and the
altar burst into a great blaze, so that everyone marvelled. As the 23
sacrifice was burning, the priests offered prayer, they and all those
present: Jonathan began and the rest responded, led by Nehemiah.

The prayer was in this style: 'O Lord God, creator of all things, 24
thou the terrible, the mighty, the just, and the merciful, the only
King, the only gracious one, the only giver, the only just, omni- 25
potent, and everlasting one, who dost deliver Israel from every evil,
who didst choose the patriarchs and set them apart: accept this 26
sacrifice on behalf of thy whole people Israel; they are thy own,
watch over them and sanctify them. Gather the dispersed, free those 27
who are in slavery among the heathen, look favourably on the
despised and detested; let the heathen know that thou art our God.
Punish our oppressors for their insolent brutality and make them 28
suffer torment; but plant thy people in thy holy place, as Moses said.' 29

Then the priests chanted the hymns. After the materials of the 30, 31

sacrifice had been consumed, Nehemiah further ordered what re-
32 mained of the liquid to be poured over some great stones.[a] At this a
flame shot up, but burnt itself out as soon as the fire on the altar
outshone it.[b]

33 These events became widely known. The king of Persia was told
that, in the place where the priests who were deported had hidden
the fire, a liquid had appeared, and that Nehemiah and his com-
34 panions had used it to burn up the materials of the sacrifice. When
he had verified the fact, the king enclosed the site and made it sacred.
35 The custodians he appointed received a share of the very substantial
36 revenue that the king derived from it. Nehemiah and his companions
called the liquid 'nephthar', which means 'purification'; but most
people call it 'naphtha'.

2 The records show that it was the prophet Jeremiah who ordered
2 the exiles to hide the fire, as has been mentioned; also that, having
given them the law, he charged them not to neglect the ordinances of
the Lord, or be led astray by the sight of images of gold and silver
3 with all their finery. In similar words he appealed to them not to
abandon the law.

4 Further, this document records that, prompted by a divine
message, the prophet gave orders that the Tent of Meeting and the
ark should go with him. Then he went away to the mountain from the
5 top of which Moses saw God's promised land. When he reached
the mountain, Jeremiah found a cave-dwelling; he carried the tent,
the ark, and the incense-altar into it, then blocked up the entrance.
6 Some of his companions came to mark out the way, but were unable
7 to find it. When Jeremiah learnt of this he reprimanded them. 'The
place shall remain unknown', he said, 'until God finally gathers his
8 people together and shows mercy to them. Then the Lord will bring
these things to light again, and the glory of the Lord will appear with
the cloud, as it was seen both in the time of Moses and when
Solomon prayed that the shrine might be worthily consecrated.'

9 It was also related that Solomon, having the gift of wisdom,
offered the dedication sacrifice at the completion of the temple;
10 and that, just as Moses prayed to the Lord and fire came down from
heaven and burnt up the sacrificial offerings, so Solomon prayed and

[*a*] what remained...stones: *so some witnesses; others read* that great stones should enclose what remained of the liquid. [*b*] *Or* but hardly had the light been reflected from the altar, when it burnt itself out.

the fire came down and consumed the whole-offerings. (Moses said: 11
'The sin-offering was burnt up in the same way because it was not
eaten.') Solomon celebrated the feast for eight days. 12
These same facts are set out in the official records and in the 13
memoirs of Nehemiah. Just as Nehemiah collected the chronicles of
the kings, the writings of prophets, the works of David, and royal
letters about sacred offerings, to found his library, so Judas also has 14
collected all the books that had been scattered as a result of our recent
conflict. These are in our possession, and if you need any of them, 15
send messengers for them.
As, then, we are about to celebrate the purification of the temple, 16
we are writing to impress upon you the duty of celebrating this
festival. God has saved his whole people and granted to all of us the 17
holy land, the kingship, the priesthood, and the consecration, as he 18
promised by the law; and in him we have confidence that he will soon
be merciful to us and gather us from every part of the world to the
holy temple. For he has delivered us from great evils and purified
the temple.

Preface to this abridgement

IN FIVE BOOKS Jason of Cyrene has set out the history of Judas 19
Maccabaeus and his brothers, the purification of the great temple,
and the dedication of the altar. He has described the battles with 20
Antiochus Epiphanes and with his son Eupator, and the apparitions 21
from heaven which appeared to those who vied with one another in
fighting manfully for Judaism. Few though they were, they ravaged
the whole country and routed the foreign hordes; they restored the 22
world-renowned temple, freed the city of Jerusalem, and reaffirmed
the laws which were in danger of being abolished. All this they
achieved because the Lord was merciful and gracious to them.
These five books of Jason I shall try to summarize in a single work; 23
for I was struck by the mass of statistics and the difficulty which the 24
bulk of the material causes to those wishing to grasp the narratives of
this history. I have tried to provide for the entertainment of those 25
who read for pleasure, the convenience of students who must commit the facts to memory, and the profit of even the casual reader.
The task which I have taken upon myself in making this summary is 26

27 no easy one. It means toil and late nights, just as it is no light task for
the man who plans a dinner-party and aims to satisfy his guests.
Nevertheless, I will gladly undergo this hard labour for the benefit
28 of[a] readers in general. I shall leave to the original author the minute
discussion of every detail, and concentrate on the main points of my
29 outline. As the architect of a new house must concern himself with
the whole of the structure, while the man who paints in encaustic on
the walls needs to discover only what is necessary for the ornamenta-
30 tion, so, I judge, it is with me also. It is the province of the original
author of a history to take possession of the field, to spread himself in
31 discussion, and to inquire closely into particular questions. The man
who makes a paraphrase must be allowed to aim at conciseness of
expression and to omit a full treatment of the subject-matter.
32 Here, then, without adding anything further, I begin my narrative.
It would be absurd to make a lengthy introduction to the history and
cut short the history itself.

Syrian oppression of the Jews

3 DURING THE RULE of the high priest Onias, the holy city enjoyed
complete peace and prosperity, and the laws were still observed
most scrupulously, because he was a pious man and hated wicked-
2 ness. The kings themselves held the sanctuary in honour and used to
3 embellish the temple with the most splendid gifts; even Seleucus,
king of Asia, bore all the expenses of the sacrificial worship from his
own revenues.
4 But a certain Simon, of the clan Bilgah,[b] who had been appointed
administrator of the temple, quarrelled with the high priest about the
5 regulation of the city market. Unable to get the better of Onias, he
went to Apollonius son of Thrasaeus, then governor of Coele-syria
6 and Phoenicia, and alleged that the treasury at Jerusalem was full of
untold riches—indeed the total of the accumulated balances was
incalculable and did not correspond with the account for the sacrifices; he suggested that these balances might be brought under the
7 control of the king. When Apollonius met the king, he reported what

[*a*] for...of: *so some witnesses; others read* to win the gratitude of... [*b*] *So some witnesses* (*compare Nehemiah 12. 5, 18*); *others read* Benjamin.

he had been told about the riches. The king selected Heliodorus,
his chief minister, and sent him with orders to remove these treasures.
Heliodorus set off at once, ostensibly to make a tour of inspection 8
of the cities of Coele-syria and Phoenicia, but in fact to carry out the
purpose of the king. When he arrived at Jerusalem and had been 9
courteously received by the high priest and the citizens, he explained
why he had come: he told them about the allegations and asked if
they were in fact true. The high priest intimated that the deposits 10
were held in trust for widows and orphans, apart from what belonged 11
to Hyrcanus son of Tobias, a man of very high standing; the matter
was being misrepresented by the impious Simon. In all there were
four hundred talents of silver and two hundred of gold. It was un- 12
thinkable, he said, that wrong should be done to those who had relied
on the sanctity of the place, on the dignity and inviolability of the
world-famous temple. But Heliodorus, in virtue of the king's orders, 13
replied that these deposits must without question be handed over to
the royal treasury.

He fixed a day and went into the temple to make an inventory. At 14
this there was great distress throughout the whole city. The priests, 15
prostrating themselves in their vestments before the altar, prayed to
Heaven, to the Lawgiver who had made deposits sacred, to keep
them intact for their rightful owners. The high priest's looks pierced 16
every beholder to the heart, for his face and its changing colour
betrayed the anguish of his soul. Alarm and shuddering gripped 17
him, and the pain he felt was clearly apparent to the onlookers.
The people rushed pell-mell from their houses to join together in 18
supplication because of the dishonour which threatened the holy
place. Women in sackcloth, their breasts bare, filled the streets; un- 19
married girls who were kept in seclusion ran to the gates or walls of
their houses, while others leaned out from the windows; all with out- 20
stretched hands made solemn entreaty to Heaven. It was pitiful to 21
see the crowd all lying prostrate in utter confusion, and the high
priest in an agony of apprehension.

While the people were calling upon the Lord Almighty to keep 22
the deposits intact and safe for those who had deposited them,
Heliodorus proceeded to carry out his decision. But at the very 23, 24
moment when he arrived with his bodyguard at the treasury, the
Ruler of spirits and of all powers produced a mighty apparition, so
that all who had the audacity to accompany Heliodorus were faint

25 with terror, stricken with panic at the power of God. They saw a
horse, splendidly caparisoned, with a rider of terrible aspect; it
rushed fiercely at Heliodorus and, rearing up, attacked him with its
26 hooves. The rider was wearing golden armour. There also appeared
to Heliodorus two young men of surpassing strength and glorious
beauty, splendidly dressed. They stood on either side of him and
27 scourged him, raining ceaseless blows upon him. He fell suddenly
to the ground, overwhelmed by a great darkness, and his men
28 snatched him up and put him on a litter. This man, who so recently
had entered the treasury with a great throng and his whole bodyguard, was now borne off by them quite helpless, publicly compelled
to acknowledge the sovereignty of God.[a]

29 While he lay speechless, deprived by this divine act of all hope of
30 recovery, the Jews were praising the Lord for the miracle he had
performed in his own house. The temple, which a short time before
was full of alarm and confusion, now overflowed with joy and
festivity, because the Lord Almighty had appeared.

31 Some of Heliodorus's companions hastily begged Onias to pray to
the Most High, and so to spare the life of their master now lying at his
32 very last gasp. The high priest, fearing that the king might suspect
that Heliodorus had met with foul play at the hands of the Jews,
33 brought a sacrifice for the man's recovery. As the high priest was
making the expiation, the same young men, dressed as before, again
appeared to Heliodorus. They stood over him and said: 'Be very
grateful to Onias the high priest; for his sake the Lord has spared
34 your life. You have been scourged by God; now tell all men of his
mighty power.' When they had said this, they vanished.

35 Heliodorus offered a sacrifice and made lavish vows to the Lord
who had spared his life; then, after taking friendly leave of Onias, he
36 led his troops back to the king. He bore witness to everyone of the
miracles of the supreme God which he had seen with his own eyes.
37 When the king asked him what sort of man would be suitable to
38 send to Jerusalem another time, Heliodorus replied: 'If you have an
enemy or someone plotting against your government, that is the
place to send him; you will receive him back soundly flogged, if he
survives at all, for beyond doubt there is a divine power surrounding
39 the temple. He whose habitation is in heaven watches over it himself

[*a*] was now...of God: *so some witnesses; others read* they, recognizing the sovereignty of God, now bore off quite helpless.

and gives it his aid; those who approach the place with evil intent he
strikes and destroys.'

So runs the story of Heliodorus and the preservation of the 40
treasury.

BUT THE SIMON mentioned earlier, the man who had made 4
allegations against his country about the money, slandered
Onias, alleging that he had attacked Heliodorus and had been the
author of these troubles. He had the effrontery to accuse him of 2
conspiracy against the government—this benefactor of the holy city,
this protector of his fellow-Jews, this zealot for the laws. The enmity 3
grew so great that one of Simon's trusted followers even resorted to
murder. Onias, realizing that Simon's rivalry was dangerous and 4
that Apollonius son of Menestheus, governor of Coele-syria and
Phoenicia, was encouraging his evil ways, paid a visit to the king. 5
He did not appear as an accuser of his fellow-citizens, but as concerned for the interests of all the Jews, both as a nation and as individuals. For he saw that unless the king intervened there could not 6
possibly be peace in public affairs, nor could Simon be stopped in his
mad course.

But when Seleucus was dead and had been succeeded by Antio- 7
chus, known as Epiphanes, Jason, Onias's brother, obtained the
high-priesthood by corrupt means. He petitioned the king and 8
promised him three hundred and sixty talents in silver coin immediately, and eighty talents from future revenue. In addition he 9
undertook to pay another hundred and fifty talents for the authority
to institute a sports-stadium, to arrange for the education of young
men there, and to enrol in Jerusalem a group to be known as the
'Antiochenes'.[a] The king agreed, and, as soon as he had seized the 10
high-priesthood, Jason made the Jews conform to the Greek way
of life.

He set aside the royal privileges established for the Jews through 11
the agency of John, the father of that Eupolemus who negotiated a
treaty of friendship and alliance with the Romans. He abolished the
lawful way of life and introduced practices which were against the
law. He lost no time in establishing a sports-stadium at the foot of 12
the citadel itself, and he made the most outstanding of the young
men assume the Greek athlete's hat. So Hellenism reached a high 13

[a] *Or* enrol the inhabitants of Jerusalem as citizens of Antioch.

point with the introduction of foreign customs through the bound-
14 less wickedness of the impious Jason, no true high priest. As a
result, the priests no longer had any enthusiasm for their duties at
the altar, but despised the temple and neglected the sacrifices; and in
defiance of the law they eagerly contributed to the expenses of the
15 wrestling-school whenever the opening gong called them. They
placed no value on their hereditary dignities, but cared above every-
16 thing for Hellenic honours. Because of this, grievous misfortunes
beset them, and the very men whose way of life they strove after,
and tried so hard to imitate, turned out to be their vindictive
17 enemies. To act profanely against God's laws is no light matter, as
will become clear in due time.

18 When the quinquennial games were being held at Tyre in the
19 presence of the king, the blackguard Jason sent, as envoys to repre-
sent Jerusalem, Antiochenes carrying three hundred drachmas in
cash for the sacrifice to Hercules. Even the bearers thought it
improper that this money should be used for a sacrifice, and con-
20 sidered that it should be spent otherwise. So, thanks to the bearers,
the money designed by the sender for the sacrifice to Hercules went
to fit out the triremes.

21 When Apollonius son of Menestheus was sent to Egypt for the
enthronement of King Philometor, Antiochus learnt that Philometor
was now hostile to his state, and became anxious for his own security.
22 So he went to Joppa, and then on to Jerusalem, where he was
lavishly welcomed by Jason and the city and received with torch-
light and ovations. After this, he quartered his army in Phoenicia.

23 Three years later, Jason sent Menelaus, brother of the Simon
mentioned above, to convey money to the king and to carry out his
24 directions about urgent business. But Menelaus established his
position with the king by acting as if he were a person of great
authority, outbid Jason by three hundred talents in silver, and so
25 diverted the high-priesthood to himself. He arrived back with the
royal mandate, but with nothing else to make him worthy of
the high-priesthood; he still had the temper of a cruel tyrant and
26 the fury of a savage beast. Jason, who had supplanted his own
brother, was now supplanted in his turn and forced to flee to
27 Ammonite territory. As for Menelaus, he continued to hold the
high-priesthood but without ever paying any of the money he had
promised the king, although it was demanded by Sostratus, the

commander of the citadel, who was responsible for collecting the re- 28
venues. In consequence they were both summoned by the king. As 29
their deputies, Menelaus left his brother Lysimachus, and Sostratus
left Crates, the commander of the Cypriots.

It was at this point that the inhabitants of Tarsus and Mallus 30
revolted, because their cities had been handed over as a gift to the
king's concubine, Antiochis. The king hastened off to restore order, 31
leaving as regent Andronicus, one of his ministers. Menelaus, think- 32
ing he had obtained a favourable opportunity, made a present to
Andronicus of some of the gold plate belonging to the temple which
he had appropriated. He had already sold some of it to Tyre and to
the neighbouring cities. When Onias heard this on good authority, 33
he withdrew to sanctuary at Daphne near Antioch and denounced
him. As a result, Menelaus approached Andronicus privately and 34
urged him to kill Onias. The regent went to Onias bent on treachery;
he greeted him, gave him assurances on oath, and persuaded him,
though still suspicious, to leave the sanctuary. Then at once, with no
respect for justice, he made away with him.

His murder filled not only Jews, but many from other nations as 35
well, with alarm and anger. So when the king returned from Cilicia, 36
the Jews of Antioch sent him a petition about the senseless killing of
Onias, the Gentiles sharing in their detestation of the crime. Antio- 37
chus was deeply grieved, and was moved to pity and tears as he
thought of the prudence and disciplined habits of the dead man. In a 38
burning fury, he immediately stripped Andronicus of the purple,
tore off his clothes, led him round the whole city to that very place
where he had committed sacrilege against Onias, and there disposed
of the murderer. Thus the Lord repaid him with the retribution he
deserved.

Lysimachus committed many acts of sacrilegious plunder in 39
Jerusalem with the connivance of Menelaus. When the news of them
became public and the people heard that much of the gold plate
had been disposed of, they banded together against Lysimachus.
Since the crowds were seething with rage and getting out of hand, 40
Lysimachus armed some three thousand men and began to launch
a vicious attack, led by a certain Auranus, a man advanced in
years and no less in folly. Realizing that the attack came from 41
Lysimachus, some of the crowd seized stones and others blocks of
wood, while others again took handfuls of the ashes that were lying

round, and there was complete confusion as they all hurled them
42 at Lysimachus and his men. As a result, they wounded many,
killed some, and routed them all; the sacrilegious man himself they
dispatched near the treasury.
43 An action was brought against Menelaus in connection with this
44 incident. When the king came to Tyre, the three men sent by the
45 Jewish senate pleaded the case before him. Menelaus's cause was as
good as lost; but he promised a large sum of money to Ptolemaeus
46 son of Dorymenes to win over the king. So Ptolemaeus led the king
aside into a colonnade, as if to take the air, and persuaded him to
47 change his mind. The king acquitted Menelaus, the cause of all the
mischief, dismissed the charges brought against him, and condemned
his unfortunate accusers to death, men who would have been discharged as entirely innocent had they appeared even before Scy-
48 thians. Without more ado those who had pleaded for their city, their
49 people, and their sacred vessels, suffered the unjust penalty. At this,
even some of the Tyrians showed their detestation of the crime by
50 providing a splendid funeral for the victims. Menelaus, thanks to
the greed of those in power, remained in office. He went from bad to
worse, this arch-plotter against his own fellow-citizens.

5 About this time Antiochus undertook his second invasion of
2 Egypt. Apparitions were seen in the sky all over Jerusalem for nearly
forty days: galloping horsemen in golden armour, companies of
3 spearmen standing to arms, swords unsheathed, cavalry divisions in
battle order. Charges and countercharges were made on each side,
shields were shaken, spears massed and javelins hurled; breastplates
4 and golden ornaments of every kind shone brightly. All men prayed
that this apparition might portend good.
5 Upon a false report of Antiochus's death, Jason collected no less
than a thousand men and made a surprise attack on Jerusalem. The
defenders on the wall were driven back and the city was finally
6 taken; Menelaus took refuge in the citadel, and Jason continued to
massacre his fellow-citizens without pity. He little knew that success
against one's own kindred is the greatest of failures, and he imagined
that the trophies he raised marked the defeat of enemies, not of
7 fellow-countrymen. He did not, however, gain control of the government; he gained only dishonour as the result of his plot, and returned
8 again as a fugitive to Ammonite territory. His career came to a
miserable end; for, after being imprisoned by Aretas the ruler of the

Arabs, he fled from city to city, hunted by all, hated as a rebel against
the laws, and detested as the executioner of his country and his
fellow-citizens, and finally was driven to take refuge in Egypt. In the 9
end the man who had banished so many from their native land himself died in exile after setting sail for Sparta, where he had hoped to
obtain shelter because of the Spartans' kinship with the Jews. He 10
who had cast out many to lie unburied was himself unmourned; he
had no funeral of any kind, no resting-place in the grave of his
ancestors.

When news of this reached the king, it became clear to him that 11
Judaea was in a state of rebellion. So he set out from Egypt in savage
mood, took Jerusalem by storm, and ordered his troops to cut down 12
without mercy everyone they met and to slaughter those who took
refuge in the houses. Young and old were murdered, women and 13
children massacred, girls and infants butchered. At the end of three 14
days their losses had amounted to eighty thousand: forty thousand
killed in action, and as many sold into slavery.

Not satisfied with this, the king had the audacity to enter the 15
holiest temple on earth, guided by Menelaus, who had turned traitor
both to his religion and his country. He laid impious hands on the 16
sacred vessels; his desecrating hands swept together the votive
offerings which other kings had set up to enhance the splendour and
fame of the shrine.

The pride of Antiochus passed all bounds. He did not understand 17
that the sins of the people of Jerusalem had angered the Lord for a
short time, and that this was why he left the temple to its fate.
If they had not already been guilty of many sinful acts, Antiochus 18
would have fared like Heliodorus who was sent by King Seleucus
to inspect the treasury; like him he would have been scourged and
his insolent plan foiled at once. But the Lord did not choose the 19
nation for the sake of the sanctuary; he chose the sanctuary for the
sake of the nation. Therefore even the sanctuary itself first had its part 20
in the misfortunes that overtook the nation, and afterwards shared
its good fortune. It was abandoned when the Lord Almighty was
angry, but restored again in all its splendour when he became
reconciled.

Antiochus, then, carried off eighteen hundred talents from the 21
temple and hastened back to Antioch. In his arrogance he was rash
enough to think that he could make ships sail on dry land and men

22 walk over the sea. He left commissioners behind to oppress the
Hebrews: in Jerusalem Philip, by race a Phrygian, by disposition
23 more barbarous than his master, and in Mount Gerizim, Andronicus,
to say nothing of Menelaus, who was more brutally overbearing to the
citizens than the others. Such was the king's hostility towards the
24 Jews that he sent Apollonius, the general of the Mysian mercenaries,
with an army of twenty-two thousand men, and ordered him to kill
25 all the adult males and to sell the women and boys into slavery. When
Apollonius arrived at Jerusalem, he posed as a man of peace; he
waited until the holy sabbath day and, finding the Jews abstaining
26 from work, he ordered a review of his troops. All who came out to
see the parade he put to the sword; then, charging into the city with
his soldiers, he killed a great number of people.

27 BUT JUDAS, also called Maccabaeus, with about nine others,
escaped into the desert, where he and his companions lived in
the mountains, fending for themselves like the wild animals. They
remained there living on what vegetation they found, so as to have
no share in the pollution.

6 Shortly afterwards King Antiochus sent an elderly Athenian to
force the Jews to abandon their ancestral customs and no longer
2 regulate their lives according to the laws of God. He was also
commissioned to pollute the temple at Jerusalem and dedicate it
to Olympian Zeus, and to dedicate the sanctuary on Mount Gerizim
to Zeus God of Hospitality, following the practice of the local
inhabitants.

3, 4 This evil hit them hard and was a severe trial. The Gentiles filled
the temple with licentious revelry: they took their pleasure with
prostitutes and had intercourse with women in the sacred precincts.
5 They also brought forbidden things inside, and heaped the altar with
6 impure offerings prohibited by the law. It was forbidden either to
observe the sabbath or to keep the traditional festivals, or to admit to
7 being a Jew at all. On the monthly celebration of the king's birthday,
the Jews were driven by brute force to eat the entrails of the sacrificial victims; and on the feast of Dionysus they were forced to wear
8 ivy-wreaths and join the procession in his honour. At the instigation
of the inhabitants of Ptolemais[a] an order was published in the neighbouring Greek cities to the effect that they should adopt the same

[a] *Some witnesses read* At the instigation of Ptolemaeus...

policy of compelling the Jews to eat the entrails and should kill those 9
who refused to change over to Greek ways.
Their miserable fate was there for all to see. For instance, two 10
women were brought to trial for having had their children circumcised. They were paraded through the city, with their babies hanging
at their breasts, and then flung down from the fortifications. Other 11
Jews had assembled in caves near Jerusalem to keep the sabbath in
secret; they were denounced to Philip and were burnt alive, since
they scrupled to defend themselves out of regard for the holiness of
the day.
Now I beg my readers not to be disheartened by these calamities, 12
but to reflect that such penalties were inflicted for the discipline of
our race and not for its destruction. It is a sign of great kindness that 13
acts of impiety should not be let alone for long but meet their due
recompense at once. The Lord did not see fit to deal with us as he 14
does with the other nations: with them he patiently holds his hand
until they have reached the full extent of their sins, but upon us he 15
inflicted retribution before our sins reached their height. So he never 16
withdraws his mercy from us; though he disciplines his people by
calamity, he never deserts them. Let it be enough for me to have 17
recalled this truth; after this short digression, I must continue with
my story.
There was Eleazar, one of the leading teachers of the law, a man of 18
great age and distinguished bearing. He was being forced to open his
mouth and eat pork, but preferring an honourable death to an un- 19
clean life, he spat it out and voluntarily submitted to the flogging,
as indeed men should act who have the courage to refuse to eat for- 20
bidden food even for love of life. For old acquaintance' sake, the 21
officials in charge of this sacrilegious feast had a word with Eleazar in
private; they urged him to bring meat which he was permitted to eat
and had himself prepared, and only pretend to be eating the sacrificial
meat as the king had ordered. In that way he would escape death and 22
take advantage of the clemency which their long-standing friendship
merited. But Eleazar made an honourable decision, one worthy of 23
his years and the authority of old age, worthy of the grey hairs he had
attained to and wore with such distinction, worthy of his perfect
conduct from childhood up, but above all, worthy of the holy and
God-given law. So he answered at once: 'Send me quickly to my
grave. If I went through with this pretence at my time of life, many 24

of the young might believe that at the age of ninety Eleazar had
25 turned apostate. If I practised deceit for the sake of a brief moment of
life, I should lead them astray and bring stain and pollution on my
26 old age. I might for the present avoid man's punishment, but, alive
27 or dead, I shall never escape from the hand of the Almighty. So if
I now die bravely, I shall show that I have deserved my long life
28 and leave the young a fine example, to teach them how to die a good
death, gladly and nobly, for our revered and holy laws.'

When he had finished speaking, he was immediately dragged away
29 to be flogged. Those who a little while before had shown him friendship now became his enemies because, in their view, what he had said
30 was madness. When he was almost dead from the blows, Eleazar
sighed deeply and said: 'To the Lord belongs all holy knowledge.
He knows what terrible agony I endure in my body from this flogging, though I could have escaped death; yet he knows also that in
my soul I suffer gladly, because I stand in awe of him.'

31 So he died; and by his death he left a heroic example and a
glorious memory, not only for the young but also for the great body
of the nation.

7 Again, seven brothers with their mother had been arrested, and
were being tortured by the king with whips and thongs to force them
2 to eat pork, when one of them, speaking for all, said: 'What do you
expect to learn by interrogating us? We are ready to die rather than
3 break the laws of our fathers.' The king was enraged and ordered
4 great pans and cauldrons to be heated up, and this was done at once.
Then he gave orders that the spokesman's tongue should be cut out
and that he should be scalped and mutilated before the eyes of his
5 mother and his six brothers. This wreck of a man the king ordered to
be taken, still breathing, to the fire and roasted in one of the pans. As
the smoke from it streamed out far and wide, the mother and her sons
6 encouraged each other to die nobly. 'The Lord God is watching',
they said, 'and without doubt has compassion on us. Did not Moses
tell Israel to their faces in the song denouncing apostasy: "He will
have compassion on his servants"?'

7 After the first brother had died in this way, the second was subjected to the same brutality. The skin and hair of his head were torn
off, and he was asked: 'Will you eat, before we tear you limb from
8 limb?' He replied in his native language, 'Never!', and so he in turn
9 underwent the torture. With his last breath, he said: 'Fiend though

you are, you are setting us free from this present life, and, since we
die for his laws, the King of the universe will raise us up to a life
everlastingly made new.'
After him the third was tortured. When the question was put to 10
him, he at once showed his tongue, boldly held out his hands, and 11
said courageously: 'The God of heaven gave me these. His laws
mean far more to me than they do, and it is from him that I trust to
receive them back.' When they heard this, the king and his followers 12
were amazed at the young man's spirit and his utter disregard for
suffering.
When he too was dead, they tortured the fourth in the same cruel 13
way. At the point of death, he said to the king: 'Better to be killed 14
by men and cherish God's promise to raise us again. There will be
no resurrection to life for you!'
Then the fifth was dragged forward for torture. Looking at the 15, 16
king, he said: 'You have authority over men, mortal as you are, and
can do as you please. But do not imagine that God has abandoned
our race. Wait and see how his great power will torment you and your 17
descendants.'
Next the sixth was brought and said with his dying breath: 'Do 18
not delude yourself. It is our own fault that we suffer these things;
we have sinned against our God and brought these appalling disasters
upon ourselves. But do not suppose you will escape the con- 19
sequences of trying to fight against God.'
The mother was the most remarkable of all, and deserves to be 20
remembered with special honour. She watched her seven sons all die
in the space of a single day, yet she bore it bravely because she put
her trust in the Lord. She encouraged each in turn in her native 21
language. Filled with noble resolution, her woman's thoughts fired
by a manly spirit, she said to them: 'You appeared in my womb, 22
I know not how; it was not I who gave you life and breath and set in
order your bodily frames. It is the Creator of the universe who 23
moulds man at his birth and plans the origin of all things. Therefore
he, in his mercy, will give you back life and breath again, since now
you put his laws above all thought of self.'
Antiochus felt that he was being treated with contempt and sus- 24
pected an insult in her words. The youngest brother was still left,
and the king, not content with appealing to him, even assured him on
oath that the moment he abandoned his ancestral customs he would

make him rich and prosperous, by enrolling him as a King's Friend
25 and entrusting him with high office. Since the young man paid no
attention to him, the king summoned the mother and urged her to
26 advise the lad to save his life. After much urging from the king, she
27 agreed to persuade her son. She leaned towards him, and flouting the
cruel tyrant, she said in their native language: 'My son, take pity on
me. I carried you nine months in the womb, suckled you three years,
28 reared you and brought you up to your present age. I beg you, child,
look at the sky and the earth; see all that is in them and realize that
God made them out of nothing, and that man comes into being in the
29 same way. Do not be afraid of this butcher; accept death and prove
yourself worthy of your brothers, so that by God's mercy I may
receive you back again along with them.'

30 She had barely finished when the young man spoke out: 'What are
you all waiting for? I will not submit to the king's command; I obey
31 the command of the law given by Moses to our ancestors. And you,
King Antiochus, who have devised all kinds of harm for the Hebrews,
32 you will not escape God's hand. We are suffering for our own sins,
33 and though to correct and discipline us our living Lord is angry for a
34 short time, yet he will again be reconciled to his servants. But you,
impious man, foulest of the human race, do not indulge vain hopes
or be carried away by delusions of greatness, you who lay hands on
35 God's servants. You are not yet safe from the judgement of the
36 almighty, all-seeing God. My brothers have now fallen in loyalty to
God's covenant, after brief pain leading to eternal life;[a] but you will
37 pay the just penalty of your insolence by the verdict of God. I, like
my brothers, surrender my body and my life for the laws of our
fathers. I appeal to God to show mercy speedily to his people and
by whips and scourges to bring you to admit that he alone is God.
38 With me and my brothers may the Almighty's anger, which has
justly fallen on all our race, be ended!'

39 The king, exasperated by these scornful words, was beside himself
40 with rage. So he treated him worse than the others, and the young
man died, putting his whole trust in the Lord, without having
41 incurred defilement. Then finally, after her sons, the mother died.

42 This, then, must conclude our account of the eating of the entrails
and the monstrous outrages that accompanied it.

[*a*] in loyalty...life: *or* after a brief time of pain, in loyalty to God's covenant of everlasting life.

The revolt of Judas Maccabaeus

MEANWHILE JUDAS, also called Maccabaeus, and his com- 8
panions were making their way into the villages unobserved.
They summoned their kinsmen and enlisted others who had
remained faithful to Judaism, until they had collected about six
thousand men. They invoked the Lord to look down and help his 2
people, whom all were trampling under foot, to take pity on the
temple profaned by impious men, and to have mercy on Jerusalem, 3
which was being destroyed and would soon be levelled to the
ground. They prayed him also to give ear to the blood that cried to
him for vengeance, to remember the infamous massacre of innocent 4
children and the deeds of blasphemy against his name, and to show
his hatred of wickedness.

Once his band of partisans was organized, Maccabaeus proved 5
invincible to the Gentiles, for the Lord's anger had changed to
mercy. He came on towns and villages without warning and burnt 6
them; he occupied the key positions, and inflicted many severe
reverses on the enemy, choosing the night-time as being especially 7
favourable for these attacks. His heroism[a] was talked about everywhere. When Philip realized that the small gains made by Judas were 8
occurring with growing frequency, he wrote to Ptolemaeus, the
governor of Coele-syria and Phoenicia, asking for his help in protecting the royal interests. Ptolemaeus immediately selected Nicanor, 9
son of Patroclus, a member of the highest order of King's Friends,
and sent him at the head of at least twenty thousand troops of
various nationalities to exterminate the entire Jewish race. With
him Ptolemaeus associated Gorgias, a general of wide experience.
Nicanor determined to pay off the two thousand talents due from the 10
king as tribute to the Romans, by the sale of the Jews he would take
prisoner; and he at once made an offer of Jewish slaves to the coastal 11
towns, undertaking to deliver them at the price of ninety to the
talent. But he did not expect the vengeance of the Almighty, which
was soon to be at his heels.

Word of Nicanor's advance reached Judas, and he informed his 12
men that the enemy was at hand. The cowards who doubted God's 13

[*a*] *Or* His numerous force.

14 justice took themselves off and fled. But the rest disposed of their
remaining possessions, and they prayed together to the Lord to save
them from the impious Nicanor, who had sold them even before they
15 met in battle; and if they could not ask this for their own merits, they
did so on the ground of the covenants God had made with their
ancestors, and of his holy and majestic Name which they bore.
16 Maccabaeus assembled his followers, six thousand in number, and
appealed to them not to flee in panic before the enemy nor to be
afraid of the great host which was attacking them without just cause.
17 Rather they should fight nobly, having before their eyes the wicked
crimes of the Gentiles against the temple, their callous outrage upon
Jerusalem, and, further, their suppression of the traditional Jewish
18 way of life. 'They rely on their weapons and their audacity,' he said,
'but we rely on God Almighty, who is able to overthrow with a nod
19 our present assailants and, if need be, the whole world.' He went on
to recount to them the occasions when God had helped their
ancestors: how, in Sennacherib's time, one hundred and eighty-five
20 thousand of the enemy had perished, and also how, on the occasion
of the battle against the Galatians in Babylonia, all the Jews engaged
in the combat had numbered no more than eight thousand, with
four thousand Macedonians, yet, when the Macedonians were hard
pressed, the eight thousand through heaven's aid had destroyed one
hundred and twenty thousand and taken much booty.

21 His words put them in good heart and made them ready to die for
their laws and for their country. He then divided the army into four
22 and gave each of his brothers, Simon, Josephus, and Jonathan,
23 command of a division of fifteen hundred men. Besides this, he
appointed Eleazar to read the holy book aloud,[a] and giving the signal
for battle with the cry 'God is our help', and taking command of the
24 leading division in person, he engaged Nicanor. The Almighty fought
on their side, and they slaughtered over nine thousand of the enemy,
wounded and disabled the greater part of Nicanor's forces, and
25 routed them completely. They seized the money of those who had
come to buy them as slaves. After chasing the enemy a considerable
26 distance, they were forced to break off because it was late; for it was
the day before the sabbath, and for that reason they called off the
27 pursuit. When they had collected the enemy's weapons and stripped
the dead, they turned to keep the sabbath. They offered thanks and

[*a*] Besides...aloud: *probable reading; Gk. obscure.*

praises loud and long to the Lord who had kept the first drops of his
mercy to shed on them that day.[a] After the sabbath was over, they 28
distributed some of the spoils among the victims of persecution and
the widows and orphans; the remainder they divided among themselves. This done, all together made supplication to the merciful 29
Lord, praying him to be fully reconciled with his servants.
The Jews now engaged the forces of Timotheus and Bacchides 30
and killed over twenty thousand of them. They gained complete
control of some high strongholds, and divided the immense booty,
giving shares equal to their own to the victims of persecution, to the
widows and orphans, and to the old men as well. They carefully 31
collected all the enemy's weapons and stored them at strategic
points; the remainder of the spoils they brought into Jerusalem. They 32
killed the officer commanding the forces of Timotheus, an utterly
godless man who had caused the Jews great suffering. During the 33
victory celebrations in their capital, they burnt alive the men who
had set fire to the sacred gates, including Callisthenes, who had taken
refuge in a small house; he thus received the due reward of his
impiety.
Thus, by the Lord's help, Nicanor, that double-dyed villain who 34–35
had brought the thousand merchants to buy the Jewish captives, was
humiliated by the very people whom he despised above all others.
He threw off his magnificent uniform, and all alone like a runaway
slave made his escape through the interior, and was, indeed, very
lucky to reach Antioch after losing his whole army. So the man who 36
had undertaken to secure tribute for the Romans by taking prisoner
the inhabitants of Jerusalem showed the world that the Jews had a
champion and were therefore invulnerable, because they kept the
laws he had given them.
It so happened that, about this time, Antiochus had returned in 9
disorder from Persia. He had entered the city of Persepolis and 2
attempted to plunder its temples and assume control. But the popu-
lace rose and rushed to arms in their defence, with the result that
Antiochus was routed by civilians and forced to beat a humiliating
retreat. When he was near Ecbatana, news reached him of what had 3
happened to Nicanor and the forces of Timotheus. Transported 4
with fury, he conceived the idea of making the Jews pay for the

[*a*] kept...day: *so some witnesses; others read* brought them safely to that day and had appointed it as the beginning of mercy for them.

injury inflicted by those who had put him to flight, and so he
ordered his charioteer to drive without stopping until the journey
was finished.

But riding with him was the divine judgement! For in his arrogance he said: 'When I reach Jerusalem, I will make it a common
5 graveyard for the Jews.' But the all-seeing Lord, the God of Israel,
struck him a fatal and invisible blow. As soon as he had said the
words, he was seized with incurable pain in his bowels and with
6 sharp internal torments—a punishment entirely fitting for one who
had inflicted many unheard-of torments on the bowels of others.
7 Still he did not in the least abate his insolence; more arrogant than
ever, he breathed fiery threats against the Jews. After he had given
orders to speed up the journey, it happened that he fell out of his
chariot as it hurtled along, and so violent was his fall that every joint
8 in his body was dislocated. He, who in his pretension to be more
than man had just been thinking that he could command the waves of
the sea and weigh high mountains on the scales, was brought to the
ground and had to be carried in a litter, thus making God's power[a]
9 manifest to all. Worms swarmed even from the eyes of this godless
man and, while he was still alive and in agony, his flesh rotted off,
10 and the whole army was disgusted by the stench of his decay. It was
so unbearably offensive that nobody could escort the man who only a
short time before had seemed to touch the stars in the sky.

11 In this broken state, Antiochus began to abate his great arrogance.
Under God's lash, and racked with continual pain, he began to see
12 things in their true light. He could not endure his own stench and
said, 'It is right to submit oneself to God and, being mortal, not to
13 think oneself equal to him.' Then the villain made a solemn promise
to the Lord, who had no intention of sparing him any longer, and it
14 was to this effect: Jerusalem the holy city, which he had been hurry-
ing to level to the ground and to transform into a graveyard, he would
15 now declare a free city; to all the Jews, whom he had not considered
worthy of burial but only fit to be thrown out with their children as
prey for birds and beasts, he would give privileges equal to those
16 enjoyed by the citizens of Athens. The holy temple which he had
earlier plundered he would adorn with the most splendid gifts; he
would replace all the sacred utensils on a much more lavish scale; he
17 would meet the cost of the sacrifices from his own revenues. In

[a] *Some witnesses read* litter. God made his power...

addition to all this, he would even turn Jew and visit every inhabited place to proclaim God's might.

When his pains in no way abated, because the just judgement of 18
God had fallen on him, he was in despair and, as a kind of olive
branch, wrote to the Jews the letter here copied:

To my worthy citizens, the Jews, warm greetings and good 19
wishes for their health and prosperity from Antiochus, King and
Chief Magistrate.

May you and your children flourish and your affairs go as you 20
wish. Having my hope in heaven, I keep an affectionate remem- 21
brance of your regards and goodwill.

As I was returning from Persia, I suffered a tiresome illness, and
so I have judged it necessary to provide for the general safety of
you all. Not that I despair of my condition—on the contrary 22
I have good hopes of recovery—but I observed that my father, 23
whenever he made an expedition east of the Euphrates, appointed
a successor, so that, if anything unexpected should happen or if 24
some tiresome report should spread, his subjects would not be
disturbed, since they would know to whom the empire had been
left. Further, I know well that the neighbouring princes on the 25
frontiers of my kingdom are watching for an opportunity and waiting on events. So I have designated as king my son Antiochus,
whom I frequently entrusted and recommended to most of you
during my regular visits to the satrapies beyond the Euphrates.
I have written to him what is here copied. Wherefore I pray 26
and entreat each one of you to maintain your existing goodwill
towards myself and my son, remembering the services I have
rendered to you both as a community and as individuals. For 27
I am sure my son will follow my own policy of moderation and
benevolence and will accommodate himself to your wishes.

Thus this murderer and blasphemer, suffering the worst of 28
agonies, such as he had made others suffer, met a pitiable end in the
mountains of a foreign land. His body was brought back by Philip, 29
his intimate friend; but he was afraid of Antiochus's son and went
over to Ptolemy Philometor in Egypt.

Maccabaeus with his men, led by the Lord, recovered the temple **10**
and city of Jerusalem. He demolished the altars erected by the 2
heathen in the public square, and their sacred precincts as well. When 3

they had purified the sanctuary, they constructed another altar;
then, striking fire from flints, they offered a sacrifice for the first time
for two whole years, and restored the incense, the lights, and the
4 Bread of the Presence. This done, they prostrated themselves and
prayed the Lord not to let them fall any more into such disasters,
but, should they ever happen to sin, to discipline them himself with
clemency and not hand them over to blasphemous and barbarous
5 Gentiles. The sanctuary was purified on the twenty-fifth of Kislev,
the same day of the same month as that on which foreigners had
6 profaned it. The joyful celebration lasted for eight days; it was like
the Feast of Tabernacles, for they recalled how, only a short time
before, they had kept that feast while they were living like wild
7 animals in the mountains and caves; and so they carried garlanded
wands and branches with their fruits, as well as palm-fronds, and
they chanted hymns to the One who had so triumphantly achieved
8 the purification of his own temple. A measure was passed by the
public assembly to the effect that the entire Jewish race should keep
these days every year.

The campaign against Eupator

9 WE HAVE ALREADY recounted the end of Antiochus called
10 Epiphanes. Now we will describe what happened under that
godless man's son, Antiochus Eupator, in a brief summary of the
11 principal evils brought about by his wars. At his accession, Eupator
appointed as vicegerent a man called Lysias who had succeeded
Ptolemaeus Macron as governor-general of Coele-syria and Phoe-
12 nicia. For Ptolemaeus had taken the lead in reversing the former
unjust treatment of the Jews and had attempted to maintain peaceful
13 relations with them, and as a result he was denounced by the King's
Friends to Eupator. On every side he was called traitor, because he
had already abandoned Cyprus, entrusted to him by Philometor, and
had gone over to Antiochus Epiphanes. He still enjoyed power, but
no longer respect, and in despair he ended his life by poison.
14 When Gorgias became governor, he engaged mercenaries and took
15 every opportunity of attacking the Jews. At the same time the
Idumaeans, who were in control of strategic fortresses, were also

harassing them; they harboured the fugitives from Jerusalem and
tried to carry on the war. Maccabaeus and his men made public 16
supplication and prayed God to fight on their side. They made an
assault on the Idumaean fortresses, pressed the attack vigorously, 17
and captured them; they drove off all who were manning the walls,
and killed all they met, to the number of at least twenty thousand.

Nine thousand or more of the enemy took refuge in two towers, 18
very strongly fortified and fully equipped against a siege. Macca- 19
baeus himself set out for the places which were being hard pressed,
but left Simon and Josephus behind, with Zacchaeus and his men,
enough to prosecute the siege. But Simon's men were too fond of 20
money, and when they were bribed with seventy thousand drachmas
by some of those in the towers, they let them slip through their lines.
When Maccabaeus was informed of this, he assembled the leaders 21
of the army and denounced these men for having sold their brothers
for money by letting their enemies escape. Then he executed the 22
men who had turned traitor, and immediately the two towers fell to
him. His military operations were completely successful; in the two 23
fortresses he destroyed over twenty thousand of the enemy.

After his previous defeat by the Jews, Timotheus collected a huge 24
force of mercenaries and Asian cavalry, and advanced to take Judaea
by storm. As he approached, Maccabaeus and his men made their 25
prayer to God. They sprinkled dust on their heads and put sackcloth
round their waists; they prostrated themselves on the altar-step and 26
begged God to favour them, 'to be an enemy of their enemies and an
opponent of their opponents', as the law clearly states.

When they had finished their prayer, they took up their weapons, 27
advanced a good distance from Jerusalem, and halted near the enemy.
At first light the two armies joined battle. For the Jews, success and 28
victory were guaranteed not only because of their bravery but even
more because the Lord was their refuge, whereas the Gentiles had
only their own fury to lead them into battle. As the fighting grew 29
hot, the enemy saw in the sky five magnificent figures riding horses
with golden bridles, who placed themselves at the head of the Jews,
formed a circle round Maccabaeus, and kept him invulnerable under 30
the protection of their armour. They launched arrows and thunderbolts at the enemy, who, confused and blinded, broke up in complete
disorder. Twenty thousand five hundred of the infantry, as well as six 31
hundred cavalry, were slaughtered.

32 Timotheus himself fled to a fortress called Gazara, commanded by
33 Chaereas and strongly garrisoned. Maccabaeus and his men wel-
34 comed this, and for four days they laid siege to the place. The garrison, confident in the strength of their position, hurled horrible and
35 impious blasphemies at them, until, at dawn on the fifth day, twenty
young men from the force of Maccabaeus, burning with rage at the
blasphemy, courageously stormed the wall and in savage anger cut
36 down all they met. Under cover of this distraction others got up the
same way, attacked the defenders, set light to the towers, and started
fires on which they burnt the blasphemers alive. Others broke
down the gates and let in the rest of the army, and thus the city was
37 occupied. Timotheus had hidden himself in a cistern, but he was
38 killed along with his brother Chaereas and Apollophanes. To celebrate their achievement, the Jews praised with hymns and thanks-
givings the Lord who showers blessings on Israel and gives them the
victory.

11 Very shortly afterwards, Lysias the vicegerent, the king's guardian
2 and relative, angered by these events, collected about eighty thousand
troops, in addition to his entire cavalry, and advanced on the Jews.
3 He reckoned on making Jerusalem a settlement for Gentiles, subjecting the temple to taxation like all gentile shrines, and putting up the
4 high-priesthood for sale annually. He reckoned not at all with the
might of God, but was elated with his myriads of infantry, his
5 thousands of cavalry, his eighty elephants. Penetrating into Judaea,
he approached Bethsura, a fortified place about twenty miles from
Jerusalem, and closely invested it.

6 When Maccabaeus and his men learnt that Lysias was besieging
their fortresses, they and all the people, wailing and weeping, prayed
7 the Lord to send a good angel to deliver Israel. Maccabaeus was the
first to arm himself, and he urged the rest to share his danger and
come to the help of their brothers. One and all, they set out eagerly.
8 They were still in the neighbourhood of Jerusalem when there
appeared at their head a horseman arrayed in white, brandishing his
9 golden weapons. Then with one voice they praised their merciful
God and felt so strong in spirit that they could have attacked not
only men but also the most savage animals, and even walls of iron.
10 They came on fully armed, with their heavenly ally, under the mercy
11 of the Lord. They hurled themselves like lions against the enemy, cut
down eleven thousand of them, as well as sixteen hundred cavalry,

and put all the rest to flight. Most of those who escaped lost their 12
weapons and were wounded, and Lysias saved his life only by
running away.
Lysias was no fool, and as he took stock of the defeat he had 13
suffered he realized that the Hebrews were invincible, because the
mighty God fought on their side. So he proposed a settlement on 14
terms entirely acceptable, promising also to win the king over by
putting pressure on him to show friendship to the Jews. Macca- 15
baeus agreed to all the proposals of Lysias out of regard for the
general welfare, for the king had accepted all the proposals from the
Jewish side which Maccabaeus had forwarded to Lysias in writing.

The letter of Lysias to the Jews ran as follows: 16

Lysias to the Jewish community, greeting.
Your representatives John and Absalom have handed to me 17
the document here copied and have asked me to ratify what is
contained in it. Whatever needed to be brought to the king's 18
knowledge, I have communicated to him, and what was within my
own competence, I have granted. If, therefore, you maintain your 19
goodwill towards the empire, I for my part will endeavour to
promote your welfare for the future. I have ordered your repre- 20
sentatives and mine to confer with you about the details. Farewell. 21
The twenty-fourth of Dioscorus in the year 148.[a]

The king's letter ran as follows: 22

King Antiochus to his brother Lysias, greeting.
Now that our royal father has gone to join the gods, we desire 23
that our subjects be undisturbed in the conduct of their own
affairs. We have learnt that the Jews do not consent to adopt 24
Greek ways, as our father wished, but prefer their own mode of
life and request that they be allowed to observe their own laws.
We choose, therefore, that this nation like the rest should be left 25
undisturbed, and decree that their temple be restored to them and
that they shall regulate their lives in accordance with their
ancestral customs. Have the goodness, therefore, to inform them 26
of this and ratify it, so that, knowing what our intentions are, they
may settle down confidently and quietly to manage their own affairs.

[*a*] *That is* 164 B.C.

27 To the people the king's letter ran thus:

King Antiochus to the Jewish Senate and people, greeting.
28 We hope that you prosper. We too are in good health.
29 Menelaus has informed us of your desire to return to your own
30 homes. Therefore we declare an amnesty for all who return be-
31 fore the thirtieth of Xanthicus. The Jews may follow their own
food-laws as heretofore, and none of them shall be charged with
32 any previous infringement. I am sending Menelaus to reassure
33 you. Farewell.

The fifteenth of Xanthicus in the year 148.[a]

34 The Romans also sent the Jews the following letter:

Quintus Memmius and Titus Manius, Roman legates, to the Jewish people, greeting.
35 We give our assent to all that Lysias, the king's relative, has
36 granted you. But examine carefully the questions which he
reserved for reference to the king; then send someone immediately,
so that we may make suitable proposals, for we are proceeding to
37 Antioch. Send messengers therefore without delay, so that we
38 also may know what your opinion is. Farewell.

The fifteenth of Xanthicus in the year 148.[a]

12 When these agreements had been concluded, Lysias went off to
2 the king, and the Jews returned to their farming. But some of the
governors in the region, Timotheus and Apollonius son of Gennaeus and also Hieronymus and Demophon, and in addition Nicanor, chief of the Cypriot mercenaries, would not allow them to enjoy security and live in quiet.

3 I MUST NOW describe an atrocity committed by the inhabitants of
Joppa. They invited the Jews living in the town to embark with
their wives and children in boats which they provided, with no
4 indication of any ill will towards them. As it was a public decision by
the whole town, and because they wished to live in peace and suspected nothing, they accepted; but when they were out at sea, the
people of Joppa sank the boats, drowning no fewer than two
5 hundred of them. When Judas learnt of this brutal treatment of his

[a] *That is* 164 B.C.

fellow-countrymen, he alerted his troops, invoked God, the just 6
judge, and fell upon their murderers. He set the harbour of Joppa
on fire by night, burnt the shipping, and put to the sword those
who had taken refuge there. But finding the town gates closed, he 7
withdrew, meaning however to return and root out the entire community. When he learnt that the people of Jamnia intended to do the 8
same to the Jews who lived among them, he attacked Jamnia by night 9
and set fire to its harbour and fleet; the light of the flames was visible
in Jerusalem thirty miles away.

When they had marched more than a mile further in their advance 10
against Timotheus, they were set upon by not less than five thousand
Arabs, with five hundred cavalry. A violent combat ensued, in which 11
by divine help Judas and his men were victorious. The defeated
nomads begged Judas to make an alliance with them, and promised to
supply him with cattle and to give the Jews every other kind of help.
Judas realized that they could indeed be useful in many ways; so he 12
agreed to make peace with them, and, after receiving assurances from
him, they went back to their tents.

Judas also attacked Caspin, a walled town, strongly fortified and 13
inhabited by a motley crew of Gentiles. Confident in the strength of 14
their walls and in their store of provisions, the defenders behaved
provocatively towards Judas and his men, abusing them and also
uttering the most wicked blasphemies. But they invoked the world's 15
great Sovereign who in the days of Joshua threw down the walls of
Jericho without battering-rams or siege-engines. They attacked the
wall fiercely and, by the will of God, captured the town. The carnage 16
was indescribable; the adjacent lake, a quarter of a mile wide,
appeared to be overflowing with blood.

Advancing about ninety-five miles from there, they reached 17
Charax, which is inhabited by the Tubian Jews, as they are called.
They did not find Timotheus there; he had by that time left the 18
district, having had no success, but in one place he had left behind
an extremely strong garrison. Dositheus and Sosipater, Macca- 19
baeus's generals, set out and destroyed the garrison, which con-
sisted of over ten thousand men. Maccabaeus for his part grouped 20
his army in several divisions, appointed commanders for them,[a] and
hurried after Timotheus, whose forces numbered a hundred and
twenty thousand infantry and two thousand five hundred cavalry.

[a] *Probable meaning, based on one Vs.; Gk.* appointed them to command the divisions.

21 When he learnt of Judas's approach, Timotheus sent off the women
and children with all the baggage to a town called Carnaim, this
being an inaccessible place, hard to storm because all the approaches
22 to it were narrow. But when Judas's first division appeared, terror
and panic seized the enemy at the manifestation of the all-seeing
One. In their flight they rushed headlong in every direction, so that
frequently they were injured by their comrades and were run through
23 by the points of their swords. Judas pressed the pursuit vigorously
24 and put thirty thousand of these criminals to the sword. Timotheus
himself was taken prisoner by the troops of Dositheus and Sosipater.
With much cunning, he begged them to let him go in safety, pointing
out that most of them had parents, and some of them brothers, who
25 were in his hands, and might never be heard of again. He pledged
himself over and over again to restore these hostages safe and sound;
and so they let him go in order to save their relatives.

26 Judas moved on Carnaim and the sanctuary of Atargatis, and killed
27 twenty-five thousand people there. After this victory and destruction
he next marched on Ephron, a fortified town inhabited by a mixed
population.[a] Stalwart young men took up their position in front of
the walls and fought vigorously, while inside there was a great supply
28 of engines of war and ammunition. But the Jews invoked the
Sovereign whose might shatters all the strength of the enemy. They
made themselves masters of the town and killed twenty-five thousand
29 of the defenders. Leaving that place, they advanced to Scythopolis,
30 some seventy-five miles from Jerusalem. The Jews who lived there
testified to the goodwill shown them by the people of Scythopolis
and the kindness with which they had treated them in their bad
31 times; so Judas and his men thanked them, and charged them to be
equally friendly to the Jewish race for the future. They returned to
Jerusalem in time for the Feast of Weeks.

32 After celebrating Pentecost, as it is called, they advanced to attack
33 Gorgias, the general in charge of Idumaea, who met them with three
34 thousand infantry and four hundred cavalry. When the ranks joined
35 battle, a small number of the Jews fell. But a cavalryman of great
strength called Dositheus, one of the Tubian Jews, had hold of
Gorgias by his cloak and was dragging the villain off by main force,
with the object of taking him alive, when a Thracian horseman bore
down on him and chopped off his arm; so Gorgias escaped to Marisa.

[a] *Some witnesses add* where Lysias had his headquarters.

Esdrias and his men had been fighting for a long time and were 36
exhausted. But Judas invoked the Lord to show himself their ally
and leader in battle. Striking up hymns in his native language as a 37
battle-cry, he put the forces of Gorgias to flight by a surprise attack.
Regrouping his forces, he led them to the town of Adullam. The 38
seventh day was coming on, so they purified themselves, as custom
dictated, and kept the sabbath there. Next day they went, as had by 39
now become necessary, to collect the bodies of the fallen in order to
bury them with their relatives in the ancestral graves. But on every 40
one of the dead, they found, under the tunic, amulets sacred to the
idols of Jamnia, objects which the law forbids to Jews. It was evident
to all that here was the reason why these men had fallen. Therefore 41
they praised the work of the Lord, the just judge, who reveals what is
hidden; and, turning to prayer, they asked that this sin might be 42
entirely blotted out. The noble Judas called on the people to keep
themselves free from sin, for they had seen with their own eyes what
had happened to the fallen because of their sin. He levied a contribu- 43
tion from each man, and sent the total of two thousand silver drachmas to Jerusalem for a sin-offering—a fit and proper act in which he
took due account of the resurrection. For if he had not been expect- 44
ing the fallen to rise again, it would have been foolish and superfluous
to pray for the dead. But since he had in view the wonderful reward 45
reserved for those who die a godly death, his purpose was a holy and
pious one. And this was why he offered an atoning sacrifice to free
the dead from their sin.

In the year 149,[a] information reached Judas and his men that **13**
Antiochus Eupator was advancing on Judaea with a large army; he 2
was accompanied by Lysias, his guardian and vicegerent, bringing in
addition a Greek force, consisting of one hundred and ten thousand
infantry, five thousand three hundred cavalry, twenty-two elephants,
and three hundred chariots armed with scythes.

Menelaus also joined them and urged Antiochus on; this he did 3
most disingenuously, not for his country's good, but because he
believed he would be maintained in office. However, the King of 4
kings aroused the rage of Antiochus against Menelaus: Lysias produced evidence that this criminal was responsible for all Antiochus's
troubles, and so the king ordered him to be taken to Beroea and there
to be executed in the manner customary at that place. Now in 5

[*a*] *That is* 163 B.C.

Beroea there is a tower some seventy-five feet[a] high, filled with
ashes; it has a circular device sloping down sheer on all sides into the
6 ashes. This is where the citizens take anyone guilty of sacrilege or
7 any other notorious crime, and thrust him to his doom; and such
was the fate of the law-breaker Menelaus, who was not even allowed
8 burial—a fate he richly deserved. Many a time he had desecrated the
hallowed ashes of the altar-fire, and by ashes he met his death.

9 So the king came on with the barbarous intention of inflicting on
10 the Jews sufferings far worse than his father had inflicted. When
Judas heard this he ordered the people to invoke the Lord day and
night and pray that now more than ever he would come to their aid,
11 since they were on the point of losing law, country, and temple; and
that he would not allow them, just when they had begun to breathe
12 again, to fall into the hands of blaspheming Gentiles. They all obeyed
his orders: for three days without respite they prayed to their merciful
Lord, they wailed, they fasted, they prostrated themselves. Then
Judas urged them to action and called upon them to stand by him.

13 After holding a council of war with the elders, he decided not to
wait until the royal army invaded Judaea and took Jerusalem, but to
14 march out and with God's help to bring things to a decision. He
entrusted the outcome to the Creator of the world; his troops he
charged to fight bravely to the death for the law, for the temple and
for Jerusalem, for their country and their way of life. He pitched
15 camp near Modin, and giving his men the signal for battle with the
cry 'God's victory!', he made a night attack on the royal pavilion
with a picked force of the bravest young men. He killed as many as
two thousand in the enemy camp, and his men stabbed to death[b] the
16 leading elephant and its driver. In the end they reduced the whole
17 camp to panic and confusion, and withdrew victorious. It was all
over by daybreak, through the help and protection which Judas had
received from the Lord.

18 Now that he had had a taste of Jewish daring, the king tried
19 stratagems in attacking their strong-points. He advanced on
Bethsura, one of their powerful forts; he was repulsed; he attacked,
20, 21 he was beaten. Judas sent in supplies to the garrison, but a soldier in
the Jewish ranks, Rhodocus by name, betrayed their secrets to the
22 enemy. However, he was tracked down, arrested, and put away. The
king parleyed for the second time with the inhabitants of Bethsura,

[*a*] some...feet: *Gk.* fifty cubits. [*b*] stabbed to death: *probable reading, based on one Vs.*

and, when he had given and received guarantees, he withdrew; he
then attacked Judas and his men, but had the worst of it. He now 23
received news that Philip, whom he had left in charge of state affairs
in Antioch, had gone out of his mind. In dismay he summoned the
Jews, agreed to their terms, took an oath to respect all their rights,
and, after this settlement, offered a sacrifice, paid honour to the
sanctuary and its precincts, and received Maccabaeus graciously. He 24
left behind Hegemonides as governor of the region from Ptolemais
to Gerra, and went himself to Ptolemais. Its inhabitants were 25
furious at the treaty he had made, and in their alarm wanted to
repudiate it. Lysias mounted the rostrum, made the best defence he 26
could, won the people over, calmed them down, and, having thus
gained their support, left for Antioch.

Such was the course of the king's offensive and retreat.

The victory of Maccabaeus over Nicanor

AFTER AN INTERVAL of three years, information reached Judas 14
and his men that Demetrius son of Seleucus had sailed into the
harbour of Tripolis with a powerful army and fleet, and, after dispos- 2
ing of Antiochus and his guardian Lysias, had taken possession of the
country.

There was a man called Alcimus, who had formerly been high 3
priest but had submitted voluntarily to pollutions at the time of the
secession. This man, realizing that there was not now the slightest
guarantee of his safety, or any possibility of access to the holy altar,
came to King Demetrius, about the year 151,[a] and presented him 4
with a gold crown and palm, and also some of the customary olive
branches from the temple. On that particular occasion he kept quiet;
but he found a chance of forwarding his own mad scheme when 5
Demetrius summoned him to his council and questioned him about
the attitude and plans of the Jews. He replied: 'Those of the Jews 6
who are called Hasidaeans and are led by Judas Maccabaeus are
keeping the war alive and fomenting sedition, refusing to leave the
kingdom in peace. Thus, although I have been deprived of my 7
hereditary dignity—I mean the high-priesthood—I am here today

[a] *That is* 161 B.C.

8 from two motives: first, a genuine concern for the king's rights; and
secondly, a regard for my fellow-citizens, since our whole race is
suffering considerable hardship as a result of the folly of the people
9 I have just mentioned. I would advise your majesty to acquaint
yourself with every one of these matters and then make provision for
our country and our beleaguered nation, as befits your universal
10 kindness and goodwill. For the empire will enjoy no peace so long as
Judas remains alive.'
11 When he had spoken to this effect, the other Friends, who were
12 hostile to Judas, immediately inflamed Demetrius still more. The
king at once selected Nicanor, commander of the elephant corps,
13 gave him command of Judaea, and sent him off with a commission
to dispose of Judas himself and disperse his forces, and to install
14 Alcimus as high priest of the great temple. The gentile population of
Judaea, refugees from the attacks of Judas, now flocked to Nicanor,
thinking that defeat and misfortune for the Jews would mean
prosperity for themselves.
15 When they learnt of Nicanor's offensive and the gentile attack, the
Jews sprinkled dust over themselves and prayed to the One who
established his people for ever, who never fails to manifest himself
16 when his chosen are in need of help. At their leader's command, they
immediately struck camp and joined battle with the enemy at the
17 village of Adasa.[a] Simon, the brother of Judas, had fought an
engagement with Nicanor, but, because the enemy came up[b] un-
18 expectedly, he had suffered a slight reverse. In spite of this, when
Nicanor learnt how brave Judas and his troops were and how
courageously they fought for their country, he shrank from deciding
19 the issue in battle. So he sent Posidonius, Theodotus, and Mattathias to negotiate a settlement.
20 After a lengthy consideration of the proposals, Judas informed his
21 men of them; they were unanimous in agreeing to make peace. A day
was fixed for a private meeting of the leaders. A chariot advanced
22 from each of the two lines, and seats were placed for them; but Judas
posted armed men at strategic points ready to deal with any unforeseen treachery on the enemy's part. The discussion between the two
23 leaders was harmonious. Nicanor stayed some time in Jerusalem and
behaved correctly; he dismissed the crowds that had flocked round

[*a*] Adasa: *probable reading; compare 1 Macc. 7. 40.* [*b*] came up: *probable reading, based on one Vs.*

him, and kept Judas always close to himself. He had acquired a real 24
affection for him, and urged him to marry and start a family. So 25
Judas married and settled down to the quiet life of an ordinary citizen.
Alcimus noticed their friendliness and got hold of a copy of the 26
agreement they had concluded. He went to Demetrius and said that
Nicanor was pursuing a policy detrimental to the interests of the
empire, by appointing that traitor Judas King's Friend designate.
The king was furious and was provoked by these villainous slanders 27
to write to Nicanor expressing his dissatisfaction with the agreement
and ordering him to arrest Maccabaeus and send him at once to
Antioch. This message filled Nicanor with dismay; he took it hard 28
that he should have to break his agreement although the man had
committed no offence, but since there was no going against the king, 29
he watched for a favourable opportunity of carrying out the order by
means of some stratagem. Maccabaeus, however, observed that 30
Nicanor had become less friendly towards him and no longer showed
him the same civility. He realized that this unfriendliness boded no
good, so he collected a large number of his followers and went into
hiding from Nicanor.

When Nicanor recognized that he had been outmanœuvred by the 31
resolute action of Judas, he went to the great and holy temple at the
time when the priests were offering the regular sacrifices, and
ordered them to surrender Judas to him. The priests declared on 32
oath that they did not know the whereabouts of the wanted man. But 33
Nicanor stretched out his right hand towards the shrine and swore
this oath: 'Unless you surrender Judas into my custody, I will raze
God's sanctuary to the ground, I will destroy the altar, and on this
spot I will build a temple to Dionysus for all the world to see.'
With these words he left; but the priests with outstretched hands 34
prayed to Heaven, the constant champion of our race: 'Lord, thou 35
hast no need of anything in the world, yet it was thy pleasure that
among us there should be a shrine for thy dwelling-place. Now, 36
Lord, who alone art holy, keep this house, so newly purified, for ever
free from defilement.'

A man called Razis, a member of the Jerusalem senate, was 37
denounced to Nicanor. He was very highly spoken of, a patriot who
for his loyalty was known as 'Father of the Jews'. In the early days 38
of the secession he had stood his trial for practising Judaism, and
with the utmost eagerness had risked life and limb for that cause.

39 Nicanor wished to give clear proof of his hostility towards the Jews,
40 and sent more than five hundred soldiers to arrest Razis; he reckoned
41 that his arrest would be a severe blow to the Jews. The troops were
on the point of capturing the tower where Razis was, and were trying
to force the outer door. Then an order was given to set the door on
fire, and Razis, hemmed in on all sides, turned his sword on himself.
42 He preferred to die nobly rather than fall into the hands of criminals
43 and be subjected to gross humiliation. In his haste and anxiety he
misjudged the blow, and with the troops pouring through the doors
he ran without hesitation on to the wall and heroically threw himself
44 down into the crowd. The crowd hurriedly gave way and he fell in
45 the space they left. He was still breathing, still on fire with courage;
so, streaming with blood and severely wounded, he picked himself up
and dashed through the crowd. Finally, standing on a sheer rock,
46 and now completely drained of blood, he took his entrails in both
hands and flung them at the crowd. And thus, invoking the Lord of
life and breath to give these entrails back to him again, he died.

15 Nicanor received information that Judas and his men were in the
region of Samaria, and he determined to attack them on their day of
2 rest, when it could be done without any danger. Those Jews who
were forced to accompany his army said, 'Do not carry out such a
savage and barbarous massacre, but respect the day singled out and
3 made holy by the all-seeing One.' The double-dyed villain retorted,
'Is there a ruler in the sky who has ordered the sabbath day to be
4 observed?' The Jews declared, 'The living Lord himself is ruler in
5 the sky, and he ordered the seventh day to be kept holy.' 'But I',
replied Nicanor, 'am a ruler on earth, and I order you to take your
arms and do your duty to the king.' However, he did not succeed in
carrying out his cruel plan.

6 Now Nicanor, in his pretentious and extravagant conceit, had
resolved upon erecting a public trophy from the spoils of Judas's
7 forces. But Maccabaeus's confidence never wavered, and he had not
8 the least doubt that he would obtain help from the Lord. He urged
his men not to be afraid of the gentile attack, but to bear in mind the
aid they had received from heaven in the past and so look to the
9 Almighty for the victory which he would send this time also. He
drew encouragement for them from the law and the prophets and, by
reminding them of the struggles they had already come through,
10 filled them with a fresh enthusiasm. When he had roused their

courage, he gave them their orders, reminding them at the same time
of the Gentiles' broken faith and perjury. He armed each one of 11
them, not so much with the security of shield and spear, as with the
encouragement that brave words bring; and he also told them of a
trustworthy dream he had had, a sort of waking vision, which put
them all in good heart.

What he had seen was this: the former high priest Onias appeared 12
to him, that great gentleman of modest bearing and mild disposition,
apt speaker, and exponent from childhood of the good life. With outstretched hands he was praying earnestly for the whole Jewish community. Next there appeared in the same attitude a figure of great 13
age and dignity, whose wonderful air of authority marked him as a
man of the utmost distinction. Then Onias said, 'This is God's 14
prophet Jeremiah, who loves his fellow-Jews and offers many
prayers for our people and for the holy city.' Jeremiah extended his 15
right hand and delivered to Judas a golden sword, saying as he did so,
'Take this holy sword, the gift of God, and with it crush your 16
enemies.'

The eloquent words of Judas had the power of stimulating every- 17
one to bravery and making men out of boys. Encouraged by them,
the Jews made up their minds not to remain in camp, but to take the
offensive manfully and fight hand to hand with all their strength until
the issue was decided. This they did because Jerusalem, their
religion, and their temple were in danger. Their fear was not chiefly 18
for their wives and children, not to mention brothers and relatives,
but first and foremost for the sacred shrine. The distress of those 19
shut up in Jerusalem was no less, for they were anxious at the
prospect of a battle on open ground.

All were waiting for the decisive struggle which lay ahead. The 20
enemy had already concentrated his forces; his army was drawn up
in order of battle, the elephants stationed in a favourable position and
the cavalry ranged on the flank. When Maccabaeus observed the 21
deployment of the troops, the variety of their equipment, and the
ferocity of the elephants, with hands upraised he invoked the Lord,
the worker of miracles; for he knew that God grants victory to those
who deserve it, not because of their military strength but as he himself decides. This was his prayer: 'Master, thou didst send thy 22
angel in the days of Hezekiah king of Judah, and he killed as many as
a hundred and eighty-five thousand men in Sennacherib's camp.

23 Now, Ruler of heaven, send once again a good angel to go in front of
24 us spreading fear and panic. May they be struck down by thy strong
arm, these blasphemers who are coming to attack thy holy people!'
Thus he ended.

25 Nicanor and his forces advanced with trumpets and war-songs,
26 but Judas and his men joined battle with invocations and prayers.
27 Fighting with their hands and praying to God in their hearts, they
killed no fewer than thirty-five thousand men, and were greatly
cheered by the divine intervention.

28 The action was over, and they were joyfully disbanding, when
29 they recognized Nicanor lying dead in his armour. Then with
tumultuous shouts they praised their Master in their native lan-
30 guage. Judas their leader, who had always fought body and soul on
behalf of his fellow-Jews, never losing his youthful patriotism, now
ordered Nicanor's head to be cut off, also his hand and arm, and
31 taken to Jerusalem. On arrival there he summoned all the people and
stationed the priests before the altar. Then he sent for the men in the
32 citadel, and showed them the head of the blackguardly Nicanor and
the hand which this bragging blasphemer had extended against the
33 Almighty's holy temple. He cut out the tongue of the impious
Nicanor, and said he would give it to the birds bit by bit; and he gave
orders that the evidence of what Nicanor's folly had brought upon
34 him should be hung up opposite the shrine. They all made the sky
ring with the praises of the Lord who had shown his power: 'Praise
35 to him who has preserved his own sanctuary from defilement!' Judas
hung Nicanor's head from the citadel, a clear proof of the Lord's
36 help, for all to see. It was unanimously decreed that this day should
never pass unnoticed but be regularly celebrated. It is the thirteenth
of the twelfth month, called Adar in Aramaic, the day before
37 Mordecai's Day. Such, then, was the fate of Nicanor, and from that
time Jerusalem has remained in the possession of the Hebrews.

38 AT THIS POINT I will bring my work to an end. If it is found
well written and aptly composed, that is what I myself hoped for;
39 if cheap and mediocre, I could only do my best. For, just as it is
disagreeable to drink wine alone or water alone, whereas the mixing
of the two gives a pleasant and delightful taste, so too variety of style
in a literary work charms the ear of the reader. Let this then be my
final word.